LAND USE, U
AN
ENVIRONMENTAL QUALITY

Brian J. L. Berry

Andrew J. Bruzewicz	Richard F. Lamb
Douglas B. Cargo	Lee F. Margerum
James B. Cummings	Marvin W. Mikesell
Donald C. Dahmann	David J. Morgan
Peter G. Goheen	Jack P. Mrowka
Charles P. Kaplan	John P. Piccininni
Dorothy B. Koopman	Judith A. Soisson

The University of Chicago

for the

Office of Research and Development
ENVIRONMENTAL PROTECTION AGENCY

THE UNIVERSITY OF CHICAGO
DEPARTMENT OF GEOGRAPHY
RESEARCH PAPER NO. 155

1974

FINAL REPORT of Project No. R–801419:
"Land Use Forms and the Environment,"
Office of Research and Development
ENVIRONMENTAL PROTECTION AGENCY

Library of Congress Catalog Card Number: 73-87830

Research Papers are available from:
The University of Chicago
Department of Geography
5828 S. University Avenue
Chicago, Illinois 60637
Price: $5.00 list; $4.00 series subscription

ACKNOWLEDGEMENTS

We wish to acknowledge our indebtedness in the preparation of this report to:

Mary Grear and Sandra Marcus, for typing the final report, and setting the manuscript in camera-ready form.

John P. Hughes, for his cartographic skills.

Marion Harr, for contract management and protecting us from paperwork.

Peter House and Philip Patterson, Director and Assistant to the Director, Environmental Studies Division, Office of Research and Development, Washington Environmental Research Center, U. S. Environmental Protection Agency, for suggesting the project, providing support, and criticizing the draft report.

PREFACE

This report is the result of an intensive fifteen month study conducted by a research team at the University of Chicago for the Office of Research and Development of the U.S. Environmental Protection Agency. Some background on individual responsibilities is appropriate, although the report is a team product. Day to day matters were handled by Donald Dahmann and Charles Kaplan, who also focussed their attention on air and water quality, respectively, and on overall questions of research design. Marvin Mikesell, Peter Goheen and Jack Mrowka served as a faculty advisory group, concerning themselves with concepts of environmental quality, urban data and physical systems analysis. Douglas Cargo dealt with solid wastes, Judith Soisson with noise, Dorothy Koopman with urban land use, John Piccininni with water quality measurements, and Donald Dahmann, additionally, with radiation and pesticides. Richard Lamb handled many of the dealings with the university's computer, David Morgan contributed the urban density analysis, Andrew Brucewicz the work on urban transport networks, Lee Margerum that on retail decentralization and James Cummings the information on the decline of public transportation. Brian J. L. Berry was project director.

A few words of caution are relevant:

The study was conducted between June, 1972 and September, 1973, with a cut off date for inclusion of new data from what is an expanding and accelerating stream occuring in April-May, 1973. Thus, newer or better data relating to source aspects of the study may have been published since the analysis was completed. Where known, these new data sets were referenced during the succeeding review period; however, the diversity of data sources undoubtedly means that some important new contributions will have been overlooked.

Also, where statistical analyses are reported that incorporate 1970 census data, variables relating to environmental quality are standardized as nearly as possible to that census date.

CONTENTS

TABLES

FIGURES

A INTRODUCTION

There is growing dissatisfaction with the operation of land use planning at the local level in the United States, and at the metropolitan level a distinguished historian of planning has observed that "the present preoccupation of many American planning agencies with alternative configuration models has no current relevance whatsoever, because the power is lacking to carry out even the least drastic departure from straight line projection of past trends. We lack not the technical skill but the political will (and) decision-making power over the place, tempo, sequence and pattern of urban development" (Reps, in Clawson, ed., 1973, pp. 16-17).

Yet there are some signs that the political will may be changing. A much larger Federal role in land-use planning has been specified in bills before the Congress. Senate bill 632, which was passed by the Senate in September, 1972, expressed a national interest in land use planning, provided grants to the States to enable them to conduct land use planning for certain critical ecological and development areas and to provide some degree of supervision to local units of government in their land use planning. Although a similar bill was not acted upon by the House, ultimate passage of national legislation on land use planning seems likely.

If a national land use policy does begin to take shape, the formulation of policy objectives will undoubtedly involve assessment of "alternative urban futures" that are held to be more desirable than the simple unfolding of present processes. Public bodies charged with promoting the general welfare under conditions that make private economic goals secondary to social benefits will be set against the traditional land use dynamic in which power has rested primarily in private hands, motivated mainly by profit and personal gain and supported rather than being modified by public controls.

It follows that any agency of government charged with achieving broader welfare goals for society, such as the Environmental Protection Agency, must develop the means for assessing these different alternative urban futures in terms of its statutory

obligations and powers. Which alternatives will reduce environmental pollution in what ways, and with what kinds of synergisms
and secondary impacts? Which alternatives should be fought by
the agency because they will make the achievement of agency goals
more difficult, and which should be supported? Such are the
questions that must be made answerable.

As a contribution to the agency's task, this study deals
with the ways in which urban form and land use affect the nature
and intensity of environmental pollution. The inquiry proceeds
at two scales: (a) from one urban region to another, and (b) on
a more detailed basis within urban regions. At the first level
of analysis, attention is directed to the effects of different
urban forms and land use mixes on the levels of environmental
pollution reported by U.S. government monitoring stations to be
characteristic of the urban regions. At the second scale, spatial patterns of pollution are related to spatial patterns of land
use within a sample of metropolitan areas that have different
urban forms and that exemplify the range of pollution types
characterizing American urban regions today. The report is
structured cumulatively, to provide an understanding of those
urban forms that naturally generate the lowest pollution levels,
the environmental consequences of contemporary urban dynamics,
and the role that urban planning may potentially play in the
achievement and maintenance of the nation's environmental quality
standards.

Chapter 1 raises basic questions about the meaning and
measurement of environmental quality, reviews some of the suggestions in the previous literature about the relationships between environmental pollution, urban form and land use, and dis-
cusses briefly the disciplinary role of geographers in studies
of such relationships. The six chapters that comprise Part B
review sources of data on environmental pollution for each of the
types of current national concern--air, water, solid wastes,
noise, pesticides and radiation, what is known about pollution
generators, the currently available environmental quality assessment systems in the United States, the standards with which pollution levels are compared to determine quality levels, and the
known health and welfare effects of pollution on which the national
standards are based.

With these materials as background, the four chapters in
Part C focus on the more general level of analysis. The assembly

of a nationwide data set is discussed, a pollution-sensitive
typology of urban regions is developed, levels of environmental
pollution are related to urban form and land use taking into account the effects of such other city characteristics as size and
the urban economic base, and finally, an attempt is made to measure
the overall incidence of agglomerative economies and environmental
diseconomies in cities of different sizes.

Next, in Part D, relationships within urban regions are considered. First, in Chapter 12, the causal links between the urban
land use pattern and the pollution map are explored, looking at
pollution generators, diffusion and transport mechanisms and the
like. Then, in Chapter 13, the correlations between pollution
and land use resulting from the causal links are studied.

Finally, Part E of the study concludes by using the findings
to outline the environmental consequences of alternative urban
futures.

Several things should be noted about the analyses undertaken.
Our studies were being conducted at the very time that the basic
EPA data systems were being established, and neither the National
Air Surveillance Network (NASN) nor STORET, the water quality data
bank, were properly functioning. Great difficulties also were
experienced with data on solid wastes because of the disarray in
that EPA office caused by funding cut backs. This was particularly
problematical for the intra-regional analyses of Part D, which in
consequence had to be conducted on an experimental and exploratory
basis, seeking to open up lines of inquiry rather than being able
to offer very definitive conclusions.

1 ENVIRONMENTAL QUALITY AND LAND USE: THE PROBLEM STATED

Most pollution is the result of wastes being introduced into environmental systems in greater concentrations than such systems can absorb. It is urbanization, produced by and combined with industrialization, that has created the excessive concentration of wastes. The industrial city, physically concentrated, core-oriented, and carrying with it a distinctive way of life not only brought with it economic growth and affluence. It also brought a variety of problems, each an outcome of size and concentration—traffic congestion, poverty, social disorganization, and both modification and pollution of the urban environment. In turn, the problems have bred responses: highway and mass transportation programs, urban renewal, public housing, community action, and environmental protection. In common, these programs have been formulated with the concentrated core-oriented city and the problems arising within it in mind; in common, many of the programs have encountered difficulty both because of the "perverse" character of complex systems and because systemic change has been taking place. Supposed solutions have thus been produced for problems related to urban forms from which we are evolving—solutions which therefore may be inappropriate today and especially tomorrow. Yet we clearly should be planning for tomorrow.

The perversity of complex systems is, of course, multifaceted, as Jay Forrester has pointed out in Urban Dynamics. Such systems, he says, are counterintuitive, insensitive to parameter changes, resistant to policy inputs, tending to counteract corrective programs, and showing opposite long term and short-term responses. But Forrester also noted that complex systems may be controlled though a few central influence points, saying that these points are generally not self-evident, but only are discernible through a careful examination of system dynamics. Such an examination is the orientation of this study.

Whenever one is dealing with complex systems, there is therefore a critical need to know about the processes that give them order—and this is all the more true because part of the perversity of complex urban systems in the U.S. today is that the very processes of urbanization appear to be undergoing transformation.

A critical need therefore is evident for a careful study of urban system dynamics, and its relationships to environmental pollution. Today's metropolises, the product of _past_ processes of population and economic concentration, have so burst their traditional high-density limits as new urbanization forces have come into play that broad _daily urban systems_ now transcend all the traditional realities in a network now blanketing all except the most sparsely settled parts of the country, embracing the daily activities and travel of ninety percent of the nation's population.

As core-oriented urban regions developed they imprinted a particular geography on the nation. To quote a description of New York:

> If we think of the region as a huge conical structure in which altitude represents the concentration of human activity, we find Newark, Jersey City, Paterson, Elizabeth, Yonkers, and Bridgeport—each with a population of over 100,000—protruding as lesser peaks from its sloping flanks. Yet by any measure one cares to devise, the apex of the whole structure is on the island of Manhattan.

The growth and spread of similar socio-economic cones around each city brought to the nation orderly rhythms of opportunity and welfare during the first half of the twentieth century: as "altitude" fell, so did population densities, income and educational levels. And parallelling the socio-economic cones came similar conical forms of environmental influence; the urban heat island is a case in point. Just as the urban density cone varied in size and shape systematically with city size, so did the heat island, subject to the influence of local microclimatological conditions.

The American people have not been ignorant of the socio-economic rhythms. Particularly in the last two decades, facilitated by changing transportation technologies, rising real incomes, and subsidized suburban housing, they have responded in several ways. Minority and rural populations in peripheral regions reacted by centralization, emigrating from low-income peripheries, resulting in population declines in the outlying regions. If the new migrant was poorly educated and/or a member of a minority group, his move placed him in a central-city ghetto, generally the zone of greatest environmental pollution, abandoned increasingly by whites and by employment. This flight of upper income white city-dwellers into the expanding peripheries of metropolitan regions, and the concentration of new workplaces, shopping facilities and services at the outer edge, is an accelerating phenomenon.

As a result, traditional core-orientation is fast on the wane. Today's daily urban systems appear to be highly dispersed multi-nodal multi-connected social systems in action. The essence of any such system is its linkages and interactions, as changed by changing modes of communication. It is the spontaneous creation of new communities, the flows that respond to new transportation arteries, the waves emanating from growth centers, the mutually-repulsive interactions of antagonistic social groups, the explicit selection of particular environmental settings and the avoidance of others, the reverse commuting resulting from increasing segregation along city boundary lines as employment decentralizes, and many other facets of social dynamics that today combine to constitute today's emergent daily urban systems, depicted in Figure 1.1.

Given such changes, the "alternative futures" speculators are in their element. Kahn and Wiener (1967) conclude that major sprawl will meet major sprawl, so that

> the United States of the year 2000 will see at least three gargantuan metropolises, Boswash, Chipitts, and Sansan, which should contain more than half the U.S. population, including an overwhelming proportion of the most prosperous and creative elements of society.

On the other hand, Friedmann and Miller (1965) say

> Looking ahead to the next generation, we foresee a new scale of urban living that will extend far beyond existing metropolitan cores and penetrate deeply into the periphery. Relations of dominance and dependency will be transcended. The older established centers, together with the inter-metropolitan peripheries that surround them, will constitute the new ecological unit of America's post-industrial society that will replace traditional concepts of the emerging spatial order. This we shall call the urban field.

> The urban field may be viewed as an enlargement of the space for urban living that extends far beyond the boundaries of existing metropolitan areas...into the open landscape of the periphery. This change to a larger scale of urban life is already underway, encouraged by changes in technology, economics, and preferred social behavior.

All of this suggests the need for careful investigation of urban forms and the changing nature of urban structure, to determine the relationships of differing types of environmental pollution to such variations and changes in form. Of particular concern is the identification of those forms that naturally generate the least pollution, and the relative tradeoffs and trends in pollution associated with one urban land use pattern

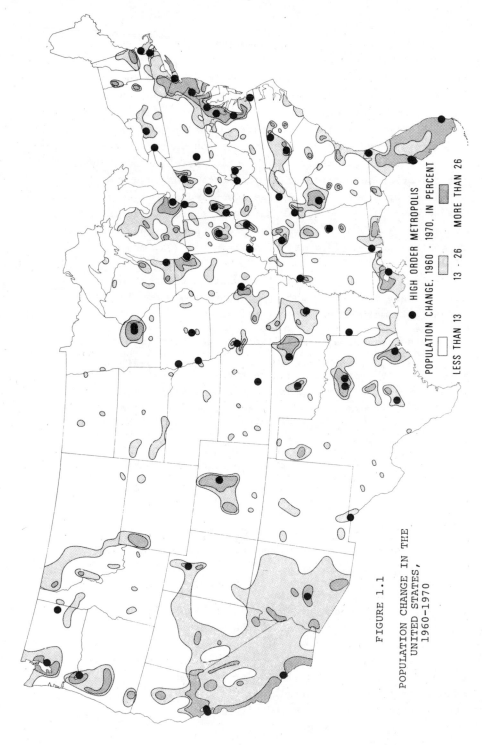

FIGURE 1.1

POPULATION CHANGE IN THE
UNITED STATES,
1960-1970

● HIGH ORDER METROPOLIS

POPULATION CHANGE, 1960 - 1970, IN PERCENT

LESS THAN 13   13 - 26   MORE THAN 26

as opposed to another.

Let us focus for a moment on the question of decentralization and densities, key variables in the differentiation of
urban forms, as an example. Geographers have noted, as have many
other observers, the universal flattening of the population density profiles of American metropolitan areas. The decentralization on an ever-increasing scale of population and employment
away from the aging cores of the large cities makes some assessment of the impact of a new suburban landscape and radically
transformed traditional central cities on pollution imperative.
Increasing reliance on growing numbers of automobiles and the
changing pattern of their use for business and recreation purposes in new metropolitan fringe communities suggests that air
and noise pollution will reflect changing human behavior patterns.
The careful segregation of land uses in new communities likewise
creates novel patterns of daily mobility, affecting environmental
pollution. Whereas certain relationships can be established
correlating pollution with atmospheric physics and individual
pollution sources, some consideration of new scale implications
of the problem seems now to be required.

How is this to be done? The orientation obviously has to
be towards codifying what is known about the impact of self-
transforming urbanization processes on the biosphere, and particularly what can be said about the undesirable consequences
(called pollution) when the environmental system becomes overloaded.

On the physical side, the principal categories of concern
must therefore be

(a) The climate of cities, and its relationship to
    pollution via the locational pattern of point,
    line and area sources of pollutants. Attention
    needs to be focussed on the nature of the urban
    heat island, including city size and land use
    distribution,effects on both daytime and night-
    time temperature differences, diurnally, seasonally
    and annually, in both vertical and horizontal
    profiles. The impact of local microclimatological
    differences also has to be taken into account.
    Attendant considerations are those of urban humi-
    dity patterns, visibility, solar radiation, at-
    mospheric turbidity, wind speeds and directions,
    and finally, precipitation (including the role
    of anthropogenically produced dust particles).

(b) Hydrologic effects of urban land use, involving
    changes in peak flow characteristics, sediment
    load and total runoff, changes in water quality
    and in ground water recharge, and changes in

      hydrologic amenities.

  (c) Questions of wastes management and land pollution, the
      interactions of air, land and water at their gaseous and
      liquid interfaces, and the resulting problems of, for
      example, heat as a residual.

Through the above physical considerations differing urban forms
and land use patterns have to be interfaced with air, water,
solid wastes, pesticides, radiation and noise pollution.

     The case of urban noise illustrates some of the problems of
specifying land use alternatives and tradeoffs. There appear to
be three principal alternatives in treating noise problems:
development of new technologies, careful choice and control of
the location of noise sources and receivers, and direct control
of noise itself. While technological innovation can be expected
to be the most productive path to eliminating any problem of concomitant effects, the long time lags typically associated with
invention and implementation usually lead to the question of
urban form--whether influencing the location of noise sources
and noise sensitive activities in urban areas represents a
viable approach. But new complexities then arise. One of the
principal tradeoffs which must be made in any urban systems
design is between the benefits derived from accessibility to
services and systems and the disbenefits which arise from proximity. People want to be near work, firehouses, hospitals, stores,
and theaters, but suffer when these are in their back yards.
Zoning ordinances are used, sometimes ineffectively, to attempt
to provide the collective benefits of accessible factories and
business, while insulating most people from their negative effects, including noise. There is reliance upon public and private transportation systems to provide this accessibility without
proximity, but these relatively ubiquitous systems themselves are
generators of a large proportion of the noise in urban areas.
Those whose residences are close to especially noisy transportation facilities bear a burden so that the population as a whole
can live in relative isolation from the noise and smoke of industry and commerce. In what ways, then, is noise pollution
affected by changing urban forms and locational choices? Which
urban forms naturally generate the least noise externalities?
The questions are those of tradeoffs. Noise is dissipated ex-
ponentially with distance from the source. For a single point
source, sound level decays approximately 6 dB for each doubling
of distance from the source. If the noise is produced by a line
source, such as a crowded highway, the sound will decrease 3 dB

for each doubling of distance. What effects then, do decentralization and reduced densities have upon the spatial incidence of
noise? Are there land use configurations that naturally minimize noise? Immediately, the whole question of tradeoffs arises,
particularly in so far as three differing sets of effects of the
initial noise pollution all must be taken into account:

    a) Direct effects--the direct and immediate externalities
       borne by the receptor

    b) Adjustments (Indirect effects)--effects which induce
       persons and firms to make certain adjustments in
       order to reduce the direct impact of the pollutants.

    c) Market effects--effects realized through the market-
       place as a result of the adjustments made.

This chapter is not the place to explore these issues further,
but should serve to illustrate the chains of questioning that
must be pursued.

I. URBAN FORMS AND THE ENVIRONMENT

What are some of the ways in which we might distinguish
urban forms and land use patterns in terms of their environmental impact? Several studies have been conducted which ask
whether different urban forms generate different levels of air
pollution (Voorhees, 1971): In Hartford, Connecticut, it was
found that air pollution concentrations were clearly related to
land use, and that a controlled linear development pattern could,
by the year 2000, produce improvements in air quality. In
Chicago, the air pollution implications of three alternative
metropolitan plans were analyzed on the basis of emission estimates for two pollutants. The alternative plans were a "Finger
Plan" for high-density corridor development, a "Multi-Towns
Plan" and a "Satellite Cities Plan." The Finger Plan was significantly better than the other two. The reason was that although the plan had high residential and industrial concentrations, large green areas bordering the development corridors
provided greater opportunities for pollutant dispersion than
under the other two plans. Similar findings were produced in
Seattle, where a "Cities and Corridors" concept produced substantially lower total emissions than a development pattern based
upon the continuation of present trends.

These studies suggest the importance of examining the different effects upon environmental pollution of the following
variations in urban form: core-oriented or multinodal; concen-

trated or dispersed; concentric or radial. Within each of these,
differing patterns and mixes of industrial, commercial and residential land use need to be explored together with their implications for urban densities, and the associations of these mixes
with different transport networks and combinations of modes. What
needs to be developed is a classification table of urban forms
through which the urban regions of the U.S. can be filtered so
that their pollution problems may be understood more clearly.
For above all, what appears to be needed at this time is a base
of knowledge about the effects of urban form differences today in
the complex world of reality, to serve as a base for comparison of
simulations that perform "abstract city analysis" on the basis of
idealized and highly simplified urban form alternatives (Voorhees,
1968).

What the research task involves is therefore:

(a) preparation of a "sorting table" in which the
"rows" are the various permutations and combinations of urban forms and land use patterns and
the "columns" are the several classes, types
and elements of environmental pollution;

(b) reviewing, assembling and evaluating the evidence
relating to each "cell" of the sorting table, i.e.
to the nature and incidence of each type of environmental effects of urbanization, and pollution with
respect to urban form;

(c) comparative analysis of the materials assembled
under (b) above to determine:
(1) trends in the nature and incidence of
pollution, across the urban forms and
land use types, establishing the relative
tradeoffs and trends in pollution associated with one land use pattern as opposed to another;
(ii) the intervening and constraining effects
of different geographic, micro-climatologi-
cal and local hydrological settings on
these trends;

(d) parallel investigation of national trends in population distribution and land use, so that in terms
of (c-1) above, some expectations can be developed
as to the likely impacts on pollution of current
patterns of regional growth and change, and so
that the likely changes in pollution of the suc-
cessful pursuit of alternative proposals for
national urban development can be evaluated.

Such is the organization of what follows. The analysis focusses
upon urban form differences as they currently exist, and the
consequences of these for different levels and patterns of
environmental pollution, holding other city characteristics
constant.

II. THE QUALITY OF LIFE

In focussing on the relationships between urban form and environmental pollution we are, of course, probing the ways in which
urban forms affect the quality of life, conceived as involving
both the well-being of people and the "well-being" of the environment in which these people live. This concern follows from the
National Environmental Policy Act, that mandates the Federal
Government to take action to "protect and enhance the quality of
the Nation's environment to sustain and enrich human life (so as
to) foster and promote the general welfare, to create and maintain conditions under which man and nature can exist in harmony,
and fulfill the social, economic, and other requirements of
present and future generations of Americans." What is expressed
is a new concern that has grown out of American affluence to go
beyond "just economics" to consider pollution, health, over-
crowding, cultural opportunities and political influence.

The very diffuseness of this concern produces imprecision,
when compared with the relative precision and acceptability of
the traditional economic indicators of the "health" and growth
of the economy. Thus, the National Environmental Protection Act
of 1969 mandated the Council on Environmental Quality to prepare
a set of indicators to measure the state of the environment. The
Council's mandate has hastened the development of environmental
indicators, particularly in areas perceived to be of greatest
urgency, notably air and water quality. These indicators, which
have the following form, as used wherever possible in this study:
$Q = \Sigma_i w_i I_i$ -- where there are i components of the indicator, I_i is
the ratio of the current status of i to the desired level or standard of i to be achieved, and w_i is a preference function (Office of
Research and Monitoring, 1973).

However, the absence of experimental indicators is not used
as an excuse for not studying a particular pollutant. In so far
as the columns of the sorting table are concerned they consider
each of the major types of environmental pollution (water, air,
solid wastes, noise, pesticides and radiation) together with
their principal sources (transportation, fuel combustion in stationary sources, industrial processes, and solid waste disposal).
Within these major types fine distinctions are drawn between particular pollutants, while across the types, interactions and
tradeoffs are specified.

III. GEOGRAPHY AS THE STUDY OF ENVIRONMENT

In considering the analysis of relationships and tradeoffs,
it should be noted that urban geographers traditionally have had
much to say about the importance of "site" and "situation" as
elements creating urban morphologies. Traditionally, an examination of the physical environment constituted the major element
in the consideration of site which was taken to be determinative
of urban land use configurations. Subsequent urban research has
stressed different ways of reaching generalizations about the
structure of urban activities and areas. More direct comparisons
of various cities have been discussed with reference to population density configurations and traffic patterns. Indeed,
fairly elaborate multivariate taxonomies of metropolitan areas,
and process-models of urban form have recently been developed
in geography. Because pollution of the urban environment is
largely a product of the joint influences of human processes
and dynamics of the biosphere, it is therefore quite appropriate
that geographers with ecological and urban interests address
themselves to these issues.

What is being implied is, of course, the reaffirmation of
some old and the development of some new disciplinary commitments. When the first departments of geography were established
in the United States shortly after the beginning of the twentieth
century their self-proclaimed charge was to function as a bridge
between the natural and social sciences. For example, the bulle-
tin of the University of Chicago for 1903 indicated that its
newly established Department of Geography offered courses "inter-
mediate between geology and climatology, on the one hand, and
history, sociology, political economy, and biology, on the other."
Three years later the first president of the Association of
American Geographers proclaimed that "any statement is of geographic quality if it contains...some relation between an element of inorganic control and one of organic response." This
conception of the nature of geography was appealing to the first
generation of American geographers, who were trained for the most
part as geologists and hoped to apply this knowledge in the
study of mankind.

But the movement from geology to physical geography and
then to human geography was denounced in time as a one-sided
determinism, an example of special pleading and selectivity in

the search for evidence. As a result, a retreat of geographers
from environmentalism began in the 1920's and within a decade
had resulted in a nearly total abandonment. For most geographers
the alternative to environmentalism was to disregard the ecological
commitments of the discipline in favor of distributional or
locational studies that paid only perfunctory attention to environment. Thus although land use and land forms might both be mapped,
the only generalization offered about a connection between the
two would be one of coincidence or correlation, e.g., steep
slopes have different uses than gentle slopes. Not a few geographers simply ignored environment and devoted themselves to
functional or classificatory studies of economic activities.

Moreover, human and physical geographers began to drift
apart in the 1930's and by the 1940's and 1950's were quite
separate. The conception of geography as a bridge between the
natural and social sciences was still proclaimed in textbooks,
but was seldom evident in research. The separation of geography's
"two cultures" is manifest in American Geography: Inventory and
Prospect, the "official" survey of the field published by the
Association of American Geographers in 1954, for although this
volume includes studies of both nature and culture no chapter is
devoted explicitly to their relationship. Between physical geography cultivated without reference to human activities and human
geography cultivated with only perfunctory reference to nature
there could be few opportunities for collaboration, especially
when both sides were influenced by a residual fear of environmentalism.

Yet concern for the operation of man in nature had not been
abandoned totally, for some geographers had devoted themselves to
studies of deforestation, erosion, reclamation, and other processes of environmental modification. These studies were in-
spired by a belief that man's role as an ecological dominant
should be a primary focus of geographic investigation.

Out of this belief emerged an Association of American
Geographers' Task Force Report on Environmental Quality in 1973.
In this report, several characteristics of geographic thought
conveying a comparative advantage in environmental analysis were
identified as follows:

(1) Synthesizing. Geographers are self-selected for their
    curiosity about, and ability to handle, a wide range
    of scholarly approaches. Geographical training
    generally fosters these traits and expands the range
    of accessible insights and materials. This is espe-

cially true for interactions between man and environment, for which geographers are apt to assume that any
subject matter may be germane and must be taken into
account more or less systematically.

(2) Complexity of explanations. The wide range of often
conflicting insights that geographers normally acquire
and the profession's past experience with simplistic
explanations--notably environmental determinism--makes
most geographers reluctant to accept single-factor
propositions about cause-and-effect relations. Already
sensitive to the need for complex and multiform explanations, geographers bring mature leadership to the study
of environmental problems that are usually less simple
and less easily resolved than they seem. The inability
of any single discipline to formulate, let alone answer,
some of the basic environmental problems suggests a
need for the synthesizing, holistic approach long and
successfully developed in geography.

(3) Range of information sources. Environmental understanding is apt to require enormously diverse kinds of
information, ranging from the location and dispersal
mechanisms of specific chemical agents, for example,
to the attitudes and behavior of individuals and groups
stemming from their images of such agents. More than
most other scholars, geographers are early exposed
to and trained in a variety of data-gathering techniques, from field observations and laboratory analyses
to interviews and questionnaires, from historical,
archival, and library sources to attitudinal surveys,
from cartographic and statistical analyses to descriptive and holistic syntheses. It is not contended that
any geographer is competent to handle all such techniques, nor that many geographers are well trained in
most of them; what is held to be significant is that
geographical education presupposes the potential utility
of any or all such techniques. Geographers are usually
willing to recognize the value of evidence drawn from
fields in which they themselves lack expertise. Catho-
licity and eclecticism of this nature are invaluable in
many problems of environmental understanding and action.

(4) Location and spatial relationships. Interest and train-
ing alert most geographers to features of distribution
and diffusion, both as to environmental factors and
information and as to value systems bearing on those
factors.

(5) Man as a part of environment, and vice versa. More
than other professions, geography is aware of the complexity of the man-nature interface. Geographers have
examined landscapes and artifacts seen to varying degrees as both 'natural' and 'cultural;' they avoid
sharp dichotomies between these realms. And geographers
are constantly reminded that the physical environment
is felt and responded to through screens of perception
and cognition, screens that deserve to be studied along
with environment and man.

The most persuasive feature of this assessment is its re-
minder of geography's unique position as a discipline devoted to
both natural and social science. On the natural science side,

geographers have the advantage of a perspective that encourages
awareness of the relationship of climate, water, land forms,
vegetation, and soils. The range of investigations conducted by
geographers who identify themselves as social scientists is
similarly broad and eclectic and has the additional advantage of
including both predictive and retrospective orientations. From a
disciplinary point of view, it was the opportunity to draw from
and weave together both of these sources of strength that made
this study for the Environmental Protection Agency a particularly
attractive undertaking.

B POLLUTANT DATA SOURCES AND ENVIRONMENTAL QUALITY ASSESSMENT SYSTEMS

Data on pollutants come from a variety of sources, federal, state, and local. These sources are gradually being linked by EPA into surveillance networks, but as yet the national coverage is highly variable from one type of pollutant to another, and no systematic guides to information or working materials are available. Before proceeding with a discussion of the relationships between city characteristics, urban form, land use, and environmental pollution, it is therefore necessary that an overview be provided of the types of effluents for which measurements are currently being made, the nature of the surveillance networks through which the measures are being collected, the quality of the data that are, as a result, being produced, and within these constraints, what is known about amounts of residuals discharged by type of source and by type of land use. In addition, it is important to be fully aware at the outset of the nature of the environmental standards that have been set, as well as the various quality assessment systems that have been proposed to measure degree of achievement of these standards. This leads to a final question that must be considered: what is known about the health and welfare effects of different pollution intensities, whether there are threshold values beneath which no known damage occurs, etc., because it is the present state of knowledge on which federal standards are based. With this background provided in turn for air, water, solid wastes, noise, pesticides and radiation in Chapters 2-7, it is possible in Part C to proceed with a series of nationwide analyses of the relationships between city characteristics, urban form, land use and environmental pollution using metropolitan areas as observations, and then in Part D to consider intra-metropolitan covariations of urban form and the spatial patterns of pollution.

We know that the summaries presented in the next six chapters seem obvious and elementary to specialists in each of the respective pollution areas, but we know of no single place where the materials have been drawn together in a way designed to help researchers avoid duplicate effort and wasted motion. It is in this spirit that Part B has been accumulated.

AIR QUALITY CONTROL REGIONS
IN THE
CONTERMINOUS UNITED STATES

Source: EPA, Federal Air Quality Control Regions (1972) p. 7.

2   AIR QUALITY

I. POLLUTANT MEASUREMENT SYSTEMS

The air pollution monitoring and air quality measurement
systems currently available in the United States vary in several
ways. One source of variation is in the types of pollutants
which are recorded. Another is in the kind of network by which
the pollutants are currently being monitored. Before considerations of the assessment of air quality can be discussed, it is
important that these basic items of the data being monitored be
reviewed.

1. TYPES OF POLLUTANTS

Air pollutants consist of gases, liquids or solid particulates. The following list covers all the currently known pollutants measured in some way by the Environmental Protection
Agency at the date of writing (March, 1973):

Gases: Carbon monoxide, methane, nitric oxide, nitrogen
oxide, pesticides, reactive hydrocarbons, sulfur oxides,
total hydrocarbons, total oxidants

Elements: Antimony, arsenic, barium, beryllium, bismuth,
boron, cadmium, chromium, cobalt, copper, iron, lead,
manganese,mmercury, molybdenum, nickel, selenium, tin,
titanium, vanadium, zinc

Radicals: Ammonium, fluorides, nitrate, sulfate

Others: Aeroallergens, asbestos, β-radioactivity, benzene-
soluble organic compounds, benzo[a]pyrene, pesticides,
respirable particulates, total suspended particulates

Documents published by EPA and HEW, or reports by Litton Industries Inc. under contract to EPA enable the nature, sources,
effects and present abatement and central methods for many of
these pollutants to be summarized in convenient tabular form
(Table 2.1). In 1973, EPA selected ten from among this total
array of pollutants as being of special concern because of their
adverse health effects, widespread use, production in large
quantities, or their toxicity. These ten, to be the objects of
the most concerted attack by EPA in the years ahead, are arsenic,
asbestos, beryllium, cadmium, fluorides, lead, mercury, carbon
monoxide, nitrogen oxides and sulfur oxides (EPA, Strategic Environmental Assessment System, 1973).

TABLE 2.1

NATURE, SOURCES AND PRINCIPAL ABATEMENT AND CONTROL METHODS OF MAJOR AIR POLLUTANTS

Description and Sources	Effects	Abatement and Control Methods

ARSENIC AND ITS COMPOUNDS
 	
A brittle, very poisonous chemical element.
Major sources are: smelters processing gold and copper; cotton ginning and the burning of cotton trash; use as pesticide; combustion of coal.
	ON HUMANS, ANIMALS AND PLANTS:
	
	Arsenic is extremely poisonous. Arsenical dusts may produce dermatitis, bronchitis, and irritation of the upper respiratory tract. Use of medicines containing arsenic has produced growths and cancers of the skin. The relationship of arsenic to other types of cancer, particularly lung tumors, is uncertain. Herbivorous animals have been poisoned after eating plants contaminated with arsenic compounds.
		1. Use of air cleaning devices to remove particulates from smelters and cotton gins. Equipment must operate at temperature low enough (160 degrees centigrade) to condense arsenic fumes.
		  Electrostatic precipitators
		  Cooling flues
		  Bag houses, especially those using wet scrubbing vacuum pumps instead of fabric filters
		
		2. No methods available to control emissions produced by burning cotton trash.

ASBESTOS General name given to a variety of fibrous minerals. Products made of asbestos are virtually indestructible. Major pollutant is a dust composed of asbestos fibers. Major sources are: asbestos mines and factories; the wearing away of brake linings, roofing, insulation and shingles; fireproofing of buildings with sprayed asbestos applications.	ON HUMANS AND ANIMALS: May cause chronic lung disease or cancer of the lung and pleural cavity.	IN MANUFACTURING: Ventilation through fabric sleeve filters; carrying out some operations (such as spinning and weaving of asbestos fabrics) as wet processes to eliminate dust. IN TRANSPORTATION: Use of plastic-coated bags to transport asbestos. IN CONSTRUCTION: Use of insulators to enclose the work area when asbestos fireproofing is blown onto steel frames. This technique is not completely effective. IN MINES AND MILLS: No information available.

BARIUM AND ITS COMPOUNDS
 	
A slightly malleable metal. Most important pollutant is in solid particle form.
Major sources are: industrial process involved in the mining, refining and production of barium and barium-base chemicals; use of barium compounds as a fuel additive for the reduction of black smoke emissions from diesel engines (producing micron-sized particles in vehicle exhaust).
	ON HUMANS:
	
	Inhalation of barium compounds can cause baritosis, a nonmalignant lung disease characterized by fibrous hardening.
		1. Use of conventional air cleaning devices to remove particulates.
		  Bag filters
		  Electrostatic precipitators
		  Wet scrubbers
		2. No information is available on control of diesel vehicle exhaust.

BERYLLIUM AND ITS COMPOUNDS A hard metallic element which forms strong, hard alloys with several metals, including copper and nickel. Major pollutant is beryllium dust. Major sources are: industrial plants engaged in the extraction, refining, machining and alloying of the metal; combustion of coals containing small quantities of beryllium; proposed use of beryllium as an additive in rocket fuels. During the 1930's, use of beryllium in production of fluorescent lamps was a major source of pollution.	ON HUMANS AND ANIMALS: Inhalation of beryllium or its compounds can cause a bodywide systemic disease, with pulmonary damage of major concern. The acute form occurs as a chemical pneumonitis, with inflammation of the respiratory tract. Chronic beryllium disease, which differs clinically from the acute form, has also caused severe respiratory damage. Bone and lung cancers have been produced experimentally in animals, and	

TABLE 2.1 (Continued)

Description and Sources	Effects	Abatement and Control Methods
	malignant tumors have been recorded in cases of human beryllium disease. ON PLANTS: There is some evidence that beryllium in soils is toxic to plant life.	
BORON AND ITS COMPOUNDS: A nonmetallic chemical element which occurs only in combination with other elements (as with sodium and oxygen in borax). Most important pollutants are boron dusts and borane fuel. Major sources are: use of borane (a compound of boron used as a high-energy fuel for rocket motors and jet engines); combustion of petroleum fuels which contain boron as an additive; burning of coal which contains boron; manufacturing processes employed to produce boron compounds (which are used as water softeners and in manufacture of soap, enamels, glass and pottery).	ON HUMANS AND ANIMALS: Inhalation of boron compounds as dusts can be moderately toxic, causing irritation and inflammation but no permanent injury. Inhalation of borane fuel can be highly toxic; it produces signs of severe central nervous system damage, and high concentrations can cause death after relatively short exposure. ON PLANTS: Kills plants if applied in more than minute quantities.	1. Prevention of accidental spilling of fuels. 2. Reduction or elimination of boron additives in vehicle fuels.
CARBON MONOXIDE A colorless, odorless, tasteless gas, about 97 percent as heavy as air. U.S. emissions in 1966: 101.6 million tons. The major source (60% of total emissions in 1966) is gasoline-powered motor vehicles; other sources are industrial (10%), including foundries, petroleum refineries and kraft pulp mills; burning of solid wastes (7.5%), forest fires, structural fires, burning banks of coal refuse and fires in underground coal mines or coal seam outcrops.	ON HUMANS: When this gas enters the bloodstream, it interferes with the ability of the blood to transport oxygen, thus impairing the functioning of the central nervous system. At high concentrations it kills quickly. At concentrations of 100 parts of carbon monoxide per million parts of air (100 ppm), most people experience dizziness, headache, lassitude, and other symptoms of poisoning. Concentrations higher than this occasionally occur in garages, in tunnels or behind automobiles in heavy traffic. Exposure to 30 ppm for 8 hours or 120 ppm for 1 hour may be a serious risk to the health of sensitive people (those suffering from impaired circulation, heart disease, anemia, asthma or lung impairment). In six U.S. cities where NAPCA measured carbon monoxide inside motor vehicles in traffic, averages ranged from 21 to 39 ppm. Animal experiments indicate that carbon monoxide exposure is a traffic safety hazard. Exposure to levels of carbon monoxide commonly found in traffic may have effects on the driver similar to those resulting from alcohol or fatigue--reduced alertness and a decrease in the ability to respond properly in a complex situation, with resultant impairment of driving ability.	FROM MOTOR VEHICLE SOURCES: 1. Factory installation of emission control systems on new-model vehicles (in effect since 1968 models of autos and light trucks, beginning with 1970 models of buses and heavy-duty trucks). these are of two types: a. Crankcase ventilation systems, in which exhaust vapors are routed back into the fuel induction system and burned in the engine. These devices remove primarily hydrocarbons. b. Exhaust emission control systems, which operate either by injecting air into the exhaust system (thereby changing the carbon monoxide into carbon dioxide) or by reducing the quantity of carbon monoxide coming out of the engine cylinders. The latter is accomplished by designing engines which have improved air-fuel mixing and distribution systems and by tailoring ignition systems to furnish the best degree of control. These devices can be effective in meeting emission standards for carbon monoxide and hydrocarbons, and preliminary studies indicate that they are also effective in reducing nitrogen oxides. NAPCA now tests manufacturers' prototype models, to determine whether federal emission standards for carbon monoxide and hydrocarbons are met. 2. Application of exhaust emission control devices on pre-1968 model cars and trucks (of special significance in Appalachia, where many used vehicles are on the roads). These devices are currently being developed by various automobile manufacturers and are designed to improve the ignition process and to cut down on the emission of carbon monoxide, hydrocarbons and nitrogen oxides by diminishing the amount

TABLE 2.1 (Continued)

Description and Sources	Effects	Abatement and Control Methods
	Susceptibility to carbon monoxide poisoning is increased by high temperature, high altitude, hifh humidity and the use of alcoholic beverages or certain drugs, such as tranquilizers.	of fuel delivered to the engine. NAPCA is currently testing three such devices. 3. Modifying vehicle fuel, changing its volatility, hydrocarbon type and additives. Under consideration: liquefied petroleum gas, liquefied and compressed natural gas. 4. Changing the power source of vehicles. Under development: automatic gas turbine, steam engine, electric drive, free-piston, and Stirling stratified-charge engines. 5. Better inspection and maintenance of vehicles, including governmental certification of maintenance and inspection personnel to protect the public from mechanics who inadvertently increase pollution from exhausts because of incorrect or incomplete work. 6. Substitution of public for private automobile transportation. 7. Planning of freeways and traffic control systems to minimize stop-and-go driving. 8. Planning for emergency actions to reduce vehicular emissions during periods when unfavorable weather conditions create an air pollution emergency. FROM STATIONARY SOURCES (INDUSTRY, POWER PLANTS, FIRES): 1. Good practice. Proper design, application, installation, operation and maintenance of combustion equipment and other systems. 2. Change of fuel or energy source. Change from oil and coal to gas, nuclear power or hydroelectric power, which can be centrally generated at installations where carbon monoxide emission can be controlled. 3. Change of waste disposal method. Use of sanitary land fill to replace open burning; treatment of burning coal waste piles.
CHLORINE GAS Chlorine is a dense, greenish-yellow gas with a distinctive, irritating odor. It is noted for its very strong oxidizing and bleaching properties. Although not flammable, it can support combustion, and many materials and metals can burn in a chlorine atmosphere - sometimes with explosive violence. Major sources are: industrial preparation, particularly the process of liquefaction before use or storage; use of chlorine in the chemical and pulp and paper industries; leakage in storage or transportation.	ON HUMANS: Low concentrations can cause irritation of the eyes, nose and throat; larger doses can cause damage to the lungs and produce pulmonary edema, pneumonitis, emphysema or bronchitis. Incidental chlorine leakage has caused injury and death to humans and animals. ON MATERIALS: Corrosion.	1. Removal of residual gases which remain after liquefaction. Liquid scrubbers (using water, alkali solutions, carbon tetrachloride or brine solution). Solid absorbents such as silica gel 2. Shunting untreated residual gases to other in-plant operations for direct use (for example, chlorination of hydrocarbons).

CHROMIUM
 	
A very hard metal which has a high resistance to corrosion and is best known for its use as a decorative finish in chrome plating. Important pollutants are the chemical chromium compounds.
Possible sources are: industries which use chromium in electroplating and in the manufacture of chemicals and stainless and austenite steels; coal burning; use of chromium compounds as fuel additives, corrosion
	ON HUMANS:
	
	Inhalation of chromium compounds may produce cancer of the respiratory tract. Workers in the chromate-producing industry have experienced deaths from cancer of the respiratory tract at a rate 28 times greater than the normal rate. Exposure to airborne chromium compounds may also produce dermatitis and ulcers on the skin.
		Use of conventional air cleaning devices to remove particulates:
		    Bag filters
		    Precipitators
		    Scrubbers (including mist eliminators and inhibitors)

TABLE 2.1 (Continued)

Description and Sources	Effects	Abatement and Control Methods
inhibitors, pigments and tanning agents.	ON MATERIALS: Chromic acid mists discolor automobile and building paints.	
FLUORIDES Compounds of the element fluorine. May occur in the atmosphere as solid particles (sodium and calcium fluoride) or as highly irritant and toxic gases (for example, hydrofluoric acid) which are usually found in the atmosphere in extremely low concentrations. Major sources are industrial plants (phosphate fertilizer, aluminum metal, brick and tile, steel), the firing of some types of rockets and combustion of coal.	ON HUMANS: Fluorides are highly active and extremely irritating to exposed surfaces of the body. In amounts emitted by industrial plants in several areas of the U.S., fluorides cause eye irritations, nosebleeds, inflammations of the respiratory tract and severe difficulties in breathing. ON ANIMALS: Fluoride emissions settle out of the air onto local pastures, building up toxic doses in the grass and other forage for cattle. When the cattle eat this forage, they develop fluorosis, an ailment which causes crippling skeletal changes, including the softening of gums, wearing away of teeth and malformation of bones and joints. ON PLANTS: Fluorides cause withering of shrubs and damage to flowers and citrus groves. Low concentrations of fluorides damage gladioluses, pine, apricots, prunes and azaleas.	IN MANUFACTURE OF PHOSPHATE FERTILIZER AND PROCESSING OF ANIMAL AND POULTRY FEED: Use of scrubbers. Waste water accumulates in ponds, where lime treatment may prevent evaporation into the air. IN ALUMINUM MANUFACTURE: Use of air cleaning devices (cyclones and electrostatic precipitators with scrubbers). IN STEEL MANUFACTURE: Partial control through use of air cleaning devices to remove particulates. IN BRICK AND TILE MANUFACTURE: No devices now used. Could use scrubbers. IN GLASS MANUFACTURE: Little or no control today. Some smaller furnaces use scrubbers and bag houses. IN COAL COMBUSTION: Little or no control at present. Could use electrostatic precipitators in combination with scrubbers to remove particulates.
HYDROCARBONS (including organic solvents) Compounds of hydrogen and carbon. Major polluting hydrocarbons are those which result from the incomplete combustion of fuels and the evaporation of fuels and industrial solvents. Polluting hydrocarbons exist in the air primarily as gases (including methane, ethylene, and acetylene); others, including cancer-inducing agents such as benzo-a-pyrene, are solid particulates. U.S. emissions in 1966: 31.5 million tons. The American Chemical Society estimates that most (approximately 85%) of all hydrocarbons in the air are emitted from natural sources (forests, vegetation and the bacterial decomposition of organic matter). The major man-made source of hydrocarbons is the processing, distribution, marketing and use of petroleum. The hydrocarbons in vehicle exhausts, which result from the incomplete burning of gasoline in the internal combustion engine, accounted for over half of the man-made hydrocarbon emissions in 1967. Other important sources were the evaporation of industrial solvents and incineration of waste.	ON HUMANS: Most hydrocarbons are toxic only at relatively high concentrations. A considerable number of hydrocarbons, including benzo-a-pyrene (a substance found in cigarette smoke), have produced cancer in laboratory animals. One study indicates that, in terms of this substance, breathing city air is the equivalent of smoking from 7 to 36 cigarettes a day, depending on the degree of concentration. Even at very low concentrations, certain types of hydrocarbons (particularly the olefins produced during incomplete combustion of fuel) react with sunshine to produce photochemical oxidants, which are the toxic and irritating compounds in smog. The effects of these compounds are described in a separate section of this table.	FROM MOTOR VEHICLE SOURCES: Same as for carbon monoxide. Emissions resulting from evaporation of gasoline from fuel tanks and carburetors can be limited by storage of the vapors within the engine itself or in a carbon canister which absorbs the fuel vapors, and then routing the vapors back to the engine, where they will be burned. Federal standards controlling these emissions will be in effect beginning with 1971 vehicle models. FROM STATIONARY SOURCES: 1. Design equipment to use or consume completely the processed materials. 2. Use materials which have a higher boiling point or are less photochemically reactive. 3. Use control equipment to reduce emissions. 4. Stop open burning of waste by use of multiple-chamber incinerators or disposing of waste in sanitary land fills.

TABLE 2.1 (Continued)

Description and Sources	Effects	Abatement and Control Methods

HYDROGEN CHLORIDE
 	
    A colorless gas with a strong, pungent and irritating odor. Because of its high solubility in water, the gas is readily converted into hydrochloric acid fumes and droplets in the air or when inhaled into the lungs.
    Major sources are: the commercial use and production of the gas and the acid; burning of paper products and fossil fuels (coal and oil); manufacture of chemicals (hydrochloric acid is a byproduct).
	ON HUMANS:
	
	    Inhalation causes coughing and choking, as well as inflammation and ulceration of the upper respiratory tract. Irritation of the eye membranes is also common, and exposure to high concentrations can cause clouding of the cornea. Erosion of teeth may also result.
	
	ON MATERIALS:
	
	    Hydrochloric acid is extremely corrosive to most materials.
	
	ON PLANTS:
	
	    Both the gas and the acid damage the leaves of a great variety of plants.
		1. <u>Use of water absorption facilities</u> which convert the gas to hydrochloric acid:
		    Water scrubbing systems
		    Rotary brush scrubbers
		    Ejector venturi scrubbers
		2. <u>Use of dry solid absorbents.</u>
		3. <u>Addition of basic salts</u> (such as sodium carbonate) to coal before burning.

LEAD
 	
    A metallic element which is a natural constituent of soil, water, vegetation and animal life, and is taken into the body in water and food as well as in air. Most air pollutants are in the form of aerosols, fumes and powders.
    The major source of airborne lead in urban areas is the exhaust from gasoline-fueled vehicles. (Lead is added to high-octane gasoline motor fuels to cut down on engine knock.) Other man-made sources are manufacturing (lead additives for gasoline, lead processing and the manufacture of lead products), combustion of coal (as in dry bottom power plants which use pulverized coal), transfer and transportation of leaded gasoline, use of pesticides and the incineration of refuse. Natural sources include silicate dusts from soils and particles from volcanoes.
	ON HUMANS AND ANIMALS:
	
	    Lead is a cumulative poison. One form of lead poisoning damages the brains of young children and may cause death. Other forms cause severe malfunctioning of the alimentary tract (loss of appetite, constipation, colic), general weakness and malaise and impaired functioning of the nervous system, with resulting weakness, atrophy and sometimes paralysis of the extensor muscles of the forearm. Auto exhaust containing lead was found to increase the concentration of lead in the bones of mice.
		FROM VEHICLE SOURCES:
		
		    Reduction or elimination of lead in fuel; use of particulate traps on vehicle exhausts.
		
		FROM LEAD PROCESSING AND THE MANUFACTURE OF LEAD PRODUCTS:
		
		    Control of operating conditions (temperature and timing); use of conventional air cleaning techniques (bag house filters, scrubbers, electrostatic precipitators).
		
		FROM COAL COMBUSTION:
		
		    Use of electrostatic precipitators.
		
		FROM MANUFACTURE OF LEAD ADDITIVES IN GASOLINE:
		
		    Use of water scrubbers and bag house filters.
		
		FROM TRANSFER AND TRANSPORTATION OF LEADED GASOLINE:
		
		    Use of vapor recovery systems; reduction or elimination of lead in gasoline.
		
		FROM USE OF PESTICIDES:
		
		    Use of pesticides which do not contain lead; improved techniques of pesticide use.
		
		FROM INCINERATION OF REFUSE:
		
		    Use of sanitary land fills instead of incineration.

MERCURY AND ITS COMPOUNDS:
 	
    A heavy metal which is liquid at ordinary temperatures, has high specific gravity and high electrical conductivity.
Major sources are: the mining and refining of mercury; industrial applications (mercury-arc rectifiers, mercury precision casting); laboratory equipment and instruments (spillage creates droplets which vaporize); agricultural use of mercury compounds as pesticides (now declining).
	ON HUMANS AND ANIMALS:
	
	    Mercury and most derivatives are lethal to man, animals and plants. Inhalation can cause acute mercury poisoning, which may be fatal or cause permanent damage to the nervous system.
	Russian experiments with animals indicate that chronic exposure to mercury vapor may cause a chronic form of mercury poisoning which is difficult to diagnose because the symptoms (exaggerated emotional response, gum infection and muscular tremors) are ambiguous and frequently appear long after exposure.
		FOR APPLICATIONS WHICH USE MERCURY AT NORMAL TEMPERATURES:
		
		1. <u>Proper ventilation in work areas.</u>
		2. <u>Cleaning up spilled mercury</u> (sweeping with special vacuum cleaners or chemical treatment).
		3. <u>Use of nonporous material</u> for floors, working surfaces and protective clothing.
		
		FOR APPLICATIONS WHICH USE MERCURY AT HIGH TEMPERATURES:
		
		1. <u>Condensing mercury vapors</u> by:
		Cold-water-jacketed condensers
		Impregnated charcoal
		Water scrubbers
		2. <u>Conventional control of pesticides</u> (see pesticides).

TABLE 2.1 (Continued)

Description and Sources	Effects	Abatement and Control Methods

NICKEL AND ITS COMPOUNDS
 	
A grayish-white metallic element - hard, tough and markedly resistant to oxidation and corrosion - which forms a variety of alloys with other metals. Major pollutants are nickel dust and vapors.
 	
Major sources are: plants producing nickel alloys (including stainless steel), catalysts and chemicals; aviation and automobile engines burning fuels containing nickel additives; burning coal and oil; nickel plating facilities; incineration of nickel products.
	ON HUMANS:
	
	Inhalation may cause cancer of the lung, cancer of the sinus, other disorders of the respiratory system and dermatitis.
		1. Use of conventional air cleaning devices.
		   Bag filters
		   Precipitators
		   Scrubbers
		2. Decomposition of gaseous emissions at high temperatures, forming nickel (which can be removed as a particulate) and carbon monoxide.
		3. No control methods currently available for vehicle engine exhausts.

NITROGEN OXIDES Compounds of nitrogen and oxygen. Most significant pollutants are two gases: nitric oxide, a colorless gas which is relatively harmless but which usually converts in the atmosphere to the more dangerous nitrogen dioxide. nitrogen dioxide, a gas which is normally brownish-red in color and which is produced during the burning of fuels and, to a lesser degree, during chemical processes. In the presence of sunshine, nitrogen oxides act as the trigger for the photochemical reactions which produce smog (see hydrocarbons and photochemical oxidants). U.S. emissions in 1966: 16.7 million tons. Most nitrogen oxides are the result of fuel combustion. Nearly half come from the use of fuels in transportation, particularly gasoline in the automobile. The second largest source (40%) is the burning of fossil fuels (coal, oil and natural gas) in generating electric power and space heating.	**ON HUMANS AND ANIMALS:** Little is known about the direct effects of nitrogen oxides at levels commonly found in polluted air (1-3 ppm). At 13 ppm, they may cause eye and nose irritation. Animals exposed to 10-20 ppm showed damage to lung tissue and increased susceptibility to infection. Major effects result from the substances formed when nitrogen oxides (in combination with hydrocarbons, discussed above) are exposed to sunlight, forming photochemical smog (see photochemical oxidants). **ON PLANTS** Nitrogen oxides restrict growth and cause injuries similar to those caused by sulfur dioxide.	**FROM MOTOR VEHICLE SOURCES:** Same as for carbon monoxide. Emissions standards for new vehicles will be effective beginning with 1973 models. Preliminary studies indicate that the exhaust emission control systems and devices used to control emissions of carbon monoxide and hydrocarbons may also be effective against nitrogen oxides. **FROM STATIONARY SOURCES:** 1. Modification of combustion methods. 2. Substitution of electricity for oil, coal and natural gas fuels. 3. Substitution of sanitary land fills for open burning of solid waste. 4. Relocation of power generating stations to remote places. 5. Burning nitrogen oxide gases to reduce them to elemental nitrogen. 6. Addition of urea to nitric acid to prevent release of nitrogen oxides.
ODOROUS COMPOUNDS Offensive smells which provoke people into complaining about air pollution. Hydrogen sulfide is a major offender. Major sources are: kraft paper mills; animal-rendering plants; chemical plants; petroleum refineries; metallurgical plants; diesel engines; sewers and sewage treatment plants.	**ON HUMANS:** Nausea, headache, loss of sleep, loss of appetite, impaired breathing, allergic reactions and emotional disturbances. **ON PROPERTY:** Discouragement of capital improvements, damaged community reputation, stifling of community growth and development, decline in property values, tax revenues, payrolls and sales.	1. Combustion. Incineration at the source. 2. Absorption. Used when odorants are soluble in water. Various devices (including spray towers, cyclone scrubbers, trays) bring vapor into contact with liquid. 3. Adsorption. Activated charcoal commonly used. 4. Masking or counteracting odors. Usually uses synthetic compounds with a pleasant smell. 5. Dilution with air. Requires favorable weather conditions. 6. Source elimination. Use of low-sulfur fuels. 7. Removal of particulates which carry odors. See particulates. 8. Chemical control. Oxidation or combination may change odorous to nonodorous compounds. 9. Biological control. Use of organisms which control sewage odor by oxidizing the odorous gases. 10. Containment. Covers on fuel tanks, sewage ponds and other open storage areas.

TABLE 2.1 (Continued)

Description and Sources	Effects	Abatement and Control Methods

ORGANIC CARCINOGENS

ON ANIMALS:

Same as for hydrocarbons.

Carbon compounds which cause cancer in experimental animals, and which are therefore suspected of playing a role in causing human cancer, particularly cancer of the lung. (This category includes some of the hydrocarbons discussed earlier in the table.) Most frequently studied is benzo-a-pyrene, a substance also found in cigarette smoke.

Major source is the incomplete combustion of matter containing carbon. Heat generation (burning coal, oil and gas) accounts for more than 85%; refuse burning, motor vehicle exhaust and industrial processes account for 5% each.

Certain organic compounds, especially benzo-a-pyrene, have been found to increase tumor incidence in experimental animals. In addition, animal studies indicate that other carbon compounds may encourage or slow the development of malignant tumors.

PARTICULATES

Any matter dispersed in the air, whether liquid or solid, that has individual particles smaller in diameter than 500 microns (approximately 1/50 of an inch). Particulates may remain airborne from a few seconds to several months. The category includes some compounds which are not solid or liquid while in industrial stacks, but which condense when dispersed into the regular atmosphere.

Included are: aerosols (solids and liquids of microscopic size which are dispersed in gas, forming smoke, fog or mist), visible particles (such as fly ash, metallic particles and dust), fumes, soot (carbon particles impregnated with tar), oil and grease. Particulates are responsible for grime. U.S. emissions in 1966: 28.6 million tons.

Of the total volume of particulates in the U.S. in 1966 (28.6 million tons), nearly one-third (primarily fly ash from coal combustion) was produced by plants generating electric power and space heating. Another one-fourth of the total came from industrial sources - dust, fumes, smoke and mists which arise from fuel combustion and the loss of materials or products into the atmosphere. Slightly more than one-third of the total particulates are the result of fires - incineration of refuse, forest fires and man-made fires. In the transportation category, the major source of particulates is the automobile exhaust, which is characterized by an extremely large number of fine particles, including lead. Diesel-fueled vehicles are particular offenders, producing approximately 10 times as much particulate matter per gallon as gasoline-fueled vehicles.

Some particulates are directly harmful - they contain poisonous or disease-producing substances (for example, hydrocarbons, arsenic, asbestos, beryllium, fluorides and lead, which are described in this table).

Other particulates multiply the potential harm of irritant gases. For example, sulfur dioxide (a pollutant described in this table) is a gas which is highly soluble in water, and if inhaled by itself it will dissolve relatively harmlessly in the upper respiratory tract. But sulfur dioxide is rarely inhaled alone; when it is absorbed on particulate matter, it will penetrate deep into the lungs, where it can cause damage to lung tissue.

Still other particulates speed chemical reactions in the atmosphere, and these reactions may produce much more harmful substances than the ingredients that went into them. For example, certain particulates speed the conversion of sulfur dioxide to sulfuric acid.

FROM MOTOR VEHICLE SOURCES:

Same as for carbon monoxide. See also lead and boron. Research on particulate emission control is being conducted by NAPCA. It has not yet been determined whether emission control systems (described under carbon monoxide) are effective in removing particulates from vehicle exhaust.

FROM STATIONARY SOURCES (INDUSTRY, POWER PLANTS, FIRES):

1. Use of air cleaning techniques and devices by industry and power plants to remove particulates:
   Inertial separators or gravitational settling chambers
   Cyclones
   Bag houses and fabric filters
   Electrostatic precipitators
   Scrubbers and venturi scrubbers
2. Control of construction and demolition (including grading of earth, paving roads and parking lots, sandblasting, spray painting). Hooding and venting to air pollution control equipment; wetting down working surfaces with water or oil.
3. Disposal of solid waste by sanitary land fill, composting, shredding and grinding rather than incineration.

PESTICIDES

ON HUMANS:

Economic poisons used to control or destroy pests that cause economic losses or adverse human health effects. Includes: poisons to kill insects, weed and brush, fungi, rodents, molluscs, algae, worms; repellents; attractants; plant growth regulators.

The primary source of pesticides

One class of insecticides (the chlorinated hydrocarbons which include DDT) may cause poisoning in humans; in mild cases symptoms include headache, dizziness, gastrointestinal disturbances, numbness and weakness of the extremities, apprehension

1. Control of pesticide drift during application.
Improved application equipment and methods;
Improved formulas for pesticides (increased use of large oil-based droplets rather than dusts);
Wider distribution and use of weather data in area where pesticides are to be used.

TABLE 2.1 (Continued)

Description and Sources	Effects	Abatement and Control Methods

in the air is from the application process; a certain amount of drift is unavoidable even under ideal conditions. Pesticides can evaporate into the air from soil, water and treated surfaces, and pesticides contained in dust from the soil can enter the air and be transported for considerable distances before falling back to the earth. Plants manufacturing pesticides also produce pollutant emissions.

and great irritability. In more severe cases, fine muscular tremors appear, and these may lead to convulsions or death from cardiac or respiratory arrest. Another category of insecticides (the organophosphates) cause loss of appetite, nausea and headache, followed by vomiting, abdominal cramps, excessive sweating and salivation. A large dose will cause gastro-intestinal symptoms and bronchial secretion that may be accompanied by pulmonary edema. In severe cases, con-vulsions, coma and death may occur.

Weed killers may cause irritation of eyes and gastro-intestinal disturbances; they have caused liver and kidney injury in experimental animals.

Fungicides cause allergic dermatitis, irritation of the mucous membranes and kidney damage.

2. Control and abatement during production.
Enclosure of grinding, mixing, packing, and filling operations;
Venting of solid emissions through bag houses and cyclones;
Venting of liquid emissions through liquid scrubbers.

PHOTOCHEMICAL OXIDANTS

Chemical compounds which are the major components of smog and which are formed when hydrocarbons and nitrogen oxides (discussed above) are exposed to sunlight. Most significant oxidants are ozone and PAN (peroxyacyl nitrates).

Sources are the same as those for hydrocarbons and nitrogen oxides.

ON HUMANS: See hydrocarbons and nitrogen oxides.

The most common effects are eye irritation and difficulty in breathing, particularly for people already suffering from respiratory disease.

At levels commonly found in city atmospheres, ozone causes irritation of mucous membranes in nose and throat. At some-what higher levels, it causes coughing, choking and severe fatigue. At relatively high levels, such as those occurring during severe photo-chemical smogs, ozone interferes with lung function for the duration of exposure and up to 24 hours beyond, and causes bronchial irritation, slight coughing, and soreness in the chest. At these high levels, ozone also reduces visual acuity and causes recurrent headache, fatigue, chest pains, difficulty in breathing and wheezing. Long-term exposure to ozone shortens the lives of experimental animals.

Preliminary studies indicate that PAN causes eye irritation and has the same effects on lung function as ozone.

ON PLANTS:

Photochemical oxidants cause lesions in the leaves of plants, thereby causing a serious decline in agricultural crops (par-ticularly citrus and leafy vegetables) in California and along the eastern seaboard from Boston to Washington, D.C. Ozone is toxic to field and forage crops (such as tobacco), leafy vegetables, shrubs, fruit and forest trees (particularly conifers). PAN is toxic to many species of field crops (spinach, beets, celery, tobacco, peppers, endive, Romaine lettuce, swiss chard and alfalfa) and to several ornamental plants (petunias, snapdragons, primroses, asters and fuchias).

ON MATERIALS:

Ozone damages textiles, discolors dyes and accelerates the cracking of rubber. Stressed rubber has cracked after less than an hour's exposure to ozone in concentrations lower than those commonly reached in metropolitan areas.

ON VISIBILITY:

Photochemical smog can reduce visibility to as low as a quarter of a mile. In Los Angeles, where smoggy days are commonplace, visibility frequently is less than three miles, which is considered the minimum visibility for safe operation of airplanes.

RADIOACTIVE SUBSTANCES

Substances which give off radiant energy in the form of particles or rays as a result of the disintegration of atomic nuclei. Major pollutants are radioactive gases and particu-lates (dust, fumes, smokes, and mists).

ON HUMANS AND ANIMALS:

Radiation causes leukemia and genetic effects. Since the genetic effects of various amounts of radiation cannot always be determined, many scientists accept the belief that there is no safe level of exposure, i.e.,

1. Limiting emissions of radio-active pollutants:
In uranium mining: wet drilling, underground drainage and clearing away ore;
In nuclear reactors: use of closed-cycle coolant systems and maintenance of high coolant purity;
In nuclear testing: choice of

TABLE 2.1 (Continued)

Description and Sources	Effects	Abatement and Control Methods
Atmospheric radiation arises from both natural sources (rocks, soils and cosmic rays) and from artificial sources (nuclear explosions and the nuclear industry in general). World population received a significant dose of radiation as a result of nuclear weapons testing (an average of 5-10% higher than the levels of natural radioactivity), resulting in contamination of food and soil. Experience to date has shown that, although there is a potential for radiation release from all facets of the nuclear industry, the amount of radiation reaching the general public from the nuclear industry is insignificant when compared with the natural radiation dose. However, because of projected expansion of nuclear industry, there is evidence that Krypton-85, which is released from nuclear fuel reprocessing, may be a problem. The U.S. Atomic Energy Commission has established maximum permissible concentrations for radionuclides that can be released from nuclear plants.	no threshold below which there is no danger of biological damage to humans.	ideal meteorological conditions. 2. Containment: a. Completely containing pollutant so it does not escape into the atmosphere by use of hermetically sealed tanks and closed-cycle process systems. b. If an accident allows fission product to escape from reactor, isolating the polluted air in a reactor containment building. 3. Dispersal. Diluting pollution by mixing with air in stacks. 4. Site location. Choosing localities where possibility of excessive radiation dose to general population is minimized (depends on type of installation, meteorological factors, distribution of population). 5. Removal of particulates and gases: a. Filtration: roughing filters, absolute filters, bag filters, deep-bed filters b. Centrifugal collection (cyclones) c. Electrostatic precipitators d. Wet collection: Wet filters, viscous filters, packed towers, cyclone scrubbers, venturi scrubbers. 6. Adsorption and chemisorption. Use of activated carbons, silica gels and chemicals based on soda lime. 7. Absorption Removing gases that react chemically with scrubbing 8. Delay for decay. Retaining gases in tanks until radioisotopes have decayed. Effective for short-lived isotopes. 9. Physically or chemically locking radioactive wastes into solid forms which can easily be stored, monitored and protected.
SELENIUM A chemical element found in soils (particularly in the Midwest) and fuels. Major pollutants are a solid (selenium dioxide), which turns to acid in moist environments, and a gas (hydrogen selenide). Major sources are: combustion of industrial and residential fuels; gases and fumes from refinery waste; incineration of trash, particularly paper products which contain minute quantities of selenium.	ON HUMANS: Selenium compounds in the air cause irritation of the eyes, nose, throat, and respiratory tract; prolonged exposure may cause gastrointestinal disorders. ON ANIMALS: Swallowing selenium compounds may cause cancer of the liver, and is known to produce pneumonia and degeneration of liver and kidneys.	1. Installation of good ventilation systems in fuel refineries and incinerators. 2. Use of personal protective equipment by workers (safety goggles, respirators). 3. Use of conventional air cleaning devices to remove particulates: Wet scrubbers Electrostatic precipitators 4. Burial of solid waste. 5. Dilution of liquid wastes by washing them away.
SULFUR OXIDES Chemical compounds of sulfur and oxygen. The most significant pollutants are: sulfur dioxide, a colorless gas, which has a pungent and irritating odor at concentrations above 3 ppm and which can be tasted at concentrations from .3 ppm to 1 ppm in air. In the atmosphere sulfur dioxide is partially converted to sulfur trioxide.	ON HUMANS: Sulfur dioxide gas alone can irritate the upper respiratory tract. If it is absorbed on particulate matter, or if it is converted into sulfuric acid, it can be carried deep into the lungs, where it can injure delicate tissue. Prolonged exposure to relatively low levels of	1. Change from high-sulfur coal and oil to low-sulfur fuels or electricity. 2. Removal of sulfur from fuel before use. For coal, cleaning techniques (crushing and flotation); for fuel oil, catalytic treatment with hydrogen or blending with low-sulfur distillate oils. 3. Increased combustion efficiency. 4. Removal of sulfur oxide from flue gases by: Reaction with calcined limestone,

TABLE 2.1 (Continued)

Description and Sources	Effects	Abatement and Control Methods

sulfur trioxide, a gas which combines with water in the atmosphere to form sulfuric acid, or with other materials in the atmosphere to form various sulfate compounds. U.S. emissions in 1967: 31.2 million tons.

Nearly three-fourths of the sulfur oxides emitted in the U.S. in 1967 resulted from the burning of sulfur-bearing fuels in order to produce electric power and space heating. (Coal combustion alone accounted for more than 60% of total emissions). Industrial processes, primarily smelting and petroleum refining, accounted for most of the remainder.

sulfur dioxide has been associated with an increase in the number of deaths from cardiovascular disease in older persons.

Prolonged exposure to higher concentrations has been associated with an increase in respiratory death rates and an increase in complaints by schoolchildren of cough, mucous membrane irritation and mucous secretion.

Very heavy concentrations of sulfur oxides (as in the four-day October 1948 air disaster in Donora, Pennsylvania) cause cough, sore throat, chest constriction, headache, a burning sensation of the eyes, nasal discharge and vomiting. During the year following the disaster, 20 people died in Donora, where the normal mortality would have been two.

ON PLANTS:

Damage to or death of trees and plants may occur as far as 52 miles from smelters discharging large amounts of sulfur oxides, and levels routinely observed in U.S. cities are damaging to plants. The plants most sensitive to sulfur pollution are those with leaves having high physiological activity - alfalfa, grains, squash, cotton, grapes, white pine, apple and endive.

ON MATERIALS:

Sulfur oxides attack and destroy even the most durable of materials. Steel corrodes two to four times faster in urban and industrial areas than it does in rural areas, where much less sulfur-bearing coal and oil are burned. Sulfur pollution also destroys zinc, silver and palladium (used in electrical contacts), paint pigments and fresh paint (thus delaying drying), nylon hose (which can be destroyed during a lunch hour in a high-sulfur atmosphere), and stone buildings and statuary.

Cleopatra's Needle, a famous sculpture from ancient Egypt, has deteriorated more in the 90 years since its arrival in New York City than it did during the more than 3,000 years it spent in Egypt. The corrosive action of the sulfur oxides is accelerated by the presence of particulates and water.

ON VISIBILITY:

When high concentrations of sulfur oxides are coupled with relatively high humidity, visibility goes down because of the formation of sulfuric acid, which scatters light. Reduced visibility is a hazard to land, water and air transportation.

then removal by fly ash control devices or wet scrubbers;

Reaction with alkalized alumina, followed by recovery of sulfur (which has commercial value);

Catalytic oxidation to sulfuric acid (which has commercial value).

5. Dispersion by use of tall stacks. Limited by local meteorological and topographic conditions.

VANADIUM AND ITS COMPOUNDS

A rare malleable metal. Major sources are: vanadium refining industries; alloy industries; power plants and utilities using vanadium-rich residual oils.

ON HUMANS AND ANIMALS:

Vanadium is toxic to humans and animals. Human inhalation of relatively low concentrations has resulted in inhibition of cholesterol synthesis; chronic exposure to environmental air containing vanadium has been statistically related to mortality rates from heart diseases and certain cancers. Exposure to high concentrations results in observable effects on the gastro-intestinal and respiratory tracts.

1. Use of additives (such as magnesium oxide) when burning high-vanadium content oils to reduce the quantity of small particulates emitted.

2. Use of conventional air cleaning devices to remove particulates:

Cyclones and other centrifugal collectors

Electrostatic precipitators

2. SURVEILLANCE NETWORKS

The surveillance networks for the sampling of atmospheric pollutants exist at several scales which range from the nation-wide level down to the local urban region.

a. THE NATIONAL AIR SURVEILLANCE NETWORK

Nationwide coverage is achieved through the National Air Surveillance Network (NASN), which maintains one sampling station in each of its reporting communities. Data obtained from this network are published by the Office of Air Programs of E.P.A. in their Air Pollution Technical Documents. These reports present valid sample data in annual cumulative frequency distributions with arithmetic and geometric means, the sampling techniques used, and station locations. The principal pollutants measured are two for which APTD reports are available, and four without inventories (etc.) as yet:

Sulfur Dioxide -- collected by bubbling air through a solution of potassium tetrachloromercurate, analysed using a West Jacke method, and sampled in 64 cities in 1971 (APTD - 1354).

Suspended Particulates -- collected with a high volume air sampler, analysed by use of gravimetric techniques, and sampled in 191 cities in 1971 (APTD - 1353).

Carbon Monoxide -- collected with a carbon monoxide analyzer using a method based on the absorption of infrared radiation by carbon monoxide.

Photochemical Oxidants -- ambient air is combined with ethylene and passed by a photomultiplier detection cell which detects a reaction of ozone from the ambient air with ethylene.

Hydrocarbons -- air is passed into a hydrogen flame ionization detector which measures its total hydrocarbon content.

Nitrogen Dioxide -- collected by bubbling air through a sodium hydroxide solution and testing for presence of nitrite ions.

b. CONTINUOUS AIR MONITORING PROJECT

A second network of nationwide significance is the Continuous Air Monitoring Project (CAMP) from which samples are obtained on a 24 hour basis in six cities: Cincinnati, Chicago, Denver, Philadelphia, St. Louis, and Washington, D.C. Readings are taken concerning five pollutants: Sulfur dioxide, nitrogen dioxide, carbon monoxide, photochemical oxidants, and suspended particulates.

c. STATE REPORTS

Air Pollution Emission Inventories have been developed as
of the time of writing for the following states in the Air Pol-
lution Technical Documents (APTD) noted: Alabama (APTD - 0746);
Alaska (APTD - 0671); Arkansas (APTD - 0795); Hawaii (APTD -
0817); Kansas (APTD - 0748); Louisiana (APTD - 0794); Minnesota
(APTD - 0771); Missouri (APTD - 0732); Montana (APTD - 0791);
Nebraska (APTD - 0771); New Jersey (APTD - 0742); New Mexico
(APTD - 0792); North Dakota (APTD - 0799); Ohio (APTD - 0756);
Oklahoma (APTD - 0773); South Carolina (APTD - 0747); South
Dakota (APTD - 0799); Vermont (APTD - 0758); Wyoming (APTD - 0801).

d. AIR QUALITY CONTROL REGION SAMPLING NETWORKS

The most important data base for regionally determining the
level of air quality is that contained in the Air Quality Control
Region system. This system of regions exhausts the national territory with a total of 247 Air Quality Control Regions. This system,
designed to determine regional levels of air quality, contains several types of units: 53 interstate regions (centered on urban cores),
182 intrastate regions (designed to evaluate state-wide levels of
air quality), and 12 regions which were established as a result of
the Clean Air Act to exhaust the national territory and include those
areas which were part of neither interstate or intrastate regions
(EPA, Office of Air Programs, 1972).

e. URBAN EMISSION INVENTORIES

EPA also has completed Air Pollution Emission Inventories
for a series of specific places which, as of the time of writing
this report, include: Albuquerque (APTD - 0809); Atlanta (APTD -
0811); Baton Rouge (APTD - 0866); Beaumont - Port Arthur (APTD -
0810); Billings (APTD - 0808); Birmingham (APTD - 0893); Boston
(APTD - 0879); Buffalo (APTD - 0877); Charlotte (APTD - 0812);
Cheyenne (APTD - 0813); Cincinnati (APTD - 0878); Columbus (APTD -
0814); Dayton (APTD - 0876); Denver (APTD - 0880); El Paso (APTD -
0815); Fargo (APTD - 0816); Houston (APTD - 0818); Indianapolis
(APTD - 0881); Kansas City (APTD - 0896, -97); Las Vegas (APTD -
0819); Louisville (APTD - 0894); Memphis (APTD - 0882); Miami
(APTD - 0821); Milwaukee (APTD - 0883); New Orleans (APTD -
0823); Oklahoma City (APTD - 0825); Omaha (APTD - 0826); Phoenix -
Tucson (APTD - 0827); Pittsburgh (APTD - 0895); Portland, Maine
(APTD - 0828); Providence (APTD - 0884); Raleigh - Durham - Chapel
Hill (APTD - 0834); Reno (APTD - 0829); Salt Lake City (APTD -

0830); San Antonio (APTD - 0885); San Juan (APTD - 0831); Seattle
(APTD - 0886); Springfield, Ohio (APTD - 0840); St. Louis (APTD -
0887); Sioux Falls, S.D. (APTD - 0832); Toledo (APTD - 0888).

II. GENERATION OF EMISSIONS

1. EMISSION SOURCES AND AMOUNTS

A variety of air pollution emission sources has been identified. The most important of these in terms of tonnages of pollutants emitted are the means of transportation, most notably
automobiles and trucks, as indicated in Table 2.2. Following behind are fuel combustion from stationary sources (especially
electric power generation), industrial processes and the burning
of solid wastes. Among the miscellaneous items are forest fires,
coal waste fires, and agricultural burning.

TABLE 2.2

THE SOURCES OF AIR POLLUTION:
1970 NATIONWIDE ESTIMATES

	Sulfur Oxides	Parti- culates	Carbon Monoxide	Hydro- Carbons	Nitrogen Oxides	TOTAL
	MILLIONS OF TONS PER YEAR					
Transportation	1.0	0.8	111.0	19.5	11.7	144.0
Fuel combustion in stationary sources: Electric Power Combustion	15.0	3.0	0.1	0.03	3.0	21.13
Industrial Combustion	9.3	3.4	0.1	0.4	6.8	20.0
Domestic Heating	2.2	0.4	0.6	0.2	0.2	3.6
Industrial Processes	6.4	13.3	11.4	5.5	0.2	36.8
Solid Waste Disposal	0.1	1.4	7.2	2.0	0.4	11.1
Miscellaneous	0.2	4.0	18.3	7.3	0.5	30.3
TOTAL	34.2	26.3	148.7	34.93	22.8	

Source: EPA, The National Air Monitoring Program: Air Quality and Emission
Trends; Annual Report (1973), p. 1-7, and Justus et al. Economic
Costs of Air Pollution Damage (1973).

2. THE INCIDENCE OF POLLUTION

Much of this pollution occurs within urban areas. There is a distinct gradient of pollution intensities of most types from urban areas into progressively more remote rural territory, as shown in Table 2.3. Furthermore, within the urban scene, pollution intensities increase with city size, as Table 2.4 indicates. But there are also important variations among cities, once the effects of size are held constant, and these have been the subject of several statistical analyses.

TABLE 2.3

URBAN-RURAL AIR POLLUTION GRADIENTS

| | URBAN (217 Stations) | | NONURBAN | | | | | |
| | | | Proximate (5) | | Intermediate (15) | | Remote (10) | |
	$\mu g/m^{3a}$	%	$\mu g/m^{3a}$	%	$\mu g/m^{3a}$	%	$\mu g/m^{3a}$	%
Suspended Particulates	102.0		45.0		40.0		21.0	
Benzene soluble org.	6.7	6.6	2.5	5.6	2.2	5.4	1.1	5.1
Ammonium ion	0.9	0.9	1.22	2.7	0.28	0.7	0.15	0.7
Nitrate ion	2.4	2.4	1.40	3.1	0.85	2.1	0.46	2.2
Sulfate ion	10.1	9.9	10.0	22.2	5.29	13.1	2.51	1.8
Copper	0.16	0.15	0.16	0.36	0.078	0.19	0.060	0.28
Iron	1.43	1.38	0.56	1.24	0.27	0.67	0.15	0.71
Manganese	0.073	0.07	0.026	0.06	0.012	0.03	0.005	0.02
Nickel	0.017	0.02	0.008	0.02	0.004	0.01	0.002	0.01
Lead	1.11	1.07	0.21	0.47	0.096	0.24	0.002	0.10

[a]Unit of measure: $\mu g/m^3$ = micrograms per cubic meter.

Source: Thomas B. McMullen, Comparison of Urban and Nonurban Air Quality, presented at 9th Annual Indiana Air Pollution Control Conference, Purdue University, Oct 13-14, 1970, Table 4, p. 7.

TABLE 2.4

AIR POLLUTION RELATED TO CITY SIZE

| Class Number and Population Class | CONCENTRATION | | | Number of Sites |
	TSP^a	SO_2	NO_2	
1. Nonurban	25	10	33	5
2. Urban < 10,000	57	35	116	2
3. 10,000	81	18	64	2
4. 25,000	87	14	63	2
5. 50,000	118	29	127	9
6. 100,000	95	26	114	37
7. 400,000	100	28	127	17
8. 700,000	101	29	146	9
9. 1,000,000	134	69	163	2
10. 3,000,000	120	85	153	2
Slope	9.152	6.103	12.109	
Intercept	41.467	0.733	44.000	
r^2	0.748	0.590	0.719	
t statistic	4.874	3.392	4.526	

[a]TSP: Total suspended particulates.

Source: The Mitre Corp., MTR-6013, p. 70. Time span-second half of 1969, first half of 1970. Cited in Council on Environmental Quality, Environmental Quality, Second Annual Report, 1971, pp. 215 and 243. Regressions: Pollutant concentration on population class number (1 through 10).

3. STATISTICAL MODELS OF CITY CHARACTERISTICS RELATED TO
   POLLUTION

Among the statistical analyses that have been completed relating variations in pollution intensities among cities to city
characteristics, perhaps the best known example is by Hoch (1972)
in his report to the Commission on Population Growth and the
American Future. Hoch's results are summarized in Table 2.5,
and they show that increases in pollution levels are consistently

TABLE 2.5

FACTORS ASSOCIATED WITH HIGH LEVELS
OF AIR POLLUTION

Dependent Variable (Geometric Mean of Pollutant Listed) and Explanatory Variable	Coefficient	t value	R^2
Particulates			
Constant	51.55	...	0.26
Log SMSA population	22.94	3.10[a]	
January temperature	−0.54	1.67[b]	
Iron and steel production workers in 000	0.66	2.41[a]	
Nitrates			
Constant	0.664		0.34
Log SMSA population	0.816	1.93[b]	
Central city density (000)	−0.127	3.44[a]	
Total central city gasoline sales, in million dollars	0.011	3.38[a]	
Sulfates			
Constant	5.84		
Central city density (000)	0.53	5.01[a]	0.48
Nonferrous metals production workers in 000	0.81	3.26[a]	

[a]Significant at 0.05 level.

[b]Significant at 0.10 level.

Source: Irving B. Hoch (1972)

related to population densities, concentrations of manufacturing, and high automobile usage when the effects of increasing city size are held constant.

Hoch's results have been confirmed by other investigations, for example Morris (1972), who fitted equations of the following form to city data:

(1) $S\hat{O}_x = s(S, M, R, W, T)$

(2) $\hat{P} = p(S, M, R, W, T)$

where

SO_x = sulfur oxides per square mile

P = particulates per square mile

S = city size (population)

M = manufacturing index

R = annual median precipitation (inches)

W = annual median wind velocity (mph)

T = annual number of degree days in excess of 65° F.

(3) $\hat{c} = f(S, SO_x, P)$

where

c = the estimated cost of controlling SO_x and P emissions on a square mile basis.

(4) $c\hat{o} = f(S, \hat{G}, R, W, T)$

(5) $\hat{G} = f(S, D)$

where

D = city density

G = gasoline sales per square mile

The parameters estimated for equations (1), (2), (3), (4), and (5) by Morris, using ordinary least squares regression on a sample of twenty-seven metropolitan areas are as follows:

(1') $S\hat{O}_x = -295.6638 + 0.4080*S - 1.8507S^2 + 3.4378R$
          (0.2079)   (1.3638)   (s.6433)

$\qquad - 3.8242W + 2.0379T + 5.6520*M \qquad R^2 = .5774$
$\quad$ (15.9449) (1.6755)   (2.6794)

(2') $\hat{P} = 32.1210 + 0.0427S - 0.2454S^2 + 1.5794R$
          (0.0862)   (0.5656)   (1.0962)

$\qquad - 10.7903W - 0.1256T + 2.3578*M \qquad R^2 = .4372$
$\quad$ (6.6129)   (0.6949)   (1.1120)

(3'$_L$) $\hat{C}_L = -0.5936 + 0.0749**S + 0.0263**SO_x + 0.0217P$
               (0.0281)   (0.0083)   (0.0219)

$\qquad\qquad\qquad\qquad\qquad\qquad\qquad R^2 = .6541$

(3'$_H$) $\hat{C}_H = -0.7432 + 0.0851**S + 0.0370**SO_x + 0.0314P$
               (0.0323)   (0.0095)   (0.0252)

$\qquad\qquad\qquad\qquad\qquad\qquad\qquad R^2 = .6790$

$$(4') \quad \hat{CO} = -55.4416 + 0.3603*S - 0.4332S^2 + 1.7805R$$
$$\phantom{(4') \quad \hat{CO} = -55.4416 +} (0.1667) \quad\quad (0.9662) \quad\quad (1.6502)$$

$$- 4.5093W + 1.0622T + 2.9983**\hat{G}$$
$$(10.0746) \quad (0.8366) \quad (0.3698) \quad\quad R^2 = .9424$$

$$(5') \quad \hat{G} = -0.4366 + 0.5956S - 0.5145**S^2 + 0.0918**D$$
$$\phantom{(5') \quad \hat{G} = -0.4366 +} (0.0349) \quad (0.2049) \quad\quad (0.0072)$$

$$R^2 = .9339$$

Figures 2.1 to 2.3 show the actual data for SO_x, P, and CO related to city size, as well as the predicted city size effects from the above models when, turning Hoch's discussion around, all the variables other than city size are held constant. Air pollution is evidently quite variable from city to city, but Morris argues that there is an underlying relation with city size that is strongly positive to a point. The lowest levels of air quality are found in large, high-density industrial cities with heavy automobile usage.

Morris' three figures, developed using data for the year 1970, are as follows:

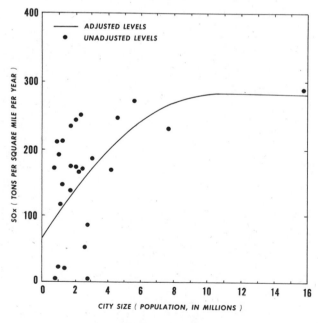

FIGURE 2.1

SULFUR OXIDES POLLUTION LEVELS BY CITY SIZE

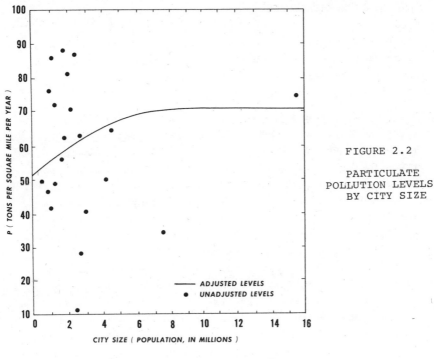

FIGURE 2.2

PARTICULATE
POLLUTION LEVELS
BY CITY SIZE

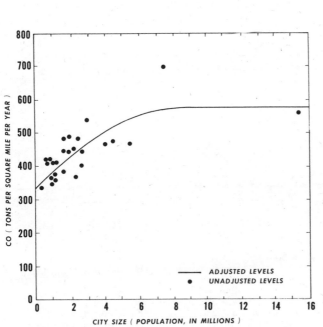

FIGURE 2.3

CARBON MONOXIDE
POLLUTION LEVELS
BY CITY SIZE

III. AIR QUALITY ASSESSMENT

The assessment of air quality involves two ingredients, the setting of clean air standards and the measurement of the extent to which these standards are being achieved.

1. CLEAN AIR STANDARDS

Primary and secondary air quality standards for ambient air in the United States were published in the Federal Register, Vol. 36, No. 84, Pt. II (Friday, April 30, 1971). These are summarized in Table 2.6. By ambient air is meant that portion of the atmosphere, external to buildings, to which the general public has access. The national primary ambient air quality standards are the levels of air quality which the Administrator of EPA judges are necessary, with an adequate margin of safety, to protect the public health. The national secondary ambient air quality standards are the levels of air quality which the Administrator judges necessary to protect the public welfare from any known or anticipated adverse effects of a pollutant. Thus, the national primary standard for carbon monoxide was based on evidence that low levels of carboxyhemoglobin in human blood may be associated with impairment of ability to discriminate time intervals. Similarly the national standards for photochemical oxidants are based upon evidence of increased frequency of asthma attacks in some asthmatic persons on days when estimated hourly concentrations of photochemical oxidant reach 200 $\mu g/m^2$ (0.10 ppm).

TABLE 2.6

NATIONAL AIR QUALITY STANDARDS

Pollutant	Primary Standards	Secondary Standards
Sulfur Oxides	(a) 80 micrograms per cubic meter (0.03 ppm) - annual arithmetic mean. (b) 365 micrograms per cubic meter (0.14 ppm) - maximum 24-hr. concentration not to be exceeded more than once per year.	(a) 60 micrograms per cubic meter (0.02 ppm) - annual arithmetic mean. (b) 260 micrograms per cubic meter (0.1 ppm) - maximum 24-hr. concentration not to be exceeded more than once per year, as a

TABLE 2.6 (Continued)

Pollutant	Primary Standards	Secondary Standards
		guide to be used in assessing implementation plans to achieve the annual standard. (c) 1,300 micrograms per cubic meter (0.5 ppm) - maximum 3-hr. concentration not to be exceeded more than once per year.
Particulate Matter	(a) 75 micrograms per cubic meter - annual geometric mean. (b) 260 micrograms per cubic meter - maximum 24-hr. concentration not to be exceeded more than once per year.	(a) 60 micrograms per cubic meter - annual geometric mean, as a guide to be used in assessing implementation plans to achieve the 24-hr. standard. (b) 150 micrograms per cubic meter - maximum 24-hr. concentration not to be exceeded more than once per year.
Carbon Monoxide	(a) 10 milligrams per cubic meter (9 ppm) - maximum 8-hr. concentration not to be exceeded more than once per year. (b) 40 milligrams per cubic meter (35 ppm) - maximum 1-hr. concentration not to be exceeded more than once per year.	
Photochemical Oxidants	160 micrograms per cubic meter (0.08 ppm) - maximum 1-hr. concentration not to be exceeded more than once per year.	
Hydrocarbons	160 micrograms per cubic meter (0.24 ppm) - maximum 3-hr. concentration (6 to 9 a.m.) not to be exceeded more than once per year.	
Nitrogen Dioxide	100 micrograms per cubic meter (0.05 ppm) - annual arithmetic mean.	

TABLE 2.7

EMISSIONS STANDARDS FOR MOTOR VEHICLES
1974, 1975 AND 1976 MODEL YEARS

		Exhaust Emissions			Fuel Evaporative Emission	Crank-Case Emission
		Hydro-carbons[1] (HC)	Nitrogen Oxides[1] (NO×)	Carbon Monoxide[1] (CO)	Hydro-carbons[1] (HC)	Hydro-carbons[1] (HC)
Light Duty	1974	3.4	3.0	39.0	2.0	0.0
Gasoline Fueled	1975	1.5	3.1	15.0	2.0	0.0
	1976	0.41	2.0	3.4	2.0	0.0
Heavy Duty	1974	sum of HC and NO for all 3 years = 16 g/BHP hour		40 g/BHP hours[2]		0.0
Gasoline Fueled	1975			40 g/BHP hours		0.0
	1976			40 g/BHP hours		0.0

[1]-Grams per vehicle mile
[2]-BHP=braking horse power

Source: Federal Register, August 7, 1973 and subsequent revisions.

    To help achieve its published standards in places with sub-
standard air quality, EPA has taken a variety of positive steps.
One is to set emissions standards that have to be met by new
motor vehicles, the greatest source of pollution, by model years
1975 and 1976. These are described in Table 2.7. The publication
of other related standards is to be expected.

    2. MEASURES OF ACHIEVEMENT OF STANDARDS, I: STATISTICAL
          INDEXES

    Given a set of clean air standards, the question naturally
arises as to how well the standards are being met. To this end,
EPA has sponsored a variety of efforts to develop air quality
indexes that measure the degree of standards-achievement. Three
of these indexes, the Mitre Air Quality Index (MAQI), the Extreme
Value Index (EVI), and the Oak Ridge Air Quality Index (ORAQI)
were given national exposure in the Second Annual Report of the
Council of Environmental Quality in 1972.

a. THE MITRE AIR QUALITY INDEX

The Mitre Air Quality Index is a combination of individual pollution indexes, each composed of a ratio of observed air pollution levels to national secondary air quality standards, viz:

$$MAQI = \sqrt{I_c^2 + I_s^2 + I_p^2 + I_n^2 + I_o^2}$$

where the I's are level-to-standard ratios for each of the five main categories of air pollution: carbon monoxide, sulfur dioxide, total suspended particulates, nitrogen dioxide, and photochemical oxidants.

Essentially, the MAQI is the root-sum-square value of the individual pollutant indexes. This method of index computation guarantees the MAQI value will be at least 1 if any pollutant included in its computation exceeds the secondary standard value. (MAQI values between 1 and 3 require inspection of the individual components, because values in this range do not necessarily imply that any standard is exceeded.) A MAQI value of less than 1 indicates that all standards are being met for those pollutants included in the MAQI computations. Because nine standards for five pollutants are involved in computing MAQI, any MAQI value greater than 3, or $\sqrt{9}$, guarantees that at least one standard value has been exceeded.

The individual components, the I's, are computed as follows:

The carbon monoxide index is the root-sum-square (RSS) value of individual terms corresponding to each of the secondary standards. The RSS value is used to ensure that the index value will be greater than 1 if either standard value is exceeded. The index is defined as $I_c = \sqrt{\left(\dfrac{C_{c8}}{S_{c8}}\right)^2 + \delta\left(\dfrac{C_{c1}}{S_{c1}}\right)^2}$

where

C_{c8} is the maximum observed eight-hour concentration of carbon monoxide,

S_{c8} is the eight-hour secondary standard value (i.e., 9ppm or 10,000 $\mu g/m^3$) consistent with the unit of measure of C_{c8},

C_{c1} is the maximum observed one-hour concentration of carbon monoxide,

S_{c1} is the one-hour secondary standard value (i.e., 35 ppm or 40,000 $\mu g/m^3$) consistent with the unit of measure of C_{c1}, and

δ is 1 if $C_{c1} \geq S_{c1}$ and is 0 otherwise.

For example, the maximum observed values of carbon monoxide in 1965 at the Chicago CAMP (Continuous Air Monitoring Program) Station were $C_{c8} = 44$ ppm and $C_{c1} = 59$ ppm. The corresponding carbon monoxide index is

$$I_c = \sqrt{\left(\frac{44}{9}\right)^2 + 1\left(\frac{59}{35}\right)^2} = 5.17.$$

The <u>sulfur dioxide index</u> component of the MAQI is computed in a fashion similar to the carbon monoxide index. This index has three rather than two terms, one for each of the Federal standards, and is given by

$$I_s = \sqrt{\left(\frac{C_{sa}}{S_{sa}}\right)^2 + \delta_1\left(\frac{C_{s24}}{S_{s24}}\right)^2 + \delta_2\left(\frac{C_{s3}}{S_{s3}}\right)^2}$$

where

C_{sa} is the annual arithmetic mean observed concentration of sulfur dioxide,

S_{sa} is the annual secondary standard value (i.e., 0.02 ppm or 60 $\mu g/m^3$) consistent with the unit of measure of C_{sa},

C_{s24} is the maximum observed twenty-four-hour concentration of sulfur dioxide,

S_{s24} is the twenty-four-hour secondary standard value (i.e., 0.1 ppm or 260 $\mu g/m^3$) consistent with the unit of measure of C_{s24},

C_{s3} is the maximum observed three-hour concentration of sulfur dioxide,

S_{s3} is the three-hour secondary standard value (i.e., 0.5 ppm or 13000 $\mu g/m^3$) consistent with the unit of measure of C_{s3},

δ_1 is 1 if $C_{s24} \geq S_{s24}$ and is 0 otherwise, and

δ_2 is 1 if $C_{s3} \geq S_{s3}$ and is 0 otherwise.

The observed levels of sulfur dioxide at the Chicago CAMP Station in 1965 were

C_{sa} = 0.13 ppm,

C_{s24} = 0.55 ppm, and

C_{s3} = 0.94 ppm.

The corresponding sulfur dioxide index is

$$I_s = \sqrt{\left(\frac{.13}{.02}\right)^2 + 1\left(\frac{.55}{.1}\right)^2 + 1\left(\frac{.94}{.5}\right)^2} = 8.72.$$

The index of total suspended particulates is computed as

$$I_p = \sqrt{\left(\frac{C_{pa}}{S_{pa}}\right)^2 + \delta\left(\frac{C_{p24}}{S_{p24}}\right)^2}$$

where

C_{pa} is the annual geometric mean observed concentration of total suspended particulate matter,

S_{pa} is the annual secondary standard value (i.e. 60 $\mu g/m^3$),

C_{p24} is the maximum observed twenty-four-hour concentration of total suspended particulate matter,

S_{p24} is the twenty-four-hour secondary standard value (i.e., 150 $\mu g/m^3$), and

δ is 1 if $C_{p24} \geq S_{p24}$ and is 0 otherwise.

For the Chicago CAMP Station in 1965, sixty-six measurements were taken with a Hi-Volume Sampler. The observed concentrations were

C_{pa} = 194 $\mu g/m^3$ and
C_{p24} = 414 $\mu g/m^3$.

The corresponding total suspended particulate index is

$$I_p = \sqrt{\left(\frac{194}{60}\right)^2 + 1\left(\frac{414}{150}\right)^2} = 4.25$$

Due to the nature of a geometric mean, a single twenty-four-hour reading of 0 would result in an annual geometric mean of 0. The EPA recommends that one half of the measurement method's minimum detectable value be substituted, in this case 0.5 $\mu g/m^3$, when a "zero" value occurs.

The nitrogen dioxide index does not require the RSS technique because only a single annual Federal standard has been promulgated. The index is

$$I_n = \frac{C_{na}}{S_{na}}$$

where

C_{na} is the annual arithmetic mean observed concentration of nitrogen dioxide, and

S_{na} is the annual secondary standard value (i.e., 0.05 ppm or 100 $\mu g/m^3$) consistent with the unit of measure of C_{na}.

For the Chicago CAMP Station in 1965, the observed annual average concentration of nitrogen dioxide was

C_{na} = 0.04 ppm

and the index is

$$I_n = \frac{0.04}{0.05} = 0.80.$$

The index of photochemical oxidants is computed in a manner similar to the nitrogen dioxide index. A single standard value is used as the basis of the index which is

$$I_o = \frac{C_{ol}}{S_{ol}}$$

where

C_{ol} is the maximum observed one-hour concentration of photo-chemical oxidants, and

S_{ol} is the one-hour secondary standard value (i.e., 0.08 ppm or 160 $\mu g/m^2$) consistent with the unit of measure of C_{ol}.

In 1965, the Chicago CAMP Station registered a maximum one-hour concentration of photochemical oxidants of C_{ol} = 0.13 ppm. The index for that year and station is

$$I_o = \frac{0.13}{0.08} = 1.62.$$

The photochemical oxidant data required for the index computation must be derived from a continuous sampler in order to obtain hourly readings. Most of the NASN and local air quality sampling sites do not presently measure this pollutant at this frequency.

The individual pollutant indexes derived from the 1965 Chicago CAMP Station data can be used to show how the total value for MAQI is derived:

$$MAQI = \sqrt{(5.17)^2 + (8.72)^2 + (4.25)^2 + (.8)^2 + (1.62)^2}$$

or

MAQI = 11.14.

If each of the individual pollutants had been at exactly the standard values, the MAQI would have been equal to $\sqrt{9}$ or 3. This value is arrived at by noting that nine standard values are defined, two for carbon monoxide, three for sulfur dioxide, two for carbon monoxide, three for sulfur dioxide, two for total suspended particulates, and one each for nitrogen dioxide and photochemical oxidants. Hence, any MAQI value in excess of 3 guarantees that at least one pollutant component has exceeded the standards. Interpretation of this index, as of any aggregate index, should be in terms of its relative (rather than absolute) magnitude with respect to a national or regional value of the index. Cost of living and umemployment indexes for a given location, for example, are frequently interpreted in this manner. It is apparent that the ambient air quality measured

by the Chicago CAMP Station in 1965 was worse than the Federal
Secondary Standard Values. It is not apparent, by inspection
of only the MAQI value, which standards were exceeded. It is
recommended, therefore, that each of the individual pollutant
indexes be considered together with the MAQI in order to obtain
a true picture of the actual situation.

b. THE EXTREME VALUE INDEX

Because extreme high air pollution values are those most
directly related to personal comfort and wellbeing, and affect
plants, animals, and property, an index based upon extreme values
also provides a meaningful measure of the ambient air quality.
The Extreme Value Index (EVI) is such a measure, an accumulation
of the ratio of the extreme values to the standard values for
each pollutant, combined using the root-sum-square method. Only
those pollutants are included for which secondary "maximum values
not to be exceeded more than once per year" are defined.

The Extreme Value Index is given by

$$EVI = \sqrt{E_c^2 + E_s^2 + E_p^2 + E_o^2}$$

where

E_c is an extreme value index for carbon monoxide,

E_s is an extreme value index for sulfur dioxide,

E_p is an extreme value index for total suspended particulates, and

E_o is an extreme value index for photochemical oxidants.

The carbon monoxide extreme value index is the root-sum-
square of the accumulated extreme values divided by the secondary
standard values. The index is defined as

$$E_c = \sqrt{\left(\frac{A_{c8}}{S_{c8}}\right)^2 + \left(\frac{A_{c1}}{S_{c1}}\right)^2}$$

where

A_{c8} is the accumulation of values of those observed eight-
hour concentrations which exceed the secondary standard and is expressed mathematically as

$$A_{c8} = \sum_i \delta_i \, (C_{c8})_i ,$$

δ_i is 1 if $(C_{c8})_i \geq S_{c8}$ and is 0 otherwise,

S_{c8} is the eight-hour secondary standard value (i.e., 9 ppm or 10,000 µg/m³) consistent with the unit of measure of the $(C_{c8})_i$ values,

A_{c1} is the accumulation of values of those observed one-hour concentrations which exceed the secondary standard value and is expressed as

$$A_{c1} = \sum_i \delta_i \, (C_{c1})_i,$$

δ_i is 1 if $(C_{c1})_i \geq S_{c1}$ and is 0 otherwise, and

S_{c1} is the one-hour secondary standard value (i.e., 35 ppm or 40,000 µg/m³) consistent with the unit of measure of the $(C_{c1})_i$ values.

At the Chicago CAMP Station in 1965, about 1 percent of the measured one-hour carbon monoxide concentrations and 93.4 percent of the measured eight-hour concentrations exceeded the respective secondary standards. From the raw EPA data, the accumulations of these values are

$A_{c8} = 16,210$ ppm and

$A_{c1} = 2,893$ ppm.

The carbon monoxide extreme value index for Chicago in 1965 is

$$E_c = \sqrt{\left(\frac{16210}{9}\right)^2 + \left(\frac{2893}{35}\right)^2} = 1803.01.$$

The <u>sulfur dioxide extreme value index</u> is computed in the same manner as the carbon monoxide extreme value index. This index also includes two terms, one for each of the secondary standards which are maximum values not to be exceeded more than once per year. No term is included for the annual standard. The index is computed as

$$E_s = \sqrt{\left(\frac{A_{s24}}{S_{s24}}\right)^2 + \left(\frac{A_{s3}}{S_{s3}}\right)^2}$$

where

A_{s24} is the accumulation of those observed twenty-four-hour concentrations which exceed the secondary standard value and is expressed as

$$A_{s24} = \sum_i \delta_i \, (C_{s24})_i,$$

δ_i is 1 if $(C_{s24})_i \geq S_{s24}$ and is 0 otherwise,

S_{s24} is the twenty-four-hour secondary standard value (i.e., 0.1 ppm or 260 µg/m³) consistent with the unit of measure of the $(C_{s24})_i$ values,

A_{s3} is the accumulation of those observed three-hour concentrations which exceed the secondary standard value and is expressed mathematically as

$$A_{s3} = \sum_i \delta_i \, (C_{s3})_i,$$

δ_i is 1 if $(C_{s3})_i \geq S_{s3}$ and is 0 otherwise, and

S_{s3} is the three-hour secondary standard value (i.e., 0.5 ppm or 1300 $\mu g/m^3$) consistent with the unit of measure of the $(C_{s3})_i$ values.

At the Chicago CAMP site in 1965, the observed sulfur dioxide concentrations resulted in accumulated values of

$A_{s24} = 37.52$ ppm and

$A_{s3} = 38.63$ ppm

where 49.9 percent of the twenty-four-hour values and 2.5 percent of the three-hour vlaues exceeded the secondary standards. The index for the Chicago CAMP Station in 1965 is

$$E_s = \sqrt{\frac{37.52}{.1}^2 + \frac{38.63}{.5}^2} = 383.07.$$

An inspection of CAMP sulfur dioxide data suggests that the three-hour standard is rarely exceeded and, when it is, the contribution of the three-hour extreme values to the sulfur dioxide extreme value index is negligible. The index, therefore, could optionally be calculated as

$$E_s = \frac{A_{s24}}{S_{s24}}$$

For example, computation in this manner using the Chicago CAMP data results in an index value of 375.20, a value which is 98 percent of the index value which includes the three-hour term.

A secondary standard single maximum value not to be exceeded more than once per year is defined for total suspended particulates. The total suspended particulates extreme value index has but one term; no annual term is included. This index is computed as

$$E_p = \frac{A_{p24}}{S_{p24}}$$

where

A_{p24} is the accumulation of values of those observed twenty-four-hour concentrations which exceed the secondary standard value and is given by

$$A_{p24} = \sum_i \delta_i \ (C_{p24})_i$$

δ_i is 1 if $(C_{p24})_i \geq S_{p24}$ and is 0 otherwise, and

S_{p24} is the twenty-four-hour secondary standard value (i.e., 150 $\mu g/m^3$).

The Chicago CAMP data for 1965 indicate that sixty-six Hi-Volume Sampler twenty-four-hour measurements were taken. Of these, approximately 74.2 percent exceeded the secondary standard value. The observed accumulated total suspended particu-

lates concentrations in excess of the twenty-four-hour standard
for 1965 at the Chicago CAMP Station were

$$A_{p24} = 111535 \ \mu g/m^3.$$

The 1965 Chicago CAMP Station data result in an index of

$$E_p = \frac{11534}{150} = 76.90.$$

The photochemical oxidants extreme value index consists of
a single term. The index is calculated as

$$E_o = \frac{A_{ol}}{S_{ol}}$$

where

A_{ol} is the accumulation of values of the observed one-hour
c   concentrations which exceed the secondary standard
value and is expressed as

$$A_{ol} = \sum_i \delta_i \ (C_{ol})_i,$$

δ_i is 1 if $(C_{ol})_i \geq S_{ol}$ and is 0 otherwise, and

S_{ol} is the one-hour secondary standard value (i.e., 0.08 ppm
or 160 $\mu g/m^3$) consistent with the unit of measure of
the $(C_{ol})_i$ values.

At the Chicago CAMP Station in 1965, 1.8 percent of the observed one-hour concentrations of photochemical oxidants exceeded
the secondary standard. The accumulation of these values was

$$A_{ol} = 9.45 \ ppm.$$

The index value is

$$E_o = \frac{9.45}{.08} = 118.12.$$

The individual pollutant extreme value indexes may then be
combined and the combined EVI calculated for the Chicago CAMP
Station in order to illustrate the method of computation. The
EVI is

$$EVI = \sqrt{(1803.01)^2 + (383.07)^2 + (76.90)^2 + (118.12)^2}$$

or

$$EVI = 1848.64.$$

Although this index tends to depict the degree to which the
secondary standards have been exceeded, it is probably most useful as an indicator of the trend over time of the air quality in
a particular locality.

A characteristic of the EVI is its tendency to increase in
magnitude as the number of observations in excess of standards
increases. This growth of the index value is desirable. The
index truly depicts the ambient air quality only if observations

are made for all periods of interest (i.e., one-hour, three-hour, eight-hour, and twenty-four-hour) during the year for which secondary standards are defined. Trend analyses using EVI values based upon differing numbers of observations may be inadequate and even misleading. Further research is required to develop statistical techniques for adjusting the index values to compensate for differing numbers of observations.

The EVI and its component indexes always indicate that all standards are not being attained if the index values are greater than zero. The index value will always be at least 1 if any standard based upon a "maximum value not to be exceeded more than once per year" is surpassed.

    c.   THE OAK RIDGE AIR QUALITY INDEX

The Oak Ridge Air Quality Index (ORAQI) is designed to incorporate the five major air pollutants, carbon monoxide, sulfur dioxide, nitrogen dioxide, photochemical oxidants, and total suspended particualtes, into one index value based on the following formula:

$$ORAQI = \left(39.02 \sum_{i=1}^{3} \left(\frac{\text{Concentration of pollutant i}}{\text{EPA standard of pollutant i}} \right) \right)^{0.967}$$

where the Concentration of pollutant i values are annual means obtained from the National Air Sampling Network, the same data as are used to compute the Mitre Air Quality Index.

The ORAQI formula of computation normalizes the data such that a value of 100 would indicate that all air pollutant concentrations are equal to the federally established secondary standards. As an index of air quality, the ORAQI yields results similar to the MAQI values utilized for computations in this present work. MAQI values were chosen in preference to the ORAQI values as they were available for the necessarily large set of urban locations.

Table 2.8 demonstrates the different values obtained from each of three indexes--Mitre Air Quality Index, Extreme Value Index, and the Oak Ridge Air Quality Index--for a set of nine urban places.

    3.   MEASURES OF ACHIEVEMENT OF STANDARDS, II: INDEXES INCORPORATING PHYSICAL PROCESSES

The problem of MAQI, EVI and ORAQI is they develop total

TABLE 2.8

AIR POLLUTION DATA UTILIZING MAQI,
EVI, AND ORAQI MEASURES

	MAQI	EVI	ORAQI
NEW YORK			
1968	6.07	20.06	246
1969	5.01	13.39	181
1970	3.48	7.38	116
BALTIMORE			
1968	3.51	6.95	127
1969	3.28	4.48	117
1970	4.17	15.15	114
BIRMINGHAM			
1968	5.09	26.67	135
1969	4.25	22.41	107
1970	5.05	16.13	76
BOSTON			
1968	2.35	3.24	84
1969	2.51	2.58	79
1970	2.12	1.09	76
PHILADELPHIA			
1968	3.84	9.15	128
1969	2.72	5.53	82
1970	3.99	13.38	150
ST. LOUIS			
1968	3.82	18.07	157
1969	5.35	27.24	163
1970	4.41	13.15	125
MILWAUKEE			
1968	4.27	30.82	119
1969	3.17	10.17	89
1970	2.69	6.41	70
ATLANTA			
1968	2.88	2.22	108
1969	2.51	1.10	91
1970	2.60	3.44	86
DETROIT			
1968	4.01	17.90	145
1969	3.68	12.11	138
1970	3.39	9.17	102

Source: U. S. Council on Environmental Quality (1972).

standard-achievement measures as the sum of achievement ratios
for the individual pollutants, without due regard being given to
the interdependencies and interactions among pollutants that arise
from their physical relationships in the environment. At least
one proposed index has been developed to include provision for
particulate matter-sulfur oxides synergisms as well as the effects
of oxidants as both primary and secondary pollutants. This is
the PINDEX, described by Babcock (1970).

   a. PINDEX

Babcock's Pindex calculation scheme is described in Figure 2.4.

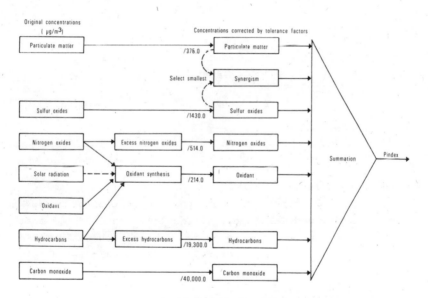

FIGURE 2.4

PINDEX CALCULATION SCHEME

   Moving from left to right, the inputs include the raw emissions plus solar radiation. Solar radiation influences the amount
of hydrocarbons and nitrogen oxides converted to oxidant. Alternatively, oxidant can be considered an input as in air quality
data. Next the revised concentrations of pollutants are weighted
by their tolerance factors. Finally each corrected pollutant
plus the particulate-nitrogen oxides synergism term are summed to

TABLE 2.9

DERIVATION OF TOLERANCE FACTORS

	California Standards	Tolerance Factors	
		(ppm)	($\mu g/m^3$)
Oxidant	0.1 ppm for 1 hr.	0.10	214
Particulate matter	Visibility below 7.5 miles for 12 hr, below 3 miles for 1 hr.	----	375
Nitrogen oxides	0.25 ppm for 1 hr. (for nitrogen dioxide)	0.25	514
Sulfur oxides	0.1 ppm for 24 hr. 0.5 ppm for 1 hr.	0.50	1430
Hydrocarbons	----	----	19300
Carbon monoxide	20 ppm for 8 hr.	32.0	40000

Source: Babcock (1970), p. 658

yield the Pindex level.

Babcock's 1970 paper describes the computation of Pindex in terms of the proposed California air quality standards of that year, thereby producing the "tolerance factors" shown in Table 2.9. Given these tolerance factors, Pindex is calculated as follows:

1. Given surveillance information:
Particulate Matter	(PM) =	143.0 $\mu g/m^3$
Sulfur Oxides	(SOX) =	123.0
Nitrogen Oxides	(NOX) =	136.0
Carbon Monoxide	(CO) =	7250.0
Hydrocarbons	(HC) =	2157.0
Oxidant	(OOO) =	43.2
Solar Radiation	(SR) =	400.0 cal/cm^2 day

2. Convert reactants to $\mu mol/m^3$

   NOX = 136.0/46.0 = 3.0 $\mu mol/m^3$
   HC = 2157.0/16.0 = 134.5
   OOO = 43.2/48.0 = 0.9

3. Determine limiting reactant for oxidant synthesis (NOX or HC): NOX is limiting

4. Create oxidant

   OOO = 0.0006 X SR X (limiting reactant)
   OOO = 0.0006 X 400.0 X 3.0 = 0.72 $\mu mol/m^3$

5. Determine total oxidant and excess HC and NOX:

$$OOO = 0.9 + 0.72 = 1.6 \ \mu mol/m^3$$
$$HC = 134.5 - 0.72 = 133.8$$
$$NOX = 3.0 - 0.72 = 2.3$$

6. Convert reactants back to weight basis

$$OOO = 1.6 \ X \ 48.0 = 77.3$$
$$HC = 133.5 \ X \ 16.0 = 2140.0$$
$$NOX = 2.3 \ X \ 46.0 = 105.0$$

7. Apply tolerance factors

$$PM = 143.0/375.0 = 0.381$$
$$SOX = 123.0/1430.0 = 0.086$$
$$NOX = 105.0/514.0 = 0.204$$
$$CO = 7250.0/40000.0 = 0.181$$
$$HC = 2140.0/19300.0 = 0.111$$
$$OOO = 77.3/214.0 = 0.361$$

8. Determine synergism term (SYN)

$$SYN = SOX \ or \ PM \ (whichever \ is \ smaller)$$
$$SYN = SOX = 0.086$$

9. Sum terms to determine Pindex

$$Pindex = PM + SOX + NOX + CO + HC + OOO + SYN$$
$$Pindex = 1.41$$

Table 2.10 describes Pindex levels for selected U.S. cities, calculated using the tolerance factors reported in the previous table.

TABLE 2.10

PINDEX LEVELS FOR SELECTED U.S. CITIES*

	PM ($\mu g/m^3$)	SO_x (ppm)	NO_x (ppm)	CO (ppm)	HC (ppm)	Oxidant (ppm)	
Chicago	124	0.14	0.14	12.0	3.0	0.01	
Cincinnati	154	0.03	0.06	6.0	3.0	0.02	
Denver	126	0.01	0.07	7.9	2.4	0.03	
Los Angeles	119	0.02	0.13	11.0	4.0	0.05	
Philadelphia	154	0.08	0.08	6.8	2.0	0.01	
Saint Louis	143	0.04	0.07	5.8	3.0	0.04	
San Diego	69	0.01	0.05	3.0	6.0	0.03	
San Francisco	68	0.01	0.14	3.2	3.0	0.02	
San Jose	92	0.01	0.12	5.0	4.0	0.02	
Washington	77	0.05	0.07	6.0	3.0	0.02	
Pindex Levels							**TOTAL**
Chicago	0.47	0.42	0.56	0.38	0.11	0.10	2.04
Los Angeles	0.34	0.06	0.52	0.34	0.15	0.50	1.91
Saint Louis	0.42	0.14	0.26	0.18	0.11	0.36	1.47
Philadelphia	0.49	0.24	0.32	0.21	0.07	0.10	1.43
San Jose	0.26	0.03	0.48	0.16	0.15	0.30	1.38
Denver	0.35	0.03	0.29	0.25	0.09	0.29	1.30
Cincinnati	0.44	0.09	0.24	0.19	0.11	0.20	1.27
San Francisco	0.19	0.03	0.56	0.16	0.11	0.20	1.25
Washington	0.26	0.15	0.28	0.18	0.11	0.20	1.18
San Diego	0.19	0.03	0.20	0.09	0.22	0.30	1.03

*(approximated from 1962 to 1967 data).   Source: Babcock (1970), p. 655

IV. THE EFFECTS OF AIR POLLUTION

Air quality standards are based upon presumed threshold effects related to <u>public health</u> (primary standards) and "any known or anticipated adverse effects" on the <u>public welfare</u> (secondary standards). What is known about such effects?

1. HEALTH EFFECTS

An initial brief summary of the health effects of various air pollutants was provided in Table 2.1. The issue is more complicated than suggested by this tabulation, however. For example, the multiple pollutant burdens that affect all individuals in an increasingly complex society are pyramidal in their effects, as diagrammed in Figure 2.5.

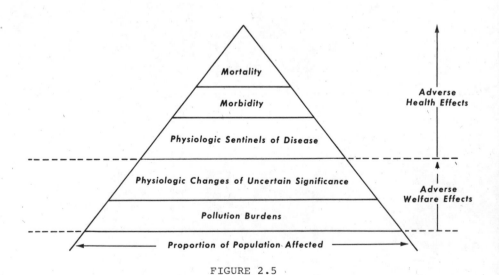

FIGURE 2.5

SPECTRUM OF RESPONSES TO POLLUTANT EXPOSURE

From a biological perspective, this figure refers to pollutant burdens in the sense of any environmental residue in tissue greater than that needed for optimal growth and development. From a more general socio-economic viewpoint, the pollution burdens can be thought of as transcending biological considerations, including a broad range of social and economic impacts that have the same pyramidal structure as the physiological residues. Specific information on the pyramidal effects of SO_2 on health and on vegetation is presented in Figures 2.6 and 2.7.

Hickey, Boyce, Harner and Clelland (1970) argue that the pyramidal structure diagrammed in these two figures may in the long run have to be reversed, however. The acute levels of pollution characteristic of major pollution episodes do, they admit, constitute substantial threats, but they go on to argue that the long-term low-concentration levels of exposure which cause relatively little irritation, discomfort or odor may in reality constitute the more serious health hazards. The central hypothesis underlying their studies is based on a mutagenic or radiomimetic theory of cumulative molecular degradation of deoxyribonucleic acid (DNA), as follows: certain environmental chemicals affect DNA by causing alterations in the sequence of purine and pyrimidine bases along the DNA strand or helix. Such alterations in the genetic code are alterations in the cell genotype which often result in changes of cell phenotype. They find support for the hypothesis both in biological theory and related literature, and their own statistical studies reveal significant statistical relationships between concentrations of a number of environmental chemicals, mostly atmospheric, and mortality rates for several categories of cancer, heart disease, and certain congenital malformations in the U.S. These significant relationships remained when effects of age, sex and race were taken into account.

2. WELFARE EFFECTS

If these are health effects, what of more general effects on the public welfare? Aside from attempts to estimate overall national costs, analyses have been undertaken at two levels: (a) using cities in nationwide investigations, and (b) using various sub-units within cities in more local analyses to study differences between neighborhoods and social groups.

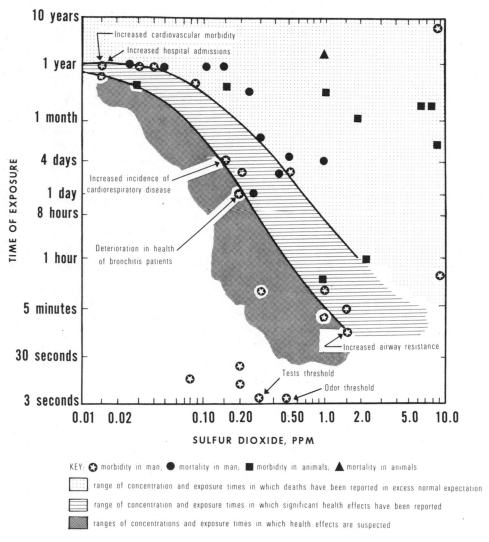

FIGURE 2.6

EFFECTS OF SULFUR DIOXIDE ON HEALTH

Source: Stern (1962)

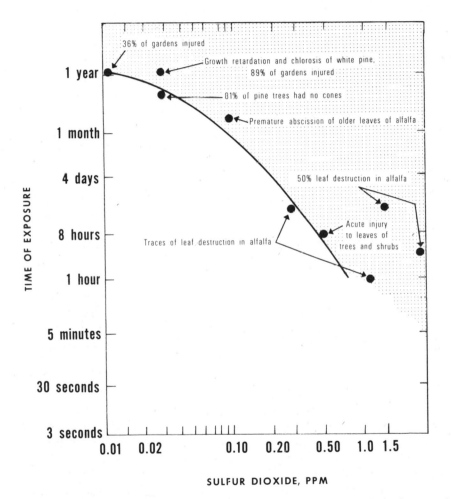

SHADED AREA: range of concentrations and exposure times in which injury to vegetation has been reported
WHITE AREA: range of concentrations and exposure times of undetermined significance to vegetation

FIGURE 2.7

EFFECTS OF SULFUR DIOXIDE ON VEGETATION

Source: Stern (1962)

a. NATIONWIDE EVIDENCE

Studies that have concentrated on the annual national total cost of air pollution have focussed on either the cost of cleaning the air or the property and health costs of not cleaning the air. One frequently quoted cost of air pollution damage, $11 billion (Schmidt, 1959), originates from an estimate of cleaning costs from the smoke damage data for Pittsburgh in 1913. The cost was estimated to be $20 per person per year. In 1958, this figure was updated by the commodity price index and multiplied by the 1958 population to arrive at the $11 billion mark. Extrapolation of these data to recent years and to cities with less air pollution seems a hazardous procedure at best. Another variation of the Pittsburgh study results in the cost of $4 billion (Seamans, 1959), obtained by multiplying the updated 1958 cost by the urban population.

Ridker (1967) identified and estimated total costs for a variety of potential effects of air pollution including maintenance costs of residential, commercial and industrial facilities; damage to trees, agricultural crops and livestock; and costs associated with illness and death of humans. The proportion of the cost due to air pollution was $5.5 billion. More recently Lave and Seskin (1970), in the most influential paper of recent years, concentrated on the health costs alone, arguing that twenty-five percent of all respiratory disease is associated with air pollution. Lave and Seskins' study also contains a comprehensive review of previous work dealing with the health costs of air pollution.

b. CITY-TO-CITY DIFFERENCES

Morris (1973) has analyzed city-to-city differences in the social cost of air pollution, following on from his analyses reported earlier. Returning to that analysis, the estimated SO_x and P emissions, on a square mile basis is expressed as a function of city size, S, and pollutant levels:

$$\hat{C} = f (S, SO_x, P)$$

The social cost of controlling SO_x and P is computed by inserting into the equation levels of SO_x and P derived from the equations described earlier, after correcting for industrial and climatic factors so that the social cost is a function of city size only—all other variables being statistically held constant. Conversion to a per capita figure is achieved by using a constant population density per square mile. A similar procedure is followed for other pollutants, to yield the results shown in the Figures 2.8 and 2.9. The first refers to the per capita social costs of controlling SO_2 and P, while the second adds in CO, using high and low cost estimates for industrially emitted pollutants and the costs of recovering constant automobile performance.

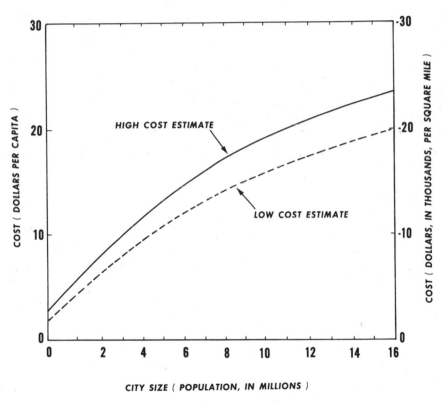

CITY SIZE (POPULATION, IN MILLIONS)

FIGURE 2.8

PER CAPITA SOCIAL COST AND SOCIAL COST PER SQUARE MILE
FOR INDUSTRIALLY EMITTED POLLUTANTS
SULFUR OXIDES AND PARTICULATES

Source: Morris (1972)

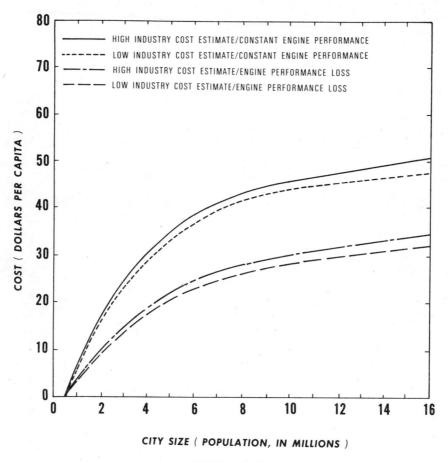

FIGURE 2.9

PER CAPITA SOCIAL COST OF AIR POLLUTION

Source: Morris (1972)

    c. INTRAURBAN VARIATIONS

    A similar analysis at the intraurban level by A. Myrick
Freeman (1973) poses the general issues of intraurban welfare-
effect analysis:

    1. Do difference in air quality across space get capital-
ized into property values?

    2. Can cross section regressions of property values on air
quality be used to predict the change in the price of a given
property when air quality changes over the whole urban area?

3. Can such a regression be used to predict the change in aggregate property values for an urban area when air quality improves?

4. Can predicted or measured changes in property values be used as a measure or an approximation of the benefits of air quality improvement?

5. Can regressions of property values on air quality be used to identify or gain information on the demand curve for air quality?

6. Can differences in property values arising because of air quality differentials provide any information on the benefits of an improvement in air quality?

Freeman argues that, theoretically at least, property values should reflect differences in air quality. Given well functioning markets, the price of a capital asset will be the present value of the anticipated stream of net benefits. If air pollution reduces the benefits or utility derived from a property, or if it increases the costs associated with it (e.g., cleaning, maintenance), the market price should reflect these changes in capitalized value.

The major empirical questions then center on whether air quality differences are perceived, and whether property markets function effectively in adjusting prices to these perceptions. The available evidence from empirical studies points to an affirmative answer. This evidence consists of cross section regressions for a given city of air quality and other independent variables thought to influence property values (primarily characteristics of the property, improvements and neighborhoods), and some measure of property value. Regressions have been run in both arithmetic and logarithmic form. Given the assumptions underlying least squares, the regression equations can be used to plot rent gradients with respect to air quality under ceteris paribus conditions.

Table 2.11 summarizes the essential features and main results of five major studies which have been reported. Comparisons of the numerical results are difficult because of differences in the data base, the equation forms, and the measures of pollution and property values used.

One of the motivating forces behind property value-air quality studies has been a line of reasoning something like this: "If we can show that air quality differentials are associated

TABLE 2.11

SUMMARY OF RELATIONSHIPS
BETWEEN PROPERTY VALUES AND AIR POLLUTION

		City	Regression Form	Pollution Measure	Pollution Coeffecient	R^2
1.	Ridker-Henning (1967)[a]	St. Louis	Linear	Sulfation		
2.	Anderson & Crocker (1971)[ab]	St. Louis	Log	Sulfation[c] Suspended Particulate	-.10 -.12*	.76
		Kansas City	Log	Sulfation[c] Suspended Particulate	-.08 -.09*	.82
		Washington D.C.	Log	Sulfation[c] Suspended Particulate	-.07 -.06**	.70
3.	Peckham (Reported in Anderson and Crocker [1972])	Philadelphia	Log	Sulfation[c] Suspended Particulate	-.10 -.12	.77
4.	Zerbe [18] (As reported in Anderson and Crocker [1972][a])	Toronto	Log of V, Arithmetic Values of (Q)	Sulfation	-.12	.94
		Hamilton	Log of V, Arithmetic Values of (Q)	Sulfation	-.08	.92
5.	Spore [14][d]	Pittsburgh	Log	Sulfation[c,e] Dustfall	+.03* -.12	.81

a) The unit of observation is the census tract. The property value variable is the mean owner estimated value as reported in the 1960 census
b) Only the results for their Type I equation for owner-occupied dwellings are shown.
c) Sulfation and suspended particulates are included in the same equation.
d) The unit of observation is the census tract. The property value variable is the mean owner estimated value as reported in the 1970 census.
e) Sulfation was converted to equivalent concentrations of sulfur dioxide in PPM.
* Not significantly different from zero at the .01 level.
**Not significantly different from zero at the .01 level.

with property value differentials, then we would expect that when air quality is improved the prices of affected properties would increase; and if we could predict how much property values would increase we could use this as an estimate of the benefit or the willingness to pay for the air quality improvement." This line of reasoning was spurred by Strotz's unpublished paper (1966). Two questions arise:

Do cross-section regressions such as those described above provide sufficient information to predict changes in values of individual properties and changes in aggregate property values? The second is, given known changes in property values, can they be related somehow to benefits?

Freeman reviews the relevant theory, and finds that when the assumptions of individual utility maximization and market equilibrium are applied to a model of property values and air quality, cross-section regression equations of property values

and air quality can be given a direct interpretation in terms
of individuals' marginal willingness to pay for air quality.
Specifically the first derivative of the regression equation with
respect to air quality provides a locus of points which are individuals' willingnesses to pay for present levels of air quality.
Aggregate marginal willingness to pay can be calculated directly;
and several alternative assumptions can be made concerning the
slope of individuals' marginal willingness to pay curves. These
assumptions enable the investigator to make reasonable approxi-
mations of the benefits of various non-marginal improvements in
air quality.

3. RATING THE POLLUTANTS BY EFFECT

Walther (1972) has proposed that, given a set of air quality
standards, it is possible to rate the various air pollutants by
effect rather than by mass. Using the national primary and secondary standards as base, he follows Babcock's (1970) computation
of "tolerance factors" related to the relative toxicity of pollutants, as shown in Table 2.12.

TABLE 2.12

AMBIENT AIR QUALITY STANDARDS, TOLERANCE
FACTORS, AND EFFECT FACTORS

Parameter	CO	HC	SO_x	NO_x	Aerosol
	National ambient air quality standards				
Primary	$10 \ mg/m^3$ (8 hr)[a]	$160 \ \mu g/m^3$ (3 hr)[a]	$80 \ \mu g/m^3$ (1 yr)	$10^2 \ \mu g/m^3$ (1 yr)	$75 \ \mu g/m^3$ (1 yr)
	$40 \ mg/m^3$ (1 hr)[a] (32 ppm)		$365 \ \mu g/m^3$ (1 day)	$(250 \ \mu g/m^3$, 1 day, recommended but deleted)	$260 \ \mu g/m^3$ (1 day)[a]
Secondary	$10 \ mg/m^3$ (8 hr)[a]	$160 \ \mu g/m^3$ (3 hr)[a]	$60 \ \mu g/m^3$ (1 yr)	$10^2 \ \mu g/m^3$ (1 yr)	$60 \ \mu g/m^3$ (1 hr)
	$40 \ mg/m^3$ (1 hr)[a] (32 ppm)		$260 \ \mu g/m^3$ (1 day)	$(250 \ \mu g/m^3$, 1 day, recommended but deleted)	$150 \ \mu g/m^3$ (1 day)[a]
	Tolerance factors based on national primary ambient air qual. stds.				
$(\mu g/m^3)$	5600	45	365	250	260
	Tolerance factors based on nat'l. secondary air quality stds.				
$(\mu g/m^3)$	5600	45	260	250	150
	Effect Factor				
(primary stds.)	1	125	15.3	22.4	21.5
(secondary stds.)	1	125	21.5	22.4	37.3

[a]Maximum concentration not to be exceeded more than once a year.

For SO_x and aerosol, the tolerance factors are simply the one-day standard that was originally recommended, but finally deleted from the national ambient air quality standards. For CO, there is no one-day standard so an extrapolation was made from the eight-hour standard (lo mg/m^3) to a one-day tolerance factor of 5.6 mg/m^3. The extrapolation was based on the two percent carbozyhemoglobin (COHb) concentration-exposure gradient presented originally by Peterson and Stewart and reproduced by NAPCA. This COHb level was chosen because it is about the minimum associated with some health effect. The gradient is linear on a logarithmic plot of both variables. For hydrocarbons, the national ambient air quality standards were set not on the direct effects of HC but on the effects of the oxidant concentration resulting from reactions of HC with other atmospheric constituents including NO_x. Therefore, the concentration-time gradient applied to the national hydrocarbon ambient air quality standard to extrapolate from the given three-hour concentration to a twenty-four-hour tolerance factor is based on oxidant data (more specifically, ozone). The actual data are the projected ozone concentrations which will produce, for short-term exposures, five percent injury to economically important vegetation grown under sensitive conditions. For sensitive plants a concentration range was plotted against exposure time on double logarithmic axes to obtain the gradient that was applied to the national HC standard.

If the air pollutant with the highest tolerance factor is taken as the reference pollutant (CO), by assigning it an effect factor of unity, then the effect factor for any other pollutant is equal to the ratio of the mass concentration tolerance factors of the reference pollutant and of that pollutant. Such effect factors also appear in the foregoing table.

If these effect factors are applied to the actual mass emissions data of Table 2.13 the very different picture of Table 2.14 emerges:

(1) the largest source of air pollution is still transportation;

(2) stationary fuel combustion drops to fourth place, compared to its second place contribution by mass;

(3) hydrocarbons are the most important pollutants by effect, accounting for about seventy-one percent of the air pollution problem compared to their thirteen percent contribution by mass;

TABLE 2.13

NATIONAL ANNUAL AIR POLLUTION EMISSIONS,
CLASSIFIED BY SOURCE AND RANKED BY MASS[a]

Source	Pollutant	Annual quantity $(10^6$ tons)	%
Transportation		144.4	51.4
	CO	111.5	77.2
	HC	19.8	13.6
	NO_x	11.2	7.7
	Aerosol	0.8	0.8
	SO_x	1.1	0.7
			100.0
Stationary fuel combustion		44.3	15.7
	SO_x	24.4	55.0
	NO_x	10.0	22.6
	Aerosol	7.2	16.3
	CO	1.8	4.1
	HC	0.9	2.0
			100.0
Miscellaneous		41.0	14.6
	CO	18.2	44.4
	Aerosol	11.4	27.8
	HC	9.2	22.4
	NO_x	2.0	4.9
	SO_x	0.2	0.5
			100.0
Industry		39.6	14.1
	Aerosol	14.4	36.4
	CO	12.0	30.3
	SO_x	7.5	18.9
	HC	5.5	13.9
	NO_x	0.2	0.5
			100.0
Solid waste disposal		11.9	4.2
	CO	7.9	66.3
	HC	2.0	16.8
	Aerosol	1.4	11.8
	NO_x	0.4	3.4
	SO_x	0.2	1.7
			100.0
	TOTAL	281.2	100%

[a] Estimated nationwide emissions for 1969 obtained from: Environmental Quality, The Second Annual Report of the Council on Environmental Quality, August 1971.

Source: Walther (1972) p. 353.

TABLE 2.14

NATIONAL ANNUAL AIR POLLUTION EMISSIONS,
CLASSIFIED BY SOURCE AND RANKED BY EFFECT[a]

Source	Pollutant	Annual quantity (10^6 tons)	Effect Factor	Effect	%	
Transportation		144.4		2876.5	43.3	
	HC	19.8	125	2480		86.3
	NO_x	11.2	22.4	251		8.7
	CO	111.5	1	111.5		3.8
	Aerosol	0.8	21.5	17.2		0.6
	SO_x	1.1	15.3	16.8		0.6
						100.0
Miscellaneous		41.0		1461.1	22.1	
	HC	9.2	125	1150		78.7
	Aerosol	11.4	21.5	245		16.8
	NO_x	2.0	22.4	44.8		3.1
	CO	18.2	1	18.2		1.2
	SO_x	0.2	15.3	3.1		0.2
						100.0
Industry		39.6		1129.0	17.0	
	HC	5.5	125	688		60.9
	Aerosol	14.4	21.5	310		27.5
	SO_x	7.5	15.3	114.5		10.1
	CO	12.0	1	12.0		1.1
	NO_x	0.2	22.4	4.5		0.4
						100.0
Stationary fuel combustion		44.3		866.5	13.1	
	SO_x	24.4	15.3	373.2		43.1
	NO_x	10.0	22.4	224		25.8
	Aerosol	7.2	21.5	155.0		17.9
	HC	0.9	125	112.5		13.0
	CO	1.8	1	1.8		0.2
						100.0
Solid waste disposal		11.9		300.1	4.5	
	HC	2.0	125	250		83.4
	Aerosol	1.4	21.5	30.1		10.0
	NO_x	0.4	22.4	9.0		3.0
	CO	7.9	1	7.9		2.6
	SO_x	0.2	15.3	3.1		1.0
						100.0
Total		281.2			100%	

[a]Effect factors based on national primary ambient air quality standards.

Source: Walther (1972) p. 353.

and

 (4) CO is only two percent of the problem by effect compared to fifty-six percent by mass.

 The picture drawn by the mass analysis and these effect analyses encourage different and conflicting priorities for control research and regulation. The key to an effect analysis is the effect factor, based on the national ambient air quality standards as an indirect assessment of the health and other effect literature.

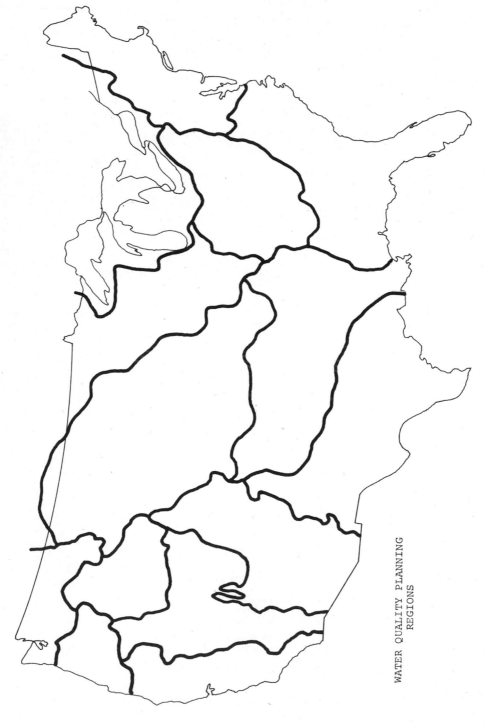

WATER QUALITY PLANNING
REGIONS

Source: U. S. G. S., Quality of Surface Waters of the United States, 1968, Geological Survey Water-Supply Paper 2099, 2.

3   WATER QUALITY

I. EFFLUENT MEASUREMENT SYSTEMS

As in the case of air pollution, water quality measurement
systems vary in purpose, the effluents that are recorded, and
the extensiveness of the monitoring networks. Thus, the purpose
of this chapter will be to summarize the types of pollution
recorded, and describe the nature of the various water quality
measurement systems, along with the monitoring networks supplying
data for analysis.

1. TYPES OF POLLUTANTS

First, it has to be recognized that regional variation in
the quality of surface waters arises naturally, determined by
two major factors: the mineral structure of the geological strata
and the chemistry of the surface soils. Urbanized areas tend
to degrade this variable natural quality of surface waters due
to the introduction of agricultural, industrial, and municipal
wastes and runoff. The effects of mineral and soil quality are
in general, uncontrollable by man at present, whereas he has the
technical knowledge and engineering capabilities to control
water quality degradation due to agricultural, industrial, and
municipal pollution.

Agricultural uses of water add dissolved minerals, sediments, fertilizers, pesticides, chemicals, and herbicides to
the surface waters. Industrial wastes add organic materials,
inorganic ions, and suspended solids from cooling and process
waters. Municipal wastes consist mainly of organic materials,
suspended solids and associated bacteria; inorganics are often
contributed by surface runoff to combined or separate storm
sewers. These several types and sources of water pollution are
described in Table 3.1.

Table 3.1 begs the question of why the presence of certain
things in water is called "pollution," however. The perception
of pollution arises when there is interference with one or more
water uses. Water quality standards, discussed in more detail
later, thus seek to establish levels of pollutants in surface

TABLE 3.1

NATURE, SOURCES AND PRINCIPAL ABATEMENT AND CONTROL METHODS OF MAJOR WATER POLLUTANTS

Pollutant and Sources	Effects on Waters	Abatement and Control Methods
SOLIDS		
Particulate		
Municipal wastewater and effluents from certain industries such as pulp and paper, food and tannery.	Degrades aesthetic appearance--utilizes oxygen resources; interferes with bottom life; prevents adequate disinfection and allows disease-causing organisms to live longer in natural waters.	Primary wastewater treatment; advance wastewater treatment by chemical coagulation and settling; filtration; industrial process m modifications.
Silt in runoff from construction sites and agricultural land.	May cover and destroy valuable fish and wildlife habitat; makes assimilation of oxygen-demanding wastes more difficult; adds to water treatment costs; degrades aesthetic appearance.	Land use control; improved soil conservation practices.
Dissolved		
Municipal and industrial wastewater, particularly the mining and chemical industry, road salting.	Interferes with agricultural and industrial water use; increases hardness of water used for domestic purposes; excessive dissolved salts can also cause a laxative action when present in potable water; adds taste to water.	Process changes and in-plant controls in industry; advance wastewater treatment processes, such as reverse osmosis and ion exchange; controlled and effective use of road salting chemicals, or use of substitutes such as sand.
ORGANIC MATERIAL		
Biodegradable		
Municipal wastewater and the wastewater from many industries such as milk, food, pulp and paper. Runoff from areas with high concentration of animals such as zoos, feedlots or barnyards.	Utilizes the oxygen resources of a stream & thus interferes with normal biological life; can cause taste, odors and colors.	Secondary wastewater treatment; in-plant industrial controls; containment, control and treatment of animal land runoff.
Non-biodegradable		
Municipal wastewater and the wastewater from many industries such as milk, food, pulp and paper. Runoff from areas with high concentration of animals such as zoos, feedlots or barnyards.	Can cause taste, odors and color in water; fish-tainting; foam; can become biodegradable.	Control use of non-biodegradable products' advance waste treatment process such as ozone or activated carbon absorption.
INFECTIOUS AGENTS		
Bacteria & Viruses		
Domestic wastewater; waste from hospitals, research laboratories and some industries such as milk processing and meat packing.	Presents a health hazard to direct and indirect reuse and to water contact recreation.	Secondary wastewater treatment, plus disinfection.
NUTRIENTS		
such as Nitrogen & Phosphorus		
Municipal wastewater; some industrial wastewater; runoff from agricultural and urban land.	Fertilizes the water and thereby stimulates the excessive growth of weeds and algae causing cultural eutrophication.	Advance waste treatment; land use controls; soil conservation practices; control use of products containing phosphorus and nitrogen.

TABLE 3.1 (Continued)

Pollutant and Sources	Effects on Waters	Abatement and Control Methods
TOXIC AGENTS		
Metals, acids & alkalides		
Industrial wastewater.	Harms surface water ecology; interferes with downstream water reuse; potential health hazard; corrodes piers, boats.	Industrial process changes and controls; industrial waste treatment.
Pesticides & Other Exotic Organics		
Agriculture, forestry, residential and commercial pest control, certain organic chemical industries.	Harms surface water ecology; interferes with downstream reuse; represents potential health hazard.	Controlled agricultural, forestry, residential and commercial pesticide use; prohibition of manufacture of certain particularly harmful organic chemical; industrial, wastewater treatment.
Radioactive waste		
Nuclear power plants, radioactive material, reprocessing, industry, medical and laboratory radioactivity material uses.	Potential health hazard; potentially harmful to aquatic life.	Nuclear power plant and industrial process changes and wastewater treatment.
HEAT		
Electric generating plants, steel mills, certain industries, large air conditioning systems.	Interferes with normal surface water life by favoring species tolerant to high temperatures; reduces the oxygen saturation concentration of water and and increases rate of biological activity thus affecting weed and algae growth.	Reuse of waste heat; cooling towers; cooling ponds; more efficient electrical generation systems; reduce demand for power.
TASTE, ODOR & COLOR		
Industrial wastewater.	Interfere with downstream recreation and reuse.	Industrial process changes and wastewater treatment.
Oil		
Oil spills during transport or storage, railroad and truck yards, some industry, bilge water and ballast water from boats, urban runoff, waste oil from automobiles.	Aesthetic damage; taints fish; kills or injures fish and wildlife; interferes with recreational use.	Design and construction of failsafe oil transportation and storage facilities; containment and treatment of bilge and ballast water and runoff from areas with high potential for oil pollution; development of a market for waste oils reuse.

waters that will not interfere with the desired uses. The problem that then arises is that water quality differs for different uses.

The water quality criteria for municipal water supplies are derived from the need for palatable and safe finished water, free from concentrations of coliform bacteria, organic compounds that may result in offensive tastes and odors, inorganic chemicals that may constitute long-term health hazards, and suspended matter (Table 3.2). Quality criteria for industrial process water vary over a very wide range depending on the industry and the nature of the product; the important parameters include color; turbidity; pH; temperature; hardness; odor; biochemical

TABLE 3.2

SURFACE WATER CRITERIA FOR PUBLIC WATER SUPPLIES

Constituent or characteristic	Permissible Criteria	Desirable Criteria
PHYSICAL:		
Color (color units)...............75		<10
Odor..............................Narrative		Virtually absent
Temperature.......................Narrative		Narrative
Turbidity.........................Narrative		Virtually absent
MICROBIOLOGICAL:		
Coliform organisms..........10,000/100ml		<100/100ml
Fecal coliforms..............2,000/100ml		<20/100ml
INORGANIC CHEMICALS:	(mg/l)	(mg/l)
Alkalinity...................Narrative		Narrative
Ammonia......................0.5 (as N)		<0.01
Arsenic......................0.05		Absent
Barium.......................1.0		Absent
Boron........................1.0		Absent
Cadmium......................0.01		Absent
Chloride..................... 250		<25
Chromium, hexavalent.........0.5		Absent
Copper.......................1.0		Virtually Absent
Dissolved oxygen............. $\geq$ 4 (monthly mean)		Near saturation
$\geq$ 3 (ind. sample)		
Fluoride.....................Narrative		Narrative
Hardness.....................Narrative		Narrative
Iron (filterable)............0.3		Virtually absent
Lead.........................0.05		Absent
Manganese (filterable).......0.05		Absent
Nitrates plus nitrites.......10 (as N)		Virtually absent
pH (range)...................6.0 - 8.5		Narrative
Phosphorus...................Narrative		Narrative
Selenium.....................0.01		Absent
Silver.......................0.05		Absent
Sulfate...................... 250		<50
Total dissolved solids....... 500		<200
(filterable residue)		
Uranyl ion................... 5		Absent
Zinc......................... 5		Virtually absent
ORGANIC CHEMICALS:		
Carbon chloroform extract(CCE). 0.15		<0.04
Cyanide...................... 0.20		Absent
Methylene blue active substances................0.5		Virtually absent
Oil and grease...............Virtually absent		Absent
Pesticides:		
Aldrin...................0.017		Absent
Chlordane................0.003		Absent
DDT......................0.042		Absent
Dieldrin.................0.017		Absent
Endrin...................0.001		Absent
Heptachlor...............0.018		Absent
Heptachlor epoxide.......0.018		Absent

TABLE 3.2 (Continued)

Constituent or characteristic	Permissible Criteria	Desirable Criteria
Lindane....................0.056 ....Absent
Methoxychlor...............0.035 ....Absent
Organic phosphate plus carbamates..............0.1 ....Absent
Toxaphene..................0.005 ....Absent
Herbicides:
2,4-D plus 2,4,5-T, plus 2,4,5-TP...............0.1 ....Absent
Phenols......................0.001 ....Absent
RADIOACTIVITY:	(pc/l)	(pc/l)
Gross beta....................1,000 ....<100
Radium - 226................. 3 ....< 1
Strontium - 90..............10 ....< 2

Source: "Water Quality Criteria," FWPCA, 1968.

oxygen demand; and concentrations of dissolved solids, dissolved oxygen, oil, iron, and manganese. The importance of each of these parameters depends on the intended use. Color and odor for example, are undesirable in water used in the food and beverage industries but are of little significance in water used by the steel industry. Temperature and pH, on the other hand, are important considerations for almost any industrial use.

Dissolved oxygen presents an interesting case of conflicts in standards defining pollution. For most industrial applications, it would be desirable to obtain water containing no dissolved oxygen. Similarly, biochemical oxygen demand is a general index of the degree of organic pollution and is of concern to such industries as food and beverages. For other industrial uses, however, it serves only as a measure of gross pollution--an indication of the presence of potentially harmful corrosion, erosion, scale formation, sludge accumulation, and the growth of slime-forming microorganisms that are particularly detrimental to industrial cooling water systems. Criteria for industrial cooling water are related to these effects and include pH; turbidity; hardness; and the concentrations of dissolved solids, dissolved oxygen, iron, manganese, chlorides, and sulfates. Temperature is important since the capacity of the cooling system is directly related to the initial tempera- ture of the cooling water. The criteria vary in importance with such factors as materials of construction and the degree of recirculation in a given system.

In water to be used for irrigation, the concentrations of dissolved salts and the bacterial quality are of primary importance. The deleterious effects of salts on plant growth can result from osmotic effects, or prevention of water uptake; chemical effects of plant metabolism; or indirect effects on the soil. The presence of coliform bacteria indicates the pos- sibility of food crop contamination. Unlike water for munici- pal and industrial use, water for irrigation cannot reasonably be treated for use if the supply is of unsatisfactory quality; the effect of pollution can be elimination of the use.

Suspended solids may deposit in streams to block naviga- tion channels or in reservoirs to reduce storage capacity. They can also cause erosion in turbines used for hydroelectric power generation. Dissolved substances, particularly acidic compounds can cause or accelerate corrosion of watercraft and dock facilities. Pollution here is measured by the costs added as a result of maintenance dredging, corrosion damage, and reservoir depletion.

Recreational uses of surface streams, such as swimming, fishing, boating, water sports, and streamside camping; use for commercial fishing; and use for esthetic enjoyment are dependent on suitable water quality. The users can alter neither the quality of the water nor eliminate the effects of pollution. Unsatisfactory quality results in elimination of these uses.

Polluting substances can be assimilated to some extent within a stream, depending on its temperature, dissolved oxygen concentration, flow rate, and other factors. The use of assi- milative capacity of a stream must assure that the resultant quality does not impair other beneficial uses. This, of course, is the crux of the water pollution problem, and the quality requirements for assimilative use cannot be stated simply.

2. COMPOSITION OF SURFACE WATERS

All natural waters contain dissolved mineral matter. The quantity of dissolved mineral matter in a natural water depends

primarily on the type of rocks or soils with which the water
has been in contact and the length of time of contact. Ground
water is generally more highly mineralized than surface runoff
because it remains in contact with the rocks and soils for much
longer periods. Some streams reflect the chemical character of
their concentrated underground sources during dry periods and
are more dilute during periods of heavy rainfall. The dissolved-
solids content in a river is frequently increased by drainage
from mines or oil fields, by the addition of industrial or municipal wastes, or--in irrigated regions--by drainage from irrigated lands.

The mineral constitutents and physical properties of natural
waters include those that have a practical bearing on water use.
They generally include silica, iron, calcium, magnesium, sodium,
potassium (or sodium and potassium together calculated as sodium),
carbonate, bicarbonate, sulfate, chloride, fluoride, nitrate,
boron, pH, dissolved solids, and specific conductance. Aluminum,
manganese, color, acidity, dissolved oxygen, and other dissolved
constituents and physical properties are reported for certain
streams. Microbiologic (coliforms) and organic components
(pesticides, total organic carbon) and minor elements (arsenic,
cobalt, cadmium, copper, lead, mercury, nickel, strontium, zinc,
etc.) are determined occasionally for some streams in connection
with specific problems and the results are reported. The
sources and significance of these different constituents and
properties of natural waters are described in Table 3.3. What
results from natural composition and from man-made effluents is
a variety of measurable properties of water thought to be of
qualitative importance. These are outlined in Table 3.4.

TABLE 3.3

MINERAL CONSTITUENTS IN SOLUTION

SILICA (SiO_2)	Silica is dissolved from practically all rocks. Some natural surface waters contain less than 5 miligrams per liter of silica and few contain more than 50 mg/l, but the more common range is from 10 to 30 mg/l. Silica affects the usefulness of a water because it contributes to the formation of boiler scale; it usually is removed from feed water for high-pressure boilers. Silica also forms troublesome deposits on the blades of steam turbines. However, it is not physiologically significant to humans, livestock, or fish, nor is it of importance in irrigation water.

TABLE 3.3 (Continued)

ALUMINUM (Al)

Aluminum is usually present only in negligible quantities in natural water except in areas where the waters have been in contact with the more soluble rocks of high aluminum content such as bauxite and certain shales. Acid waters often contain large amounts of aluminum. It may be troublesome in feed waters where it tends to be deposited as a scale on boiler tubes.

IRON (Fe)

Iron is dissolved from many rocks and soils. On exposure to air, normal basic waters that contain more than 1 mg/l of iron soon become turbid with the insoluble reddish ferric compounds produced by oxidation. Surface waters, therefore, seldom contain as much as 1 mg/l of dissolved iron, although some acid waters carry large quantities of iron in solution. Iron causes reddish-brown stains on porcelain or enaeled ware and fixtures and on fabrics washed in the water. Concentrations of more than 0.3 mg/l are not acceptable for drinking and culinary use. (U.S. Public Health Service, 1962.)

MANGANESE (Mn)

Manganese is dissolved in appreciable quantities from rocks in some sections of the country. It resembles iron in its chemical behavior and in its occurrence in natural waters. However, manganese is much less abundant than iron. As a result the concentration of manganese is much less than that of iron and is not regularly determined in many areas. It is expecially objectionable in water used in laundry work and in textile processing. Concentrations as low as 0.2 mg/l may cause a dark-brown or black stain on fabrics and porcelain fixtures. Appreciable quantities of manganese are often found in waters containing objectionable quantities of iron.

CALCIUM (Ca)

Calcium is dissolved from almost all rocks and soils, but the highest concentrations are usually found in waters that have been in contact with limestone, dolomite, and gypsum. Calcium and magnesium make water hard and are largely responsible for the formation of boiler scale. Most waters associated with granite or silicious sands contain less than 10 mg/l of calcium; waters in areas where rocks are composed of dolomite and limestone contain from 30 to 100 mg/l; and waters that have come in contact with deposits of gypsum may contain several hundred mg/l.

MAGNESIUM (Mg)

Magnesium is dissolved from many rocks, particularly from dolomitic rocks. Its effect in water is similar to that of calcium. The magnesium in soft waters may amount to only 1 or 2 mg/l, but water in areas that contain large quantities of dolomite or other magnesium-bearing rocks may contain from 20 to 100 mg/l or more of magnesium.

SODIUM and POTASSIUM (Na and K)

Sodium and potassium are dissolved from practically all rocks. Sodium is the predominant cation in some of the more highly mineralized waters found in the western United States. Natural waters that contain only 3 or 4 mg/l of the two together are likely to carry almost as much potassium as sodium. As the total quantity of these constituents increases, the proportion of sodium becomes greater. Moderate quantities of sodium and potassium have little effect on the usefulness of the water for most purposes, but waters that carry more than 50 to 100 mg/l of the two may require careful operation of steam boilers to prevent foaming. More highly mineralized waters that contain a large proportion of sodium salts may be unsatisfactory for irrigation.

BICARBONATE, CARBONATE, and HYDROXIDE (HCO_3, CO_3, OH)

Bicarbonate, carbonate, or hydroxide is sometimes reported as alkalinity. The alkalinity of a water is produced by anions or molecular species of weak acids which are not fully dissociated above a pH of 4.5. Since the major causes of alkalinity in most natural waters are carbonate and bicarbonate ions dissolved from carbonate rocks, the results are usually reported in terms of these constituents. Although alkalinity may suggest the presence of definite amounts of carbonate, bicarbonate or hydroxide, there are other ions that contribute to alkalinity such as silicates, phosphates, borates, possibly fluoride, and certain organic anions which may occur in colored waters. The significance of alkalinity to the domestic, agricultural, and industrial user is usually dependent upon the nature of the cations (Ca, Mg, Na, K) associated with it. Alkalinity in moderate amounts does not adversely affect most users. Hydroxide may occur in water that has been softened by the lime process. Its presence in streams usually can be taken as an indication of contamination and does not represent the natural chemical character of the water.

SULFIDE (S)

Sulfide occurs in water as a result of bacterial and chemical processes. It usually is present as hydrogen sulfide. Variable amounts may be found in waters receiving sewage and (or) industrial wastes, such as from tanneries, papermills, chemical plants, and gas manufacturing work (California State Water Quality Control Board, 1963). Waters containing sulfides, especially hydrogen sulfide, may be considered undesirable because of their odor. The U.S. Public Health Service (1962) states that water on carriers subject to Federal quarantine regualtions shall have no objectionable taste or odor. The toxicity to aquatic organisms differs significantly with the species and the nature of associated ions.

TABLE 3.3 (Continued)

SULFATE (SO_4)

Sulfate is dissolved from most sedimentary rocks. Large quantities may be derived from beds of gypsum, sodium sulfate deposits, and some types of shale. Organic material containing sulfur adds sulfate to the water as a phase of the sulfur cycle. In natural waters, concentrations range from a few mg/l to several thousand mg/l. The U.S. Public Health Service (1962) recommends that the sulfate concentration not exceed 250 mg/l in drinking and culinary water on carriers subject to Federal quarantine regualtions. Sulfates are less toxic to crops than chlorides.

CHLORIDE (Cl)

Chloride is dissolved from rock materials in all parts of the country. Surface waters in the humid regions are usually low in chloride, whereas streams in arid or semiarid regions may contain several hundred mg/l of chloride leached from soils and rocks, especially where the streams receive return drainage from irrigated lands or are affected by ground-water-inflow carrying appreciable quantities of chloride. Large quantities of chloride in water that contains a high content of calcium and magnesium increases the water's corrosiveness. The presence of abnormal concentrations of chloride and nitrogenous material together in water supplies indicates possible pollution by human or animal wastes.

FLUORIDE (F)

Fluoride has been reported as being present in some rocks to about the same extent as chloride. However, the quantity of fluoride in natural surface waters is ordinarily very small compared to that of chloride. Investigations have proved that fluoride concentrations of about 0.6 to 1.7 mg/l reduced the incidence of dental caries and that concentrations greater than 1.7 mg/l also protect the teeth from cavities but cause an undesirable black stain (Durfor and Becker, 1964, p. 20). Public Health Service, 1962, states, "When fluoride is naturally present in drinking water, the concentration should not average more than the appropriate upper control limit (0.6 to 1.7 mg/l). Presence of fluoride in average concentration greater than two times the optimum values shall constitute grounds for rejection of the supply." Concentration higher than the stated limits may cause mottled enamel in teeth, endemic cumulative fluorosis, and skeletal effects.

BROMIDE (Br)

Bromine is a very minor element in the earth's crust and is normally present in surface waters in only minute quantities. Measurable amounts may be found in some streams that receive industrial wastes, and some natural brines may contain rather high concentrations. It resembles chloride in that it tends to be concentrated in sea water.

IODIDE (I)

Iodide is considerably less abundant both in rocks and water than bromine. Measurable amounts may be found in some streams that receive industrial wastes, and some natural brines may contain rather high concentrations. It occurs in sea water to the extent of less than 1 mg/l. Rankama and Sahama (1950) report iodide present in rainwater to the extent of 0.001 to 0.003 mg/l and in river water in about the same amount. Few waters will contain over 2.0 mg/l.

NITROGEN, ORGANIC (N)

Organic nitrogen includes all nitrogenous organic compounds, such as amino acid, polypeptides, and proteins. It is present naturally in all surface waters as a result of inflow of nitrogenous products from the watershed and the normal biological life of the stream. Organic nitrogen is not pathologically significant but is sometimes an indication of pollution.

NITROGEN, AMMONIA (NH_4, as N)

Ammonia nitrogen includes nitrogen in the forms of NH_3 and NH_4^{+1}. As a component of the nitrogen cycle, it is often present in water, but usually in only small amounts. More than 0.1 mg/l usually indicates orgnaic pollution (Rudolph, 1931). There is no evidence that ammonia nitrogen in water is physiologically significant to man or livestock. Fish, however, cannot tolerate large quantities.

NITRITE (NO_2)

Nitrite is unstable in the presence of oxygen and is, therefore, absent or present in only minute quantities in most natural waters under aerobic conditions. The presence of nitrite in water is sometimes an indication of organic pollution. Recommended tolerances of nitrite in domestic water supplies differ widely. A generally accepted limit is 2 mg/l, but as little as 0.1 mg/l has been proposed (California State Water Quality Control Board, 1963).

NITRATE (NO_3)

Nitrate in water is considered a final oxidation product of nitrogenous material and may indicate contamination by sewage or other organic matter, such as agricultural runoff, or industrial waste. The quantities of nitrate present in surface waters are generally less than 5 mg/l (as NO_3) and have no effect on the value of the water for ordinary uses. It has been reported that as much as 2 mg/l of nitrate in boiler water tends to decrease intercrystalline cracking of boiler steel. Studies made by Faucett and Miller (1946), Waring (1949) and by the National Research Council (Maxcy, 1950) concluded that drinking water containing nitrates in excess of 44 mg/l (as NO_3) should be regarded as unsafe for infant feeding. U.S. Public Health Services (1962) sets 45 mg/l as the upper limit.

TABLE 3.3 (Continued)

PHOSPHORUS (P)

Phosphorus is an essential element in the growth of plants and animals. It occurs in water as organically bound phosphorus or as phosphate (PO_4). Some sources that contribute nitrate, such as organic wastes are also important sources of phosphorus. The addition of phosphates in water treatment constitutes a possible source although the dosage is usually small. In some areas phosphate fertilizers may yield some phosphorus to water. Another important source is the use of phosphates in detergents. Domestic and industrial sewage effluents often contain considerable amounts of phosphorus. Concentrations of phosphorus found in water are not reported to be toxic to man, animal, or fish. However, the element can stimulate the growth of algae, which may cause taste and odor problems in public water treatment and esthetic problems in recreation areas.

BORON (B)

Boron in small quantities has been found essential for plant growth, but irrigation water containing more than 1 mg/l is detrimental to citrus and other boron-sensitive crops. Boron is reported in Survey analyses of surface water in arid and semiarid regions of the Southwest and West where irrigation is practiced or contemplated, but few of the surface waters analyzed have harmful concentrations of boron.

DISSOLVED SOLIDS

The reported quantity of dissolved solids--the residue on evaporation--consists mainly of the dissolved mineral constituents in the water. It may also contain some organic matter and water of crystalization. Waters with less than 500 mg/l of dissolved solids are usually satisfactory for domestic and some industrial uses. Water containing several thousand mg/l of dissolved solids are sometimes successfully used for irrigation where practices permit the removal of soluble salts through the application of large volumes of water on well-drained lands, but generally water containing more than about 2,000 mg/l is considered to be unsuitable for long-term irrigation under average conditions.

ARSENIC (As)

Arsenic compounds are present naturally in some waters, but the occurence of quantities detrimental to health is rare. Weed killers, insecticides and many industrial effluents contain arsenic and are potential sources of water pollution. The U.S. Public Health Service (1962) states that the concentration of arsenic in drinking water on carriers subject to Federal quarantine regulations should not exceed 0.01 mg/l and concentrations in excess of 0.05 mg/l are grounds for rejection of the supply. Concentrations of 2-4 mg of arsenic per liter are reported not to interfere with the self-purification of streams (Rudolfs and others, 1944) but concentrations in excess of 15 mg/l may be harmful to some fish.

BARIUM (Ba)

Barium may replace potassium in some of the igneous rock minerals, especially feldspar, and barium sulfate (barite) is a common barium mineral of secondary origin. Only traces of barium are present in surface water and sea water. Because natural water contains sulfate, barium will dissolve only in trace amounts. Barium sometimes occurs in brines from oil-well wastes. The U.S. Public Health Service (1962) states that water containing concentrations of barium in excess of 1.0 mg/l is not suitable for drinking and culinary use because of the serious toxic effects of barium on heart, blood vessels, and nerves.

CADMIUM (Cd)

This element is found in nature largely in the form of the sulfide, and as an impurity in zinc-lead ores. The carbonate and hydroxide are not very soluble in water and will precipitate at high pH values; the chloride, nitrate, and sulfate are soluble and remain in solution under most pH conditions. The extensive use of the element and its salts in metallurgy electroplating, ceramics, and photography make it a frequent component of industrial wastes. The U.S. Public Health Service (1962) established as grounds for rejection any water containing more than 0.01 mg/l of cadmium.

CHROMIUM (Cr)

Few if any waters contain chromium from natural sources. Natural waters can probably contain only traces of chromium as a cation unless the pH is very low. When chromium is present in water, it is usually the result of pollution by industrial wastes. Concentrations of more than 0.05 mg/l of chromium in the hexavalent form constitute grounds for rejection of a water for domestic use on the basis of the standards of the U.S. Public Health Service (1962).

COBALT (Co)

Cobalt occurs in nature in the minerals smaltite, $(Co, Ni)AS_2$, and cobaltite, $CoAsS$. Alluvial deposits and soils derived from shales often contain cobalt in the form of phosphate or sulfate, but other soil types may be markedly deficient in cobalt in any form (Baer, 1955) Ruminant animals may be adversely affected by grazing on land deficient in cobalt. For domestic water supplies, no maximum safe concentration has been established.

COPPER (Cu)

Copper is a fairly common trace constituent of natural water. Small amounts may be introduced into water by solution of copper and brass water pipes and other copper-bearing equipment in contact with the water, or from copper salts added to control algae in open reservoirs. Copper salts such as the sulfate and chloride are highly soluble in waters with a low pH but in water of normal alkalinity the salts hydrolyze and the copper may be precipitated. In the normal pH range of natural water containing carbon dioxide, the copper might be precipitated as carbonate. The oxidized portions of sulfide-copper ore bodies contain other copper compounds. The presence of copper in mine water is common. Copper imparts a disagreeable metallic

TABLE 3.3 (Continued)

COPPER (cont'd) taste to water. As little as 1.5 mg/l can usually be detected, and 5 mg/l can render the water unpalatable. Copper is not considered to be a cumulative systemic poison like lead and mercury; most copper ingested is excreted by the body and very little is retained. The pathological effects of copper are controversial, but it is generally believed very unlikely that humans could unknowingly ingest toxic quantities from palatable drinking water. The U.S. Public Health Service (1962) recommends that copper should not exceed 1.0 mg/l in drinking and culinary water.

LEAD (Pb) Lead seldom occurs in most natural waters, but industrial mine and smelter effluents may contain relatively large amounts of lead which contaminates the streams. Also, atmospheric contamination which is produced from several types of engine exhausts has considerably increased the availability of this element for solution in rainfall, resulting in contamination of lead in streams (Hem, 1970). Lead in the form of sulfate is reported to be soluble in water to the extent of 31 mg/l (Seidell, 1940) at 25° C. In natural water this concentration would not be approached, however, since a pH of less than 4.5 would probably be required to prevent formation of lead hydroxide and carbonate. It is reported (Pleissner, 1907) that at 18° C water free of carbon dioxide will dissolve the equivalent of 1.4 mg/l of lead and the solubility is increased nearly four fold by the presence of 2.8 mg/l of carbon dioxide in the solution. Presence of other ions may increase the solubility of lead. Reports on human tolerance of lead vary widely, but the U.S. Public Health Service (1962) states that lead shall not exceed 0.05 mg/l in drinking and culinary water on carriers subject to Federal quarantine regulations.

LITHIUM (Li) Lithium is present in some minerals but it is not abundant in nature. From available information, most fresh waters rarely contain lithium of concentrations exceeding 10 mg/l, but larger quantities may be present in brines and thermal waters. Lithium is used in metallurgy, medicinal water, and some types of glass and storage batteries. Waste from such industries may contain lithium.

MERCURY (Hg) Mercury is the only common metal which is liquid at ordinary temperatures. It occurs free in nature but its chief source is cinnabar (HgS). Mercury compounds are virulent culminative poisons which are readily absorbed through the respiratory and gastrointestinal tracts or through unbroken skin (Weast and Selby, 1967). The main source of high concentrations of dissolved mercury in water, in the form of highly toxic methyl mercury, $Hg(CH_3)_2$, comes from waste discharges from industrial users of mercury and from mercurial pesticides. Fish from streams and lakes subject to mercury contamination have been found to contain amounts of mercury above the safe limits for food consumption. The U.S. Public Health Service has proposed that the upper limits of dissolved mercury in water for domestic use should not exceed 5 micrograms per liter (0.005 mg/l).

NICKEL (Ni) Elemental nickel seldom occurs in nature, but its compounds are found in many ores and minerals. Many nickel salts are quite soluble and may contribute to water pollution, especially when discharged from metal-plating industries. The U.S. Public Health Service (1962) has not placed a limit on nickel concentration in public water supplies.

STRONTIUM (Sr) Strontium is a typical alkaline-earth element and is similar chemically to calcium. Strontium may be present in natural water in amounts up to a few mg/l much more frequently than the available data indicate. In most surface water the amount of strontium is small in proportion to calcium. However, in sea water the ratio of strontium to calcium is 1:30.

ZINC (Zn) Zinc is abundant in rocks and ores but is only a minor constituent in natural water because the free metal and its oxides are only sparingly soluble. In most alkaline surface waters it is present only in trace quantities, but more may be present in acid water. Chlorides and sulfates of zinc are highly soluble. Zinc is used in many commercial products, and industrial wastes may contain large amounts. Zinc in water does not cause serious effects on health, but produces undesirable esthetic effects. The U.S. Public Health Service (1962) recommends that the zinc content not exceed 5 mg/l in drinking and culinary water.

TABLE 3.4

PROPERTIES AND CHARACTERISTICS OF WATER

DISSOLVED SOLIDS

Theoretically, dissolved solids are anhydrous residues of the dissolved substances in water. All solutes affect the chemical and physical properties of the water and result in an osmotic pressure. Water with several thousand mg/l of dissolved solids is generally not palatable, although those accustomed to highly mineralized water may complain that less concentrated water tastes flat. The U.S. Public Health Service (1962) recommends that the maximum concentration of dissolved solids not exceed 500 mg/l in drinking and culinary water on carriers subject to Federal quarantine regualtions, but permits 1,000 mg/l if no better water is available. Reported livestock tolerances range from 3,000 mg/l (Colorado Agricultural Experiment Station, 1943) to 15,000 mg/l (Heller, 1933).

Industrial tolerances for dissolved solids differ widely, but few industrial processes will permit more than 1,000 mg/l. The Geological Survey classifies the degree of salinity of these more mineralized bodies of water as follows (Swenson and Baldwin, 1965):

Dissolved solids (mg/l)	Degree of Salinity
Less than 1,000	Nonsaline.
1,000 to 3,000	Slightly saline.
3,000 to 10,000	Moderately saline.
10,000 to 35,000	Very saline.

HARDNESS

Hardness is the characteristic of water that receives the most attention in industrial and domestic use. It is commonly recognized by the increased quantity of soap required to produce lather. The use of hard water is also objectionable because it contributes to the formation of scale in boilers, water heaters, radiators, and pipes, with the resultant decrease in rate of heat transfer, possibility of boiler failure, and loss of flow.

Hardness is caused almost entirely by compounds of calcium and magnesium. Other constituents--such as iron, manganese, aluminum, barium, strontium, and free acid--also cause hardness, although they usually are not present in quantities large enough to have any appreciable effect.

Generally, bicarbonate and carbonate determine the proportions of "carbonate" hardness of water. Carbonate hardness is the amount of hardness chemically equivalent to the amount of bicarbonate and carbonate in solution. Carbonate hardness is approximately equal to the amount of hardness that is removed from water by boiling.

Noncarbonate hardness is the difference between the hardness calculated from the total amount of calcium and magnesium in solution and the carbonate hardness. The scale formed at high temperatures by the evaporation of water containing non-carbonate hardness commonly is tough, heat resistant, and difficult to remove.

Although many people talk about soft water and hard water, there has been no firm line of demarcation. Water that seems hard to an easterner may seem soft to a westerner. In this report hardness of water is classified as follows:

Hardness range (calcium carbonate in mg/l)	Hardness description
0 – 60	Soft
61 – 120	Moderately hard
121 – 180	Hard
More than 180	Very hard

Source: Durfor and Becker, 1964.

ACIDITY (H^{+1})

The use of the terms acidity and alkalinity is widespread in the literature of water analysis and is a cause of confusion to those who are more accustomed to seeing a pH of 7.0 used as a neutral point. Acidity of a natural water represents the content of free carbon dioxide and other uncombined gases, organic acids and weak bases that hydrolyze to give hydrogen ions. Sulfates of iron and aluminum in mine and industrial wastes are common sources of acidity.

SODIUM ADSORPTION RATIO (SAR)

The term "sodium adsorption ratio (SAR)" was introduced by the U.S. Salinity Laboratory Staff (1954). It is a ratio expressing the relative activity of sodium ions in exchange reaction with soil and is an index of the sodium of alkali hazard to the soil. Sodium adsorption ratio is expressed by the equation:

$$SAR = \frac{Na^+}{\sqrt{\dfrac{Ca^{++} + Mg^{++}}{2}}}$$

where the concentrations of the ions are expressed in milliequivalents per liter.

Waters are divided into four classes with respect to sodium or alkali hazard: low, medium, high, and very high, depending upon the SAR values of 10, 18, and 26, but at 5,000 micromhos the corresponding dividing points are SAR values of approximately 2.5, 6.5, and 11. Waters range in respect to sodium hazard from those which can be used for irrigation on almost all soils to those which are generally unsatisfactory for irrigation.

TABLE 3.4 (Continued)

SPECIFIC CONDUCTANCE
(micromhos per centi-
meter at 25° C)

Specific conductance is a convenient, rapid determination used to estimate the amount of dissolved solids in water. It is a measure of the ability of water to transmit a small electrical current. The more dissolved solids in water that can transmit electricity the greater the specific conductance of the water. Commonly, the amount of dissolved solids (in mg/l) is about 65 percent of the specific conductance (in micromhos). This relation is not constant from stream to stream or from well to well and it may even vary in the same source with changes in the composition of the water (Durfor and Becker, 1964, p. 27-29).

Specific conductance of most waters in the eastern United States is less than 1,000 micromhos, but in the arid western parts of the country, a specific conductance of more than 1,000 micromhos is common.

HYDROGEN-ION CONCENTRATION
(pH)

Hydrogen-ion concentration is expressed in terms of pH units. The values of pH often are used as a measure of the solvent power of water or as an indicator of the chemical behavior certain solutions may have toward rock minerals.

The degree of acidity or alkalinity of water, as indicated by the hydrogen-ion concentration, expressed as pH, is related to the corrosive properties of water and is useful in determining the proper treatment for coagulation that may be necessary at water-treatment plants. A pH of 7.0 indicates that the water is neither acid or alkaline. pH readings progressively lower than 7.0 denote increasing acidity and those progressively higher than 7.0 denote increasing alkalinity. The pH of most natural surface waters ranges between 6 and 8. Some alkaline surface waters have pH values greater than 8.0 and waters containing free mineral acid or organic matter usually have pH values less than 4.5.

The investigator who utilizes pH data in his interpretations of water analyses should be careful to place pH values in their proper perspective.

TEMPERATURE

Temperature is an important factor in properly determining the quality of water. This is very evident for such a direct use as an industrial coolant. Temperature is also important, but perhaps not so evident, for its indirect influence upon aquatic biota, concentrations of dissolved gases, and distribution of chemical solutes in lakes and reservoirs as a consequence of thermal stratification and variation.

Surface water temperatures tend to change seasonally and daily with air temperatures, except for the outflow of large springs. Superimposed upon the annual temperature cycle is a daily fluctuation of temperature which is greater in warm seasons than in cold and greater in sunny periods than with a cloud cover. Natural warming is due mainly to absorption of a solar radiation by the water and secondarily to transfer of heat from the air. Condensation of water vapor at the water surface is reported to furnish measureable quantities of heat. Heat loss takes place largely through radiation, with further losses through evaporation and conduction to the air and to the streambed. Thus the temperature of a small stream generally reaches a maximum in mid- to late afternoon due to solar heating and reaches a minimum from early to mid-morning after nocturnal radiation.

COLOR

In water analysis the term "color" refers to the appearance of water that is free from suspended solids. Many turbid waters that appear yellow, red, or brown when viewed in the stream show very little color after the suspended matter has been removed. The yellow-to-brown color of some waters is usually caused by organic matter extracted from leaves, roots, and other organic substances in the ground. In some areas objectionable color in water results from industrial wastes and sewage. Clear deep water may appear blue as the result of a scattering of sunlight by the water molecules. Water for domestic use and some industrial use should be free from any perceptible color. A color less than 15 units generally passes unnoticed (U.S. Public Health Service, 1962). Some swamp waters have natural color in excess of 300 units.

The extent to which a water is colored by material in solution is commonly reported as a part of a water analysis because a significant color in water may indicate the presence of organic material that may have some bearing on the dissolved solids content. Color in water is expressed in terms of units between 0 and 500 or more based on the above standard.

TURBIDITY

Turbidity is the optical property of a suspension with reference to the extent to which the penetration of light is inhibited by the presence of insoluble material. Turbidity is a function of both the concentration and particle size of the suspended material. It is reported in terms of mg/l of silica or Jackson turbidity units (JTU).

Turbid water is abrasive in pipes, pumps, and turbine blades. Althoug turbidity does not directly measure the safety of drinking water, it is related to the consumer's acceptance of the water. A level of 5 JTU of turbidity becomes objectionable to a considerable number of people (U.S. Public Health Service, 1962).

DENSITY AT 20° C

Density is the mass of any substance per unit volume at a designated standard temperature. Density should not be confused with specific gravity, which is a mass-to-mass relation.

The density value has some use in industries that utilize brines and whose basic unit of concentration of dissolved material is density. Density is used primarily by the chemist in the computation of milligrams per liter for highly mineralized waters.

TABLE 3.4 (Continued)

DISSOLVED OXYGEN (DO)

Oxygen dissolved in water is derived from the air and from the oxygen given off in the process of photosynthesis by aquatic plants. Dissolved oxygen is responsible for many of the corrosion problems in industry.

CHEMICAL OXYGEN DEMAND (COD)

Chemical oxygen demand is a measure of the chemically oxidizable material in the water, and furnishes an approximation of the amount of organic and reducing material present. The determined value may correlate with natural-water color or with carbonaceous organic pollution from sewage or industrial wastes.

BIOCHEMICAL OXYGEN DEMAND (BOD)

Biochemical oxygen demand is a measure of the oxygen required to oxidize the organic material usable as a source of food by aerobic organisms.

BIOLOGICAL AND MICROBIOLOGICAL INFORMATION

Biological and microbiological information is an important aspect in the evaluation of water quality. The kinds and amount of aquatic biota in a stream or lake can be useful "indicators" of environmental conditions and particularly of the degree of pollution of water with organic wastes (Doudoroff and Warren, 1957). Biological information includes qualitative and quantitative analyses of plankton, bottom organisms, and particulate inorganic and amorphous matter present. Microbiological information includes quantitative identification of certain bacteriological indicator organisms.

CHLOROPHYLL (Plant pigment)

The concentrations of photosynthetic pigments in natural waters vary with time and changing aquatic conditions. Concentrations of chlorophyll a, b, and c (spectrophotometric determination) are used to estimate the biomass and photosynthetic capacity of phytoplankton (blue-green algae). Ratios between the different forms of chlorophyll are thought to indicate the taxonomic composition or the physiological state of the algae community (Slack, 1970).

PLANKTON

Plankton is the floating (or weakly swimming) animal or plant life in a body of water consisting, chiefly of minute plants (as diatoms and blue-green algae) and of minute animals (as protozoan, entomostracans and various larvae). Algae are know to cause tastes and odor in water supply.
Plankton population in water is obtained by count level (the number of organisms per milliliter).

COLIFORM BACTERIA

Coliform organisms have long been used as indicators of sewage pollution, though the group includes bacteria from diverse natural sources and habitats. For example, members of the coliform group are indigenous to soil and vegetation as well as feces. Standards for drinking-water quality provide definite minimums as to number of samples examined and the maximum number of coliform organisms allowable per 100 milliliters (ml) of finished water (Slack, 1970). The coliform population of water is determined either by the most probable number (MPN), or by the incubation membrane filter method, a direct count of coliform colonies per plate.

FECAL COLIFORM BACTERIA

Fecal coliform is that portion of the coliform group that is present in the intestinal tract of warm-blooded animals and is capable of producing gas from lactos in suitable culture medium at 44.5° C. Organisms from other sources generally cannot produce gas in this manner. (American Public Health Assoc. and others, 1965). Thus, in general, the presence of fecal coliform organisms indicates recent pollution (Slack, 1970).

PHENOLS

Phenolic material in water resources is invariably the result of pollution. Phenols are widely used as disinfectants and in the synthesis of many organic compounds. Waste products from oil refineries, coke areas, and chemical plants may contain high concentrations. Fortunately, phenols decompose in the presence of oxygen and micro-organisms, and their persistence downstream from point of entry is relatively short lived. The rate of decomposition is dependent on the environment.
Very low concentrations impart such a disagreeable taste to water that it is highly improbable that harmful amounts could be consumed unknowingly. Reported thresholds of detection of taste and odor range from 0/001 to 0.01 mg/l.

CYANIDE (CN)

Cyanides are not found free in nature, but may become contaminants of water supplies by means of effluents from gasworks, coke ovens, steel mills, electroplating processes, and chemical industries. In natural streams and organic soils, simple cyanides are decomposed by bacterial action, whereas the metal-cyanide complexes are often quite stable and more resistant to degradation. The U.S. Public Health Service (1962) set a recommended limit of 0.01 mg cyanide per liter and a mandatory limit of 0.2 mg/l for waters subject to interstate regulations.

DETERGENTS (methylene blue active substance, MBAS)

Anionic surfactants in detergents resist chemical oxidation and biological breakdown. Soap is an example of this class and the synthetic members are sodium salts of organic sulfonates or sulfates (Rose, 1966). Their persistence in water over long periods of time contributes to pollution of both ground water and surface water. Some

TABLE 3.4 (Continued)

DETERGENTS (cont'd)

of the effects produced from detergent pollution are unpleasant taste, odor, and foaming (Wayman, and others, 1962). Although the physiological implications of MBAS to human beings is unknown, prolonged ingestion of this material by rats is believed to be nontoxic (Paynter, 1960). The U.S. Public Health Service (1962) recommends that MBAS should not exceed 0.5 mg/l in drinking and culinary waters.

TOTAL ORGANIC CARBON (TOC)

Total organic carbon is a measure of the organically related carbonaceous content of water. It includes all natural and manmade organic compounds which are combustable at a temperature of 950° C.

SEDIMENT

Fluvial sediment generally is regarded as that material which is transported by, suspended in, or deposited by water. Suspended sediment is that part which remains in suspension in water owing to the upward components of turbulent currents or by colloidal suspension. Much fluvial sediment results from the natural process of erosion, which in turn is part of the geologic cycle of rock transformation. This natural process may be accelerated by agricultural practices. Sediment also is contributed by a number of industrial and construction activities. In certain sections, waste materials from mining, logging, oilfield, and other industrial operations introduce large quantities of suspended material.

The quantity of sediment, transported or available for transportation, is affected by climatic conditions, form or nature of precipitation, character of the solid mantle, plant cover, topography, and land use. The mode and rate of sediment erosion, transport, and deposition is determined largely by the size distribution of the particles or more precisely by the fall velocities of the particles in water. Sediment particles in the sand size range (larger than 0.062 mm) do not appear to be affected by flocculation or dispersion resulting from the mineral constituents in solution. In contrast, the sedimentation diameter of clay and silt particles in suspension may vary considerably from point to point in a stream or reservoir, depending on the mineral matter in solution and in suspension and the degree of turbulence present. The size of sediment particles in transport at any point depends on the type of erodible and soluble material in the drainage area, the degree of flocculation present, time in transport, and characteristics of the transporting flow. The flow characteristics include velocity of water, turbulence, and the depth, width, and roughness of the channel. As a result of these variable characteristics, the size of particles transported, as well as the total sediment load, is in constant adjustment with the characteristics and physical features of the stream and drainage area.

3. SURVEILLANCE NETWORKS

Several surveillance networks for the sampling of water quality are to be found in the United States, ranging in scale from national to local. Inconsistencies in parameter selection, sample point location, observation frequency, instrumentation, and coordinated data storage and retrieval do not permit the coordinated use of all published data. However, despite these difficulties Federal, State, and local governmental agencies as well as private firms and universities are attempting systematic surveillance of water quality. Additionally, models for evaluating the collected data have been developed for certain purposes.

Within urban areas water quality surveillance as an organized reporting network hardly exists. A principal flaw for urban network analysis lies in the lack of monitoring stations on main channels immediately down-stream from metropolitan areas. Some tributary stations provide particular point information but do not allow for an analysis of total water quality adjustments from a metropolitan area. Published materials resulting from the efforts of regional surveillance networks are available in the following documents:

Approved Interstate Water Quality Standards and plans for the implementation and enforcement within the study area.

Comprehensive River Basin Surveys published by the Corps of Engineers with the cooperation and assistance of numerous governmental agencies.

Proceedings of conferences on interstate water pollution conducted by FWPCA and the U.S. Public Health Service.

Quality of Surface Waters of the United States published by the Geological Survey and the various States.

Quantity of Water Records published by the Geological Survey and the various States.

Publications concerning water quality by the various State Departments of Health or their analogs.

Pollution Surveys published by FWPCA Regional Basin Offices.

Studies of the Federal Power Commission.

    a.   THE NATIONAL WATER SURVEILLANCE NETWORK

The effective conduct of a national pollution control program requires that reliable information on water quality be collected, analyzed, and evaluated in a timely and efficient manner. The STORET system was developed to meet this challenge and provide comprehensive evaluation of water quality at the Federal, State, or local level of concern. STORET is the acronym used to identify the computer-oriented U.S. Environmental Protection Agency Water Quality Control Information System for STOrage and RETrieval of the following information: water quality; water quality standards; fish kill; municipal and industrial waste discharge; and waste abatement needs, costs and implementation schedules.

STORET system capabilities provide a national repository for all water quality control data collected by EPA and cooperating agencies. This data bank constitutes the largest single storehouse of information for research available from any agency. Water quality data may be retrieved from STORET in a statistical format; compared to State and Federal standards; or as a digital plotting of the data on maps.

As the national data-bank, STORET incorporates many data collection efforts, data files, and unique computer programs. On a historical and a technical basis, the computer programs

may be divided into two major groups: water quality data
programs and waste discharge inventories and other programs.

The water quality data programs are used to store, update,
retrieve, and analyze water quality data. The programs of the
system analyze two basic types of data:

1. Station location data are identified with the site
at which water quality samples are collected. Two methods
for determining station locations are, (a) the hydrologic index
which locates a station on a defined river system and (b) the
geographical coordinates by latitude and longitude. This latter
station location method allows storage and retrieval of data
collected from large open bodies of water and locations which
cannot be readily associated with points on a stream.

2. Water quality data consists of the date, time, type
sample, and the water quality analyses reported in terms of
parameter measurements. Chemical, physical, and biological
water quality parameters are identifiable with the system.

The second STORET system capability includes waste discharge inventories and other programs. These programs store,
update, retireve, and analyze municipal and industrial facility
data related to a facility's location, treatment practice,
effluent, and scheduled implementation of new treatment practice.

Several hundred agencies and monitoring networks supply
STORET data on a continuing basis (Table 3.5). The information
is identifiable by more than one thousand specific parameters
although not all parameters are available for every region of
the country. Because of this limitation on information regarding certain locations several alternative but specific regional
surveillance sources are worth noting.

(i)   FEDERAL AGENCIES

Federal agencies participating at various levels in the
national water surveillance network are listed in Table 3.5

(ii)   STATE AND LOCAL AGENCIES

Non-Federal agencies reporting information on water quality
data acquisition are listed in Table 3.6.

TABLE 3.5

FEDERAL SOURCES OF WATER QUALITY DATA

DEPARTMENT OF AGRICULTURE

ARS Agricultural Research Service
ERS Economic Research Service
FS Forest Service
SCS Soil Conservation Service

AF DEPARTMENT OF THE AIR FORCE

DEPARTMENT OF THE ARMY

CE Corps of Engineers

DEPARTMENT OF COMMERCE

CEN Bureau of the Census
CGS Coast and Geodetic Survey - ESSA
WB Weather Bureau - ESSA
BDS Business and Defense Services Administration

DEPARTMENT OF HEALTH, EDUCATION, AND WELFARE

IHS Indian Health Service
PHS Public Health Service

HUD DEPARTMENT OF HOUSING AND URBAN DEVELOPMENT

DEPARTMENT OF THE INTERIOR

BPA Bonneville Power Administration
BCF Bureau of Commercial Fisheries
BIA Bureau of Indian Affairs
BLM Bureau of Land Management
BM Bureau of Mines
BOR Bureau of Outdoor Recreation
BR Bureau of Reclamation
SFW Bureau of Sport Fisheries and Wildlife
WQA Federal Water Quality Administration
GS Geological Survey
NPS National Park Service
OSW Office of Saline Water

DEPARTMENT OF THE NAVY

NFE Naval Facilities Engineering Command
MC Marine Corps

DEPARTMENT OF TRANSPORTATION

BRP Bureau of Public Roads - FHWA

INDEPENDENT AGENCIES

AEC Atomic Energy Commission
FPC Federal Power Commission
IBW International Boundary and Water Commission
IJC International Joint Commission
NOD National Oceanographic Data Center
TVA Tennessee Valley Authority

TABLE 3.6

STATE AND LOCAL SOURCES FOR WATER QUALITY DATA

ALASKA

Chugah Electric Association

ARIZONA

Salt River Vally Water Users Association
Water Resources Research Center
Roosevelt Irrigation District
Arizona Game and Fish Department
Maricopa County Municipal Water Conservation
    District Number One
Gila Water Commissioner

ARKANSAS

Arkansas State Department of Health
Arkansas Game and Fish Commission
Arkansas Pollution Control Commission
Arkansas Geological Commission

CALIFORNIA

California Department of Water Resources
Alameda County Water District
Marine Municipal Water District
Humboldt Bay Municipal Water District
California Water Quality Control Board

COLORADO

Board of Water Commissioners
    City and County of Denver
Division of Water Resources
    Office of State Engineer
Department of Public Utilities
    City of Colorado Springs
Boulder City County Health Department
Pueblo Board of Water Works

CONNECTICUT

State Department of Health
The Water Bureau of the Metropolitan District
Bridgeport Hydraulic Company

DELAWARE

Delaware Geological Survey

DISTRICT OF COLUMBIA

Department of Sanitary Engineering
    Government of the District of Columbia
Department of Public Health
    Government of the District of Columbia

FLORIDA

Hollywood Reclamation District
Hillsborough County Health Department
Manatec County Health Department
Central & Southern Florida Flood Control District
Bureau of Geology,
    Department of Natural Resources

GEORGIA

Savannah Department of Water & Sewage
Thomasville Water & Light Department
Valdosta Water & Sewage Department
City of Gainesville Water Works
City of Rome Water Works
City of Griffin Water Works
Macon Board of Water Commissioners
Atlanta Water Works
Columbus Water Works

HAWAII

Board of Water Supply
    City and County of Honolulu
Department of Water, County of Kauai
Board of Water Supply, County of Maui
Board of Water Supply, County of Hawaii
Department of Hawaiian Home Lands
    State of Hawaii
Division of Fish & Game
    State of Hawaii
Division of Water & Land Development
    State of Hawaii
Public Utility Agency Water Division
    Government of Guam
Ryukyu Industrial Research Institute
    Government of Ryukyu Islands
Ryukyu Meteorological Agency
    Government of Ryukyu Islands

IDAHO

Idaho State Fish Hatchery
Water Resources Research Institute
Idaho Department of Health

ILLINOIS

Illinois Department of Public Health
Metropolitan Sanitary District of Greater Chicago
Illinois Department of Registration and Education
Illinois Department of Public Works and Buildings

INDIANA

Indiana State Board of Health
Indiana Department of Natural Resources

IOWA

Iowa State Hygenic Laboratory
Director of Lakeside Laboratory
    University of Iowa
Des Moines Water Works
Ottumwa Water Works
Department of Civil Engineering University of Iowa
Iowa Department of Preventive Medicine & Environmental
    Health
Agricultural Engineering Department
    Iowa State University

TABLE 3.6 (Continued)

Fort Dodge Department of Municipal Utilities
Council Bluffs Water Works
Des Moines County Drainage District No. 7
Green Bay Levee & Drainage District No. 2
Department of Civil Engineering
   Iowa State University
Department of Geography
   University of Iowa
Institute of Geography
   University of Iowa
Engineering Research Institute
   Iowa State University
Iowa State Agricultural Experimental Station
Department of Earth Sciences
   Iowa State University

KANSAS

Kansas State Department of Health
Kansas City Board of Public Utilities
Kansas State Board of Agriculture
Topeka Water Department
Kansas Forestry, Fish & Game Commission

KENTUCKY

Kentucky State Department of Health
   Division of Environmental Health
Kentucky State Department of Health
   Water Pollution Control Commission
Louisville Water Company
Kentucky Department of Fish & Wildlife
Kentucky Department of Natural Resources
Water Resources Laboratory

LOUISIANA

Rapides Parish Water Works District No. 3
Louisiana State Department of Health
Houma Light & Water Plant
Jefferson Water Works District No. 2
Lafourche Water Works District No. 1
East Jefferson Water Works District No. 1
New Orleans Sewerage & Water Board
Bossier City Water Plant
Monroe Water Treatment Plant
Louisiana Wild Life & Fisheries Commission
City of Shreveport Department of Water Utilities

MARYLAND

Baltimore County Health Department
City of Baltimore Department of Public Works

MICHIGAN

Michigan Water Resources Commission

MINNESOTA

Hennepin County Highway Department
Eveleth Taconite Company
Minnesota Conservation Department
Otter Tail Power Company
Ramsey County Engineer's Department
Northern States Power Co.
City of Duluth
   Water, Gas & Sewage Treatment Department

Minnesota Ore Operations, USS Corporation
Blandin Paper Company
Minnesota Power and Light Co.
Minneapolis-St. Paul Sanitary District
Minnesota Pollution Control Agency
Washington County Highway Department

MISSISSIPPI

City of Vicksburg Water Treatment Plant
City of Jackson Water Works
Pearl River Valley Water Supply District
City of Meridian Water & Sewer Department
City of Columbus Light & Water Department
Mississippi State Board of Health

MISSOURI

Missouri Division of Health
Kansas City Sanitary Sewer District
University of Missouri at Rolla
Metropolitan St. Louis Sewer District
Little River Drainage District
Missouri Geological Survey & Water Resources

MONTANA

Montana Fish & Game Department
Montana University Joint Water Resources
   Research Center
Montana State Board of Health
Montana Water Resources Board
Montana Bureau of Mines and Geology

NEBRASKA

Nebraska Game & Parks Commission
Nebraska Department of Health
Omaha Metropolitan Utilities District
Soil & Water Testing Laboratory
   University of Nebraska

NEVADA

Nevada Department of Health, Welfare & Rehabilitation
Walker River Irrigation District
State Department of Conservation & Natural Resources

NEW JERSEY

Passaic Valley Water Commission
New Jersey State Department of Conservation &
   Economic Development
North Jersey District Water Supply Commission
Pasaic County
Delaware River Joint Toll Bridge Commission
New Jersey State Department of Health

NEW MEXICO

State Engineers Office

NEW YORK

New York State Department of Health
Nassau County Department of Public Works

NORTH CAROLINA

North Carolina State Board of Health
North Carolina Department of Water & Air Resources

TABLE 3.6 (Continued)

NORTH DAKOTA

North Dakota Game & Fish Department
North Dakota State Department of Health
Minot Water Treatment Plant
City of Bismarck Water Department
City of Dickinson Water Treatment
Grand Forks Water Treatment Plant

OHIO

Ohio Department of Natural Resources
The Miami Conservancy District
Ohio River Valley Water Sanitation Commission
Ohio Department of Health

OKLAHOMA

Oklahoma State Department of Health

OREGON

School of Forestry
   Oregon State University
Oregon State Game Commission
Douglas County Water Resources Survey
Oregon State Engineer
Fish Commission of Oregon

PENNSYLVANIA

Pennsylvania Department of Health

PUERTO RICO

Puerto Rico Water Resources Authority

SOUTH CAROLINA

Agricultural Engineering Department
   Clemson University
Greenville Water Works
Spartanburg Water Works

SOUTH DAKOTA

Water Resources Research Institute
East Dakota Conservancy Subdistrict
South Dakota Geological Survey

TENNESSEE

Tennessee Game & Fish Commission
Tennessee Department of Public Health
Cleveland Water System
City Water Company of Chattanooga
Bristol Water Plant
University of Tennessee Experiment Station
Memphis Light, Gas & Water Division
Water Resources Research Center

TEXAS

Texas Water Development Board

UTAH

Utah State Health Department
Metropolitan Water District of Salt Lake City
Utah Division of Fish & Game
Salt Lake County Water Conservancy District
Salt Lake City Water Supply & Waterworks
Ogden Bay Waterfowl Management Area
Clear Lake Waterfowl Management Area
Utah Department of Natural Resources
Utah Geological & Mineralogical Survey
Ogden River Water Users
Weber River Distribution System
Utah Water Research Laboratory
   Utah State University

WASHINGTON

Washington Department of Water Resources
Skagit County PUD No. 1
Chelen County PUD No. 1
College of Fisheries
   University of Washington
College of Engineering Research
   Washington State University
Department of Zoology
   University of Washington
City of Bremerton Water Department
City of Everett Department of Water
City of Seattle Water Department
Tacoma Department of Public Utilities

WEST VIRGINIA

West Virginia Department of Natural Resources
West Virginia Department of Health

WISCONSIN

Wisconsin Department of Natural Resources
Northeastern Wisconsin Regional Planning Commission

WYOMING

City of Casper Board of Public Utilities
Sheridan Water Department
Wyoming State Engineer
Water Resources Research Institute

(iii)   FEDERAL, STATE, AND LOCAL CONFERENCES

A joint Federal, State, and local effort to evaluate the nation's water quality resulted in a series of Federal Water Pollution Enforcement Conferences held between January 1957 and February 1971. The conference proceedings and reports are excellent sources of information on polluters and pollution, are published, and the standards developed from these conferences are available from the Environmental Protection Agency. Figure 3.1 which maps conference sites, and the listing of conference titles presented in Table 3.7 indicates the national coverage for this effort.

FIGURE 3.1

FEDERAL WATER POLLUTION ENFORCEMENT CONFERENCES
February 1971

TABLE 3.7

FEDERAL WATER POLLUTION ENFORCEMENT CONFERENCES
January 1957-February 1971

1. Corney Creek Drainage System (Ark.-La.): January 16-17, 1957.

2. Big Blue River (Neb.-Kan.): May 3, 1957.

3. Missouri River-St. Joseph, Missouri Area (Mo.-Kan.): June 11, 1957 (Court Order: October 31, 1961).

4. Missouri River-Omaha, Nebraska Area (Neb.-Kan.-Mo.-Ia.): June 14, 1957 (Session 2: July 21, 1964).

5. Potomac River-Washington Metropolitan Area (D.C.-Md.-Va.): August 22, 1957 (Progress meeting: December 8-9, 1970).

6. Missouri River-Kansas Cities Metropolitan Area (Kan.-Mo.): December 3, 1967 (Hearing: June 13-17, 1960).

7. Mississippi River-St. Louis Metropolitan Area (Mo.-Ill.): March 4, 1958.

TABLE 3.7 (Continued)

8. Animas River (Colo.-N.M.): April 29, 1958 (Session 2: June 24, 1959).

9. Missouri River-Sioux City Area (S.D.-Ia.-Neb.-Kan.-Mo.): July 24, 1958 (Hearing: March 23-27, 1959).

10. Lower Columbia River (Wash.-Ore.): September 10-11, 1958 (Session 3: September 8-9, 1965).

11. Bear River (Ida.-Wyo.-Utah): October 8, 1958 (Session 2: July 19, 1960).

12. Colorado River and All Tributaries (Colo.-Utah-Ariz.-Nev.-Calif.-N.M.-Wyo.): January 13, 1960 (Session 6: July 26, 1967)

13. North Fork of the Holston River (Tenn.-Va.): September 28, 1960 (Session 2: June 19, 1962).

14. Raritan Bay (N.J.-N.Y.): August 22, 1961 (Session 3: June 13-14, 1967).

15. North Platte River (Neb.-Wyo.): September 21, 1961 (Session 3: November 20, 1963).

16. Puget Sound (Wash.): January 16-17, 1962 (Session 2: September 6-7, October 6, 1963).

17. Mississippi River-Clinton, Iowa Area (Ill.-Ia.): March 8, 1962.

18. Detroit River (Mich.): March 27-28, 1962 (Session 2: June 15-18, 1965).

19. Androscoggin River (N.H.-Me.): September 24, 1962 (Session 2: October 21, 1969).

20. Escambia River (Ala.-Fla.): October 24, 1962.

21. Coosa River (Ga.-Ala.): August 27, 1963 (Session 2: April 11, 1968).

22. Pearl River (Miss.-La.): October 22, 1963 (Session 2: November 7, 1968).

23. South Platte River (Colo.): October 29, 1963 (Session 2: November 10, 1966).

24. Menominee River (Mich.-Wisc.): November 6-8, 1963.

25. Lower Connecticut River (Mass.-Conn.): December 2, 1963 (Session 2: September 27, 1967).

26. Monongahela River (W. Va.-Pa.-Md.): December 17-18, 1963.

27. Snake River-Lewiston, Idaho-Clarkston, Washington Area (Ida.-Wash.): January 15, 1964.

28. Upper Mississippi River (Minn.-Wisc.): February 7-8, 1964 (Session 2: February 28, March 1 and 20, 1967).

29. Merrimack & Nashua Rivers (N.H.-Mass.): February 11, 1964 (Workshops: October 20-21, 1970).

30. Lower Mississippi River (Ark.-Tenn.-Miss.-La.): May 5-6, 1964.

31. Blackstone and Ten Mile Rivers (Mass.-R.I.): January 26, 1965 (Session 2: May 28, 1968).

32. Lower Savannah River (S.C.-Ga.): January 26, 1965 (Session 2: October 29, 1969).

33. Mahoning River (Ohio-Pa.): February 16-17, 1965.

34. Grand Calumet River, Little Calumet River, Calumet River, Wolf Lake, Lake Michigan, and Their Tributaries (Ill.-Ind.): March 2-9, 1965 (Technical Session: January 4, 5, 31, February 1, 1966).

35. Lake Erie (Mich.-Ind.-Ohio-Pa.-N.Y.): August 3-5, 1965 (Session 5: June 3-4, 1970).

36. Red River of the North (Minn.-N.D.): September 14-15; January 18, March 4, 1966.

37. Hudson River (N.Y.-N.J.): September 28-30, 1965 (Session 3: November 25, 1969).

38. Chattahoochee River and Its Tributaries (Ga.-Ala.): July 14-15, 1966 (Session 2: February 17, 1970).

39. Lake Tahoe (Calif.-Nev.): July 18-20, 1966.

40. Moriches Bay and Eastern Section of Great South Bay and Their Tributaries (N.Y.): September 20-21, 1966 (Session 2: June 21, 1967).

41. Penobscot River and Upper Penobscot Bay and Their Tributaries (Me.): April 20, 1967.

42. Eastern New Jersey Shore-from Shark River to Cape May (N.J.): November 1, 1967.

43. Lake Michigan (Mich.-Ind.-Ill.-Wisc.): January 31, 1968 (Conference is scheduled to reconvene March 23-24, 1971).

44. Boston Harbor (Mass.): May 20, 1968 (Session 2: April 30, 1969).

45. Lake Champlain (N.Y.-Vt.): November 13, 1968 (Session 2: June 25, 1970).

46. Lake Superior and Its Tributary Basin (Wisc.-Minn.-Mich.): May 13-15, 1969 (Session 2: January 14-15, 1971).

47. Escambia River Basin (Ala.-Fla.): January 20-21, 1970.

48. Perdido Bay (Fla.-Ala.): January 22, 1970.

49. Mobile Bay (Ala.): January 27-28, 1970.

50. Biscayne Bay (Fla.): February 24-26, 1970.

51. Dade County (Fla.): October 20-21, 1970.

II. GENERATION OF THE EFFLUENTS

1. DISCHARGE SOURCES AND AMOUNTS

Water pollution comes from a variety of sources. Regional sources include coal mining in Appalachia, where acidity is a problem, and areas of the West with unusually high salinity content in irrigation areas. Taking these regional variations into account, it is in urban areas that industrial and municipal wastes discharged into the waterways are the principal contributors to the degradation of water quality. The Committee on Pollution of the National Academy of Sciences suggests that research be directed towards the following eight contributors to water quality degradation:

Domestic sewage and other oxygen-demanding wastes;

Infectious agents;

Plant nutrients, particularly nitrogen and phosphorus;

Organic chemical exotics, particularly insecticides, pesticides, and detergents;

Other mineral and chemical substances from industrial, mining, and agricultural operations;

Sediments from land erosion;

Radioactive substances;

Heat.

Each of these categories can be subsumed under the two principal components of urban water degradation--industrial and municipal waste discharge.

a. INDUSTRIAL WASTES

The more than 300,000 domestic water-using factories discharge three to four times as much oxygen-demanding wastes, many toxic, as all the sewered population of the United States. At the same time industry demands billions of gallons of water meeting standards appropriate to the productive process. In 1968 about 15.5 trillion gallons of water were withdrawn in the United States by manufacturers (Table 3.8)--an increase of 27.5 percent from 1959. According to U.S. Geological Survey sources, industry, exclusive of electrical utilities, accounted for 14.5 percent of withdrawals in the United States from 1950 to 1965. Water provides a number of productive services within manufacturing processes. A number of products, notably beverages and prepared foods, incorporate water directly into the product.

TABLE 3.8

VOLUME OF INTAKE AND PERCENT
CONSUMED BY INDUSTRY GROUPS, 1968

Industry	Intake, 1968 (Billions of Gallons)	Percent Consumed, 1968
Food and Kindred Products	811	7.2
Textile Mill Products	154	11.7
Lumber	118	21.2
Paper	2252	7.7
Chemicals	4476	6.7
Petroleum and Coal	1435	15.2
Rubber	135	5.2
Leather	16	6.3
Stone, Clay, and Glass	251	13.1
Primary Metals	5005	6.2
Fabricated Metals	68	4.4
Machinery	189	4.2
Electrical Equipment	127	7.1
Transportation Equipment	313	6.4
All Manufacturing	15467	9.6

TABLE 3.9

COMPOSITION OF INDUSTRIAL WATER INTAKE AND WASTE
CONCENTRATION BY INDUSTRY GROUPS, 1968

	PERCENT OF INTAKE, 1968			WASTE CONCENTRATION OF PROCESS WATER (in p.p.m.)[1]		
Industry	Cooling	Process	Other	BOD	COD	SS
Food and Kindred Products	52.6	35.8	11.6	87	114	703
Textile Mill Products	15.3	70.7	14.0	304	327	70
Paper	28.9	65.6	5.5	336	3565	388
Chemicals	78.9	16.4	4.7	130	378	225
Petroleum and Coal	85.7	6.6	7.7	52	210	76
Rubber	70.9	17.6	11.5	17	57	30
Primary Metals	72.6	24.1	3.3	18	80	259
Fabricated Metals	28.4	54.8	16.8	N.A.[2]	N.A.	N.A.
Machinery	72.0	15.3	12.7	N.A.	N.A.	N.A.
Electrical Equipment	38.4	36.8	24.8	N.A.	N.A.	N.A.
Transportation Equipment	25.6	20.2	54.2	N.A.	N.A.	N.A.
All Manufacturing	65.5	27.8	6.7	N.A.	N.A.	N.A.

[1]Source: Conference Board Survey of 800 manufacturing establishments.

[2]N.A.--not available.

Tables from EPA, The Economics of Clean Water, Vol. 1 (1972).

Water can be used to transport materials in a manufacturing process; for example, water is used to carry partially prepared fruits and vegetables between stages of production. But the most common use of water by industry is to transport or flush away residual matter, the inevitable by-products of manufacturing processes that must be carried away in order to prevent counter-productive effects.

Much of the intake of water by industry is directed toward cooling; in 1968, the percentage of initial intake for the purpose of cooling amounted to 65.5 percent (Table 3.9). Cooling water is used to absorb the heat arising from the difference between thermal energy generated and that used in production. Although cooling tends to be the major use of water in industry, process water carries almost all residuals other than heat. Under the sponsorship of the Federal Water Quality Administration, a Conference Board (formerly the National Industrial Conference Board) survey indicated that 93.4 percent of the BOD, 89 percent of suspended solids contained in wastewater was contributed directly by the production process. Table 3.9 indicates waste concentrations in process water, generally highest for paper and allied products.

A number of economic and institutional changes in the last decade lead to the expectation that incentives have been provided for industry to curtail and treat liquid-borne wastes. Offsetting these incentives are growth of production and consequent residuals production. Publication of Water Use in Manufacturing, 1967 permits a survey of trends over the period 1959 to 1968 and re-examination of findings reported in Volume II of the Cost of Clean Water for 1967. Also available for analysis of industrial practices with respect to handling of liquid-borne wastes is the recent survey conducted by the Conference Board of establishments in the seven heaviest water-using manufacturing groups. [The industry groups surveyed were Food and Kindred Products (SIC 20), Textile Mills Products (SIC 22), Paper and Allied Products (SIC 26), Chemical and Allied Products (SIC 28), Petroleum and Coal Products (SIC 29), Rubber and Plastics Products (SIC 30), and Primary Metals (SIC 33).] From the almost 800 responses, a number of significant findings emerged.

Important changes in institutions and attitudes with respect to industrial waste discharges, and discharge of pollutants generally, occurred during the sixties. The Federal Water

Pollution Control Act of 1966 required the States, in consul-
tation with all users of interstate waterways and to the satisfaction of the Secretary of the Interior, to set standards for
interstate waterways. The standards were to account for all
uses of the waterways except as a medium for the disposal of
wastes. Continued pressures on existing supplies of freshwater,
both surface and ground, have, in a large portion of the conti-
nental United States, increased the cost of obtaining additional
units of water suitable for industrial application. In order
to obtain additional units of water, industry has had to turn
to poorer quality water, such as brackish water or treated sewage effluent, and to sink deeper wells. In effect, the price
to industry of obtaining water has generally increased during
the last decade and has provided an incentive to economize on
water intake. Although the above developments might be expected
to provide an incentive to industry to curtail and treat liquid-
borne wastes, other trends mitigate against reduction in the
discharge of industrial pollutants. The sheer growth of manufacturing output and the associated production of residuals
continues to create waste handling problems. Over the period
1959-1968 the Federal Reserve Board Index of Industrial Production for manufacturing increased 59 percent, and for the five
major water-using industries--food products, paper, chemicals,
petroleum, and primary metals--the index grew by 29, 48, 94, 33
and 52 percent, respectively. In addition to water demand growing directly out of production growth, industry's continued ac-

TABLE 3.10

U.S. ELECTRIC POWER--PAST USE, FUTURE ESTIMATES

Year	In billion kilowatt-hours
1912	12
1960	753
1965	1,060
1970	1,503
1975	2,022
1980	2,754
1985	3,639

Source: Federal Water Pollution Control Administration, Industrial Waste Guide on Thermal Pollution, September 1968.

cumulation of capital created both a direct demand for cooling water and indirect demand by increasing the consumption of thermally generated power used by industry.

Some perspective on power usage and future estimates is shown above in Table 3.10.

(i) INDUSTRIAL WATER USE AND DISCHARGE, 1959-1968

According to the Water Use in Manufacturing, 1967 14,276 billion gallons of wastewater were discharged in 1968 by manufacturing establishments using 20 million gallons of water or more. The 1968 figure represents an 8.5 percent increase over 1964 and 24.7 percent increase over 1959. However, as Tables 3.11 and 3.12 indicate, discharge across the nation and for most industries over the period 1959 to 1968 grew at a slower rate than did value added (in constant dollars), as is also the case for most of the industrial water use regions.

The geographical incidence of industrial waste discharges

TABLE 3.11

INDUSTRIAL WASTEWATER DISCHARGE
BY INDUSTRIAL WATER USE REGIONS, 1959-68

Industrial Water Use Region	Total Industrial Wastewater Discharges, 1968 (Billions of Gal.)	1968 Industrial Wastewater Discharge as a Percentage of 1959 Discharge
New England	558.4	113.0
Delaware and Hudson	1191.9	98.1
Chesapeake Bay	754.7	133.8
Ohio	2295.4	111.2
Eastern Great Lakes	1459.7	112.0
Tennessee-Cumberland	535.9	185.7
Southeast	1099.6	140.1
Western Great Lakes	1811.3	131.4
Upper Mississippi	581.6	144.7
Lower Mississippi	744.6	175.6
Missouri	141.9	102.1
Arkansas-White-Red	184.6	114.0
Western Gulf	1899.1	135.8
Colorado Basin	18.3	261.4
Great Basin	26.8	116.5
California	314.1	110.6
Pacific Northwest	532.5	119.4
National[1]	14150.5	124.6

[1] Excludes Hawaii and Alaska.

Source: EPA, The Economics of Clean Water

TABLE 3.12

INDUSTRIAL WASTEWATER DISCHARGE
BY TYPE OF INDUSTRY, 1959-68

Industry	Total Industrial Wastewater Discharges, 1968 (Billions of Gal.)	1968 Industrial Wastewater Discharge as a Percentage of 1959 Discharge
Food and Kindred Products	752.8	131.9
Textile Mill Products	136.0	113.3
Lumber	92.7	73.8
Paper	2077.6	113.9
Chemicals	4175.1	136.4
Petroleum and Coal	1217.0	101.1
Rubber	128.4	107.9
Leather	14.9	125.0
Stone, Clay, and Glass	218.4	82.6
Primary Metals	4695.5	132.2
Fabricated Metals	65.0	158.5
Machinery	180.8	109.6
Electrical Equipment	118.4	134.5
Transportation Equipment	293.1	128.0

Source: see Table 3.11.

in 1968 is shown in Table 3.13. Not surprisingly, the industrial Northeast and Midwest are the largest repositories of industrial discharges, with the Western Gulf area also receiving
a significant portion. The industrial sources of discharges
within regions are indicated in Table 3.14. With the exception
of the petroleum industry in the Delaware-Hudson and California
regions, paper, chemicals, and primary metals are the principal
sources of industrial discharges. These industries in the industrialized areas create the largest demand for curtailment of
waste discharges.

(i) INDUSTRIAL WASTE TREATMENT, 1959-68

Although industrial wastewater dishcharge has not grown as
rapidly as industrial production the volume of industrial waste
discharge must still be handled to attain, or maintain, acceptable levels of water quality. Four broad methods of curtailing
the polluting effects of industrial liquid-borne wastes can be
distinguished: (1) Waste treatment facilities can be added
prior to discharge; (2) A plant can also discharge its wastes
for treatment upon a political jurisdiction; (3) Application to
land, either through surface irrigation or well injection, can
be a very thorough treatment technique, provided that precau-
tions to prevent ground water contamination or run-off of pollutants are exercised; (4) Process change is, from both an en-

TABLE

REGIONAL INCIDENCE OF INDUSTRIAL WASTE
PERCENT OF DISCHARGE OF INDUSTRY'S

	Regionally Assignable Discharge	New Eng.	Del. & Hud.	Chesa. Bay	East. Gr. Lak. St. Law.	Ohio Riv.	Tenn. Cum.
Meat Products	99.0	.5	4.2	2.7	1.0	8.6	1.5
Dairy Products	98.8	7.5	4.3	4.9	8.9	5.1	.6
Canned & Frozen Foods	93.1	1.4	3.2	2.5	3.9	2.3	D
All Other Food Products	84.4	3.7	5.9	.7	1.0	4.0	.2
Textile Mill Products	98.5	13.5	4.7	2.9	.5	2.4	6.3
Paper & Allied Products	98.7	11.9	3.3	4.9	3.2	2.4	3.1
Chemical & Allied Products	99.0	1.2	7.3	5.7	6.4	16.6	9.3
Petroleum & Coal	92.0	.1	26.4	D	5.8	2.3	--
Rubber & Plastic, n.e.c.	92.9	15.8	7.4	2.5	35.7	6.8	D
Primary Metals	96.6	.7	6.1	6.9	17.5	29.4	.5
Machinery except Electrical	99.9	14.9	34.0	1.2	4.8	9.0	.8
Electrical Machinery	96.9	9.6	18.	10.8	8.5	25.6	1.0
Transportation Equipment	97.0	31.4	3.	5.1	33.3	4.6	.6
Assignable Discharge	96.5	93.2	96.7	82.6	95.9	98.1	91.5
Percent of Industrial Discharge, 1968	100.0	3.9	8.3	5.3	10.2	16.1	3.8
Percent of Industrial Discharge, 1959	100.0	4.3	10.7	5.0	11.5	18.1	2.5

[1]Includes Hawaii   [2]Includes Alaska   D = Disclosure not available due to constraints on

TABLE

SOURCES OF INDUSTRIAL WASTE DISCHARGE,
PERCENT OF REGIONAL

	New Eng.	Del.	Chesa. Bay	East Gr. Lak.	Ohio Riv.	Tenn. Cumb.
Meat Products	.1	.4	.4	.1	.4	.3
Dairy Products	.7	.2	.3	.3	.1	-
Canned & Frozen Products	.3	.6	.4	.3	.1	-
All Other Food Products	2.5	4.0	.5	.3	.8	.2
Textile Mill Products	3.3	.5	.5	-	.1	1.6
Paper & Allied Products	44.1	5.8	13.4	4.5	2.1	11.8
Chemical & Allied Products	9.3	25.7	31.7	18.4	30.2	72.6
Petroleum & Coal	.1	26.9	D	4.8	1.2	-
Rubber & Plastics, n.e.c.	3.6	.8	.4	3.1	.4	-
Primary Metals	5.9	24.0	31.0	56.1	60.1	4.1
Machinery except Electrical	4.8	5.2	.3	.6	.7	.3
Electrical Machinery	2.0	1.8	1.7	.7	1.3	.2
Transportation Equipment	16.5	.8	2.0	6.7	.6	.4
Assignable Discharge	93.2	96.7	82.6	95.9	98.1	91.5

Source of tables: see Table 3.11.

3.13

DISCHARGE, BY MAJOR INDUSTRIAL SECTORS, 1968
WASTEWATER, BY INDUSTRIAL WATER USE REGION

S.E.	West Gr. Lak.	Upper Miss.	Lower Miss.	Mo.	Ark. W&R	West. Gulf	Colo. Basin	Gr. Basin	Cal.	Pacf. N.W.
11.6	2.8	30.9	1.7	17.9	6.7	2.8	D	D	3.5	2.6
2.3	12.5	24.7	2.8	4.3	4.7	1.	D	1.3	7.0	6.4
29.0	5.3	2.9	1.9	.9	1.8	.8	D	D	20.5	16.7
3.4	9.8	14.0	11.7	6.7	.3	1.5	D	D	20.3	1.2
65.7	D	.5	1.4	--	D	D	D	D	.6	D
28.9	7.8	6.0	2.7	1.0	3.8	2.5	.1	D	2.1	15.0
4.7	2.7	2.1	8.0	.4	.9	31.5	D	D	.6	1.6
2.0	12.0	1.2	10.2	1.6	1.1	27.5	D	.1	8.4	.2
6.9	8.4	4.3	3.3	D	.9	D	D	D	.9	D
1.7	25.2	2.6	D	.4	.6	3.4	.2	D	.2	1.2
.7	12.5	19.8	.3	.2	.3	.7	D	D	.7	D
4.1	9.0	5.	.5	.8	.9	D	D	D	3.0	D
1.7	7.1	2.1	D	D	.5	5.0	D	D	2.2	D
97.8	96.1	88.7	78.7	81.3	95.7	99.3	61.7	8.2	81.6	87.6
7.7	12.7	4.1	5.2	1.0	1.3	13.3	0.1	0.2	2.8	4.0
6.9	12.1	3.5	3.7	1.2	1.4	12.3	0.1	0.2	2.5	3.9

U.S. Bureau of Census.

3.14

BY MAJOR INDUSTRIAL SECTORS, 1968
DISCHARGE BY INDUSTRY

S.E.	West. Gr. Lak.	Upper Miss.	Lower Miss.	Mo.	Ark. W&R	West. Gulf	Colo. Basin	Gr. Basin	Cal.	Pacf. N.W.
1.0	.2	5.3	.2	12.5	3.6	.1	D	D	1.1	.5
.1	.4	2.3	.2	1.6	1.4	-	D	2.6	1.2	
3.2	.4	.6	.3	.8	1.2	-	D	D	7.8	3.8
1.5	2.4	11.6	7.6	22.6	.7	.4	D	D	9.1	1.1
8.1	D	.1	.3	-	D	D	-	-	.3	D
54.6	9.0	21.4	7.7	14.3	42.7	2.7	D	-	14.1	58.5
18.0	6.2	15.0	45.0	12.3	20.9	69.2	15.3	D	8.5	12.3
2.3	8.7	2.5	16.6	13.6	7.4	17.6	D	5.6	32.4	.5
.8	.6	.9	.6	D	.6	D	-	D	.4	D
7.2	65.3	20.7	D	14.0	15.5	8.4	46.4	D	3.2	10.3
	1.2	6.2	.1	.3	.3	.1	D	D	.4	D
.4	.6	1.0	.1	.6	.6	D	D	D	1.1	D
.5	1.1	1.1	D	D	.8	.8	D	D	2.0	D
97.8	96.1	88.7	78.7	81.3	95.7	99.9	61.7	8.	81.6	87.6

vironmental and administrative standpoint, perhaps the most attractive technique because of its reliability, predictability,
and potential for recycling of waste materials.

Available data do not permit estimation of the degree of
treatment received by final industrial waste discharge. In the
absence of inventories of industrial treatment facilities analogous to the Municipal Waste Inventories, it is presently impossible to estimate the amount and rate of change of the discharge of industrial liquid-borne pollutants.

A reason that the apparent increases in wastewater treatment by industry do not necessarily imply a decrease in industrial pollutants is that treatment of industrial wastewater is
often a requirement for discharge to sewers, as presented in the
1968 Water Use in Manufacturing, the data did not allow an estimate of treatment prior to sewer discharge or application to
land. In 1964 the volume of industrial waste receiving treatment prior to discharge to sewers or ground appears to have been
about 5 percent of the total treated discharge. This percentage
may have increased by 1968 because of the growth in municipal
waste treatment and associated pretreatment requirements for industrial connections.

One finding which emerges from an examination of the data
over the period 1959 to 1968 is that treatment of wastes by industry grew at a considerably faster rate from 1959 to 1964
(10.5 percent annual rate) than from 1964 to 1968 (only a 3.1
percent annual rate) (cf. Tables 3.15 and 3.16). In fact, in
five of the seventeen water use regions and five of the fourteen industries there was both a relative and absolute decline
in the amount of industrial wastewater receiving some kind of
treatment over the period 1964-1968. As a consequence of the
differing rates of growth in treatment, the amount of untreated
wastewater discharged by industry grew at an annual rate of
1.- percent over the 1964-1968 period, even though total discharge of industrial wastewater grew at a slower rate in the
later period (2.1 percent annual rate of growth) than in the
earlier period (2.8 percent).

(iii) PUBLIC TREATMENT OF INDUSTRIAL WASTES

Discharge of industrial wastewater to public sewers places
the requirement for adequate waste treatment upon local public
agencies responsible for municipal waste treatment. As wastewater treatment at the secondary level (i.e., about 80 to 90

TABLE 3.15

PERCENTAGE OF INDUSTRIAL WASTEWATER RECEIVING TREATMENT
AND GROWTH IN TREATMENT BY INDUSTRIAL
WATER USE REGIONS, 1959-68

| | Industrial Wastewater Discharge | | | Annual Rate of Growth of Treated Discharge | | |
| | Percent Treated | | | | | |
Water Use Region	1959[1]	1964[2]	1968	1959-68	1959-64	1964-68
New England	4.7	11.4	10.0	10.4	19.1	.4
Delaware-Hudson	25.0	40.2	42.0	5.7	9.6	.8
Chesapeake Bay	24.5	25.6	28.5	5.1	5.8	4.1
Ohio	14.5	17.7	23.3	6.6	6.7	6.5
Eastern Great Lakes	20.3	31.7	22.0	2.2	11.6	-8.3
Tennessee-Cumberland	18.0	31.3	26.4	11.8	19.6	2.9
Southeast	17.3	36.8	43.1	14.9	19.3	9.6
Western Great Lakes	19-4	34.8	41.7	12.2	15.3	8.5
Upper Mississippi	16.9	35.0	23.7	8.2	21.0	-5.5
Lower Mississippi	6.4	23.8	21.0	21.6	38.0	2.9
Missouri	16.5	48.1	45.5	12.2	22.0	1.0
Arkansas-White-Red	30.9	50.6	67.0	10.6	15.2	8.9
Western Gulf	31.3	22.6	23.2	.1	-2.6	3.5
Colorado Basin	14.3	31.3	19.1	14.9	38.0	-8.5
Great Basin	13.0	58.6	42.9	16.1	41.0	-9.3
California	51.8	59.7	55.4	1.9	5.3	-2.2
Pacific Northwest	14.3	29.6	36.3	13.1	20.0	4.8
National[3]	20.3	29.2	30.4	7.2	10.5	3.1

[1] Volume of treated discharge derived from 1958 Census of Manufacturers.
[2] Volume of treated discharge derived from 1963 Census of Manufacturers.
[3] Excludes Alaska and Hawaii.

TABLE 3.16

PERCENTAGE OF INDUSTRIAL WASTEWATER RECEIVING
TREATMENT AND GROWTH IN TREATMENT BY
INDUSTRY GROUPS, 1959-68

| | Percent of Industrial Wastewater Discharge Treated | | | Annual Rate of Growth of Treated Discharge | | |
Industry Group	1959	1964	1968	1959-68	1959-64	1964-68
Food and Kindred Products	13.0	22.9	24.6	10.7	16.4	4.0
Textile Mill Products	14.2	25.9	39.7	13.7	15.5	11.5
Lumber	24.6	27.6	20.4	-5.3	1.9	-13.5
Paper	41.8	36.4	44.0	2.1	-1.0	6.7
Chemicals	16.3	16.0	16.1	3.4	3.4	3.4
Petroleum and Coal	54.5	76.4	75.4	3.8	8.9	-1.8
Rubber	3.4	7.8	5.4	6.4	17.6	-6.3
Leather	16.7	63.6	66.7	19.6	28.5	9.3
Stone, Clay and Glass	4.2	18.8	16.5	14.1	30.0	-3.2
Primary Metals	15.1	26.9	30.8	11.5	16.7	5.4
Fabricated Metals	7.3	12.0	13.8	13.0	14.9	10.7
Machinery	18.8	8.0	13.8	-2.3	-17.4	20.0
Electrical Equipment	8.0	17.0	23.7	16.7	16.5	16.9
Transportation Equipment	9.6	10.3	7.8	.5	1.8	-1.1

Source of tables: see Table 3.11.

percent BOD reduction) or above becomes more prevalent among
municipalities, the degree of treatment of sewered industrial
wastewater should generally increase. However, as municipalities
raise their target rates of waste removal they must become more
discriminating about the types and timing of industrial discharges that they will accept in order to prevent adverse consequences on the operation of their treatment works. Increased
selectivity of acceptable discharge to sewers generally means
outright prohibition on the discharges of certain industrial
residuals and/or pretreatment requirements. For the sewered
manufacturing plant, greater selectivity can translate into separation of waste streams and/or treatment of discharges bound
for the sewer, both of which entail an increase in costs. From
the data reported in the Water Use in Manufacturing series it
appears that these developments have been an offset to the sub-
sidies provided by Federal and State grants for municipal wastewater treatment plant construction.

From 1959 to 1968 the percentage of industrial wastewater
discharged to sewers declined from 8.7 percent to 7.2 percent
(cf. Table 3.17). However, all of this decline took place in
the 1959-1964 period, and over the 1964-1968 span relative discharge to sewers remained virtually constant, with the absolute
amount of sewered discharge increasing slightly. Although the
relative amount of industrial discharge going to sewers is
rather small, it can be inferred from Table 3.17 that municipal
waste treatment is the primary method of curtailing industrial
liquid-borne pollutants from the food processing, textiles, rubber, leather, and the various metal manufacturing industries.

The percentages in Table 3.18 probably understate the relative amount of industrial discharge going to sewers by a percentage point, however, because municipal waste treatment is
also the primary method by which the waterborne wastes of minor
urban manufacturing establishments whose intake is less than 20
million gallons a year are handled.

(iv) GROUND DISPOSAL OF INDUSTRIAL WASTES

Discharge to the ground can be an effective method of treating industrial wastewater. Direct application to land utilizes
the evaporative powers of the atmosphere and the filtering action
of soil and rock strata to eliminate and purify industrial wastewater. Deepwell injection is a method of withholding and iso-
lating particularly dangerous or conservative industrial wastes

TABLE 3.17

PERCENTAGE OF INDUSTRIAL WASTEWATER DISCHARGED
TO SEWERS AND GROWTH OF SEWERED DISCHARGE
BY INDUSTRIAL WATER USE REGION, 1959-68

Water Use Region	Industrial Wastewater Discharge Percent Discharged to Sewers			Annual Rate of Growth of Sewered Discharge		
	1959	1964	1968	1959-1968	1959-1964	1964-1968
New England	12.6	10.0	8.4	-3.0	-5.0	-.5
Delaware-Hudson	7.4	4.0	7.3	- .4	-11.8	16.1
Chesapeake Bay	5.0	5.6	4.3	1.7	7.4	-5.1
Ohio	5.4	7.1	7.5	4.9	3.1	7.1
Eastern Great Lakes	10.1	10.7	13.9	4.9	3.1	7.1
Tennessee-Cumberland	3.5	2.7	2.6	3.7	1.9	6.0
Southeast	5.0	5.4	5.2	4.3	4.3	4.3
Western Great Lakes	17.7	9.8	7.4	-6.5	-8.9	-3.3
Upper Mississippi	26.4	21.1	18.5	.2	- .4	.9
Lower Mississippi	6.4	3.5	3.1	-1.9	-5.8	3.2
Missouri	20.1	27.9	17.8	-1.2	5.1	-8.5
Arkansas-White-Red	4.9	8.0	7.9	6.8	11.8	.7
Western Gulf	.9	.8	.8	1.7	1.5	2.1
Colorado Basin	42.9	25.0	20.2	2.4	5.9	-2.0
Great Basin	4.4	6.9	6.3	6.1	14.9	-4.0
California	15.1	15.1	16.8	2.3	2.2	2.5
Pacific Northwest	9.6	6.7	5.7	-3.8	-3.5	-4.5
National[1]	8.7	7.3	7.2	.3	-.9	1.9

[1] Excludes Alaska and Hawaii.

TABLE 3.18

PERCENTAGE OF INDUSTRIAL WASTEWATER DISCHARGED
TO SEWERS AND GROWTH OF SEWERED DISCHARGE BY
INDUSTRY GROUPS, 1959-68

Industry Group	Industrial Wastewater Discharge Percent Discharged to Sewers			Annual Rate of Growth of Sewered Discharge		
	1959	1964	1968	1959-1968	1959-1964	1964-1968
Food and Kindred Products	36.6	35.0	31.6	1.4	2.9	- .3
Textile Mill Products	31.7	32.6	37.2	3.2	3.0	3.6
Lumber	6.3	3.3	2.7	-12.1	-13.0	-11.1
Paper	4.4	4.2	3.5	- 1.2	0	- 2.7
Chemicals	3.5	4.2	4.3	6.0	7.4	4.3
Petroleum and Coal	.9	2.4	.6	- 4.1	23.0	-43.0
Rubber	19.3	15.5	17.4	- .3	.9	- 1.7
Leather	50.0	63.6	68.0	6.1	3.1	9.9
Stone, Clay and Glass	8.0	8.7	9.4	- .3	- 2.0	1.8
Primary Metals	7.4	3.6	3.1	- 6.5	- 9.8	- 2.2
Fabricated Metals	70.7	64.0	59.4	3.2	2.0	4.8
Machinery	22.4	26.8	24.6	2.1	1.6	2.7
Electrical Equipment	46.6	53.8	62.8	6.8	3.6	11.0
Transportation Equipment	36.2	33.3	26.3	- .8	- 1.0	- .6

Source of tables: see Table 3.11.

from surface streams. The use of disposal to land as a technique
is constrained by the cost availability of land, the possible
contamination of ground waters, and the possible nuisances of
noxious odors and aesthetic degradation.

Discharge of industrial wastewater to the ground is not a
prevalent disposal technique; according to the data presented

in the Water Use in Manufacturing, 1968 only 1.3 percent of industrial wastewater was discharged to the ground (cf. Table 3.19).
The use of land as a disposal medium has grown however; between
1959 and 1968 industrial discharges going to the ground grew at
an annual rate of 7.8 percent. From Table 3.19 it appears that
ground discharge is a significant technique of disposal in the
sparsely populated and arid regions of the Colorado Basin and
Great Basin, where the wastes may have an economic value for
irrigation use. Ground discharge is generally least used in the
humid and often densely populated areas east of the Mississippi
River and in the Western Gulf. Among industries, the food and
kindred industry groups discharged the largest percentage of
its wastewater to the ground--5.8 percent in 1968 (cf. Table
3.20)--and the chemicals and primary metals groups discharged
to the ground 40.3 billion gallons and 38.1 billion gallons,
respectively.

           b. MUNICIPAL WASTES

     Municipal waste and sewage accounts for the second largest
category of urban water pollution. Sewage is by far the largest
urban influence in the eutrophication of adjacent water bodies
even though much sewage is treated in some manner. On a nationwide average, about 55 percent of wastes processed by municipal
treatment plants comes from homes and commercial establishments
and about 45 percent from industries.

     Less than one-third of the Nation's population is served
by a system of sewers and an adequate treatment system. The
greatest municipal waste problems exist in the areas with the
heaviest concentrations of population, particularly the Northeast.

     Three levels of treatment are employed in municipal treat-
ment plants. Primary treatment is a simple gravity process that
separates and settles solids in a big tank. Such primary plants
provide BOD removal levels of 25 to 30 percent. Secondary
treatment is a biological process that speeds up what nature does
in natural water bodies. In the activated sludge process used
by many large cities, bacteria and air are mixed with sewage to
accelerate decomposition of wastes. The other secondary treatment process--the trickling filter--involves spraying wastes
uniformly over a rock bed. Bacteria formed on the rocks, in
the presence of air, accelerate decomposition of wastes. Good
secondary treatment plants remove 90 percent of measured BOD.

TABLE 3.19

PERCENTAGE OF INDUSTRIAL WASTEWATER DISCHARGED TO
THE GROUND AND GROWTH OF GROUND DISCHARGE BY
INDUSTRIAL WATER USE REGIONS, 1959-68

Water Use Region	Industrial Wastewater Discharge Percent Discharged to Ground			Annual Rate of Growth of Discharge to Ground		
	1959	1964	1968	1959-1968	1959-1964	1964-1968
New England	.4	.4	.9	10.9	0	26.0
Delaware-Hudson	1.1	1.3	1.5	3.7	4.2	3.0
Chesapeake Bay	1.2	1.5	.6	1.7	7.4	- 5.0
Ohio	.6	.6	.5	- .3	2.9	- 4.5
Eastern Great Lakes	.6	.6	.5	- 1.8	2.4[2]	- 6.8[2]
Tennessee-Cumberland	.4	2.5	.3	6.8	N.C.[2]	N.C.[2]
Southeast	.9	1.3	1.7	11.3	11.4	11.3
Western Great Lakes	.4	.5	.6	6.6	5.9	7.5
Upper Mississippi	1.7	1.2	4.3	15.9	- 3.0	43.0
Lower Mississippi	.2	.5	1.5	35.0	25.0	39.0
Missouri	.7	1.6	1.4	8.0	14.9	0
Arkansas-White-Red	1.2	1.7	2.8	11.2	8.4	14.7[2]
Western Gulf	.2	.1	.5	13.0	- 7.8	N.C.[2]
Colorado-Basin	28.6[3]	6.3	44.3	16.8[3]	-12.9[3]	N.C.[2]
Great Basin	N.R.[3]	6.9	21.3	N.R.[3]	N.R.[3]	30.0
California	4.6	6.0	6.1	4.3	7.9	0
Pacific Northwest	2.2	3.7	4.1	10.8	14.9	5.9
National[1]	.8	1.1	1.3	7.8	7.7	7.9

[1]Excludes Alaska and Hawaii.

[2]Exceeds 50 percent in absolute value

[3]Calculation not possible because the necessary datum was not reported.

Source of tables: see Table 3.11.

TABLE 3.20

PERCENTAGE OF INDUSTRIAL WASTEWATER DISCHARGED TO
THE GROUND AND GROWTH OF GROUND DISCHARGE
BY INDUSTRY GROUPS, 1959-68

Industry Group	Industrial Waste Discharge Percent Discharged to Ground			Annual Rate of Growth of Discharge to Ground		
	1959	1964	1968	1959-1968	1959-1964	1964-1968
Food and Kindred Products	4.2	11.5	5.8	6.8	27.0	-13.9
Textile Mill Products	1.7	3.7	1.0	-3.9	20.0	-27.3
Lumber	1.6	2.4	4.1	7.4	8.4	6.1
Paper	.5	.6	.8	6.5	4.1	9.7
Chemicals	.6	1.0	1.0	8.7	14.9	1.5
Petroleum and Coal	.4	.4	1.1	11.5	0	28.0
Rubber	1.7	1.7	2.0	2.5	0	5.7
Leather	8.3	0	2.7	-9.7	--	--
Stone, Clay and Glass	1.9	8.3	5.3	9.8	29.0	-10.4
Primary Metals	.6	1.3	.9	5.4	14.9	- 5.4
Electrical Equipment	1.1	3.4	3.3	14.9	24.6	6.1
Transportation Equipment	1.7	2.1	2.5	6.9	4.6	9.9

That does not mean that 90 percent of total oxygen-demanding
wastes are removed, but only the part that is measured by certain laboratory tests.

Advanced waste treatment, often called _tertiary_ treatment,
involves a wide variety of processes tailored for specific treatment needs. For example, one advanced waste treatment process

is lime-alum precipitation, which removes 80 percent of phosphates from wastewater, compared to an average of 30 percent in
normal secondary treatment. Other processes, using carbon absorption and sand filtering, remove up to 99 percent of measured
BOD.

Among other municipal waste problems that will grow more
apparent as conventional treatment reduces gross pollution loads
are those caused by storm or combined sewers and by nutrients.
Many cities have combined sewers, which discharge raw sewage
along with street runoff directly to streams when treatment systems become overloaded during storms or thaws. Even where sewers
are separated, pollution from storm sewer discharges carrying
a variety of wastes from the streets is possible. Although
combined sewer problems exist in most regions of the country, the
most severe are centered in the Northeast, Midwest, and to some
degree, the Far West.

Municipal wastes contribute the major load of usable phosphates and significant amounts of nitrates to water bodies. Already nutrient pollution has led to a strict requirement for
very high treatment levels for waste discharges to the Great
Lakes and several other areas. Secondary treatment plants remove an average of 30 percent of the phosphorous and up to 20
percent of the nitrogenous materials, although with modifications
higher levels of treatment are possible.

An overview of sewage treatment and population served will
summarize the discussion. Table 3.21 presents accomplishments

TABLE 3.21

SEWAGE TREATMENT AND POPULATION SERVED

	1968	1969	1970	1971[1]	1972[1]
Sewered Population (millions, persons)	140	144	148	152	156
Waste Strength gross wastes treated by municipal plants (million/pounds/year BOD's)	14,137	14,773	15,438	16,133	16,859
Level of Treatment (Percent)					
Sewered Population Untreated	7	7	6	6	5
Sewered Population Primary	31	30	28	25	24
Sewered Population Secondary	62	63	66	68	70
Sewered Population Advanced	1	1	1	1	2

[1] Based upon Historical Growth Trends 1962-1970.

Source: U. S. Department of Interior, Inventory of Municipal Waste
Facilities, 1970.

in terms of population sewered and increases in wastes treated.
The table also indicates the level of treatment and the decrease
in population receiving primary treatment. The percentage of
population receiving advanced treatment has not significantly
increased.

III. WATER QUALITY ASSESSMENT

The assessment of water quality requires the setting and
measurement of specific standards, as was discussed earlier.

1. CLEAN WATER STANDARDS

The current regulatory structure was established by the
Federal Water Pollution Control Act of 1972. However, the Federal government has been active in the abatement of water pollution for over three-quarters of a century. Section 13 of the
Rivers and Harbors Act of 1899 prohibited the discharge of wastes,
other than liquids from sewers, into the navigable waters of the
United States. The Public Health Service Act of 1912 directed
that organization to conduct research into the health effects
of water pollution. In the process of virtually eliminating
major health threats from waterborne diseases, the work of the
Public Health Service over the years has provided a solid base
of knowledge for the establishment of quality standards. In
1924 the Oil Pollution Act prohibited the dumping of oil into
navigable waters except in the cases of emergency threatening
life or property, unavoidable accident, or as permitted by regulations.

Recent legislative history begins with the Water Pollution
Control Act of 1948 which was an experimental and temporary
measure designed to expire after five years. This act marked
the first in a series of acts building the present body of laws.
It specifically recognized the primacy of the States in the field
of water pollution control, provided for Federal research, and
technical and planning assistance through the Public Health Service and Federal Works Agency. The Federal Water Pollution Control Act of 1956, as amended in 1961, 1965, 1966, 1970 and 1972,
is the legal backbone for the national water cleanup effort. In
essence, this legislation provides for construction and other
grants, enforcement procedures, and research programs.

This progressive legislative development, culminating in

the Federal Water Pollution Control Act Amendments of 1972, mandated a sweeping Federal-State campaign to prevent, reduce and
eliminate water pollution. Two general goals were proclaimed
for the United States:

> (1) To achieve, wherever possible, by July 1, 1983,
> water that is clean enough for swimming and other
> recreational uses, and clean enough for the propa-
> gation of fish, shellfish and wildlife.

> (2) By 1985, to have no discharges of pollutants
> into the nation's waters.

The goals were set within the framework of a series of specific
actions that must be taken, with strict deadlines and enforcement provisions, by Federal, State and local governments and by
industries. While most responsibility for eliminating water
pollution still resides in the States, the framework of a new
national program was provided, with supervision of the States
by the Environmental Protection Agency, and the Federal control
responsibility was extended from interstate waters to all U.S.
waters. The Federal government was granted power to seek court
injunctions against polluters creating health hazards or endangering livelihood, and Federal aid to local governments to build
sewage treatment facilities was provided.

The specifics of the 1972 Amendments relate to industrial
and municipal pollution, the setting of water quality standards,
licensing discharges into the nation's waters, and to the enforcement provisions.

a. INDUSTRIAL POLLUTION

The law set deadlines for actions to control water pollution
from industrial sources:

(1) Industries discharging pollutants into the Nation's
waters must use the "best practicable" water pollution control
technology by July 1, 1977, and the "best available" technology
by July 1, 1983.

(2) EPA must issue guidelines for "best practicable" and
"best available" technologies for various industries by October,
1973. The guidelines can be adjusted by several factors, including the cost for pollution control, the age of the industrial
facility, the process used and the environmental impact (other
than on water quality) of the controls. EPA also has to identify
pollution control measures for completely eliminating industrial
discharges.

(3) By May, 1974, new sources of industrial pollution must

use the "best available demonstrated control technology." This
will be defined by EPA in the form of "standards of performance"
for various industries no later than May, 1974. Where practicable, EPA may require no discharge at all of pollutants from new
industrial facilities.

(4) Discharges of toxic pollutants will be controlled by
effluent standards to be issued by EPA no later than January,
1974. EPA is required to provide an ample margin of safety in
setting effluent standards for toxic pollutants. EPA is also
empowered to prohibit discharges of toxic pollutants, in any
amount, if deemed necessary. EPA had already established, under
earlier water pollution control legislation, strict limits on
the discharge of such toxic pollutants as lead and mercury. The
new law strengthened control of toxic pollutant discharges.

(5) Discharge into the Nation's waters of any radiological,
chemical or biological warfare materials, or high-level radioactive waste was prohibited.

(6) Any industry that discharges its wastes into a municipal
treatment plant was required to pre-treat its effluent so that
the industrial pollutants do not interfere with the operation
of the plant or pass through the plant without adequate treatment. This requirement takes effect no later that May, 1974,
for new industrial sources of pollution, and no later than July,
1976, for existing industrial facilities.

(7) The law also authorized loans to help small businesses
meet water-pollution control requirements. The loan program is
designed for firms that would be likely to suffer "substantial
economic injury" unless they receive financial assistance to
comply with the law. EPA was required to issue regulations for
the loan program by April, 1973.

b. MUNICIPAL POLLUTION

The law also provided for more Federal aid to local governments and set deadlines for stronger control measures:

(1) Federal construction grants were authorized over the
next three years to help local governments build needed sewage
treatment facilities.

(2) Federal grants were authorized to reimburse local governments for treatment plants built earlier in anticipation of
Federal aid.

(3) In order to qualify for a Federal construction grant,
sewage treatment plants approved before June 30, 1974, must pro-

vide a minimum of secondary treatment. After that date, Federal grants may be made only to plants that will use "best practicable" treatment.

(4) All sewage treatment plants in operation on July 1, 1977--whether or not built with the aid of a Federal grant, and no matter when built--must provide a minimum of secondary treatment. Exception: A plant being built with the help of a Federal grant that was approved before June 30, 1974, must comply with the secondary-treatment requirement within four years, but no later than June 30, 1978.

(5) Also by July 1, 1977, all sewage treatment plants must apply whatever additional, more stringent, effluent limitations that may be established by EPA or a State to meet water quality standards, treatment standards or compliance schedules.

(6) All publicly owned waste treatment plants--whether or not built with the aid of a Federal grant, and no matter when built--will have to use "best practicable" treatment by July 1, 1983.

(7) Areawide waste treatment management plans are to be established by July, 1976, in urban industrial areas with substantial water pollution problems. Federal grants are authorized to help areawide agencies develop and operate integrated water pollution control programs.

(8) In order to be eligible for a Federal construction grant after July, 1976, a waste treatment plant in one of these urban industrial areas must be part of, and in conformity with, the areawide plan.

c. WATER QUALITY STANDARDS

The law continued and expanded the water quality standards program initiated under earlier legislation. Water quality standards define, of course, the uses of specific bodies of water-- such as public water supply, propagation of fish and wildlife, recreation, and agricultural and industrial water supply. The standards also include "criteria" based on those uses and a plan to implement and enforce the criteria. The standards must protect public health and welfare, and enhance water quality. The new standards program will operate as follows:

(1) Water quality standards previously established by States for interstate waters, subject to EPA approval, remain in effect unless they are not consistent with the objectives of the old law.

(2) The States must now also adopt water quality standards for intrastate waters and submit them to EPA for approval by April, 1973. EPA is required to set standards for intrastate waters if the States fail to do so.

(3) If a State finds that the use of "best practicable" or "best available" controls are not adequate to meet water quality standards, more stingent controls must be imposed. To this end, the States must establish the total maximum daily load of pollutants, including heat, that will not impair propagation of fish and wildlife. EPA will identify by October, 1973, pollutants for which maximum daily loads might be set.

(4) EPA is required to submit a report to Congress by January 1, 1974 on the quality of the Nation's waters. The report must identify water bodies that, in 1973, met the standards for 1983 or any later date. The report will also include an inventory of sources of water pollution.

(5) The States are required to submit to EPA similar reports each year on the quality of bodies of water within their borders. The first report is due by January 1, 1975.

(6) EPA is required to submit the State water quality reports to Congress each year, along with its own analyses, beginning no later than October 1, 1975.

(7) At least once every three years, the States must hold public hearings to review their water quality standards and, if necessary, update the standards subject to EPA approval.

d. PERMITS AND LICENSES

The 1972 law also established a new system of permits for discharges into the Nation's waters, replacing the 1899 Refuse Act permit program. No discharge of any pollutant from any point source is permitted without a permit, and publicly-owned sewage treatment plants and municipally controlled discharge points as well as industrial discharges must obtain permits. The permit program operates as follows:

(1) Until March, 1973, EPA or a State with an existing permit program deemed adequate by EPA, could issue permits for discharges. State permits issued during this period were subject to EPA veto.

(2) EPA had to issue guidelines for State permit programs by the end of 1972 and approve by March, 1973, State permit programs that meet those guidelines.

(3) After a State permit program goes into effect, EPA will

retain the right, unless waived, to review and approve any permit that affects another state. EPA will also have authority, unless waived, to review proposed permits to determine if they meet the requirements of the new Federal legislation.

(4) A State's permit program is subject to revocation by EPA, after a public hearing, if the State fails to implement the law adequately.

(5) The Army Corps of Engineers retains authority to issue permits for the disposal of dredge-and-fill material in specified disposal sites, subject to EPA veto of disposal sites if the discharge will have an adverse effect on municipal water supplies, fishery resources or recreation.

(6) Disposal of sludge from sewage treatment plants into water bodies or on land where it affects water quality is prohibited except under a permit issued by EPA. After EPA establishes regualtions for issuing sludge-disposal permits, a State may take over the permit program if it meets EPA requirements.

(7) Anyone applying for a Federal license or permit for any activity that might produce discharge into the Nation's waters must obtain certification from the State involved that the discharge will be in compliance with the new law. State must give public notice of all applications for certification and may hold public hearings on certification applications.

(8) If a certification by one State will result in a discharge that may affect water quality in another State, a public hearing must be held by the Federal agency that issues the license or permit, if requested by the second State. If the permit or license will result in discharges that are not in compliance with water quality requirements, the license or permit cannot be issued.

  e. ENFORCEMENT

The law eliminates the earlier system of abatement conferences and hearings to compel compliance with water pollution control regulations. Stringent enforcement machinery, with heavy penalties, now exists to speed compliance with the law. For example:

(1) EPA has emergency power to seek an immediate court injunction to stop water pollution that poses "an imminent and substantial endangerment" to public health, or that endangers someone's livelihood.

(2) Polluters must keep proper records, install and use

monitoring equipment, and sample their discharges.

(3) EPA has the power to enter and inspect any polluting facility, to check its records and monitoring equipment and to sample its discharges. A State may assume this authority if approved by EPA.

(4) Except for trade secrets, any information obtained by EPA or a State about a polluter's discharges must be made available to the public.

(5) EPA may enforce permit conditions and other requirements of the law by issuing administrative orders that are enforceable in court, or by seeking court action.

(6) The 1972 law extends the oil pollution control, liability and enforcement provisions of earlier legislation to other "hazardous substances." These are defined as substances that "present an imminent and substantial danger to the public health or welfare, including, but not limited to, fish, shellfish, wildlife, shorelines, and beaches."

(9) Finally, to assist in enforcement as well as to measure the effectiveness of the water pollution control program, a national surveillance system to monitor water quality, STORET, was established by EPA in cooperation with other Federal agencies and State and local governments, to extend the present 20 percent coverage of the Nation's streams provided in the past by the Federal Water Quality Administration, the U.S. Geological Survey, and the States into a complete monitoring and surveillance network.

f.   TWO APPROACHES TO STANDARD SETTING

The setting of water quality control standards involves a reconciliation of economic, environmental, and social goals (Westman, 1972). While the legislative activity attempts to resolve competing goal assignments it is worth pointing out two internally coherent but mutually antipathetic philosophies in environmental matters. The first is a technological perspective and the second is the ecological view. The dual conceptualization is illustrated in Table 3.22.

g.   MEASUREMENT RATIONALES

How should water pollution be measured? There are many organic and inorganic parameters potentially disruptive of water quality for a given use. The task is one of making an objective assessment of the data that are available and a mechanism for evaluating the data. It must be asked whether measureable trends

TABLE 3.22

APPROACHES TO LEGISLATIVE ISSUES

LEGISLATIVE ISSUE	TECHNOLOGICAL APPROACH	ECOLOGICAL APPROACH
Water quality goal	Use to which water body is to be put by man	Restoration and maintenance of physical, chemical, and biological integrity of water bodies
Mode of treatment of pollutants	Removal of materials by sewage treatment (physical filter); liquid remainder placed in water body (assumes assimilative capacity of water body)	1. Recycling of liquid materials by land disposal (living filter) 2. Elimination of discharge into waters, based on nonreliance on assimilative capacity 3. Land-use controls for nonpoint sources of pollution
Mode of classification of pollutants	Physical and chemical parameters as they are affected by the control technology (e.g. settleable solids, suspended solids)	Chemical and biological parameters as they affect the biology of the stream (e.g. nutrients, nonnutrients, toxic substances, pathogens)
Mode of monitoring the success of pollutant removal	In-plant monitoring of effluent	Biological monitoring in stream
Legal point of control	Ability to meet water quality standards based on use	Achievement of integrity of water body by elimination of discharge; application of best available technology before discharge

Source: Westman (1962).

exist in the data and whether the variables being measured are those providing the best measure of water condition. There are shortcomings both in the collected data and in alternative evaluation mechanisms.

Few studies have been directed toward determining changes in specific parameters over long periods of time. Hydrologic records rarely go back even 50 years. At the same time techniques

of observation and of analysis have changed becoming more so-
phisticated and comprehensive. Caution should be taken as to
instrument location and accuracy. Complicating the above are
problems associated with the systematic correlation of hydrologic
behavior, difficulty in establishing trends, and a paucity of
knowledge regarding the natural background, economy, and land
use of an area.

In anticipation then of variations in data quality and availability and trend quality several rationales for choice of locations and compilation index should be advanced. First, past and
present sampling programs emphasize measurement of specific
characteristics primarily related to water use by industry and
municipality, not water quality or environment. The dynamics
of river system processes cannot easily be inferred from either
surrogate measure of quality or easily measured parameters. This
second drawback suggests the limited value such measures may be
in estimating the likelihood of reversing specific observed
trends in the absence of knowledge of their causes. Additional
attention must be given to the measurement of parameters related
to models of river behavior and to estimates of inputs based on
budgets of materials derived from industrial outputs and land
use. A third caution points to the lack of attention given to
variability of biological activity as well as physical variability associated with natural cycles in rivers and other waterways.

The State of Illinois can be used as an example to show
how effluent standards, water quality standards, and legislation
are related in determining what the actual standards for a state
might be. Table 3.23 extracts relevant background materials
from the Rules and Regulations of the Illinois Pollution Control
Board; paragraph numbers refer to that document.

IV. MEASURES OF ACHIEVEMENT OF STANDARDS

1. STATISTICAL INDEXES

Three statistical methods of water quality evaluation have
been proposed to date:

(1) Prevalence - Duration - Intensity Index (PDI).
This measure considers the relationship of actual water
quality to State standards. It has been computed for a
nationwide network of 10,000 stations, leading, however,
to a single judgmental decision as to whether water at
each station is polluted or not polluted.

TABLE 3.23.

ILLINOIS POLLUTION CONTROL BOARD
RULES AND REGULATIONS

Authority

Pursuant to the authority contained in Section 13 of the Environmental Protection Act, which authorizes the Board to issue regulations "to restore, maintain, and enhance the purity of the waters of this State in order to protect health, welfare, property, and the quality of life, and to assure that no contaminants are discharged into the waters without being given the degree of treatment or control necessary to prevent pollution," and to adopt water quality standards, effluent standards, standards for the certification of sewage works operators, standards or emergencies, lating to water pollution episodes or emergencies, and requirements for the inspection of pollution sources and for monitoring the aquatic environment, the Board adopts the following rules and regulations.

Policy

The General Assembly has found that water pollution "constitutes a menace to public health and welfare, creates public nuisances, is harmful to wildlife, fish, and aquatic life, impairs domestic, agricultural, industrial, recreational, and other legitimate beneficial uses of water, depresses property values, and offends the senses." It is the purpose of these rules and regulations to designate the uses for which the various waters of the State shall be maintained and protected; to prescribe the water quality standards required to sustain the designated uses; to establish effluent standards to limit the contaminants discharged to the waters; and to prescribe additional regulations necessary for implementing, achieving and maintaining the pre-

scribed water quality. These regulations were developed in close cooperation with the Federal Environmental Protection Agency in order that, consistent with Illinois law, they may also serve the purposes of the Federal Water Pollution Control Act.

Definitions

As used in this Chapter, the following terms shall have the meanings specified.

"Act" means the Illinois Environmental Protection Act;

"Agency" means the Illinois Environmental Protection Agency;

"Aquatic Life" means native populations of fish and other aquatic life;

"Basin" means the area tributary to the designated body of water;

"Board" means the Illinois Pollution Control Board;

"Calumet River System" means the Calumet River, the Grand Calumet River, the Little Calumet River downstream from its confluence with the Grand Calumet, the Calumet-Sag Channel, and the Calumet Harbor Basin;

"Chicago River System" means the Chicago River and its Branches, the North Shore Channel, and the Chicago Sanitary and Ship Canal;

"Combined Sewer" means a sewer receiving both wastewater and land runoff;

"Construction" means commencement of on-site fabrication, erection, or installation of a treatment works, sewer, or wastewater source; or the

reinstallation at a new site of any existing treatment works, sewer, or wastewater source;

"Dilution Ratio" means the ratio of the seven-day, once in ten years low flow of the receiving stream to the average dry weather flow of the treatment works for the design year.

"Effluent" means any wastewater discharged, directly or indirectly, to the waters of the State or to any storm sewer, and the runoff from land used for the disposition of wastewater or sludges, but does not otherwise include land runoff;

"Industrial Wastes" means any solid, liquid, or gaseous wastes resulting from any process or excess energy of industry, manufacturing, trade, or business or from the development, processing, or recovery, except for agricultural crop raising, of any natural resource;

"Institute" means the Illinois Institute for Environmental Quality;

"Interstate Waters" are all waters which cross or form part of the border between Illinois and other states;

"Intrastate Waters" are all the waters of Illinois which are not interstate waters;

"Land Runoff" means water reaching the waters of the State as runoff resulting from precipitation;

"Marine Toilet" means any toilet on or within any watercraft;

"Modification" means

1) Any physical change in a treatment works which involves different or additional processes or equipment or which increases or decreases the capacity or efficiency of the treatment works; or

TABLE 3.23 (Continued)

2) any change in the number or location of sewer points where effluent is discharged, directly or indirectly, to the waters; or

3) any change in any components of a sewer system which alters the quantity of wastewater capable of being conveyed, or which increases or decreases the quantity of wastewater capable of being discharged at overflow or bypass structures; or

4) any increase in quantity or strength of a discharge from any wastewater source, unless such increase does not exceed an upper limit specifically allowed by an existing Permit granted by the Agency and does not involve any additional contaminants contained in standards set by this Chapter that are not itemized and approved in an existing Agency permit.

"New Source" means any wastewater source, the construction of which is commenced on or after the effective date of the applicable provisions of this Chapter;

"Other Wastes" means garbage, refuse, wood residues, sand, lime, cinders, ashes, offal, night soil, oil, tar, dye stuffs, acids, chemicals and all other air, or any sewage or industrial waste whose discharge would cause water pollution or a violation of the effluent or water quality standards;

"Person" means any individual, partnership, co-partnership, firm, company, corporation, association, joint stock company, trust, estate, political subdivision, state agency, or any other legal entity, or their legal representative, agent or assigns;

"Population Equivalent" is a term used to evaluate the impact of industrial or other waste on a treatment works or stream. One population equivalent is 100 gallons of sewage per day, containing 0.17 pounds of BOD_5 and suspended solids parameters;

"Primary Contact" means any recreational or other water use in which there is prolonged and intimate contact with the water involving considerable risk of ingesting water in quantities sufficient to pose a significant health hazard, such as swimming and water skiing;

"Public and Pool Processing Water Supply" means any water use in which water is withdrawn from surface waters of the State for human consumption or for processing of food products intended for human consumption;

"Restricted Use" means certain designated waters which are not protected for aquatic life;

"Sanitary Sewer" means a sewer that carries wastewater together with incidental land runoff;

"Secondary Contact" means any recreational or other water use in which contact with the water is either incidental or accidental and in which the probability of ingesting appreciable quantities of water is minimal, such as fishing, commercial and recreational boating and any limited contact incident to shoreline activity;

"Sewage" means water-carried human and related wastes from any source together with associated land runoff;

"Sewer" means a pipe or conduit for carrying either wastewater or land runoff, or both;

"STORET" means the national water quality data system of the Federal Environmental Protection Agency;

"Storm Sewer" means a sewer intended to receive only land runoff;

"Treatment Works" means individually or collectively those constructions or devices, except sewers, used for collecting, pumping, treating, or disposing of wastewaters or for the recovery of by-products from such wastewater;

"Underground Waters" means any waters of the State located beneath the surface of the earth;

"Wastewater" means sewage, industrial waste, or other waste, or any combination of these, whether treated or untreated, plus any admixed land runoff;

"Wastewater Source" means any equipment, facility, or other point source of any type whatsoever which discharges wastewater, directly or indirectly (except through a sewer tributary to a treatment works), to the waters of the State;

"Water craft" means every type of boat, ship or barge used or capable of being used as a means of transportation on water;

"Waters" means all accumulations of water, surface and underground, natural, and artificial, public and private, or parts thereof, which are wholly or partially within, flow through, or border upon the State of Illinois, except that sewers and treatment works are not included except as specifically mentioned; provided, that nothing herein contained shall authorize the use of natural or otherwise protected waters as sewers or treatment works.

All methods of sample collection, preservation, and analysis used in applying any of the rules and regulations in this Chapter shall be in accord with those prescribed in "Standard Methods for the Examination of Water and Waste Water," Thirteenth Edition, or with other generally accepted procedures.

TABLE 3.23 (Continued)

WATER QUALITY STANDARDS

This part of the rules and regulations concerning water pollution describes the water quality standards that must be met to maintain the specified beneficial uses. References to STORET numbers identify the specific parameter as defined in the STORET system Handbook published by the Federal Environmental Protection Agency.

Mixing Zones

(a) In the application of any of the rules and regulations in this Chapter, whenever a water quality standard is more restrictive than its corresponding effluent standard then an opportunity shall be allowed for the mixture of an effluent with its receiving waters. Water quality standards must be met at every point outside of the mixing zone. The size of the mixing zone cannot be uniformly prescribed. The governing principle is that the proportion of any body of water or segment thereof within mixing zones must be quite small if the water quality standards shall have any meaning. This principle shall be applied on a case-by-case basis to ensure that neither any individual source nor the aggregate of sources shall cause excessive zones to exceed the standards. The water quality standards must be met in the bulk of the body of water, and no body of water may be used totally as a mixing zone for a single outfall or combination of outfalls. Moreover, except as otherwise provided in this Chapter, no single mixing zone shall exceed the area of a circle with a radius of 600 feet. Single sources of effluents which have more than one outfall shall be limited to a total mixing area no larger than that allowable if a single outfall were used.

In determining the size of the mixing zone for any discharge, the following must be considered:

1. The character of the body of water,

2. the present and anticipated future use of body of water,

3. the present and anticipated water quality of the body of water,

4. the effect of the discharge on the present and anticipated future water quality,

5. the dilution ratio, and

6. the nature of the contaminant.

(b) In addition to the above, for waters designated for aquatic life (General Standards), the mixing zone shall be so designed as to assure a reasonable zone of passage for aquatic life in which the water quality standards are met. The mixing zone shall not intersect any area of any such waters in such a manner that the maintenance of aquatic life in the body of water as a whole would be adversely affected.

Stream Flows

Except as otherwise provided in this Chapter with respect to temperature, the water quality standards in this Paragraph shall apply at all times except during periods when flows are less than the average minimum seven day low flow which occurs once in ten years.

General Standards

The General Standards listed below will protect the State's water for aquatic life, agricultural use, primary and secondary contact use, and most industrial uses, and ensure the aesthetic quality of the State's aquatic environment. Except as otherwise provided in this Chapter, all waters of the State shall meet the following standards:

(a) Freedom from unnatural sludge or bottom deposits, floating debris, visible oil, odor, unnatural plant or algal growth, unnatural color or turbidity, or matter in concentrations or combinations toxic or harmful to human, animal, plant or aquatic life of other than natural origin.

(b) pH (STORET number - 00400) shall be within the range of 6.5 to 9.0 except for natural causes.

(c) Phosphorus (STORET number - 00665): Phosphorus as P shall not exceed 0.05 mg/l in any reservoir or lake, or in any stream at the point where it enters any reservoir or lake.

(d) Dissolved oxygen (STORET number - 00300) shall not be less than 6.0 mg/l during at least 16 hours of any 24 hour period, nor less than 5.0 mg/l at any time.

(e) Radioactivity:

(1) Gross beta (STORET number - 03501) concentration shall not exceed 100 pico curies per liter (pCi/l).

(2) Concentrations of radium 226 (STORET number - 09501) and strontium 90 (STORET number - 13501) shall not exceed 1 and 2 pico curies per liter respectively.

(f) The following levels of chemical constituents shall not be exceeded:

TABLE 3.23 (Continued)

LIMITS OF CHEMICAL CONSTITUENTS OF
ILLINOIS WATERWAYS

CONSTITUENT	STORET NUMBER	CONCENTRATION (mg/l)
Ammonia Nitrogen (as N)	00610	1.5
Arsenic (total)	01000	1.0
Barium (total)	01005	5.0
Boron (total)	01020	1.0
Cadmium (total)	01025	0.05
Chloride	00940	500.
Chromium (total hexa-valent)		0.05
Chromium (total tri-valent)		1.0
Copper (total)	01040	0.02
Cyanide	00720	0.025
Fluoride	00950	1.4
Iron (total)	01046	1.0
Lead (total)	01049	0.1
Manganese (total)	01055	1.0
Mercury	71900	0.0005
Nickel (total)	01065	1.0
Phenols	32730	0.1
Selenium (total)	01145	1.0
Silver (total)	01075	0.005
Sulfate	00945	500.
Total Dissolved Solids	00515	1000.
Zinc	01090	1.0

(g) Based on a minimum of five samples taken over not more than a 30-day period, fecal coliforms (STORET number - 31616) shall not exceed a geometric mean of 200 per 100 ml, nor shall more than 10% of the samples during any 30-day period, exceed 400 per 100 ml.

(h) Any substance toxic to aquatic life shall not exceed one-tenth of the 48-hour median tolerance limit (48-hr. TLm) for native fish or essential fish food organisms.

(i) Temperature (STORET numbers (F°) 00011 and (C°) 00010):

(1) There shall be no abnormal temperature changes that may adversely affect aquatic life unless caused by natural conditions.

(2) The normal daily and seasonal temperature fluctuations that existed before the addition of heat due to other than natural causes shall be maintained.

(3) The maximum temperature rise above natural temperatures shall not exceed 5°F.

(4) In addition, the water temperature at representative locations in the main river shall not exceed the maximum limits in the following table during more than one percent of the hours in the 12-month period ending with any month. Moreover, at no time shall the water temperature at such locations exceed the maximum limits in the following table by more than 3°F.

MAXIMUM LIMITS OF WATER TEMPERATURES AT REPRESENTATIVE LOCATIONS

	JAN.	FEB.	MAR.	APR.	MAY	JUN.	JUL.	AUG.	SEPT.	OCT.	NOV.	DEC.
Mississippi River (Wisc. Border to Iowa Border) (°F)	45°	45°	57°	68°	78°	85°	86°	86°	85°	75°	65°	52°
Mississippi River (Iowa Border to Alton Lock and Dam) (°F)	45°	45°	57°	68°	78°	86°	88°	88°	86°	75°	65°	52°
Mississippi River (So. of Alton Lock & Dam) (°F)	50°	50°	60°	70°	80°	87°	89°	89°	87°	76°	79°	57°
Ohio River (°F)	50°	50°	60°	70°	80°	87°	89°	89°	87°	78°	70°	57°
Wabash River & Its interstate Tributaries (°F)	50°	50°	60°	70°	80°	90°	90°	90°	90°	78°	70°	57°
Other Waters	60°	50°	60°	60°	90°	90°	90°	90°	90°	90°	90°	60°

TABLE 3.23 (Continued)

PUBLIC FOOD AND PROCESSING WATER SUPPLY:
LIMITS OF CHEMICAL CONSTITUENTS

CONSTITUENT	STORET NUMBER	CONCENTRATION (mg/l)
Arsenic (total)	01000	0.01
Barium (total)	01005	1.0
Cadmium (total)	01025	0.01
Chlorides	00940	250.
Carbon Chloroform Extract (CCE)	32005	0.2
Cyanide	00720	0.01
Iron (total)	01046	0.3
Lead (total)	01049	0.05
Methylene Blue Active Substance (MBAS)	38260	0.5
Nitrates plus Nitrites as N	00630	10.0
Oil (Hexane-solubles or equivalent)	00550	0.1
Phenols	32730	0.001
Selenium (total)	01145	0.01
Sulfates	00945	250.
Total Dissolved Solids	00515	500.

(c) Other contaminants that will not be adequately reduced by the treatment processes noted in paragraph (a) of this Rule shall not be present in concentrations hazardous to human health.

Restricted Use Standards

Waters designated in Part III of this Chapter for Restricted Use shall meet the following standards:

(a) Freedom from unnatural sludge or bottom deposits, floating debris, visible oil, odor, unnatural plant or algal growth, or unnatural color or turbidity.

found at any time that any heated effluent causes significant ecological damage to the receiving stream.

Public and Food Processing Water Supply

In addition to the General Standards, waters designated in Part III of this Chapter for public and food processing water supply shall meet the following standards at any point at which water is withdrawn for treatment and distribution as a potable supply or for food processing:

(a) Waters shall be of such quality that with treatment consisting of coagulation, sedimentation, filtration, storage and chlorination, or other equivalent treatment processes, the treated water shall meet in all respects both the mandatory and the recommended requirements of the Public Health Service Drinking Water Standards - 1962.

(b) The following levels of chemical constituents shall not be exceeded:

Main river temperatures are temperatures of those portions of the river essentially similar to and following the same thermal regime as the temperatures of the main flow of the river.

(5) The owner or operator of a source of heated effluent which discharges 0.5 billion British thermal units per hour or more shall demonstrate in a hearing before this Board not less than 5 nor more than one year after the effective date of these regulations or, in the case of new sources, after the commencement of operations, that discharges from that source have not caused and cannot be reasonably expected to cause significant ecological damage to the receiving waters. If such proof is not made to the satisfaction of the Board appropriate corrective measures shall be ordered to be taken within a reasonable time as determined by the Board.

(6) Permits for heated effluent discharges, whether issued by the Board or the Environmental Protection Agency, shall be subject to revision in the event that reasonable future development creates a need for reallocation of the assimilative capacity of the receiving stream as defined in the regulation above.

(7) The owner or operator of a source of heated effluent shall maintain such records and conduct such studies of the effluents from such source and of their effects as may be required by the Environmental Protection Agency or in any permit granted under the Environmental Protection Act.

(8) Appropriate corrective measures will be required if, upon complaint filed in accordance with Board rules, it is

TABLE 3.23 (Continued)

ADDITIONAL STANDARDS FOR LAKE MICHIGAN

CONSTITUENT	STORET NUMBER	CONCENTRATION (mg/l)
Ammonia Nitrogen	00610	0.02
Chloride	00540	12.0
Sulfate	00945	24.0
Phosphorus (as P)	00665	0.007
Total Solids (Dissolved)	00515	180.0

(b) pH (STORET number - 00400) shall be within the range of 6.0 to 9.0 except for natural causes.

(c) Dissolved oxygen (STORET number - 00300) shall not be less than 3.0 mg/l during at least 16 hours in any 24-hour period, nor less than 2.0 mg/l at any time.

(d) Based on a minimum of five samples taken over not more than a 30-day period, fecal coliforms (STORET number - 31616) shall not exceed a geometric mean of 1,000 per 100 ml, nor shall more than 10% of the samples during any 30-day period exceed 2,000 per 100 ml.

(e) Concentrations of other substances shall not exceed the applicable effluent standards prescribed in Part IV of this Chapter.

(f) Temperature (STORET numbers - (OF) 00011 and (OC) 00010) shall not exceed 93OF (34OC) more than 5% of the time, or 100OF (37.8OC) at any time.

Lake Michigan

The waters of Lake Michigan shall meet the following standards in addition to the General and Public and Food Processing Water Supply Standards:

(a) Dissolved oxygen (STORET number - 00300) shall not be less than 90% of saturation except due to natural causes.

(b) pH (STORET number - 00400) shall be within the range of 7.0 to 9.0 except for natural causes.

(c) The following levels of chemical constituents shall not be exceeded:

(d) Based on a minimum of five samples taken over not more than a 30-day period, fecal coliforms (STORET number - 31616) shall not exceed a geometric mean of 20 per 100 ml.

(e) Temperature (STORET numbers - (OF) 00011 and (OC) 00010):

(1) (A) All sources of heated effluents in existence as of January 1, 1971 shall meet the following restrictions outside of a mixing zone which shall be no greater than a circle with a radius of 1000 feet or an equal fixed area of simple form.

(i) There shall be no abnormal temperature changes that may affect aquatic life.

(ii) The normal daily and seasonal temperature fluctuations that existed before the addition of heat shall be maintained.

(iii) The maximum temperature rise at any time above natural temperature shall not exceed 3OF. In addition, the water temperature shall not exceed the maximum limits (OF) indicated in the following table:

JAN.	FEB.	MAR.	APR.	MAY	JUN.	JUL.	AUG.	SEPT.	OCT.	NOV.	DEC.
45	45	45	55	60	70	80	80	80	65	60	50

(B) The owner or operator of a source of heated effluent which discharges 0.5 billion British Thermal Units per hour (BTU/HR.) or more shall demonstrate in a hearing before this Board not less than 5 nor more than six years after the adoption of this regulation, that discharges from that source have not caused and cannot be reasonably expected in future to cause significant ecological damage to the Lake. If such proof is not made to the satisfaction of the Board, backfitting of alternative cooling devices shall be accomplished within a reasonable time as determined by the Board.

(C) The owner or operator of a source of heated effluent shall maintain such records and conduct such studies of the effluents from such source and of their effects as may be required by the Environmental Protection Agency or in any permit granted under the Environmental Protection Act.

TABLE 3.23 (Continued)

(D) Backfitting of alternative cooling facilities will be required if, upon complaint filed in accordance with Board rules, it is found at any time that any heated effluent causes significant ecological damage to the Lake.

Any effluent source under construction as of January 1, 1971, but not in operation, shall meet all the requirements of Section 1 of this regulation and in addition shall meet the following restrictions:

(A) Neither the bottom, the shore, the hypolimnion, nor the thermocline shall be affected by any heated effluent.

(B) No heated effluent shall affect spawning grounds or fish migration routes.

(C) Discharge structures shall be so designed as to maximize short-term mixing and thus to reduce the area significantly raised in temperature.

(D) No discharge shall exceed ambient temperatures by more than 20°F.

(E) Heated effluents from more than one source shall not interact.

(F) All reasonable steps shall be taken to reduce the number of organisms drawn into or against the intakes.

(G) Cleaning of condensers shall be accomplished by mechanical devices. If chemicals must be used to supplement mechanical devices, the concentration at the point of discharge shall not exceed the 96-hour TLm for fresh water organisms.

(3) (A) No source of heated effluent which was not in operation or under construction as of January 1, 1971, shall discharge more than a daily average of 0.1 billion BTU/Hr.

(B) Sources of heated effluents which discharge less than a daily average of 0.1 billion BTU/Hr. not in operation or under construction as of January 1, 1971 shall meet all requirements of sections 1 and 2 of this regulation.

Underground Waters

The underground waters of Illinois which are a present or potential source of water for public or food processing water supply shall meet the General and Public and Food Processing Water Supply Standards except due to natural causes.

Nondegradation

Waters whose existing quality is better than the established standards at the date of their adoption will be maintained in their present high quality. Such waters will not be lowered in quality unless and until it is affirmatively demonstrated that such change will not interfere with or become injurious to any appropriate beneficial uses made of, or presently possible in such waters and that such change is justifiable as a result of necessary economic or social development.

WATER USE DESIGNATIONS

This part of the rules and regulations concerning water pollution designates the water uses for which particular waters of the State are to be protected. Waters designated for specific uses must meet the most restrictive standards listed in Part II of this Chapter for any specified use, in addition to meeting the General Standards.

General Use Waters

All waters of the State of Illinois are designated for general use except those designated as Restricted Use Waters.

Restricted Use Waters

The following are designated as restricted use waters:

(a) The Chicago Sanitary and Ship Canal;

(b) The Calumet-Sag Channel;

(c) The Little Calumet River from its junction with the Grand Calumet River to the Calumet-Sag Channel;

(d) The Grand Calumet River;

(e) The Calumet River;

(f) Lake Calumet;

(g) The South Branch of the Chicago River;

(h) The North Branch of the Chicago River from its confluence with the North Shore Channel to its confluence with the South Branch;

TABLE 3.23 (Continued)

(i) The Des Plaines River from its confluence with the Chicago Sanitary and Ship Canal to the Interstate 55 bridge;

(j) The North Shore Channel, except that dissolved oxygen in said Channel shall be not less than 5 mg/l during 16 hours of any 24 hour period, nor less than 4 mg/l at any time;

(k) All waters in which, by reason of low flow or other conditions, a diversified aquatic biota cannot be satisfactorily maintained even in the absence of contaminants.

Public and Food Processing Water Supply

All waters of Illinois are designated for Public and Food Processing Water Supply use except those designated as Restricted Use Waters, and except for the following:

(a) The Chicago River;

(b) The Little Calumet River.

EFFLUENT STANDARDS

This Part prescribes the maximum concentrations of various contaminants that may be discharged to the waters of the State.

General Provisions

(a) Dilution. Dilution of the effluent from a treatment works or from any wastewater source, is not acceptable as a method of treatment of wastes in order to meet the standards set forth in this part. Rather, it shall be the obligation of any person discharging contaminants of any kind to the waters of the state to provide the best degree of treatment of wastewater consistent with technological feasibility, economic reasonableness and sound engineering judgment. In making determinations as to what kind of treatment is the "best degree of treatment" within the meaning of this paragraph, any person shall consider the following:

(1) what degree of waste reduction can be achieved by process change, improved housekeeping, and recovery of individual waste components for reuse; and

(2) whether individual process wastewater streams should be segregated or combined.

In any case, measurement of contaminant concentrations to determine compliance with the effluent standards shall be made at the point immediately following the final treatment process and before mixture with other waters, unless another point is designated by the Agency in an individual permit, after consideration of the elements contained in this paragraph. If necessary the concentrations so measured shall be recomputed to exclude the effect of any dilution that is improper under this Rule.

Background Concentrations. Because the effluent standards in this Part are based upon concentrations achievable with conventional treatment technology that is largely unaffected by ordinary levels of contaminants in intake water, they are absolute standards that must be met without subtracting background concentrations. However, it is not the intent of these regulations to require users to clean up contamination caused essentially by upstream sources or to require treatment when only traces of contaminants are added to the background. Compliance with the numerical effluent standards is therefore not required when effluent concentrations in excess of the standards result entirely from influent contamination, evaporation, and/or the incidental addition of traces of materials not utilized or produced in the activity that is the source of the waste.

(c) Averaging. Except as otherwise specifically provided in this Part, compliance with the numerical standards in this Part shall be determined on the basis of 24-hour composite samples. In addition, no contaminant shall at any time exceed five times the numerical standard prescribed in this Part.

Violation of Water Quality Standards

In addition to the other requirements of this Part, no effluent shall, alone or in combination with other sources, cause a violation of any applicable water quality standard. When the Agency finds that a discharge that would comply with effluent standards contained in this Chapter would cause or is causing a violation of water quality standards, the Agency shall take appropriate action under Section 31 or Section 39 of the Act to require the discharge to meet whatever effluent limits are necessary to ensure compliance with the water quality standards. When such a violation is caused by the cumulative effect of more than one source, several sources may be joined in an enforcement or variance proceeding, and measured for necessary effluent reductions will be determined on the basis of technical feasibility, economic reasonableness, and fairness to all dischargers.

Offensive Discharges

In addition to the other requirements of this Part, no effluent shall contain settleable solids, floating debris, visible oil, grease, scum, or sludge solids. Color, odor and turbidity must be reduced to below obvious levels.

Deoxygenating Wastes

Except as provided in Rule 602 of this Chapter,

TABLE 3.23 (Continued)

all effluents containing deoxygenating wastes shall meet the following standards:

(a) On and after July 1, 1972, or such earlier date as may have been specified in Rules and Regulations SWB-7 through SWB-15, no effluent shall exceed 30 mg/l of five-day biochemical oxygen demand (BOD$_5$) (STORET number 00310) or 37 mg/l of suspended solids, except as follows:

(i) sources discharging to the Mississippi or Ohio Rivers shall comply with this paragraph (a) by December 31, 1973; and

(ii) sources discharging to the Wabash River may discharge up to 40 mg/l of BOD$_5$ and 45 mg/l of suspended solids until December 31, 1974.

(b) On and after July 1, 1972, or such earlier date as may have been specified in Rules and Regulations SWB-7 through SWB-15, no effluent from any source whose untreated waste load is 10,000 population equivalents or more, or from any source discharging into the Chicago River System or into the Calumet River System, shall exceed 20 mg/l of BOD$_5$ or 25 mg/l of suspended solids, except as follows:

(i) sources discharging to the Mississippi or Ohio Rivers shall comply with this paragraph (b) by December 31, 1973; and

(ii) sources discharging to the Illinois or Wabash Rivers, or to the Des Plaines River downstream from its confluence with the Chicago Sanitary and Ship Canal, shall comply with this paragraph (b) by December 31, 1974.

(c) On and after December 31, 1973, no effluent whose dilution ratio is less than five to one shall exceed 10 mg/l of BOD$_5$ or 12 mg/l of suspended solids, except as follows:

(i) sources within the Metropolitan Sanitary District of Greater Chicago whose untreated waste load is 500,000 population equivalents or more shall comply with this paragraph (c) by December 31, 1977;

(ii) sources whose dilution ratio is two to one or more but less than five to one shall comply with this paragraph (c) by December 31, 1974;

(iii) sources employing third-stage treatment lagoons shall be exempt from this paragraph (c), provided all the following conditions are met:

(A) the untreated waste load is less than 2500 population equivalents; and

(B) the source is sufficiently isolated that combining with other sources to aggregate 2500 population equivalents or more is not practicable; and

(C) the lagoons are properly constructed, maintained, and operated; and

(D) the effluent does not, alone or in combination with other sources, cause a violation of applicable water quality standards.

(d) On or after December 31, 1974, no effluent discharged to the Lake Michigan basin shall exceed 4 mg/l of BOD$_5$ or 5 mg/l of suspended solids.

(e) On or after December 31, 1977, no effluent from any source whose untreated waste load is 500,000 population equivalents or more shall exceed 4 mg/l of BOD$_5$ or 5 mg/l of suspended solids.

(f) Except as provided in paragraphs (d) and (e) of this Rule 404, on or after December 31, 1973, no effluent whose dilution ratio is less than one to one shall exceed 4 mg/l of BOD$_5$ or 5 mg/l of suspended solids, except as follows:

(i) sources employing third-stage treatment lagoons shall be exempt from this paragraph (f), provided all of the conditions of subparagraph (c) (iii) of this Rule 404 are met.

(ii) other sources not within paragraphs (d) and (e) of this Rule 404 shall be exempt from this paragraph provided all of the following conditions are met:

(A) the effluent shall not, alone or in combination with other sources, cause a violation of any applicable water quality standard; and

(B) the effluent shall not, alone or in combination with other sources, cause dissolved oxygen in the waters of the State to fall below 6.0 mg/l during at least 16 hours of any 24-hour period, or below 5.0 mg/l at any time; and

(C) the effluent shall not exceed 10 mg/l of BOD$_5$ or 12 mg/l of suspended solids; and

(D) on or before September 1, 1972, the owner or operator of such source shall file with the Agency the Project Completion Schedule required by Rule 1002 of this Chapter. In addition to the requirements of Rule 1002, such schedule shall include a program for achieving compliance with the above conditions and with applicable water quality standards, including, but not limited to, dissolved oxygen, bottom deposits, ammonia nitrogen, and phosphorus, with particular reference to nitrogenous oxygen demand and to the control of stormwater overflows; and

(E) the Agency finds that the program will within the compliance dates otherwise applicable assure compliance with the conditions of this subparagraph.

(g) Notwithstanding any other provision of this Rule, any source affected by this Rule 404 and relying in good faith upon the dilution rules of Rules and Regulations SWB-7 through SWB-15 to comply with applicable effluent standards need not comply with the dilution standard of Rule 401 (a) until December 31, 1974.

TABLE 3.23 (Continued)

LEVELS OF CONTAMINANTS NOT TO BE EXCEEDED BY ANY EFFLUENT

CONSTITUENT	STORET NUMBER	CONCENTRATION (mg/l)
Arsenic (total)	01002	0.25
Barium (total)	01007	2.0
Cadmium (total)	01027	0.15
Chromium (total hexavalent)		0.3
Chromium (total trivalent)		1.0
Copper (total)	01042	1.0
Cyanide	00720	0.025
Fluoride (total)	00951	2.5
Iron (total)	01045	2.0
Iron (dissolved)	01046	0.5
Lead (total)	01051	0.1
Manganese (total)	01055	1.0
Mercury (total)	71900	0.0005
Nickel (total)	01067	1.0
Oil (hexane solubles or equivalent)	00550	15.0
pH	00400	range 5-10*
Phenols	32730	0.3
Selenium (total)	01145	1.0
Silver	01077	0.1
Zinc (total)	01092	1.0
Total Suspended Solids (from sources other than those covered by Rule 404)	00530	15.0

*The pH limitation is not subject to averaging and must be met at all times.

(h) Compliance with the numerical standards in this Rule 404 shall be determined on the basis of 24-hour composite samples averaged over any consecutive 30-day period. In addition, no more than 5% of the samples collected shall exceed 2.5 times the numerical limits prescribed by this Rule.

Bacteria

No effluent shall exceed 400 fecal coliforms per 100 ml after July 31, 1972, or such concentrations as may have been prescribed for earlier dates by SWB-7 through SWB-15.

Nitrogen

Ammonia Nitrogen as N. (STORET number 00610). No effluent from any source which discharges to the Illinois River, the Chicago River System, or the Calumet River System, and whose untreated waste load is 50,000 or more population equivalents shall contain more than 2.5 mg/l of ammonia nitrogen as N during the months of April through October, or 4 mg/l at other times, after December 31, 1977.

Phosphorus (STORET number 00665)

(a) No effluent discharged within the Lake Michigan Basin shall contain more than 1.0 mg/l of phosphorus as P after December 31, 1971.

(b) No effluent from any source which discharges within the Fox River Basin and whose untreated waste load is 1500 or more population equivalents shall contain more than 1.0 mg/l of phosphorus as P after December 31, 1973.

Additional Contaminants

(a) The following levels of contaminants shall not be exceeded by any effluent:

(A) New sources shall comply on the effective date of this regulation:

(B) Existing sources shall comply by December 31, 1973.

(b) Total Dissolved Solids (STORET number 00515) shall not be increased more than 750 mg/l above background concentration levels unless caused by recycling or other pollution abatement practices, and in no event shall exceed 3500 mg/l at any time.

(c) Compliance with the limitations of this Rule 408 shall be achieved by the following dates:

(i) with respect to mercury, by April 25, 1971;

(ii) with respect to all other specified contaminants,

(2) Enviro-Control Water Pollution Measurement System.
This measurement system focusses on DOD as a criterion,
and has been computed for 140 selected stations with the
reliable DOD data. A problem is that the 142-station network is not closely correlated with the urban system.

(3) Syracuse Pollution Index (SPI).
The important feature of this index is that it provides a
single measure of water quality relative to permissible
use standards. This is perhaps the most inclusive index
available.

    a. PREVALENCE - DURATION - INTENSITY INDEX - (PDI
        INDEX)

As noted above, this index allows any water body to be described in terms of the prevalence, duration, and intensity of
its water pollution, corrected for natural background pollutant
levels, and taking into account the flow characteristics of
the water courses for which it is computed. The index is based
on how much water quality deviates from Federal-State water quality standards, which vary from place to place, depending on
locally established designations as to use, for drinking, swimming, industrial waste discharge, etc.

The prevalence of water pollution was first assessed systematically on a nationwide basis in 1970 and reported in The
Annual Report of the Council on Environmental Quality. The 1970
figures indicated that 27 percent of the U.S. stream and shoreline miles were polluted. EPA assessed it again a year later
and found that, despite improved field reporting, the prevalence
of pollution was about the same nationally (29 percent) in 1971.

Table 3.24 summarizes the EPA data for major drainage basins. Unfortunately, of the four apparently significant shifts
in reported water pollution that took place--in the Ohio, Gulf,
Missouri, and Northeastern Basins--three are so obscured by
variations in procedure that it is impossible to evaluate the
degree of real change. Both the Gulf and Missouri Basins reported an enormous improvement in compliance with State water
quality standards, but the apparent improvement between 1970
and 1971 is almost certainly due to more accurate reporting, not
to better water. In the case of the Ohio River Basin, the 1970
assessment overlooked a large number of smaller tributaries
which were polluted.

The last column of Table 3.24 shows the duration-intensity
factor for the 1971 figures. Whereas the prior columns simply
indicate what portion of the stream was polluted, the duration-

TABLE 3.24

WATER POLLUTION INDEX SUMMARIZED FOR MAJOR DRAINAGE
AREAS, 1970 AND 1971

Major Watershed	Stream Miles	Polluted miles			1971 Duration-Intensity Factor
		1970	1971	Change	
Ohio	28,992	9,869	24,031	+13,746	0.42
Southeast	11,726	3,109	4,490	+ 1,381	.74
Great Lakes	21,374	6,580	8,771	+ 2,191	.45
Northeast	32,431	11,895	5,823	- 6,072	.61
Middle Atlantic	31,914	4,620	5,627	+ 869	.47
California	28,277	5,359	8,429	+ 2,499	.27
Gulf	64,719	16,605	11,604	- 5,001	.35
Missouri	10.448	4,259	1,839	- 2,420	.31
Columbia	30,443	7,443	5,685	- 1,758	.12
UNITED STATES	260,324	69,739	76,299	+ 5,435	.41
UNITED STATES LESS OHIO	231,332	59,870	52,263	- 8,311	.40
UNITED STATES LESS COLUMBIA	229,881	62,296	70,614	+ 7,193	.43

Source: Environmental Protection Agency, "The Cost
of Clean Water" (1972).

intensity factor indicates how badly polluted it was and for
how long during the year it was in violation of the standards.
To obtain the complete PDI index, the number of polluted stream
miles is multiplied by the duration-intensity factor. Thus the
higher the factor is, the worse the pollution.

The PDI index has several advantages. It covers all U.S.
surface waters. It considers the relationship of actual water
quality to State standards of desirable water quality. And it

allows for judgment as to the effects of the water pollution in any particular stream. It has proved a useful management tool for planning, for directing resources to the most polluted areas and for suggesting improvements in monitoring coverage.

However, the index also has major disadvantages. Most important, its estimates of water quality conditions are based primarily upon judgmental evaluation by regional EPA personnel, although data are used from the approximately 10,000 stations that collect water quality data. Thus, although the data from the stations are examined by EPA personnel, they are not used in a systematic manner which could be replicated. Second, the index does not identify the type of pollutant responsible for the pollution, e.g., BOD, suspended solids, or nutrients.

The basic element of the index is a simple measurement or judgment. Once standards have been determined for a set of water quality parameters, the procedure calls for a comparison of those standards with measured quality. Where any variable or combination of variables does not meet or exceed the standard, then a state of pollution exists--by definition.

This rather rudimentary test was first applied in 1970, when a ratio of polluted waters to total waters was established for the nation, using the simple formula:

$$\frac{P}{M} = \text{prevalence of pollution}$$

where P = number of stream and shoreline miles in which one or
more of the established chemical and biological criteria had not been met one or more times.

  M = total stream and shoreline miles, to and including
third-order tributaries.

See Tables 3.25 and 3.26.

An assessment of pollution in terms of mere prevalence is essentially unsatisfactory. The degree of pollution and its persistence are significant dimensions of the phenomenon--perhaps the more significant, given the range of uncertainties that attach to the water quality criteria. The water pollution index takes these factors into accout by establishing separate weighting values to a circumstance of pollution, according to its seasonal characteristics and its interference with uses sanctioned by the water quality standards. The simple formula for determining the prevalence of pollution becomes only slightly more complex, but the level of effort and judgment required to apply the formula is increased enormously when it becomes:

TABLE 3.25

RELATIVE INCIDENCE OF WATER POLLUTION

EPA Region	Percent of Stream Miles Polluted	Duration Intensity Factor	Duration-Intensity As a Percent of U.S. Mean	Percent Polluted U.S. Miles
I Boston	16.4	.62	151	6.4
II New York	42.4	.45	110	2.7
III Philadelphia	34.7	.58	141	11.7
IV Atlanta	37.9	.45	110	19.4
V Chicago	64.5	.43	105	24.3
VI Dallas	21.5	.37	90	13.1
VII Kansas City	12.5	.33	81	3.1
VIII Denver	25.0	.23	56	7.4
IX San Francisco	23.5	.20	49	5.2
X Seattle	19.4	.11	27	7.2
Contiguous U.S.	29.3	.41	100	100.0
East of Mississippi River	38.5	.48	117	63.9
West of Mississippi River	20.6	.28	68	36.1

TABLE 3.26

WATER POLLUTION INDEX SUMMARIZED FOR MAJOR
DRAINAGE AREAS, 1970 AND 1971

| Major Watershed | Stream Miles | Polluted Miles | | | 1971 D.I. Factor |
		1970	1971	Change	
Ohio	28,992	9,869	24,031	+13,746	.42
Southeast	11,726	3,109	4,490	+ 1,381	.74
Great Lakes	21,374	6,580	8,771	+ 2,191	.45
Northeast	32,431	11,895	5,823	− 6,072	.61
Middle Atlantic	31,914	4,620	5,627	+ 869	.47
California	28,277	5,359	8,429	+ 2,499	.27
Gulf	64,719	16,605	11,604	− 5,001	.35
Missouri	10,448	4,259	1,839	− 2,420	.31
Columbia	30,443	7,443	5,685	− 1,758	.12
U.S.	260,324	69,739	76,299	+ 5,435	.41
U.S. Less Ohio	231,332	59,870	52,268	− 8,311	.40
U.S. Less Columbia	229,881	62,296	70,614	+ 7,193	.43

Source of tables: EPA, The Economics of Clean Water.

$$\frac{P \cdot D \cdot I}{M} = \text{Water Pollution Index}$$

where D = a factor ranging from 0.4 to 1.0 to express the inter-
        seasonal duration of pollution.

    I = a factor ranging from 0.1 to 1.0 to express the in-
        tensity of water pollution in terms of damage.

    b.   ENVIRO-CONTROL WATER POLLUTION ANALYSIS

While judgmental factors inherent in the PDI index help to
adjust for the numerous inadequacies of the actual water quality
monitoring data, CEQ considered it desirable to explore a different approach to gauging water quality trends, based more
heavily on readings from water quality sampling stations. The
Council thus contracted with a consulting firm, Enviro Control,
Inc., to develop trend information based on the monitoring data
collected by EPA, the U.S. Geological Survey, and other Federal
and State agencies.

A sample of 142 Federal and State water quality stations
across the country was picked on the basis of how long the station had been collecting data and how adequate the data were.
Streams of all sizes were included as well as a number of estu-
arine, reservoir and Great Lakes locations. The stations represent a variety of types of areas, ranging from highly urbanized
and industrialized to completely undeveloped. However, because
of the limited number of stations from which the sample could
be selected, it does not represent a complete and properly
weighted cross section of all U.S. waters.

To understand the Enviro Control approach, one must understand the several major problems in using existing water quality
measurements for trend assessment. First, only periods of record that are relatively short (in a hydrologic sense, i.e.,
less than 10 years) are available in any quantity if one is in-
terested in national coverage. Second, the data are generally
not sampled at fixed intervals, nor are the parameters sampled
constant within and between stations. Third, the basic data at
a station show a typical spread of one order of magnitude in
pollutant concentration and two orders of magnitude in flow. If
one uses only the pollutant concentration data, uncorrected for
flow, it will be unclear whether changes are due to variations
in flow or in pollution emissions. Finally, the data are, in
general, non-Gaussian, i.e., they do not follow the normal statistical bell-shaped curve of distribution.

The Enviro Control analysis attempted to deal with these

problems by using the following method:

a. Stations were selected on the basis of adequate coverage of key parameters, adequate sample size for each parameter, and locations of some interest nationally, e.g., major rivers or their tributaries.

b. The stations were categorized approximately by the drainage areas they represent, i.e., little effect of man, mostly agricultural, dense population and only light industry, dense population with heavy industrial concentrations.

c. For each station and each water quality variable of interest, the concentration versus flow function and its uncertainty for a number of time periods was estimated. Figure 3.2 shows the nonparametric approach used for the basic estimation, which consists of categorizing pollutant readings (plotted on log-log paper) into classes of flow levels (e.g., 3 classes per order of magnitude), taking the median pollutant concentration in each class, then fitting a function (not necessarily straight line) through the resultant medians. To analyze variability, upper and lower 15th percentiles were also estimated in each flow category, as seen in the dashed lines of Figure 3.2. Finally, concentration versus flow functions are compared for succeeding time periods to establish percentage change in concentration per unit times high, and low flow, as shown in Figure 3.3. The percentage change is, in general, different for each of these points.

This basic method permited a number of investigations of interest beyond simple time trends:

a. The method proved to be quite powerful for detecting differences before and after major events such as construction, abatement of a pollution source, etc. In this case, the C versus Q functions are fitted for the before and after periods, rather than arbitrary 2- or 3-year blocks of time.

b. Where stations measure related variables, e.g., BOD and COD, the method determines which one is a more sensitive trend indicator.

c. By iterating the method for decreasing sample sizes (or sampling frequencies), minimum frequencies to achieve given levels of trend detection can be established.

d. Of considerable interest is the analysis of trends in the upper 15th percentile of pollutant concentrations, rather than medians (where sufficient sample sizes are available). Such trends represent percent exceedances of given levels of pollution concentrations which are probably of even greater interest than median performance.

The Enviro Control analysis revealed some surprising relationships between water quality and flow: Some quality parameters are roughly proportional to flow (e.g., suspended solids and turbidity), while others are inversely related to flow (e.g.,

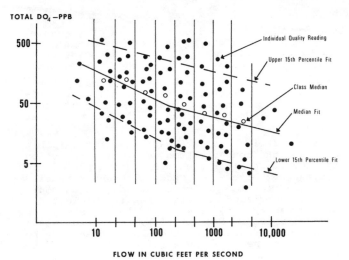

TOTAL DO₄ —PPB

FLOW IN CUBIC FEET PER SECOND

FIGURE 3.2

ESTIMATION OF CONCENTRATION VS. FLOW FUNCTION
(Example=Willamette River, Oregon.   Quality Readings--1966 to 1968

Source of figures: Council
on Environmental Quality
National Assessment of Trends
in Water Quality, 1972.

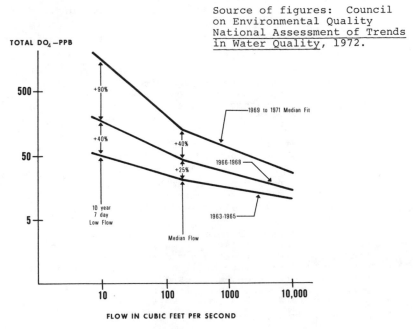

FLOW IN CUBIC FEET PER SECOND

FIGURE 3.3

QUALITY TIME TRENDS AT LOW AND MEDIAN FLOWS
(Example=Willamette River, Oregon)

total dissolved solids). The examples indicate that oxygen-demanding load (biochemical oxygen demand, chemical oxygen, total organic carbon) and nutrients (phosphorus and nitrogen and their most common chemical forms) are directly related to flow (i.e., pollution loadings increase with increasing flow). In addition, three types of relationship between flow and pollution loadings were discovered and classified as follows:

a. Dilution effect--Water quality improves as flow increases. A fairly constant point source of pollution is diluted by the larger volume of water at high flow; or the major source of the pollutant in question is groundwater inflow into the stream (which generally increases as streamflow decreases).

b. Runoff effect--Water quality is degraded as flow increases. The precipitation that causes high flow elutes large quantities of polluting materials into flowing streams; or (less likely) the high turbulence that may be associated with higher flows scours bottom deposits of pollutants (that may have come from point sources) from the streambed.

c. "Mixed" effect--Water quality shows no consistent relation to changes in flow, as when point sources and runoff sources contribute approximately equal pollutant loads.

Enviro Control tables of results aggregated the fourteen pollution parameters analyzed into seven broader classes: dissolved oxygen (DO), oxygen demanding load (biochemical oxygen demand, chemical oxygen demand, and total organic carbon), salinity (total dissolved solids and conductivity), suspended solids (frequently measured as turbidity), and three classes of nutrients (total phosphorus, organic nitrogen, and ammoniacal nitrogen; soluble phosphates; and nitrate plus nitrite). Many of the relationships that are ordinarily expected to exist among these types of pollutants were absent; instead, they found a fairly consistent pattern of relationships that had been suspected by some, but never before demonstrated in a national assessment based on actual water-quality records.

c. THE SYRACUSE INDEX

The Syracuse method of water quality evaluation has several important structural features. It is an overall expression of pollution quality, considering all uses and the overall effects of multiple items of pollutants for specific uses.

The number of pollutants included in the index varies: "the number of pollutants which may be used in calculation of the index is limited only by the availability of data concerning the particular pollutant's concentration, distribution and permissible standards." A maximum number of fourteen water quality measures was evaluated in the index as originally formulated.

Inherent in the index are several shortcomings, however, the most important of which is that the index does not correct for variable flow rates and thus is not sensitive to rapid or short term trends. The importance of major events of hydrological consequence can easily be over- or under-estimated, especially in geographic areas where such events are more pronounced or more variable.

However, the Syracuse water quality index, despite its shortcomings, is perhaps the most useful statistical index currently available due to the paucity and erratic nature of available water quality data, even through the STORET system.

The basic problem in the index is how to integrate the independent multiple items of pollutants in water into a common expression. There is often little correlation between the significance as well as the dimension of each pollutant: For instance, 1,000 (MPN/100 ml) in coliform count 6 (mg/l) in DO, and 80 (°F) in temperature. Each value may be compared only with the same item of quality. However, if the values are related to some <u>standard</u>, developed for each of the respective items such as coliform number of 500/100 ml, DO of 5 mg/l, and temperature of 50° F, the relative value can be expressed as 2.0 (1000/5000 = 2.0), 1.2 (6/5 - 1.2), and 1.6 (80/50 = 1.6) respectively, as <u>non-dimensional relative values</u>.

Thus, when the multiple items of water quality are expressed as C_i's and the permissible levels of the respective items for a use are expressed as L_{ij}'s, the Pollution Index for use j, PI, may be expressed as a function of the relative values (C_i/L_{ij})'s, i.e. PI = f $(C_1/L_{1j}, C_2/L_{2j}, C_3/L_{3j}, \ldots C_n/L_{nj})$. This approach is similar to that used in describing toxicity of multiple items of toxic materials. When several toxic materials $(T_1, T_2, T_3, \ldots)$ coexist in water, it is suggested that the total toxicity may be evaluated, applying the respective permissible levels (TL_1), (TL_2), (TL_3), by the relation total toxicity = $T_1(TL_1) + T_2/(TL_2) + T_3/(TL_3) + \ldots$. As in the case of the toxicity measures, a value of 1.0 is the "critical" value for each (C_i/L_{ij}). Values greater than 1.0 signify a condition of pollution under which a treatment is necessary for the water use. The major problem is how to get an overall index value from the multiple relative values. Theoretically, there is a large number of possible methods, the simplest of which is to compute the arithmetic average value of all the calculated (C_i/L_{ij}) values. For example, when the quality of a water is expressed as BOD (C_1) as 10 mg/l, coliform bacteria (C_2) as 1,3000/100 ml, and hardness (C_3) as 80 mg/l, and their permissible levels for a use j are given as BOD (L_{1j}) as 20 mg/l, coliform (L_{2j}) as 1,000/100 ml, and hardness (L_{3j}) as 100 mg/l, then the (C_i/L_{ij}) values are expressed as follows: $(C_1/L_{ij}) = 0.5$, $(C_2/L_{2j}) = 1.3$, and $(C_3/L_{3j}) = 0.8$. The average value of the above three values is about 0.9 which indicates that the water is just under the critical condition for the use j with no treatment of the water.

However, this average value may not satisfactorily measure pollution, because the need for water treatment is often determined by the _maximum_ of the (C_i/L_{ij}) values rather than the mean. Even if the mean is very small, the water cannot be used for use j without treatment if one of the (C_i/L_{ij}) values is over 1.0. As shown in the above example, the water needs treatment because one item, coliform bacteria, is over the permissible level $(C_2/L_{2j} = 1.3)$. Therefore, the maximum C_i/L_{ij} value is another element that must be included in any overall index. How might the mean and maximum be combined in a simple index? If the two are graphed, with the abcissa representing the maximum C_i/L_{ij}'s and the ordinate the means, the overall PI_j will be a point somewhere in the space between the two axes, as shown in Figure 3.4. It may generally be agreed that the larger the values of maximum C_i/L_{ij} and/or the mean, the more the water is polluted. Therefore the length of the vector from the origin to the point PI_j in Figure 3.4 may be proposed as a measurement of pollution. Another factor in Figure 3.4, (θ), is determined by the ratio of values of the maximum and mean. But it is difficult from a practical standpoint to discuss the significance of the ratio, or to determine which is relatively more important in regard to pollution, despite the fact that many existing data plotted in the way described are distributed within a limited angle as seen in Figure 3.5. Thus, ignoring the angle θ, the general quality expression of pollution for use j is assumed to be related to the length of a line between the origin and each point. The length is determined by the two values of the maximum and mean of (C_i/L_{ij}) values shown in Figure 3.4, or the lengths of the radii of the concentric circles as shown in Figure 3.6. Therefore, the relation shown in Figure 3.6 can be expressed as follows:

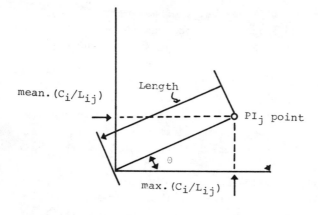

FIGURE 3.4

STEPS IN THE
SYRACUSE INDEX
CALCULATION: 1

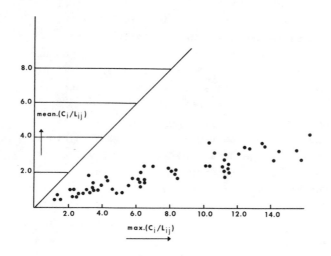

FIGURE 3.5

2: AN EXAMPLE OF
DATA DISTRIBUTION
FOR HUMAN CONTACT
USE

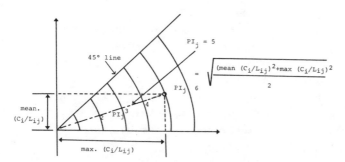

FIGURE 3.6

3: A GENERAL
QUALITY EXPRESSION
OF POLLUTION FOR
USE j.

$$PI_j = m \max. \ (C_i/L_{ij})^2 + \text{mean} \ (C_i/L_{ij})^2$$

where m = the proportionality constant.

The condition for determining the coefficient m is as follows:

$$PI_j = 1.0, \text{ when max. } (C_i/L_{ij}) = 1.0$$
$$\text{and mean } (C_i/L_{ij}) = 1.0$$

This means that the index for use j is expressed as 1.0 when all items of water quality are just equal to their respective permissible levels for the use. Where there is only one pollutant, $1.0 = m\sqrt{1^2 + 1^2}$, therefore $m + 1/\sqrt{2}$.

The index is best employed only for a particular use j. However, with some modification, it may be employed for grouped uses, depending upon what kind of permissible levels are employed as L_{ij}'s. If the L_{ij}'s are determined from the general permissible levels for swimming, boating, sport fishing, and hiking, as an example, the index PI_j, may be defined as the Pollution Index for outdoor recreation use. All existing water uses in the regions should be taken into consideration in regional benefit analyses of pollution control problems. An overall Pollution Index, PI, can be used for such problems. If an overall permissible level for all uses in a region can be determined, the overall Pollution Index could be easily determined.

When pollution is quantified for several uses, for example, 5.0 for drinking, 1.0 for swimming, and 0.9 for an industrial use, because it is a nondimensional number, an overall index, PI_j, may be obtained as a weighted average value of the individual PI_j'a as follows:

$$PI = \sum_{j=1}^{j=n} (w_j \cdot PI_j)$$

where w_j = a weighting coefficient reflecting the relative importance of water use j in the region,

   n = number of water uses,

and

$$\sum_{j}^{j=n} w_j = 1.0$$

Some problems of actual application now need to be considered. First, every item of water quality, C_i, does not increase in concentration as pollution increases. For example, pH values vary in both directions with pollution, generally within a range from 2 to 12, and in addition, it is common practice to specify the permissible level by a range of values such as pH from 6.4

to 7.5. In such cases, C_i/L_{ij} cannot be calculated as previously
suggested. When such special cases arise, special procedures
are then needed, as follows:

a. For the contaminant which decreases in value as pollution
   increases, such as transparency, DO, the theoretical or
   practical maximum value C_{im} of the C_i should be determined, such as DO concentrations at saturation. The
   C_i/L_{ij} value may be replaced by C_i/L_{ij}, where C_i/L_{ij} =
   $C_{im} - C_i/C_{im} - L_{ij}$. Thus, when maximum DO = 8.0 and the
   maximum permissible DO level is 4.0, and the existing
   level is 5.0, C_1/L_{1j} = (8.0 - 5.0)/(8.0 - 4.0) = 3/4 =
   0.75.

b. For the contaminant qualities which have permissible
   levels ranging from $L_{ij} \cdot min$ to $L_{ij} \cdot max$ the mean of the
   ranged levels, $\bar{L}_{ij}$, should be calculated, $\bar{L}_{ij}$= ($L_{ij} \cdot min$
   + $L_{ij} \cdot max$)/2 and the C_i/L_{ij} value may be substituted by
   the following: $(C_i/\bar{L}_{ij})$ = $(C_i - L_{ij})/[\bar{L}_{ij} \cdot min$ or
   $L_{ij} \cdot max - \bar{L}_{ij}]$. Thus, if the maximum pH allowable level
   is 8.5 and the range is 6.5 to 8.5 when the existing pH
   is 10.0, then C_i/L_{ij} = (10.0 - 7.5)/(8.5 - 7.5) =
   2.5/1.0 = 2.5.

Since an increase or decrease in acids or alkalis causing a pH
change occurs on a logarithmic rather than an arithmetic scale,
modification of the procedure using a log value of C_i/L_{ij} may
be in order. More study of this point is necessary since a log
value will greatly affect the magnitude of the computed index.

The C_i/L_{ij} value indicates relative pollution as compared
to the respective permissible level. At the same time, this
value also may express how damaging the water may be for use j,
especially when the value is over 1.0. To illustrate the possibility, compare C_i/L_{ij} values of 0.9 and 1.1. The waters are
almost equally polluted. However, the necessary expenses for
pollution treatment are likely to be significantly different,
and not always proportional to the quality of the raw water.
If an index is expected to reflect the relative damage of pollution rather than a numerical ratio of the pollution, different
methods of calculation may be needed, as shown in Figure 3.7.

Assuming that the shape of the curve in Figure 3.7 is valid,
the following calculation provides for the substitution of C_j/L_{ij}
values:

When $(C_i/L_{ij}) \leq 1.0$, $(C_i/L_{ij}) = (C_i/L_{ij})$

When $(C_i/L_{ij}) \geq 1.0$, $(C_i/L_{ij} = 1.0 + p \cdot \log_{10} (C_i/L_{ij})$

where p = a constant value.

In the previous discussion, PI_j was proposed for each use j,
(j=1, 2, 3, ...j...n), but the number of water uses is so numerous
that a collective general grouping of water uses may be used for

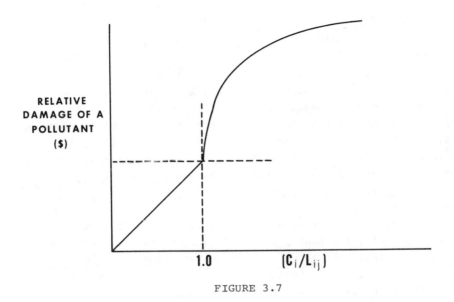

FIGURE 3.7

EFFECT OF INCREASING CONCENTRATION OF POLLUTANT
ON THE DAMAGE COSTS

practical purposes. If a reasonable common permissible level can
be determined for similar water uses, groupings of water uses may
be possible and facilitate calculation of the pollution indices.
The following three groups are recommended for separate index ex-
pressions:

1. Human Contact Use (j = 1) which includes drinking, swimming, beverage manufacturing, etc.
2. Indirect Contact Use (j = 2) which includes fishing, industrial food preparation, agricultural use, etc.
3. Remote Contact Use (j = 3) which includes industrial
   cooling, aesthetic (picnicing, hiking and plain visita-
   tion), navigation, etc.

The overall permissible levels L_{ij}'s should be determined for
the three grouped uses by applying the present permissible contamination levels for each particular use. The following contaminant items (i's) are recommended for the index computations,
although as many items of water quality as possible should be
utilized:

1. Temperature	8. Total Nitrogen
2. Color	9. Alkalinity
3. Turbidity	10. Hardness
4. pH	11. Chloride
5. Fecal coliform bacteria	12. Iron and Manganese
6. Total dissolved solids	13. Sulfate
7. Suspended solids	14. Dissolved Oxygen

Tables 3.27-3.32 illustrate computations made of the Syracuse index for the surface water resources in New York State with respect to human contact use (PI_1), indirect contact use (PI_2), remote contact use (PI_3), and for general overall use ($\underline{PI}$). The permissible quality levels for the above three grouped uses, (L_{i1}, L_{i2}, and L_{i3}), are determined as average permissible levels shown in Tables 3.27, 3.28, and 3.29, respectively, selected after careful study of the FWPCA, Interim Report of the National Technical Advisory Committee on Water Quality Criteria, June 30, 1967.

An example calculation of the pollution index for human contact use, PI_1, for Oneida Lake in New York State is described in detail. First, the water quality measures for Oneida Lake shown in Table 3.30 are divided by the respective permissible levels in Table 3.27. The calculations are summarized in Table 3.31. From this table, the max. C_1/L_{ij} and mean C_i/L_{ij} are computed as 2.9 and 0.87 respectively.

Therefore, $PI_1 = \dfrac{2.9^2 + 0.87^2}{2} = 2.1$

In the same way, PI_2 and PI_3 can be calculated using L_{i2} and L_{i3} in Table 3.28 and 3.29, to yield $PI_2 = 0.8$ and $PI_3 = 0.6$. The overall pollution index, $\underline{PI}$, is calculated using the computed PI_1, PI_2, and PI_3 values. Since no relative weights, w_j's, are known, it is assumed that all water uses are equally important, i.e., $w_1 = w_2 = w_3 = 1/3$. However, the current mix of water uses in Oneida Lake is 40% for swimming use, 40% for fishing use and 20% for navigation, aesthetic, and others. From these figures, relative wieghts might possibly be used as follows: $w_1 = 0.4$, $w_2 = 0.4$, and $w_3 = 0.2$. In the latter case, the overall pollution index for Oneida Lake is:

$\underline{PI} = w_1 PI_1 + w_2 PI_2 + w_3 PI_3$

$= 0.4 \times 2.1 + 0.4 \times 0.8 + 0.2 \times 0.6 = 1.28^n = 1.3$

Pollution indices for other surface water resources in New York State are quantified in a manner similar to that used for Oneida Lake. In the calculations, the w_j's are each given a value of 1/3. The results shown in Table 3.32 indicate the relative pollution of each water resource for each water use.

TABLE 3.27

PERMISSIBLE QUALITY LEVELS FOR HUMAN CONTACT WATER USE
(J = 1) (F.W.P.C.A., 1967)

	1	2	3	4	5	6	7	8	9	10	11	12	13	14
	Temp	Color	Turb	pH	F.Coli	TS	SS	NO_2	Alk	Hard	Chl	Fe	Sulf	DO
	F	UNIT			100 ml	ppm	ppm	ppm	ppm	ppm	ppm	ppm	ppm	ppm
Drinking Use	-	15	5	-	5	500	-	45	-	-	250	0.35	250	
Swimming Use	85	-	-	6.5 8.3	-200	-	-	-	+	+	+	-+	-	-
Beverage Manufacturing	-	10	-	-	-	-	-	-	85	-	250	0.35	-	-/
Average; L_{ij}	85	13	5	6.5 8.3	-103	500	-	45	/	/	/	/	250	4.0*

Note: 1. (Temp.) Temperature; 2. (Color) Color; 3. (Turb.) Turbidity;
   5. (Coli); Coliform Bacteria count; 6. (TS) Total Solids; 7 (SS) Total Suspended Solids;
   8. (NO_3) Total Nitrate; 9. (Alk) Alkalinity; 10. (Hard) Hardness, 11. (Chl) Chloride;
   12. (Fe) Iron and Manganese; 13. (Sulf) Sulfate; 14. (D.O.) Dissolved Oxygen

  - ; Now under discussion
  + ; No special limit
  / ; L_{ij} is not determined because of the presence of (+) mark.
  * ; Assumed

Note: Tables 3.27 and 3.30 may be incorrect in the original Syracuse formulation. See
   list of contaminant items on page 74. We adjusted our parameters as follows:
   5. Fecal Coliform; 6. Total Dissolved Solids; 8. Total Nitrogen; 12. Fe and Mn.

TABLE 3.28

PERMISSIBLE QUALITY LEVELS FOR INDIRECT CONTACT USE
(j = 2) (F.W.P.C.A., 1967)

	1	2	3	4	5	6	7	8	9	10	11	12	13	14
Fishing Use	55	-	30	6.0 to 9.0	-2000	-	-	-	-	+	-	-	-	-
Agricultural Use	-	+	-	6.0 to 8.5	-	500	-	45.	-	+	+	1.0	-	-
Fruit and Vegetable	+	5	5	6.5	-	500	.10	10	250	250	250	0.4	250	-
Industrial Use				6-8										
Average; L_{ij}	/	/	18	6.2 to 8.1	-2000	500		28	250	/	/	0.7	250	3.0*

Note: Agricultural Use is Farmstead and Irrigation

Source of tables: EPA, Benefits of Water Quality Enhancement, 1970

TABLE 3.29

PERMISSIBLE QUALITY LEVELS FOR REMOTE CONTACT USE

	1	2	3	4	5	6	7	8	9	10	11	12	13	14
Iron & Steel (cooling)	100	+	+	5-9	+	-	10	+	-	-	-	-	-	-
Cement	-	-	+	6.5 9.0	+	600	500	+	400		250	25.5	250	-
Petroleum				6.0 9.0	+	1000	10	+	-	350	300	1.0	+	-
Pulp**	95	10	-	6.1	+	-	10	+	-	100	200	1.1	+	-
Textile***	-	5	-	6.4 10.3	+	100	5	+	-	25	-	0.2	-	-
Chemical****	-	5	-	6.5 8.1	+	338	5	-	145	210	28	0.2	85	-
Navigation	-	-	-	-	-	-	-	-	-	-	-	-	-	-
Aesthetic	-	-	-	-	-	-	-	-	-	-	-	-	-	-
Average; L_{ij}	90	/	/	6.1 9.1	/	510	90	/	274	171	195	5.6	/	2.0*

**; Bleached
***; Average of sizing, scouring, bleaching and dying
****; Average of organic and inorganic matters

Note: For Navigation and Aesthetic uses, data for permissible levels are not available yet.

Source: F.W.P.C.A., 1967.

TABLE 3.30

WATER QUALITY IN ONEIDA LAKE

Item		Quality	Item		Quality
Temperature	C_1	63.3° F	Total Nitrogen	C_8	-
Color	C_2	12.0 unit	Alkalinity	C_9	86 ppm
Turbidity	C_3	12.0	Hardness	C_{10}	128 ppm
pH	C_4	8.2	Chloride	C_{11}	26 ppm
Coliform	C_5	72 MPN	Fe, Mn	C_{12}	neg.
Total Solids	C_6	209 ppm	Sulfate	C_{13}	84.4 ppm
Suspended Solids	C_7		Dissolved Oxygen	C_{14}	8 ppm

neg. = neglibible

Source: New York State Department of Health, 1964; Average data, 1960-1964.

TABLE 3.31

CALCULATION OF INDEX PI_1 FOR ONEIDA LAKE

	(C_i/L_{ij})	$\log_{10}(C_i/L_{ij})$	$(C_i/L_{ij}) = (C_i/L_{ij})$ or $= 1.0 + 5 \times \log_{10}(C_i/L_{ij})$
1	63.3/85.0=0.75	--	0.75
2	12.0/12.5=0.96	--	0.96
3	12.0/ 5.0=2.40	0.38	2.9 (max.)
4	** =0.89	--	0.89
5	72/103 =0.7	--	0.7
6	209/500 −0.42	--	0.42
7	-/-	-	-
8	-/4.5	-	-
9	86/-	-	-
10	128/-	-	-
11	26.0/-	-	-
12	0/-	-	-
13	84.4/250=0.34	--	0.34
14	*** =0.01	--	0.1
		TOTAL	6.97

Average (C_i/L_{ij})=6.97/8=<u>0.87</u>

Note: - ; Datum is not available

    -- ; Calculation is not necessary

    * ; Saturated concentration

    **; (8.2 - (6.5 + 8.3) / 2) / (8.3 - (6.5 + 8.3) / 2) = 0.8/0.9 = 0.89

    ***; (8.4* - 8.0) / (8.4* - 4.0) = 0.1

Source of tables: see p. 143.

TABLE 3.32

WATER POLLUTION OF SURFACE WATER RESOURCES
IN NEW YORK STATE
EXPRESSED BY POLLUTION INDICES

Surface Water	Location	Pl_1	Pl_2	Pl_3	Pl
Niagara Ri.	Youngstown	6.0	1.4	0.2	2.5
Niagara Ri.	Buffalo	7.9	2.5	0.6	3.6
Erie L.	Buffalo	4.5	2.4	0.6	2.5
Cattaraugua Cr.	Gowanda	2.4	0.7	0.8	1.3
Buffalo Ri.	Buffalo	10.6	6.1	2.2	6.3
Cazenovia Cr.	Buffalo	9.4	4.8	1.0	5.1
Buffalo Ri.	W. Seneca	9.3	6.0	2.3	5.9
Buffalo Ri.	W. Seneca	11.8	7.8	0.9	6.8
Tonawanda Cr.	W. Seneca	3.2	1.7	2.1	2.3
Allegheny Ri.	Indian Res.	0.7	0.6	0.6	0.6
Conewango	Carroll	3.3	2.2	0.8	2.1
Cassadaga	Palconer	4.3	3.3	0.4	2.7
Ontario L.	Rochester	8.1	3.5	0.6	4.1
Allens Cr.	Brington	3.0	2.6	0.8	2.1
Ontario L.	Oswego	4.5	0.7	0.6	1.9
Genesee Ri.	Rochester	2.6	1.2	0.6	1.5
Genesee Ri.	Rochester	2.3	0.8	0.8	1.3
Genesee Ri.	Chili	2.6	1.3	1.5	1.8
Genesee Ri.	Wellsville	8.1	2.5	0.5	3.7
Chemung Ri.	Elmira	8.2	4.0	0.6	4.3
Cohocton Ri.	Campbell	3.4	0.8	0.7	1.6
Tioga Ri.	Lindley	2.7	0.6	0.7	1.3
Susquehanna Ri.	Binghamton	9.2	4.6	0.5	4.8
Chenango Ri.	Chenango	2.3	0.6	0.6	1.2
Toughnioga Ri.	Barber	2.6	0.7	0.6	1.3
Chenango	Chenango	0.8	0.6	0.6	0.7
Susquehanna	Unadilla	0.4	0.5	0.4	0.4
Seneca Ri.	Waterloo	4.7	0.7	0.6	2.0
Seneca Ri.	Geneva	1.1	0.8	0.7	0.9
Cayuga L.	Cayuga	8.1	1.5	0.6	3.4
Cayuga L.	Fayette	1.8	0.6	0.7	1.0
Owasco L.	Fleming	2.0	0.8	0.5	1.1
Skaneateles L.	Skaneateles	1.7	0.6	0.5	0.9
Canandaigua L.	Canandaigua	0.9	1.2	0.6	0.9
Seneca Ri.	Montezuma	4.7	0.8	0.6	2.0
Oswego Ri.	Oswego	10.3	5.5	4.0	6.6
Oneida L.	Cicero	2.1	0.8	0.6	1.1
Seneca Ri.	Clay	4.9	2.6	2.9	3.5
Black Ri.	Watertown	8.2	3.6	0.4	4.1
Black Ri.	Lyons Falls	8.3	3.7	0.4	4.1
Lawrence Ri.	Massena	4.7	2.6	0.6	2.6
Lawrence Ri.	Cape Vincent	0.8	1.1	0.4	0.8
Raquette Ri.	Massena	5.2	0.6	0.6	2.1
Gross Ri.	Massena	5.9	1.2	0.6	2.6
Oswegatchie Ri.	Ogdensburgh	6.5	2.0	0.4	3.0
Saranac Ri.	Shuyler Falls	8.3	3.7	0.5	4.2
Ausable Ri.	Ausable	6.1	1.4	0.5	2.7
Hudson Ri.	Waterford	8.1	3.5	0.6	4.1
Hosic Ri.	Schaghticoke	2.3	0.8	0.6	1.2
Hudson Ri.	Fort Edward	7.9	3.3	0.7	4.0
Battenkooll	Greenwich	5.9	1.4	0.6	2.6
Hudson Ri.	Orinth	6.1	1.5	0.6	2.7
Mohawk Ri.	Cohoes	4.3	1.3	0.5	2.0
Mohawk Ri.	Schenectady	0.6	0.7	0.4	0.6
Sheoharie Cr.	Frerida	7.4	2.8	0.5	3.6
Mohawk Ri.	Frerida	7.5	2.8	0.5	3.6
E. Canada Cr.	Manheim	8.3	3.7	0.3	4.1
Mohawk Ri.	St. Johnsville	8.1	3.6	0.5	4.1
W. Canada Cr.	Herkimer	8.3	3.7	0.5	4.2

TABLE 3.32 (Continued)

Surface Water	Location	Pl_1	Pl_2	Pl_3	Pl
Mohawk Ri.	Shuyler	1.8	0.8	0.7	1.1
Hudson	Poughkeepsie	4.6	2.7	0.7	2.7
Frishkill Cr.	Beacon	11.4	6.8	0.7	6.3
Wappinger Cr.	Lagrange	3.8	0.5	0.6	1.6
Wallkill	Rosendale	8.9	4.2	0.6	4.6
Hudson Ri.	Poughkeepsie	9.9	5.4	0.4	5.2
Hudson Ri.	Bethlehem	11.4	6.6	0.3	6.1
Delaware Ri.	Port Jervis	0.4	0.1	0.3	0.3
Neversink Ri.	Deer Park	0.4	0.2	0.2	0.3
Delaware Ri.	Deposit	2.8	0.8	0.5	1.4
Hackensack Ri.	Orange Town	2.7	0.5	0.5	1.2
Pascack Cr.	Ramapo	10.2	5.3	0.5	5.3
Pascack Cr.	Clarkstown	11.9	7.3	0.5	6.6

Cr.:   creek

Ri.:   river

L. :   lake   Source: see p. 143.

V.   THE EFFECTS OF WATER POLLUTION

Sec. 101 (a) of the 1972 Federal Water Pollution Act de-
clares its objective "is to restore and maintain the chemical,
physical, and biological integrity of the Nation's waters.   In
order to achieve this objective it is hereby declared that, consistent with the provisions of this Act--

(1) it is the national goal that the discharge of pollutants into the navigable waters be eliminated by 1985;

(2) it is the national goal that wherever attainable,
an interim goal of water quality which provides for the
protection and propagation of fish, shellfish, and wildlife and provides for recreation in and on the water be
achieved by July 1, 1983;

(3) it is the national policy that the discharge of
toxic pollutants in toxic amounts be prohibited;

(4) it is the national policy that Federal financial
assistance be provided to construct publicly owned waste
treatment works;

(5) it is the national policy that area wide waste

treatment management planning processes be developed and implemented to assure adequate control of sources of pollutants in each state; and

(6) it is the national policy that a major research and demonstration effort be made to develop technology necessary to eliminate the discharge of pollutants into the navigable waters of the contiguous zone, and the oceans."

It appears, then, that the Act was designed to protect the water resource while restoring the maximum possible number of uses of our national waterways. The effect of water pollution is to inhibit the possible number of uses. This emphasis on uses was emphasized earlier in Senate Report No. 10, The Federal Water Pollution Control Amendments of 1965, 89th Congress, 1st Session, as follows: "Economic, health, esthetic, and conservation values which contribute to the social and economic welfare of an area must be taken into account in determining the most appropriate use or uses of a stream. There ought to be a constant effort to improve the quality of the water supply, it being recognized that the improvement of quality of water makes it available for more uses."

Research materials available for a substantive evaluation of water quality-urbanized place relationships do not adequately cover the diverse uses and the chemical, physical, and biological bases of our national waterways. Therefore this section will only highlight what the effects of water pollution mean to the resource itself and then generalize about the pollution impact on a variety of urban uses.

1. IMPORTANT WATER SUPPLY RESIDUALS

Water pollution can be thought of in terms of residuals from urban processes. Table 3.33 notes with an asterisk those residuals which are highly toxic, having adverse health effects for humans and biota, are in widespread use, and have established water quality standards. Other pollutants are noted along with known health or other effects. An earlier section in this chapter on the Rules and Regulations of the Illinois Pollution Control Board provides specific STORET identification coding and current acceptable levels for individual chemical constituents. Additional health and welfare effects were described earlier in this chapter.

TABLE 3.33

IMPORTANT WATER SUPPLY RESIDUALS

Pollutant	Source	Health Effects	Other Effects
Alkalinity	a) from carbonate and bicarbonate in common natural waters b) hydroxides rare in nature-- presence due to water treatment or to contamina- tion		
Aluminum	natural or in- dustrial waste	none shown for human beings	may affect laun- dries or textile manufacture
Arsenic*	rare in natural waters but found in a) weed killers b) insecticides c) industrial ef- fluent	lethal to animals at 20 mg/animal pound; harmful to some fish in quantities above 15 mg/l	
Barium	a) certain types of brines b) industrial wastes c) normal waters if very low sul- fate content	extremely pois- onous, although studies are lack- ing to determine tolerance levels	
Beryllium	from beryl crys- tal; rare in natural waters	toxic to animals possibly toxic to humans; found re- sponsible for pulmonary ail- ments of workers exposed to beryl- lium dusts	
Boron*	natural in soil but rare in water and form uncertain	not considered hazardous to humans	may affect citrus trees and other crops when in high concentrations
Bromide	a) trace element in natural wa- ters; b) industrial wastes c) natural brines		
Cadmium*	a) found in na- ture as a sulfide and impurity in zinc-lead ores b) metallurgy, electroplating, ceramics, pho- tography--in- dustrial wastes	toxic to humans	undesirable in water used for domestic, irriga- tion, and recrea- tional purposes

TABLE 3.33 (Continued)

Pollutant	Source	Health Effects	Other Effects
Calcium	common in natural waters in varying amounts--levels higher in areas of limestone,dolomite, gypsum and gysiferous shale	beneficial in small amounts but is responsible for hardness property and associated responses (see Hardness)	1) good for soil structure in irrigation 2) may cause boiler scale when present with alkalinity or sulfate
Carbon Dioxide	respiration product of aquatic plants and animals and is a byproduct of decomposition of organic matter. Acids from natural sources or pollution liberate carbon dioxide from bicarbonate	not important to man or livestock but does affect fish	corrodes calcareous material
Chloride	1) brines 2) industrial wastes 3) human and animal excreta	indicates possible pollution by human and animal wastes; gives salty taste, but known to be harmful to humans	accelerates corrosion; may damage crops
Chlorine, residual	1) products of chlorination of drinking water 2) sewage effluents 3) industrial wastes	harmless to humans (in small amounts) but might be toxic to fish depending on other variables	1) not known to be harmful to crops 2) controls bacteria 3) may harm paper manufacture
Chromium*	industrial wastes	toxic to aquatic life under some circumstances	
Cobalt	trace concentrations from natural sources	beneficial in small amounts but toxic to both plant and animal life	
Color	due only to substances in solution (animal, vegetable, mineral, industrial)	aesthetically unpleasing to humans	undesirable in most industrial waters
Copper	1) trace amounts from natural sources 2) industrial wastes 3) corroded copper pipes	1) imparts disagreeable metallic taste to water 2) harmful to some aquatic organisms	both beneficial and deleterious to crops

TABLE 3.33 (Continued)

Pollutant	Source	Health Effects	Other Effects
Cyanide	industrial effluents (from gasworks, coke ovens, steelmills, chemical industries	harmful to humans and animals	harmful to various industries
Fluoride	1) in trace amounts in natural waters (saline water from oil wells and water from areas of recent volcanic activity)	1) can produce chronic fluorosis in humans 2) may cause discoloration in teeth of children although it does reduce tooth decay	1) found only occasionally in industrial wastes and sometimes as spillage; 2) not significant in irrigation in normal concentrations
Hardness	1) solution of alkaline earth minerals from soil and rocks; 2) direct pollution by wastes	believed harmless to humans, although possibly related to urinary concretions	1) creates boiler deposits 2) forms curd with soap 3) good for irrigation
Iodide	1) trace element in natural waters 2) industrial wastes 3) some natural brines		
Iron	common in nature but rare in water	1) imparts noticeable taste and color 2) may harm fish in concentrated amounts	1) causes staining on porcelain and laundry 2) of limited use for industry
Lead*	1) rare in natural waters 2) present in industrial and mine wastes	1) cumulative poison to humans and animals 2) toxic to fish	
Lithium	1) brines and thermal water 2) industrial wastes	used in medicinal water	
Magnesium	1) in natural waters from weathering of ferromagnesian minerals and magnesium carbonate (dolomite) 2) industrial wastes from many industries	1) magnesium salts act as cathartics and diuretics 2) may cause scouring diseases among livestock	1) responsible for hardness in water and its consequences for industry 2) good for irrigation and soil structure

TABLE 3.33 (Continued)

Pollutant	Source	Health Effects	Other Effects
Manganese	common in small amounts in natural waters	1) forms deposits in higher concentrations 2) not regarded as toxically significant	limited industrial use
Molybdenum	trace amounts from weathering of molybdenite	no limiting concentration established for potable water	
Nickel	very soluble in water discharged from metalplating industries	no limiting concentration established for potable water	
Nitrogen; ammonia	more than 0.1 mg/l indicates organic pollution in natural water	1) toxic to fish depending on pH 2) not considered significant to man or livestock	
Nitrogen, nitrate*	1) fertilizers 2) human and animal wastes	may cause cyanosis due to methemoglobinemia in infants	1) injurious of dyeing of wool and silk 2) undesirable in fermenting processes
Nitrogen, nitrite	indicator or organic pollution	no limit proposed	1) undesirable for dyeing of wool and silk 2) undesirable in brewing
Nitrogen, organic	1) common in natural water from normal biological activity 2) sewage and waste from slaughterhouses and chemical plants	not pathologically significant, except to aquatic biology	
Oxygen demand (COD)	sewage or industrial wastes	can be aesthetically unpleasing due to odor imparted	1) imparts odor to textiles 2) limited concentrations required for beverages and brewing
Oxygen, dissolved (DO)	1) product of air and photosynthesis by aquatic plants 2) low levels of DO sometimes indicative of pollution in form of oxygen-demanding wastes	no adverse physiological effect-- sometimes beneficial; lack of it has adverse effect on some fish	responsible for corrosion in industry

TABLE 3.33 (Continued)

Pollutant	Source	Health Effects	Other Effects
pH	relative value indicative of acids or bases in water--modified by dissolved gases and temperature; extreme ranges indicative of industrial waste source	extremes are toxic to some forms of life; pH of potable water not important except for taste changes	1) can damage crops depending on type to be grown and physical and chemical properties of soil
Phosphorous	1) leaching of soil and rocks 2) fertilizer 3) normal decomposition of plants and animals 4) sewage 5) industrial effluents 6) phosphate-treated waters	not known to be toxic to man, animals or fish	stimulates growth of algae
Potassium	rare in natural waters	1) may be toxic to some fish 2) essential to animal nutrition	causes foaming but does not affect industrial waters
Selenium	trace amounts in water are from rocks and plants	cumulative poison to man and animals; responsible for blind staggers and alkali disease; high levels toxic to some plants	not known harmful in irrigation
Silica	from decomposition or metamorphism of silicate minerals	not significant to humans, livestock or fish	1) not important for irrigation 2) causes boiler scale
Silver	1) small amounts in natural waters 2) industrial wastes	toxic in extreme amounts	
Sodium	1) natural salts very soluble in natural water 2) industrial wastes	affects people with abnormal sodium metabolism	1) causes foaming when associated with potassium 2) harmful to soil structure
Solids, dissolved	anhydrous residues of dissolved substances in water	1) change in concentration may cause gastric disturbances; 2) high levels harmful to fish	1) maximum tolerance by industry --1000 mg/l 2) may affect irrigation

TABLE 3.33 (Continued)

Pollutant	Source	Health Effects	Other Effects
Solids, suspended	product of weathering or of wastes	gives unpleasing appearance to water when related to turbidity and color	
Strontium	trace amounts in natural waters		can impart color to water
Sulfide	result of bacterial and chemical processes--from sewage or industrial wastes	1) undesirable odor 2) toxic to some aquatic organisms	
Turbidity	reduction of transparency due to suspended particulate matter (clay, silt, organic matter)	1) affects fish-food cycle by limiting light to aquatic plants 2) imparts clouded effect to water--is associated with color	unpleasing effect for some recreation uses
Vanadium	1) common minor soil element leached into water 2) industrial wastes	possibly beneficial to human health	
Zinc	1) trace amounts in natural water 2) large amounts from industrial wastes	1) not known to be harmful to humans or livestock 2) small amounts toxic to some aquatic plants and animals 3) may harm natural purifying agents in stream	high concentrations detrimental to some crops

Source: <u>Techniques of Water-Resources Investigations of the United States Geological Survey, Book 5, Laboratory Analysis</u>. United States Department of the Interior, 1970.

2. CATEGORIES OF USE

In any assessment of water supplies, special attention must
be given to health protection for the ultimate users and intended
beneficiaries--the people. Human disease and illness are attributable to a large variety of factors associated with water and
related land resources. Major factors are discussed within the
following categories: (1) water supplies, (2) food supplies,
and (3) other environmental factors.

a. WATER SUPPLIES

As municipal water supplies are used for the domestic purposes of drinking and cooking, health and safety considerations
are directly associated with those supplies. The considerations
include epidemiological analysis, problems in public systems,
and problems in individual systems.

Epidemiological data are inadequate and do not indicate the
full extent of health damages resulting from water supply deficiencies nor do they adequately emphasize the needed remedial
measures. However, a recent review of the period 1946-1960 dis-
closed 228 outbreaks of disease or poisoning, with 25,984 cases
attributed to drinking water (Table 3.34).

More disease outbreaks occurred in private and semipublic
water systems (158) than in public water systems (70); but, because of the much larger populations served, the number of individual cases in public systems (19,928) far exceeded tha number
of cases in the private and semipublic systems (6,056). Distribution of outbreaks according to source is shown in Table 3.35.

In 1968, there was a major outbreak of salmonellosis in
which 18,000 cases were reported. The source of this disease
was a public system using groundwater without treatment by disinfection.

Epidemiological data indicate multiple causes of waterborne
disease for community or private treatment and distribution systems. An improved program for gathering epidemiological data is
badly needed. A qualitative and quantitative expansion of information would undoubtedly reveal new areas needing attention.

One of the most significant achievements in the past 100
years in the United States has been the provision of safe and
potable community water supplies. This initial achievement,
however, was followed by a sense of complacency, and deficiencies
and inadequacies in water supplies now exist. The solution to

TABLE 3.34

WATERBORNE DISEASES IN THE UNITED STATES,
1946-60

Disease	Outbreaks	Cases
	Number	Number
Gastroenteritis	126	13,630
Typhoid	39	506
Infectious hepatitis	23	930
Diarrhea	16	5,160
Shigellosis	11	5,653
Salmonellosis	4	24
Amebiasis	2	36
Other	7	45
Total........................	228	25,984

TABLE 3.35

PERCENTAGE DISTRIBUTION OF SOURCES OF WATERBORNE DISEASE
IN THE UNITED STATES, 1946-60

Source	Outbreaks	Cases
	Percent	Percent
Untreated surface water	9.6	3.2
Untreated ground water	41.7	33.9
Contamination of reservoir or cistern	1.3	0.7
Contamination of collection or conduit system	3.1	4.6
Inadequate control of treatment	15.4	41.4
Contamination of distribution system	16.7	12.9
Miscellaneous	12.2	3.3
Total	100.0	100.0

present domestic water supply problems has two aspects. First, data gathering must be improved so that present and potential problems, their scopes, and their dangers can be better defined; and, second, the necessary steps must be taken to reduce or eliminate known health hazards in our supply systems.

Figures 3.8 and 3.9 show that a substantial reduction in illness resulting from the ingestion of water contaminated with pathogenic microorganisms can occur. Melvin A. Benarde wrote in Our Precarious Habitat (1973) that for the city of Philadelphia, "there were from six thousand to ten thousand typhoid cases each year between 1890 and 1907. With the introduction in 1907 of so simple a device as sand filtration of drinking water, a precipitous reduction in illness was achieved. Six years later, the introduction of chlorination, over the strident protests of those opposed to the addition of synthetic chemicals to water, caused another abrupt drop in typhoid cases. Clearly, mechanical and chemical treatment could control waterborne disease."

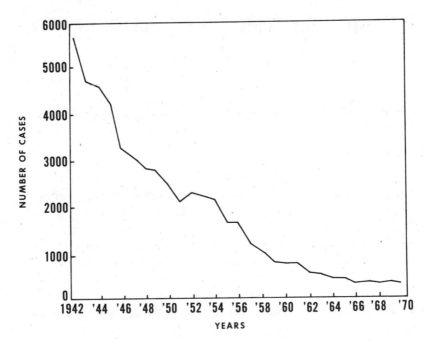

FIGURE 3.8

REPORTED CASES OF TYPHOID FEVER IN THE UNITED STATES,
1942-1970

Source: after Benarde (1973).

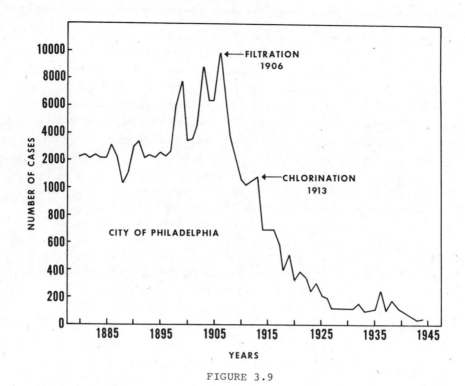

FIGURE 3.9

REDUCTION OF TYPHOID FEVER IN PHILADELPHIA
FOLLOWING TREATMENT OF THE WATER SUPPLY

Source: after Benarde (1973).

b.   WATER AND MUNICIPAL HEALTH

Waterborne disease from municipal drinking water appears to be a relatively minor problem.   Wolman argues "water-borne and water-associated diseases are at a low ebb and have been near the vanishing point for some years."   Other experts support the general conclusion, but often add that viruses can be a problem. Occasional outbreaks of gastroenteritis (intestinal flu) and hepatitis may be caused by waterborne viruses.   Such viruses can also cause polio, meningitis, rashes, and the grippe.   Viruses commonly get into water through inadequate treatment of sewage. Testing procedures for viruses are difficult to carry out, and knowledge of effects of the relatively small numbers of viruses in water supplies is limited.

The U.S. Environmental Protection Agency, Bureau of Water

Hygiene, classifies municipal water supplies serving interstate carriers--trains, planes, buses, and ships in interstate commerce. In March 1970, classification occurred for 678 cities serving 81 million persons. Three classifications are used: approved, provisionally approved, and prohibited. No supply was prohibited, but 81 cities were classified as provisionally approved, indicating the existence of some water-supply problem. Table 3.36 exhibits the distribution of these 81 cities by population size, and by three types of supply problem. Problem III

TABLE 3.36

NUMBER OF CITIES WITH WATER SUPPLY PROBLEM,
MARCH, 1970

1970 population in 000	Water Supply problem			Estimated total of U.S. cities in class[b]
	I	II	III	
	Number of cities with problem[a]			
<25	20	12	12	5,000+
25 - <100	8	12	4	600
100 - <500	5	3	3	110
500+	1	1	0	25

Water supply problems are listed in order of increasing severity:

I. Inadequate monitoring program or failure to send sampling reports to Public Health Service and/or failure to meet PHS chemical standards or provide adequate data. Note that group I includes reporting failure.

II. Low pressure in distribution system and/or inadequate cross-connection code or inspection.

III. Samples do not meet PHS bacteriological requirements and/or inadequate disinfection.

[a]Coverage here limited to 678 municipal water supplies serving interstate carriers, with total population of 81 million. Cities with problems received only "provisional approval."

[b]Estimated number in each class based on 1960 distribution. In 1960, the Census listed 4,680 urban places as having populations of 2,500 to 25,000; and 596 urban places with populations under 2,500. In the sample of cities with problems, the "under 25,000" category includes 30 cities above 2,500 and 14 below 2,500.

Sources: Water problem data from U.S. Environmental Protection Agency, Bureau of Water Hygiene, reported in Sally Lindsay "How Safe is the Nation's Drinking Water?" Saturday Review, May 2, 1970, pp.54-55. City size distribution based on U.S. Bureau of the Census, U.S. Census of Population: 1960, Vol. 1, Part A, Table 7, pp.1-13.

may be the only serious problem, since it consists of not meeting bacteriological or disinfection standards. The other problems can involve inadequate reporting or inspection.

The occurence of only 19 cities under Problem III, with 12 of those having a population less than 25,000, lends support to the argument that health problems are relatively minor. It is difficult to infer much about quality as a function of city size, but it seems reasonable to argue that trouble occurs more frequently for small cities, with little in the way of scale effects above a population of 25,000. This is based on the assumption that the 678-city sample includes all cities over 100,000 in population (135); half the cities over 25,000 (300); and the remainder from the below 25,000 category (243).

That there is often a price for progress is illustrated by municipal water quality improvement. The elimination of typhoid fever meant that young children were no longer immunized to polio through exposure to its virus in sewage contaminated water, and hence, they became susceptible to the paralytic form of the disease.

c. FOOD SUPPLIES

Man's food supplies may be contaminated by water contact during their growth period if (1) they are grown in contaminated water media, or (2) if they are irrigated with contaminated water. Experience has shown that ingestion of shellfish grown in contaminated water can result in disease, and that ingestion of raw food crops grown with the direct use of night-soil can result in enteric disease.

The earliest health hazard identified with eating raw shellfish grown in contaminated waters was typhoid fever. In recent years, however, infectious hepatitis has been the predominant known health hazard associated with their ingestion. During the four years, 1961 through 1964, four major epidemics involving more than 1,000 individual cases were attributed to ingestion of raw or partially cooked shellfish grown in contaminated waters. A significant number of isolated cases of infectious hepatitis, which continue to appear during non-epidemic periods, are thought to be attributable to this source. Better delineation of this disease aspect of shellfish production will depend on improved epidemiological surveillance and data gathering.

A cooperative Federal-State-industry program is operated for the sanitary classification of active shellfish growing areas. Table 3.37 indicates that 80% of the total acreage is fully ap-

TABLE 3.37

ACTIVE SHELLFISH GROWING AREAS

Status	Areas	Acres	
	Number	Thou.	Percent
Fully approved	388	7,211	80
Conditionally approved	40	88	1
Sub-total approved	(428)	(7,299)	(81)
Closed	401	1,752	19
Total	829	9,051	100

Source: U. S. Department of Interior: The Nation's Water Resources, 1968.

proved; 1% is conditionally approved; but that 19% is closed because those areas do not meet the sanitary standards for growing waters. Disease problems attributable to clams and oysters are often associated with unauthorized harvesting in closed areas.

In addition to known health hazards associated with shellfish, there are unknown hazards posed by the accumulation of toxic substances in the tissues of fish and shellfish.

d. OTHER ENVIRONMENTAL FACTORS

Public health aspects of domestic water supply and food crops have already been discussed generally, but there are other features of our environment associated with water and related land resources, not entirely separable from the aforementioned broad considerations, that harbor health hazards. These include solid waste disposal and provision of recreation area facilities. Improper location of solid waste disposal sites or inadequate treatment of solid wastes can contribute to surface-water and

to groundwater pollution. Good health should be assured in recognized public recreation areas in much the same way it is in
permanent communities. A safe potable water supply, vector control, and adequate waste disposal facilities are essential in
such areas because, as the number of picnickers and campers utilizing these areas increases, the health hazards and the potentials for disease outbreaks increase. It should be recognized,
however, that seasonal operation and a variable population are
two recreation area features which make public health protection
more complicated.

In the future, air pollution and radiological hazards may
become significant problems associated with water and related
land resources development. Expansion of facilities using radioactive materials and increasing industrialization along the
Nation's waterways, together with increasing knowledge of the
interrelationships between elements of the environment, portend
new dimensions for public health. Today, the primary problem
with regard to public health aspects of water and related land
resources is that insufficient information and data exist to de-
lineate and quantify many of the factors of health significance.

Categories of pollution can directly influence the condition
of a city's water supply. For example a 1968 report by Rodney
Cummins for the Department of Health, Education and Welfare, Effects of Solid Waste Disposal on Water Quality, demonstrated how
solid wastes disposal can directly and indirectly contaminate
surface water and ground water supplies. Surface sources of water for leaching in a finished landfill include rainfall, runoff,
and irrigation. Subsurface sources are high ground water levels
and breaks in water mains and sewers.

Major factors involved in the introduction of contaminants
through the use of land disposal sites are: infiltration and
percolation, solid wastes decomposition processes, gas production
and movement, leaching, groundwater travel and direct runoff.

These factors may also be examined from the standpoint of
three basic mechanisms for the contamination of groundwater:
direct, horizontal leaching of refuse by groundwater; vertical
leaching by percolating water; and transfer by diffusion and con-
vection of gases produced during decomposition.

These mechanisms and factors may be combined at random and
work together. Each of the factors is important and may have an
effect upon water quality. The retention or spread of any pro-

ducts from these factors and mechanisms is determined by the particular meteorologic, geologic, and hydrologic conditions at the
landfill site.

(i)   INFILTRATION AND PERCOLATION

Infiltration and percolation of rainfall and runoff can
produce leachates that may cause groundwater contamination.
Flooding of surface water and saturation of the solid wastes by
this process are also factors that must be considered. To produce contamination, possible pollutants must have a means of access to an aquifer.

(ii)   SOLID WASTE DECOMPOSITION PROCESSES

Many factors, such as time, composition, availability of
oxygen, temperature, moisture, and salinity, will affect decomposition of solid wastes. Decomposition of the organic constituents by bacterial action results in a broad array of chemical
and biochemical products available for potential distribution in
a water system.

(iii)   GAS PRODUCTION AND MOVEMENT

Gas production is closely related to solid wastes decomposition. Aerobic action produces a rise in temperature, water
(H_2O), ammonia (NH_3), and carbon dioxide (CO_2), which is heavier
than air and remains in the fill. Carbon dioxide and water combine to make carbonic acid (H_2CO_3), which is a very weak acid.
The ammonia, which is oxidized to nitrates and/or nitrites and
water, is always present.

Anaerobic action, through a deficiency in oxygen, produces
a rise in temperature and creates ammonia and methane gas.

(iv)   LEACHING AND GROUNDWATER MOVEMENT

Three conditions must exist in order to have contamination
by the process of leaching and groundwater travel: the site must
be over adjacent to, or in an aquifer; there must be saturation
within the fill; leached fluids must be produced, and the leachate
must be capable of entering an aquifer.

When leaching does occur, the groundwater in the immediate
vicinity of the fill, approximately 1,000 feet downstream, can
become polluted and unfit for human and animal consumption, or
for industrial and irrigation uses.

(v)   DIRECT RUNOFF

The direct surface runoff of water from a solid waste disposal site may affect water quality. The effect of the runoff

will vary according to the source of the water, its quality, the quantity of solid wastes, the site, and the operational conditions.

Evidence that physical characteristics, biological quality, and chemical composition of surrounding waters are affected by quality and quantity of solid wastes conditions is well known. These factors that govern water quality will be discussed, presuming that the disposed solid wastes are not in direct contact with the water.

(vi) PHYSICAL CHARACTERISTICS

Physical characteristics of water include turbidity, odor, taste, and color. Turbidity would be initially present in both surface runoff and leachate, but usually would be a problem only in the immediate vicinity of the disposal site. The taste and odor of water contaminated by solid wastes may be impaired under anaerobic conditions where hydrogen sulfide is produced. Color may be present because of the heterogeneous nature of solid wastes, and, in most cases, it would be removed by natural purification processes.

(vii) BIOLOGICAL QUALITY

Biological water quality refers to bacteria present in the water, usually by leaching. Bacteria normally do not persist in underground water in the direction of flow for more than fifty yards, and seemingly important bacteria are seldom found below four-foot depths, and never below seven feet, even in highly permeable soil. The pumped recharge of polluted water to underground aquifers has been shown to result in travel of bacteria for less than 1,000 feet.

(viii) CHEMICAL COMPOSITION

Solid wastes contain mineral and organic substances in quantities capable of causing gross pollution of underground water supplies. The finer the composition, or grain, and the greater the surface area of the waste material, the heavier will be the potential concentration of chemicals in the leachate.

Chlorides and other inorganics do persist in water and are only reduced in concentration by dilution with unaffected water. Free and saline ammonia also show appreciable increase in water traveling underground, and are slowly oxidized and diluted.

Organic matter in wastes undergoes both aerobic and anaerobic decomposition, thereby producing large volumes of carbon dioxide (CO_2) and methane (CH_4), with small amounts of ammonia

(NH_3) and hydrogen sulfide (H_2S).

Hydrogen sulfide has an offensive taste and odor, but, by dilution with water containing oxygen and/or by diffusing atmospheric oxygen, the sulfide is oxidized to tasteless and odorless sulfur and sulfates.

The effect of carbon dioxide, which increases water hardness, and the effects of ammonia, which on oxidation increases the nitrate content, are among the most significant chemical characteristics of decomposing organic matter in a landfill operation. The nitrate-nitrogen thus produced can exceed by 10 to 20 times the safe level for consumption by infants.

The methane has a low solubility and diffuses out of the refuse site, presenting little or no contamination potential to water.

Carbon dioxide has a high solubility and combines with water to form carbonic acid with an associated increase in hardness. The acid formed will dissolve magnesium, iron from tin cans, lime from calcareous materials and deposits, and other substances, all of which are undesirable at high concentration in water resources.

3. EFFECTS ON THE RESOURCE SYSTEM

In 1968 the National Technical Advisory Committee presented their Water Quality Criteria. This document notes that while oxygen requirements of aquatic life have been studied extensively most of the research on freshwater organisms has been devoted to fish. It is assumed that fish depend upon other aquatic species for food and would not remain in an area with an inadequate food supply. The Report points out that it is not sufficient to know how long an animal can resist death by asphyxiation at low dissolved oxygen concentrations; one must know the oxygen concentration necessary to permit an aquatic population to thrive. This data requirement includes oxygen needs for egg development, for newly hatched larvae, for normal growth and activity, and for completing all stages of the reproductive cycle and the life cycle. The Committee recommends that for a diversified warmwater biota, including game fish, daily DO concentration should be above 5 mg/l, assuming that there are normal seasonal and daily variations above this concentration. For cold water biota, it is desireable that DO concentrations be at or near saturation. This is especially important in spawning areas where DO levels must not be below 7 mg/l at any time. For good growth and the general well-being of trout, salmon, and other species of the biota, DO concentrations should not be below 6 mg/l.

a. ORGANIC WASTES AND BIOCHEMICAL OXYGEN DEMAND

Natural organic wastes such as vegetation decompose by bacterial action. Bacteria attack wastes dumped into rivers and lakes, using up oxygen in the process. Thus organic wastes are measured in units of biochemical oxygen demand (BOD), the amount of oxygen needed to decompose them. Expressed most simply, BOD is defined as "the amount of oxygen that is needed by any unit volume of water to oxidize all organic matter within it."

Certain aerobic bacteria which require free oxygen will break down organic matter to relatively harmless, stable, and odorless end products in well diluted oxygenated water. This process allows the stream to recover naturally from the effects of small pollution loads, and is sometimes described and "self-purification." The oxidation reactions which occur are represented on the left side of Table 3.38. When excessive pollution by organic matter causes depletion of dissolved oxygen, the remaining organic and dead fish are acted upon by a different set of bacteria which do not require free oxygen. Anaerobic bacteria utilize combined oxygen in the form of nitrates, sulphates, phosphates, and organic compounds. The anaerobic decomposition of organic matter results in a different set of end products, among which methane and hydrogen sulfide are quite objectionable. The reactions are shown on the right side of Table 3.38. Putrefication is the general term applied to an anaerobic decomposition of organic matter and is one of the more easily recognized indicators of water pollution in its advanced stages.

Table 3.39 illustrates the difference between two urban land uses using a five-day BOD measure in Chicago (American Public Works Association, 1969). When dissolved oxygen falls below a certain critical level (in the case of many fish about 5 ppm), mortality may occur. If the waste loads are so great that large amounts of oxygen are spent in their decomposition, certain types of fish can no longer live in that body of water. A pollution-resistant, lower order of fish, such as carp, replaces the original fish population.

Obviously, BOD is increased by the addition of raw sewage to lakes and rivers; in fact, it is increased by any ingredient

TABLE 3.38

BACTERIAL REACTIONS IN WATER POLLUTION

Aerobic Reactions	Anaerobic Reactions
Carbon, $C \rightarrow CO_2$ + carbonates + bicarbonates	$C \rightarrow$ organic $\rightarrow CH_4 \rightarrow CO_2$ acids methane
Nitrogen, $N \rightarrow NH_3 \rightarrow HNO_2 \rightarrow$ ammonia nitrous acid ** HNO_3 nitric acid **	$N \rightarrow$ amino $\rightarrow NH_3$ + amines acids
Sulfur, $S \rightarrow H_2SO_4$ sulfuric acid **	$S \rightarrow H_2S$ + organic S compound
Phosphorus, $P \rightarrow H_3PO_4$	$P \rightarrow PH_3$ + organic P compound

TABLE 3.39

BOD CONCENTRATION OF STORM WATER
HELD IN SELECTED CATCH BASINS*

Land Use	BOD in mg/liter
Commercial	225
Commercial	160
Commercial	150
Residential	50
Residential	85

*Source: Modified from p.85, American Public Works
Association (1969)

which may utilize oxygen. In this respect, increasing urbanization is particularly critical. The hydrological effects of
increasing urbanization increase volume and speed of storm water
runoff, increase peak flows and flooding; increase sediment loads
and decrease groundwater recharge (Turk, 1970). A recent study
of Lubbock, Texas revealed that storm water drainage had an average BOD concentration equivalent to secondary sewage treatment
effluent (Brownlee, et. al., 1970).

TABLE 3.40

CONSTITUENT CONCENTRATIONS FOUND IN THE RUNOFF
FROM AN URBAN AREA IN CINCINNATI, OHIO

Constituent	Range in Values	Mean Storm Values
Turbidity (J.u.)	30 - 1,000	176
Color (C.u.)	10 - 460	87
pH	5.3 - 8.7	7.5
Alkalinity (mg/l.)	10 - 210	59
Total hardness (as $CaCO_3$) (mg/l.)	19 -, 364	81
Chloride (mg/l.)	3 - 428	12
SS (mg/l.)	5 - 1,200	227
VSS (mg/l.)	1 - 290	57
COD (mg/l.)	20 - 610	111
BOD (mg/l.)	1 - 173	17
$\Sigma N+$ (mg/l.)	0.3 - 7.5	3.1
Inorganic N (mg/l.)	0.1 - 3.4	1.0
Hydrolyzable PO_4 (mg/l.)	<0.02 - 7.3	1.1
Organic chlorine (g/l.)[‡]	0.38 - 4.72	1.70
Coliform organisms number per 100 ml	2,900 - 460,000	------

*January and February 1963 not included.
+Arithmetic sum of the four forms of nitrogen.
‡From 11 storms, August 1963 to February 1964.

Source: Berry and Horton (1974).

b. EUTROPHICATION

Several case studies have demonstrated that while etrophica-
tion is a natural process resulting from drainage containing nutrients, drainage from urban sources can accelerate the process.
Tables 3.40, 3.41, and 3.42 suggest what the additional increments might be.

c. HEAT

The amount of dissolved oxygen is affected by water temperature thereby influencing aquatic life processes. Additionally,
temperature is critical to chemical and biochemical reactions.
Heat pollution influences self-purification of streams, recovery

TABLE 3.41

NUTRIENTS IN URBAN STREET DRAINAGE IN
SEATTLE, WASHINGTON

Type of Street	Antecedent Rainfall in inches (one week)	Nitrogen (mq/l.) Total Kjel. N/Nitrates		Phosphorus (ppb) Sol./Total	
Residential	0.0	6.68	0.65	14	166
Major Highway	0.0	9.06	2.24	54	352
Major Highway	0.0	7.45	2.80	72	404
Arterial St.	0.0	8.01	0.52	14	81
Residential	0.55	0.39	0.02	70	98
Major Highway	0.55	0.91	0.03	08	21
Arterial St.	0.55	0.22	0.12	20	21
Residential	0.78	2.78	1.10	16	154
Arterial St.	0.78	1.43	0.29	10	108

Source: modified from Sylvester (1960).

TABLE 3.42

NUTRIENTS IN SEWAGE

Nutrient	Concentration, ppm
Nitrogen	20 - 50
NH_3	7 - 40
NO_3	0 - 4
NO_2	0 - .3
Organic	3 - 42
Carbon	66 - 176
Soluble Phosphorus	1 - 13
Potassium	13 - 44

Source: Bartsch (1961), using data from Fitzgerald and
Rohlich (1958).

rates from organic pollution, the oxygen-carrying capacity of a stream, and anaerobic decomposition.

d. DISSOLVED AND SUSPENDED SOLIDS

Dissolved solids posing pollution and health threats are pesticides, herbicides, salt and detergents. Salt used for snow removal, detergents containing ABS (alkyl benxene sulfonate), LAS (linear alkylate sulfonate) and forms of phosphates are common examples. Suspended solids include sediments and street litter. The intensities of both dissolved and suspended solids as additive features to a given state of water quality can be seen from the following examples of cities using salt for snow control, detergents, and the amounts of urban street sediment yield.

In northern cities large quantities of salt are used for snow control. This can be an appreciable pollutant from street drainage (Veissman, 1969). Typical applications vary widely, from 100 to 2,000 pounds per lane mile, yet several states may apply as much as twenty tons per lane mile (APWA, 1969), potentially increasing the salinity of water supplies.

Some detergents used to contain ABS (alkyl benzene sulfonate) which does not break down. It therefore could travel long distances causing foam in streams (Swenson and Baldwin, 1965). The sight problem has been corrected by the use of the new chemical called LAS (linear alkylate sulphonate), but pollutants now exist in the form of phosphates from detergents still on the market.

The major sources of suspended materials from urban areas are sediment yield and street litter. In a Chicago street sweeping survey the amount of street refuse for eighteen handswept test areas over a ten-week period in 1967 ranged from 0.5 lbs. to 8.0 lbs./110 ft. of linear feet per day. The average amount of street refuse for the test areas was 2.4 lbs./day/100 ft. of curb for single family area, 3.5 lbs./day/100 ft. of curb for multiple family areas, and 4.7 lbs./day/100 ft. of curb for commercial areas (APWA, 1969, p. 49). The components of street litter from the sweeping were, in order, dirt (65%), rock (10%), paper (7%), smaller amounts of glass, wood, and metal, and extremely variable amounts of vegetation (American Public Works Association, 1969, pp. 46-47). The Chicago study suggests that street litter can add significantly to the impact of urban areas on water quality. However, the study also highlights the need for systematic studies of these effects in terms of city size, location, functions, and climatic factors.

e.   BACTERIAL AND VIRAL POLLUTANTS

In addition to the previously mentioned pollutants bacteria and viruses are introduced to water bodies and constitute actual or potential health hazards. Especially of concern are coliform and streptococcus. Serious hazards, of course, accompany flood waters and storm runoff from urban areas.

4.   WATER POLLUTION AND ITS RELATION TO THE URBAN ENVIRONMENT

In summary there are three aspects of water pollution vital to an understanding of the problem:
- types of pollutants
- generation of sources
- short and long term effects.

The types of pollution which threaten our waterways include:

Oxygen-Demanding Materials--Such as are found in sewage and industrial wastes. These reduce the level of dissolved oxygen necessary to sustain aquatic life and increase the concentration of bacteria.

Disease-Bearing Agents--From raw or partly-treated human and animal wastes. These threaten all forms of life.

Plant Nutrients--From sources such as sewage effluent. Such materials may lead to excessive growth of algae and weeds through over enrichment and premature aging of the watercourse (eutrophication).

Inorganic and Synthetic Organic Chemicals--Including oil, pesticides, and detergents. These materials are often toxic to aquatic and to human users.

Sediment--From land runoff. Destructive to bottom organisms, and interference with plant photosynthesis may result.

Heat--Imparted to a waterway by a power plant or industrial process cooling water discharge. This can modify or even destroy the entire aquatic ecology.

Major sources of water pollution include municipal wastes, direct industrial wastes, and urban runoff.

Municipal Wastes--Municipal wastes rank first in terms of pollution sources affecting the country and specifically the inner-city populace.

Municipal wastes are significant because they contain: large amounts of organic materials which lower the dissolved oxygen content of the water, large concentrations of bacteria and virus representing a potential health hazard, and nutrients that accelerate eutrophication of rivers, lakes, and esturaries.

Most municipal systems handle waste from residential, commercial, and industrial establishments. Nationally, about 55% of the wastes processed by municipal treatment plants comes from homes and businesses and about 45% from industries.

As of 1968, an estimated 50% of the biochemical oxygen demand (BOD) in municipal sewage was produced by industry.

Direct Industrial Wastes--In addition to discharges into municipal systems, industry adds to the pollution problem in inner-city areas by discharging large volumes of untreated or partly-treated wastes directly into our watercourses. The toxic wastes that industry adds to our waters include oils, metals, pesticides, poisons, dyes, and chemical catalysts that can strain a sewage treatment plant to the breaking point. The output of industrial wastes is growing several times faster than the volume of sanitary sewage. Over half the volume of wastes discharged to water comes from four major industry groups--paper manufacturing, organic chemicals, petroleum refinery, and basic steel production.

Other Urban Wastes--In addition to sewered municipal and industrial wastes, other urban runoff, such as from land erosion, is a serious source of water pollution which must be controlled to achieve water quality standards. In large metropolitan regions, where water-based recreational de-

mand is especially high, control of "other urban wastes"
will be the keystone in meeting water quality standards and
preventing closure of beaches during wet weather flows.

Pollution from these sources produce both short-term and
long-term detrimental effects:

Endangered Health--The physical effects of polluted water
on the individual range from bad taste and minor discom-
forts to major diseases causing death. Bacteria in polluted
waters may cause typhoid fever and kidney disease. Mercury, arsenic, and other chemicals in water may be fatal to
those drinking the waters. Nitrates have been found to
interact in the stomach with compounds in drugs, food fla-
voring, or decaying meat in ways that may endanger health.

Deteriorated Water Supply Quality--Small amounts of poten-
tially-toxic materials, the effects of which have not been
conclusively determined, are not removed by many drinking
water treatment plants. This pollution, in turn, increases
the costs of tretingg water at intake for domestic uses.
Several forms of water pollution, such as algae, adversely
affect the taste and odor of water; and, for reasons of
taste and custom, people are often reluctant to draw water
from such sources.

Reduced Recreational Resources--The reduction of recreational
opportunities for the public represents a widespread consequence of water pollution. Such pollution effects as floating
solids, gas bubbles, odors, and oil spills make boating add
water skiing unpleasant. If bacterial levels are sufficiently high, the health of water sportsmen can be endangered.
When the count reaches certain levels, public health authorities close beaches. Inadequately disinfected wastes from
municipalities and overflows from combined sewers are principal bacterial polluters in populated areas. The highest
water quality is needed to maintain populations of certain
types of game fish. When the quality of water declines,
fish die. For example, the trout, the most popular fresh
water sport fish, requires cold water and dissolved oxygen
levels in excess of five parts per million to live and reproduce. Although trout and other fish can die from all
types of pollution, the majority of fish kills are caused
by lack of dissolved oxygen, pesticides, and by toxic
wastes from industrial operations.

Decreased Aesthetic Appeal--Pollution can cause unpleasant
odors when algae clog the water or when anaerobic conditions
exist. Also, sediment, which can turn water murky and dark,
reduces the aesthetic appeal.

4   SOLID WASTES

I. RESIDUALS MEASUREMENT SYSTEMS

1. TYPES OF REFUSE

At present, there exists no systematic measurement of solid
wastes in the United States. While private haulers may estimate
numbers of truck loads, and some municipal landfills may actually
measure in cubic yards and tons, the vast majority of disposal
agencies and sites do not measure or weigh quantities of solid
wastes received. Part of the problem lies in the diversity of
the types of solid wastes which are produced (Table 4.1). Part
also lies in the variety of sources and the diverse methods of
disposal that have been institutionalized.

There are four municipal sources of solid wastes:

Domestic Refuse: includes all those types which normally
originate in the residential household or apartment house.

Municipal Refuse: embraces all the types which originate
on municipally owned property. These include street
sweepings and litter, catch-basin dirt, refuse from parks,
playgrounds, zoos, schools and other institutional buildings;
solid wastes from sewerage systems.

Commercial Refuse: includes all solid wastes which originate in businesses operated for profit such as office
buildings, stores, markets, theaters and privately owned
clinics, hospitals, and other institutional buildings.

Industrial Refuse: includes all solid wastes which result
from industrial processes and manufacturing operations
such as factories, processing plants, repair and cleaning
establishments, refineries and rendering plants.

Because of this diversity by type and source, no one disposal
site handles all solid wastes for any bounded area, contributing
to the lack of measurement by any agency or agencies.

2. SURVEILLANCE NETWORKS

a. NATIONAL

Because of the lack of reliable information on solid wastes,
the Environmental Protection Agency undertook a National Survey
of Community Solid Waste Practices in 1968. This is the only
national study of solid wastes which has been completed in the
United States to date. The survey was composed of three ques-

TABLE 4.1

SOLID WASTE SOURCES AND CONSTITUENTS

Municipal Refuse

Source	Waste	Composition	Means of Treatment or Disposal
Households, restaurants, institutions, stores, markets	Garbage	Wastes from preparation, cooking and serving of food; market wastes from handling, storage and sale of food	Grinding, incineration, landfill, composting, hog feeding
	Rubbish	Paper, cartons, boxes, barrels, wood, excelsior, tree branches, yard trimmings, wood furniture, bedding, dunnage, metals, tin cans, metal furniture, dirt, glass, crockery, minerals	Salvage, incineration, landfill, composting, dumping
	Ashes	Residue from fires	Landfill, dumping
Streets, sidewalks, alleys, vacant lots	Street refuse	Sweepings, dirt, leaves, catch basin dirt, contents of litter receptacles, bird excreta	Incineration, landfill, dumping
	Dead animals	Cats, dogs, horses, cows, marine animals, etc.	Incineration, rendering, explosive destruction
	Abandoned vehicles	Unwanted cars and trucks left on public property	Salvage, dumping
Factories, power plants	Industrial wastes	Food processing wastes, boiler house cinders, lumber scraps, metal scraps, shavings, etc.	Incineration, landfill, salvage
Urban renewal, express-ways, etc.	Demolition wastes	Lumber, pipes, brick masonry, asphaltic material and other construction materials from razed buildings and structures; bat guano, pigeon excreta	Incineration, landfill, dumping, salvage
New construction, remodeling	Construction wastes	Scrap lumber, pipe, concrete, other construction materials	Incineration, landfill, dumping, salvage
Household, hotels, hos-pitals, institutions, stores, industry	Special wastes	Hazardous solids and liquids, ex-plosives, pathologic wastes, ra-dioactive wastes	Incineration, landfill, burial, salvage
Sewage treatment plants, lagoons, septic tanks	Sewage treat-ment residue	Solids from coarse screening and grit chambers, sludge	Incineration, landfill, composting, fertilizing

Agriculture Refuse

Farms, ranches, live-stock feeders, and growers	Refuse	Same as Municipal Refuse	Same as Municipal Refuse
Farms, ranches, live-stock feeders and growers	Crop residue	Cornstalks, tree pruning, pea vines, sugarcane stalks (bagasse), green drop, cull fruit, cull vegetables, rice, barley, wheat and oats stubble, rice hulls. Fertilizer and insecticide residue	Plowed back into the land, incineration, stock feed.
	Animal manure (Paunch ma-nure	Lignaceous and fibrous organic matter, nitrogen, phosphorous, potassium, volatile acids, pro-teins, fats, carbohydrates	Fertilizer, composting Stock feed
	Poultry ma-nure	Same as animal manure	Fertilizer, composting, lagooning

TABLE 4.1 (Cont'd)

Industrial Wastes

Source	Waste	Characteristics	Composition	Means of Treatment or Disposal
Food and kindred product industries	Fruit, vegetable and citrus		Hull, rinds, cores, seeds, vines, leaves tops, roots, trimmings, pulps, peelings, hydrochloric acid (used in processing)	Screening, lagooning, soil absorption, spray irrigation, reclamation
Canning	Cobs, shells, stalks, straws	High in suspended solids (liquid waste) colloidal and dissolved organic matter		
Vegetable oil refining			"Still pitch"--tarry residue, fatty acids, sodium hydroxide, trichol-ethylene	Reclamation
Dairy	Dilutions of whole milk, separated milk, buttermilk and whey	High in dissolved organic matter, mainly protein, fat, and lactose	N, CaO, K_2O, P_2O_5, Fe, Cl, SiO_2	Aeration, trickling filter, activated sludge
Slaughtering of animals, rendering of bones and fats, residues in condensates, grease and wash water	Manure, paunch manure, blood, flesh, fat particles, hair, bones, oil, grease		N, NH_3, NH_2, NO_3, NaCl	Reclamation, screening, trickling filter, chlorination
Breweries and distilleries	Spent grain, spent hops, yeast, alkalis, amyl alcohol, dissolved organic solids containing nitrogen and fermented starches	High in dissolved organic solids, containing nitrogen and fermented starches or their products	Amyl alcohol (from processing)	Recovery, centrifugation and evaporation, trickling filtration, stock feeds, fertilizer
Pharmaceutical	Microorganisms, organic chemicals	High in suspended and dissolved organic matter, including vitamins	Aniline, phenols	Evaporation, incineration, stock feeds
Textile mill products	Textiles, i.e., cotton, wool, and silk	Highly alkaline, colored, high BOD and temperature, high suspended solids	H_2SO_4, NaOH, aniline chlorine Starch, malt, tin & iron salts, dyes, bleach, fibers, minerals	Neutralization, precipitation, trickling, filtration, aeration, recovery
Cooking of fibers, desizing of fabrics		Same as textile mill products	For complete list of chemicals used in textile industry, see reference	
	Rayon, other man-made materials, i.e., Acrilan, Dynel, Orlon, Nylon, etc.	Acidic, alkaline, inorganic	Sulfides and polysulfides, colloidal sulfur, NaOH, H_2SO_4, $ZnSO_4$, HCl, $NaHSO_4$, H_2S, $CaSO_4$, acrylonitrile, phenol, HNO_3, ammonia, adiponitrile, hexamethylenediamine, sodium carbonate, alcohols, ketones	Reclamation, neutralization, trickling, filtration, lagooning
Laundry		High turbidity, and alkalinity	Spent soaps, synthetic detergents, bleaches, dirt and grease	Screening, precipitation, flotation, adsorption
Lumber and wood products (forest, mills, factories)	Pulp and paper	High or low pH; colored; high suspended, colloidal, and dis-	Sawmill usage (sawdust, shavings, wood chips), wood flour;	Reclamation, incineration, soil conditioning

TABLE 4.1 (cont'd)

Source	Waste	Characteristics	Composition	Means of Treatment, or Disposal
Lumber and wood products (forest, mills, factories) (continued)		solved solids; inorganic fillers	soda, sulfate, sulfite	
	Organic, inorganic, toxic, suspended and dissolved solids of lignin, resins, soda, ash, fiber, adhesive, ink, fats, soaps, tallow		Sodium lignate, sodium resinate, complex organo-sulfur compounds, some fiber in relatively dilute solutions, sulfites, mercaptans, sulfides, disulfides, sulfates, terpenes, carbohydrates, CaO, SO_2, N, PO_4	Reclamation, settling, lagooning, biological treatment, aeration
Chemical plants (general)		Toxic	Acrylonitrile, aniline, amyl alcohol, carbon disulfide, carbon tetrachloride, chlorine, hydrogen cyanide, hydrochloric acid, phenol, sulfuric acid, touene, xylene, dinitrobenzene, dimethyl sulfate, ethylene, chlorohydrin, benzene, metallic compounds of lead, arsenic and mercury	Reclamation, lagooning and all other methods of treatment
	Fumes and/or dust		Arsenic	
	Particulate clouds and dusts		Mn, Va, Cd, Be, Fe, Zn, and their oxides	
	Weed killer		2-4-D	Sewage
	Cyanide waste	Toxic to aquatic life	Cyanides	Ponding
	Plastics, synthetic resins		Acrolein, acrylonitrile, formaldehyde, phenols, trichlorethylene	Reclamation, incineration
Aircraft manufacturing industry	Cd and Cr+	Traces of metals	Cd and Cr+	Leaching pits
Waste treatment plants	Well-digested sludge	Blackish, amorphous, nonplastic material	Mg, Ca, Zn, Cr, Sn, Mn, Fe, Cu, Pb	Anaerobic decomposition of organic waste solids
Petroleum industry	Spent chemical	Liquid wastes with oil, acid and alkaline solutions, inorganic salts, organic acids and phenols, etc.	Clays, H_2SO_4, H_3PO_4	Streams
Drilling		Oil, brine, chemicals	Sodium, calcium, magnesium, chlorine, SO_4, bromine	Separation, evaporation, lagooning
Storage	Muds, salt, oils, natural gas			Separation, evaporation, lagooning
Distillation	Acid sludges, miscellaneous oils	Insoluble organic and inorganic salts, sulfur compounds, sulfonic and napthenic acids, insoluble mercaptides,	Na_2CO_3, $(NH_4)_2S$, Na_2S sulfates, acid sulfates, H_2S, NaOH, $Ca(OH)_2$, $(NH_4)_2SO_4$, NH_4Cl, phenols	Settling, filtration, reclamation, evaporation

TABLE 4.1 (Cont'd)

Source	Waste	Characteristics	Composition	Means of Treatment or Disposal
Distillation (cont'd)		oil-water emulsions, soaps, waxy emulsions, oxides of metal, phenolic compounds		
Treating		See "Distillation"	See "Distillation"; also lead, copper, calcium	Reclamation, settling filtration, evaporation, neutralization
Recovery		See "Distillation"; also organic esters	See "Distillation"; also iron	See "Treating"
Leather and leather products	Tanneries	Organic and inorganic, high BOD--lime, sludge, hair, fleshing, tan liquor, bleach liquor, salt, blood, dirt, chrome	Chromium, sulfuric acid, nitrogen, $CaCO_3$, D_2O_5, K_2O, Fe	Sedimentation, lagooning
Energy-producing industry	Fly-ash	Hollow spheres of fused or partially fused silicate glass or as small solid spheres of fused silicates, iron oxides or silica, unburned carbon and mineral	Silicates, iron oxide, silica	Sold for use in concrete, landfills, etc.
Pulverized coal-fired plants; stoker-fired, cyclone-fired plants; and wet-bottom pulverized coal-fired plants				
Electrical industry	Ash	Dust	Silicates and aluminates of Fe, Cu, Mg with small percentages of Na, K	
Metal finishing industry	Pickling and washing liquors	Toxic, waste waters	Cu and Cu alloys	Sewage
	Acid wastes	Harmful to aquatic life, salts of metals	Cu, Ni, Zn, Cr, Fe	Sewage
Rubber and miscellaneous products	Rubber	High BOD, odor, high suspended solids, variable pH, high chlorides	Sulfuric acid, trichlorethylene, xylene, amyl alcohol, aniline benzene, chromium formaldehyde	Aeration, chlorination, sulfonation, biological treatment
Washing of latex; coagulated rubber; exuded impurities from crude rubber; rejects, cuttings, mold flashings, trims, excess extrusions	Scraps from molding, extrusion, rejects, trimming and finishing			
Explosives Washing TNT and guncotton for purification, washing and pickling of cartridges		TNT, colored, acid, odorous, and contains organic acids and alcohol from powder and cotton, metals, acid, oils and soaps	H_2SO_4, HNO_3, NO_2SO_3, picric acid, TNT isomers, copper, zinc, nitrogen, toluene	Dilution, neutralization, lagooning, flotation, precipitation, aeration, chlorination
Phosphates and phosphorous	Washing, screening, floating rock, condenser bleed-off	Clays, slimes, tallows, low pH, high suspended solids	Phosphorous, silica, flouride	Settling, clarification (mechanical), lagooning

TABLE 4.1 (Cont'd)

Source	Waste	Characteristics	Composition	Means of Treatment or Disposal
Fertilizers			Nitrogen, phosphorous, potassium, sulfuric acid, traces of other chemicals	
Coke by-products	Slag from ovens, ammonia still waste, spent acids and phenols	Suspended solids, volatile suspended solids, organic and NH_3-N, phenol, cyanide, acids, alkalis	Ammonia, benzene, H_2SO_4, phenol	Discharged to sewers, dumped, incineration
Industrial, not otherwise identified	Inorganic industrial waste or stabilization	Metals and compounds thereof	Na, K, Ca, chlorides, sulfates, bicarbonates, nitrates, phosphates, fluorides, borates, chromates, etc.	
	Metallic fumes and dusts		Pb, Va, As, Be and compounds thereof	
	Industrial wastes	Mineral fines	Chromates, heavy metals	Underground aquifers
	Laboratory wastes		Metallic ions, phenolics, cyanides, oils, synthetic fibers, pharmaceuticals, rubber chemicals	Landfill or dump
	Industrial wastes	Toxic metals	Pb, Be	
Insecticides	Washing and purification of products	High organic matter, toxic, acidic Chlorinated hydrocarbons: Toxaphene, benzene, hexachloride, DDT, aldrin, endrin, dieldrin, lindane, chlordane, methoxychlor, heptachlor	Carbon, hydrogen, chlorine, carbon disulfide, carbon tetrachloride	See Chemical plants (general)
		Organic phosphorous compounds: parathion, Malathion, phosdrin, tetraethyl, pyrophosphate	Phosphorous, oxygen, carbon, hydrogen, carbon disulfide, carbon tetrachloride	
		Other organic compounds:	Carbonates, dinitrophenols, organic sulfur compounds, organic mercurials, rotenone, pyrethrum, nicotine, strychnine	
		Inorganic substances	Copper sulfate, arsenate of lead, compounds of chlorine and fluorine, thallium sulfate, sodium fluoroacetate	

Source: Thrift G. Hanks, Solid Waste/Disease Relationships, U.S. Department of Health, Education and Welfare, Solid Waste Program, 1967, Appendix B, pp. 160-167.

tionnaires which were distributed to 33 states and the District
of Columbia, covering solid wastes generated by 46% of the population of the United States (6,259 communities), of which about
75% is considered to be urban: (a) The Community description
Report, which covered four broad areas: storage, collection,
disposal, budget; (b) The Land Disposal Report; (c) the Facility
Investigation Report. Each of the latter two reports focussed
upon three main areas: descriptions of site, quantitative data,
and fiscal data. All states were not involved in the survey and
the degree of participation of those states that were included
varied greatly. For example, the state of Illinois submitted
only 19 questionnaires, whereas other states undertook complete
surveys.

b.   STATE

As provided by the 1965 Solid Waste Disposal Act, grant
monies are available to individual states for solid waste
planning. Most of the planning reports completed to date
lack data, however.

c.   SUB-STATE REGIONS

Similarly, regional reports have been published using grant
monies provided under the 1965 Solid Waste Act. These reports
cover metropolitan regions (e.g. Louisville, Ky. - Ind. Metropolitan Region Solid Waste Disposal Study). Few of these have
been published, however, and most of them focus on the actual
disposal techniques and operations rather than the amounts and
compositions of solid wastes. Even when good data have been
produced, they tend not to be comparable with data in other reports, however. Thus, the only data which are comparable from
one region to another are those provided by the 1968 National
Survey. Unfortunately, because of economic cuts by the Federal
government,   the publication of even these data by regions and
states has been terminated, after publications for only four
states. Likewise, the acquisition of specific data from the
computer memory bank may be limited as of mid-summer of 1973
because of the reduction of E.P.A.'s Solid Waste Program staff.
No updating of the 1968 data has taken place, nor is any planned.

II. GENERATION FACTORS

1. SOURCES OF SOLID WASTES

Every aspect of urban life generates solid wastes. Combining all sources, it is estimated that 3.5 billion pounds of
solid wastes are being produced in the United States each year
(Table 4.2).

TABLE 4.2

TOTAL SOLID WASTES PRODUCED IN THE U.S.

Household, Commercial, Municipal	250 million tons/yr.
Industrial	110 million tons/yr.
	360 million tons/yr.
Agriculture	550 million tons/yr.
Animal wastes	1,500 million tons/yr.
Mineral wastes	1,100 million tons/yr.
TOTAL	3,510 million tons/yr.
	3.5 billion tons/yr.

Source: Richard D. Vaughan, National Solid Wastes Survey Report:
Summary and Interpretation, 1970.

2. AMOUNTS BY SOURCE

The most comprehensive state analysis of solid wastes has
been conducted by the State of California (California Solid
Waste Management Study 1968 and Plan 1970, U.S. Environmental
Protection Agency Report (SW-2Tsg) Solid Waste Management Office,
Washington: U.S. Government Printing Office, 1971). In this
study, a complete county and city analysis of sources and total

amounts of solid waste generated was undertaken. The results
of this analysis are summarized in Tables 4.3 and 4.4. In addi-

TABLE 4.3

MUNICIPAL SOLID WASTE PRODUCTION IN CALIFORNIA

County	Residential Tons/Year	Commercial Tons/Year	Demolition Tons/Year	Special Tons/Year	Annual Total Tonnage	Ranking in State
Alameda	477,900	582,100	202,000	84,900	1,347,000	4
Alpine	200	100	0	0	<1,000	58
Amador	5,300	3,600	200	500	10,000	50
Butte	46,300	35,300	4,600	3,600	90,000	27
Calaveras	5,600	3,700	200	200	10,000	50
Colusa	5,800	4,100	300	500	11,000	49
Contra Costa	241,800	222,100	50,900	34,000	549,000	10
Del Norte	7,300	4,900	300	300	13,000	47
El Dorado	21,900	15,100	1,000	1,800	40,000	36
Fresno	191,600	203,900	60,200	23,000	479,000	12
Glenn	8,700	6,300	600	800	16,000	43
Humboldt	52,600	39,300	5,000	4,200	101,000	24
Imperial	37,000	31,300	6,000	5,000	79,000	28
Inyo	6,800	4,800	400	400	12,000	48
Kern	155,100	129,200	24,000	13,500	322,000	14
Kings	31,000	23,700	3,300	2,400	60,000	33
Lake	8,700	5,500	200	300	15,000	44
Lassen	7,900	5,500	400	600	14,000	45
Los Angeles	3,214,200	3,883,500	1,338,800	548,200	8,985,000	1
Madera	20,400	15,900	2,500	1,900	41,000	35
Marin	89,900	78,100	15,200	12,900	196,000	18
Mariposa	2,700	1,600	0	0	4,000	55
Mendocino	24,600	17,000	1,200	1,800	45,000	34
Merced	49,100	40,400	7,300	4,900	102,000	23
Modoc	3,800	2,500	100	200	7,000	54
Mono	2,200	1,300	0	0	4,000	55
Monterey	109,500	96,600	20,800	13,400	240,000	17
Napa	34,900	29,900	5,600	4,100	74,000	30
Nevada	11,600	8,000	600	800	21,000	41
Orange	589,000	658,200	208,400	101,800	1,557,000	3
Placer	34,300	25,600	3,200	2,900	66,000	32
Plumas	5,400	3,900	400	300	10,000	50
Riverside	202,800	201,000	53,100	25,700	483,000	11
Sacramento	289,700	315,700	96,300	31,200	733,000	7
San Benito	7,800	5,500	400	800	14,000	45
San Bernardino	304,600	296,000	75,800	37,500	714,000	8
San Diego	571,000	671,600	224,000	92,400	1,559,000	2
San Francisco	341,300	477,800	187,000	65,100	1,071,000	6
San Joaquin	127,200	111,300	22,900	15,600	277,000	15
San Luis Obispo	45,900	37,100	5,900	5,900	95,000	26
San Mateo	246,600	238,800	61,700	42,000	589,000	9
Santa Barbara	114,000	98,100	19,800	13,400	245,000	16
Santa Clara	423,100	508,100	173,100	70,000	1,174,000	5
Santa Cruz	48,500	39,500	6,600	5,100	100,000	25
Shasta	37,100	27,100	3,100	2,300	70,000	31
Sierra	1,100	700	0	100	2,000	57
Siskiyou	16,100	11,600	1,000	1,700	30,000	39
Solano	72,900	69,600	17,500	13,100	173,000	19
Sonoma	83,800	65,200	9,800	7,800	167,000	22
Stanislaus	83,100	66,300	10,500	7,900	168,000	21
Sutter	18,200	14,400	2,200	1,600	36,000	38
Tehama	13,700	9,800	800	1,200	26,000	40
Trinity	4,300	2,900	200	100	8,000	53
Tulare	88,000	68,000	9,800	7,400	173,000	19
Tuolumne	9,900	6,600	400	400	17,000	42
Ventura	157,300	143,700	32,500	20,000	353,000	13
Yolo	34,200	31,600	7,500	4,200	77,000	29
Yuba	20,800	15,800	2,100	1,400	40,000	36
TOTAL	8,866,000	9,717,000	2,988,000	1,343,000	22,914,000	

Source: see p. 182.

TABLE 4.4

TOTAL SOLID WASTE PRODUCTION IN CALIFORNIA

County	Municipal Tons/Year	Industrial Tons/Year	Agri-cultural Tons/Year	Annual Total Tonnage	Rank in State
Alameda	1,347,000	388,000	125,000	1,860,000	15
Alpine	<1,000	3,000	<1,000	3,000	58
Amador	10,000	62,000	15,000	87,000	54
Butte	90,000	114,000	456,000	660,000	30
Calaveras	10,000	84,000	11,000	105,000	53
Colusa	11,000	0	540,000	551,000	35
Contra Costa	549,000	253,000	378,000	1,180,000	21
Del Norte	13,000	372,000	33,000	418,000	38
El Dorado	40,000	318,000	19,000	377,000	40
Fresno	479,000	254,000	2,876,000	3,609,000	2
Glenn	16,000	53,000	526,000	595,000	33
Humboldt	101,000	1,802,000	250,000	2,153,000	12
Imperial	79,000	9,000	2,493,000	2,580,700	6
Inyo	12,000	1,000	11,000	23,000	56
Kern	322,000	82,000	2,117,000	2,521,000	7
Kings	60,000	15,000	1,396,000	1,471,000	17
Lake	15,000	69,000	43,000	127,000	52
Lassen	14,000	147,000	28,000	189,000	49
Los Angeles	8,985,000	1,881,000	1,779,000	12,645,000	1
Madera	41,000	107,000	635,000	783,000	27
Marin	196,000	9,000	313,000	518,000	36
Mariposa	4,000	10,000	42,000	56,000	55
Mendocino	45,000	901,000	89,000	1,035,000	23
Merced	102,000	15,000	2,101,000	2,218,000	11
Modoc	7,000	92,000	77,000	176,000	50
Mono	4,000	0	2,000	6,000	57
Monterey	240,000	73,000	777,000	1,090,000	22
Napa	74,000	6,000	140,000	220,000	46
Nevada	21,000	102,000	18,000	141,000	51
Orange	1,557,000	223,000	456,000	2,236,000	9
Placer	66,000	198,000	91,000	355,000	41
Plumas	10,000	364,000	5,000	379,000	39
Riverside	483,000	88,000	1,539,000	2,110,000	13
Sacramento	733,000	73,000	847,000	1,653,000	16
San Benito	14,000	5,000	175,000	194,000	48
San Bernardino	714,000	920,000	1,535,000	3,169,000	3
San Diego	1,559,000	107,000	741,000	2,407,000	8
San Francisco	1,071,000	122,000	0	1,193,000	20
San Joaquin	277,000	182,000	1,773,000	2,232,000	10
San Luis Obispo	95,000	8,000	457,000	560,000	34
San Mateo	589,000	99,000	29,000	717,000	29
Santa Barbara	245,000	39,000	328,000	612,000	32
Santa Clara	1,174,000	343,000	387,000	1,904,000	14
Santa Cruz	100,000	142,000	97,000	339,000	42
Shasta	70,000	659,000	153,000	882,000	24
Sierra	2,000	208,000	2,000	212,000	47
Siskiyou	30,000	687,000	157,000	874,000	26
Solano	173,000	41,000	511,000	725,000	28
Sonoma	167,000	216,000	915,000	1,298,000	18
Stanislaus	168,000	156,000	2,277,000	2,601,000	5
Sutter	36,000	16,000	577,000	629,000	31
Tehama	26,000	288,000	152,000	466,000	37
Trinity	8,000	260,000	2,000	270,000	44
Tulare	173,000	182,000	2,629,000	2,984,000	4
Toulumne	17,000	310,000	8,000	335,000	43
Ventura	353,000	68,000	820,000	1,241,000	19
Yolo	77,000	31,000	769,000	877,000	25
Yuba	40,000	38,000	180,000	258,000	45
Additional Statewide		392,000		392,000	
TOTAL[1]	22,914,000	13,687,000	34,901,000	71,502,000	

Source: see p. 182.

[1] The data in this and the following tables may not balance
due to errors inherent in maintaining significant figures.

tion, amounts by source units, city size, or per capita were calculated for all of the major solid waste source categories (i.e.
commercial, industrial, etc.), as shown in Tables 4.5 and 4.6.
These calculations allowed the California staff to arrive at
solid waste multipliers, or solid-waste amounts per individual
source units. Such individual source units are single family
residences, multiple family units, number of industrial employees,
and number of pounds of commercial wastes produced per capita
(Tables 4.7-4.10). This allowed forecasting, by the use of a
simple linear weighting formula, of future amounts by type and
land useage of solid wastes for the entire state.

TABLE 4.5

MULTIPLIERS FOR NONMANUFACTURING INDUSTRY,
COMMERCIAL AND PUBLIC FACILITIES

Waste Source	Annual[a] Wastes, Volume cu yd	Employment[b]	Annual[c] Wastes, Volume per Employee cu yd	Annual[a] Wastes, 1000 lb	Annual[a] Wastes, lb per Employee	Annual[e] Wastes, ton per Employee
	1	2	3	4	5	6
Commercial[f] and Public Facilities	3,946,928	184,153	21.433	1,403,287.1	7,620.22	3.81011
Demolition and Construction	2,115,717	22,079	95.824	1,821,607.7	82,504.08	41.25205

[a]Columns 1 and 4: Food Machinery Corporation (FMC) Santa Clara Study, 1967, unpublished data

[b]Column 2: Tabulation of data obtained from California Department of Employment, San Francisco Office, Research and Statistics

[c]Column 3: Column 1/Column 2

[d]Column 5: Column 4/Column 2

[e]Column 6: Column 5/2000

[f]This group includes all wholesale and retail trade, transportation, utilities and other services, churches, shopping centers, and all publicly-owned facilities.

Source: see p. 182

TABLE 4.6

INDUSTRIAL MULTIPLIERS

Standard Industrial Classification		Small Firms		Large Firms		Annual Waste: All Firms			
No.	Title	Total[a] Employment	Annual Waste[b] Volume per Employee (cu yd)	Total[a] Employment	Annual Waste[c] Volume per Employee (cu yd)	Volume per[d] Employee (cu yd)	Densities[e] lb/cu yd	Pounds per[f] Employee	Tons per[g] Employee
		1	2	3	4	5	6	7	8
19	Ordnance and Accesseries	h	h	29,499	4.476	4.476	294.4	1,317.7	0.65885
203	Canning and Preserving	-	-	-	8.977	8.977	1,240.0	11,131.4	5.5657
20	Other Food Processing (Except 203)	920	20.961	4,306	8.720	10.875	885.8	9,633.1	4.81655
21	Tobacco	-	-	-	-	-	-	-	2.49365[i]
22	Textiles	-	-	-	-	-	-	-	0.52575[j]
23	Apparel	98	35.360	623	2.077	6.601	159.3	1,051.5	0.52575
24	Lumber and Wood Products	455	48.492	217		48.492	894.5	43,376.1	21.68805
25	Furniture and Fixtures	385	86.877			86.877	464.0	40,310.9	20.15545
26	Paper and Allied Products	570	65.442	1,535	37.440	45.022	557.0	25,077.3	12.53865
27	Printing, Publishing and Allied	1,744	25.230	1,923	7.252	15.802	1,671.0	26,405.1	13.20255
28	Chemicals and Allied	701	18.348	937		18.348	895.0	16,421.1	3.21075
29	Petroleum Refining	k	k	k	k	k	k	k	k
30	Rubber and Plastics	173	28.583	653	18.854	20.892	148.2	3,096.2	1.54810
31	Leather	-	-	-	-	-	-	-	2.49365[l]
32	Stone, Clay, Glass and Concrete	960	29.235	1,696	5.260	13.926	2,601.5	36,228.5	18.11425
33	Primary Metals	h	4.443	-	-	-	-	-	6.7300[l]
34	Fabricated Metal Products	1,259	21.214	1,304	13.206	17.140	785.3	13,460.0	6.7300
35	Nonelectrical Machinery	2,838	17.909	9,805	11.401	12.862	650.3	8,364.2	4.18210
36	Electrical Machinery	2,337	16.645	37,814	7.333	7.875	756.5	5,957.4	2.97870
37	Transportation Equipment	557	14.348	4,183	24.580	23.378	290.3	6,786.6	3.39330
38	Instruments	825	8.943	926	NA	8.943	562.9	5,034.0	2.51700
39	Miscellaneous Manufacturing Industries	517	5.946	149	NA	10.493	475.3	4,987.3	2.49365[l]

[a]Columns 1 and 3--Tabulated from data obtained from California Department of Employment,(Research and Statistics), San Francisco office

[b]Column 2--From Column 4 of Table 66 (Appendix E)

[c]Column 4--From Column 3 of Table 65 (Appendix E)

[d]Column 5--The average multiplier (cu yd/employee) for the industry as a whole was obtained for each SIC as the weighted average of small and large firm multipliers (Columns 2 and 4),

Source: see p. 182.

TABLE 4.6 (Cont'd)

using employment (Columns 1 and 3) as weights

[e]Column 6--Unpublished data furnished by FMC Santa Clara study, 1967

[f]Column 7--Column 5 multiplied by Column 6

[g]Column 8--Column 7 divided by 2,000

[h]Data not available

[i]The multiplier for the SIC 39, Miscellaneous Manufacturing Industries, calculated as weighted average of all industry multipliers available. This multiplier is used wherever an industry had no data available, e.g. Tobacco (SIC 21). Leather (SIC 31).

[j]Same as the multiplier for Apparel (SIC 23)

[k]Omitted from calculations

[l]Same as the multipler for Fabricated Metals (SIC 34)

TABLE 4.7

ESTIMATION PROCEDURES AND ESTIMATES OF MUNICIPAL WASTES

Waste Source	Multipliers	Source Units	Tons/year
Household Garbage and Rubbish			
Single Family Unit	1.42910 tons/unit/year[a]	173,819[g]	248,405
Multiple Family Unit	0.62755 tons/unit/year[a]	106,984[g]	70,347
City Streets: Leaves, Litter, Sweepings, and Tree Trimmings	42.9 lb/capita/year[b]	758,230[h]	16,264[h]
Refuse Collected Along Highway Right-of-Way			
Freeway Refuse	8.0 tons/mile/year[c]	62[i]	496
County Roads Refuse	3.3 tons/mile/year[d]	200[d]	660
Sewage Treatment Residue	87.1 lb/capita/year[e]	805,930[g]	35,098[j]
Local Parks and Playgrounds	5.4 lb/capita/year[f]	805,930[g]	2,176
Regional Parks			415[k]
TOTAL WASTE			373,861

[a]Multiplier for household garbage and rubbish are from FMC Corporation Santa Clara Study, Systems Analysis for Solid Waste Disposal by Incineration (1968), page 22, 25. Single family unit multiplier includes estimate of refuse hauled to disposal site by householder himself.

[b]FMC Corporation Santa Clara Study, pages 52, 53. The multiplier is obtained by dividing total street sweepings and tree trimming wastes (1,758 tons) by the population (82,482).

[c]Multiplier for freeway refuse developed from weight and volume data from FMC study.

[d]Multiplier for county roads refuse computed from information about mileage and volume of refuse, which was supplied by Road Division of Alameda County.

[e]FMC Corporation Santa Clara Study, page 51.

[f]FMC Corporation Santa Clara Study, pages 54, 55.

[g]Estimate of population and occupied housing units are from Alameda County Planning Department and are for July 1967. The population of Castro Valley, and unincorporated area is excluded from this total. Is street refuse is listed under county roads refuse.

[h]Excluding Castro Valley street sweepings.

[i]Data on total freeway mileage in the county was supplied by State of California Division of Highways, District 4. The study area's proportion of the county total (57%) was determined by use of a contour meter.

[j]Including Castro Valley street sweepings.

[k]Mr. Lynch, Acting Chief of Maintenance Department, East Bay Regional Park District.

Source: see p. 182

TABLE 4.8

ALTERNATE ESTIMATES OF WASTES GENERATED BY COMMERCIAL
ORGANIZATIONS AND SERVICES[a]

Size of City Population	Waste Multiplier lb/cap/day	Applicable Population	Waste tons/yr
>100,000	3.5[b]	635,100	405,670
(1) 10,001 - 100,000	2.5[b]	167,980	76,641
1,001 - 10,000	2.0[b]	2,850	1,040
		805,930	483,351
(2) 3.81011 tons/employee/year[c] x 265,401 employment = 1,011,207			

[a]Standard Industrial Classification 40-94.

[b]Dept. of Public Health, State of California, Status of Solid
Waste Management in California, 1968.

[c]Multiplier developed from employment data from Dept. of Employment and unpublished data from FMC Corp. Santa Clara
Study.

TABLE 4.9

ALTERNATE ESTIMATES OF WASTES GENERATED BY CONSTRUCTION
AND DEMOLITION[a]

Size of City Population	Waste Multiplier lbs/capita/yr	Applicable Population	Waste tons/yr
>100,000	500[b]	635,100	158,775
(1) 10,001 - 100,000	250[b]	167,980	20,997
1,001 - 10,000	100[b]	2,850	142
			179,914
			(rounded)
		805,930	180,000
(2) 41.25205 ton/employee/year[c] x (19,262) employment = 794,597			

[a]Standard Industrial Classes 15, 16, 17.

[b]Dept. of Public Health, State of California, Status of Solid
Waste Management in California, 1968.

[c]Multiplier developed from construction employment data from
Dept. of Employment and unpublished data from FMC Corp.
Santa Clara Study.

Source of tables: see p. 182

TABLE 4.10

WASTE MULTIPLIERS USED IN 76 CITY DATA NET CALCULATIONS

Single Family	2858.0	lb/unit/yr.
Multiple Family	1315.0	lb/unit/yr.
Commercial	3.5	lb/cap/yr.
Manufacturing	7.6	tons/emp/yr.[*]
Demolition and Construction	500.0	lb/cap/yr.
Sewage	87.1	lb/cap/yr.

*Calculated by averaging multiplier of manufacturing waste from Table 23 of California Study (tons/employee/year)

Source: see p. 182

III. QUALITY ASSESSMENT

1. NATURE OF STANDARDS

At the present time there exist no solid waste standards. Solid wastes are now often treated as secondary pollutants with the only limiting criterion one with respect to   disposal site, where there may be ground water contamination and air pollution, so that water and air quality regulations limit how the solid wastes are disposed of. Thus, local rules and regulations focus on the proper handling of solid wastes. For example, the regulations for the State of Washington specify that "the purpose of this regulation is to set minimum functional standards for the proper handling of all solid wastes originating from residences, commercial, agricultural, and industrial operations, and other sources..." in order to, "...prevent land, air and water pollution, breeding of flies, harboring of rodents, fire hazards; and to prevent damage to recreational values, to conserve resources, and to maintain esthetic values, and prevent damage to the environment, and to prevent nuisances." (Washington State Department of Ecology, Regulation Relating to Minimum Functional Standards for Solid Waste Handling, effective 11/27/72, p. 1).

IV.   THE EFFECTS OF SOLID WASTES

The diversity of solid wastes results in a variety of
potential health and welfare effects, the treatment of which is
complicated by the fact that each waste often demands specific
and yet different methods of disposal and recycling.

1.   HEALTH EFFECTS

a.   HAZARDOUS SOLID WASTES

Recently, national attention has been focussed on hazardous
materials in solid wastes in Section 212 of the Solid Waste Disposal Act, as amended. This act called for the planning and
creation of a system of national disposal sites for the storage
and disposal of hazardous wastes, including radioactive, toxic,
chemical, biological, and other wastes which may endanger public
health or welfare. The effects of many of these wastes have already been discussed in the previous two chapters. According
to Section 212 such planning would involve:

(1) a list of materials which should be subject to disposal
in any such site;
(2) current methods of disposal of such materials;
(3) recommended methods of reduction, neutralization, recovery, or disposal of such materials;
(4) an inventory of possible sites including existing
land or water disposal sites operated or licensed by
Federal agencies;
(5) an estimate of the cost of development and maintenance
of sites including consideration of means for distribu-
ting the short- and long-term costs of operating such
sites among the users thereof.

The development of national disposal sites for hazardous wastes
will help to alleviate the burden from public disposal sites,
and provide the special handling and treatment necessary.

b.   DISEASE RELATIONSHIPS

Solid wastes have been demonstrated conclusively to be
sources of certain diseases (Hanks, 1967). According to Hanks,
the lack of proper disposal techniques helps to create suitable
environments from which diseases can be transmitted. The modes
of transmission (pathways) are:

1.   Biological Vectors
2.   Physical and Mechanical
3.   Airborne Solids
4.   Direct Contact
5.   Water Supply
6.   Food Supply
7.   Socioeconomic Factors

Such pathways demand attention in the disposal of any solid
waste. The elimination of all is necessary for total solid
waste/disease safety. Each of the pathways/solid waste associations is described in the following illustrations (Figures
4.1-4.5).

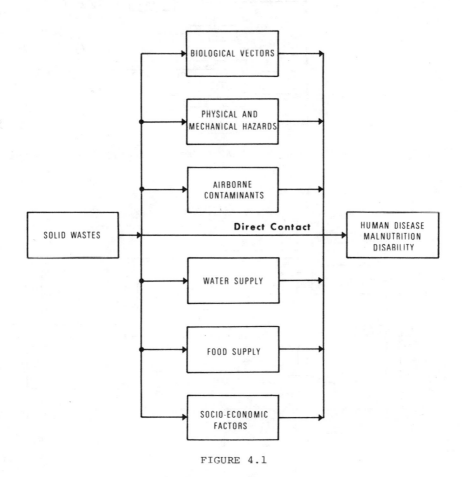

FIGURE 4.1

SOLID WASTE/HUMAN DISEASE PATHWAYS (POSTULATED)
(after Hanks, 1967)

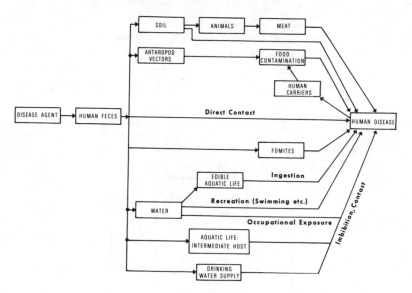

FIGURE 4.2: HUMAN FECAL WASTE/HUMAN DISEASE PATHWAYS (POSTULATED)

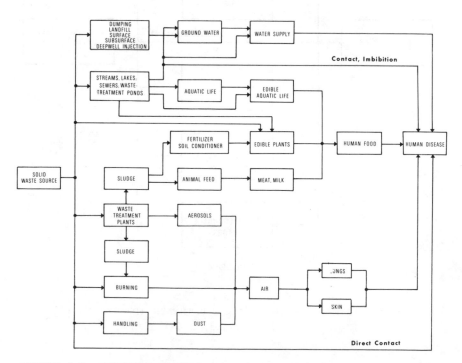

FIGURE 4.3: CHEMICAL WASTE/HUMAN DISEASE PATHWAYS (POSTULATED)

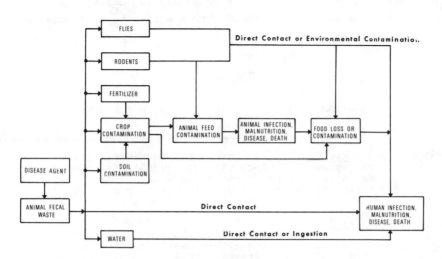

FIGURE 4.4

ANIMAL FECAL WASTE/DISEASE PATHWAYS (POSTULATED)

Note: all figures after Hanks (1967).

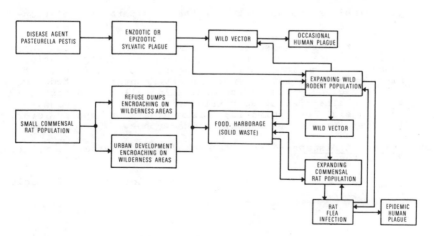

FIGURE 4.5

SOLID WASTE/PLAGUE PATHWAYS (POSTULATED)

While these are pathways by which disease can travel, many
types of diseases are associated with specific types of wastes.
These are summarized in Table 4.11.

TABLE 4.11

COMMUNICABLE DISEASES ASSOCIATED WITH SOLID WASTES

Fly-Borne Diseases--typhoid, dysentery, diarrheas, Asiatic
   Cholera, myiasis, onclocerciasis, Ozyard's filariasis,
   leishmaniasis, African sleeping sickness, yaws, tularemia,
   bartonellosis, catarrial, sandfly fever, conjunctivitis,
   salmonelloses.

Human Fecal Waste (3)

      Bacterial Infection (1)--typhoid, cholera, dysentery.
      Viral Infection (2)--poliomyelitis, Coxsackie infec-
   tion, infectious hepatitis.
      Protozoal Infection (1)--Entamoeba histalytica
      Helminthiasis (1)--fish tapeworm, beef tapeworm, pork
   tapeworm, pinworm, whipworm, hookworms.

   (1) Direct contact necessary
   (2) Pathway still being investigated
   (3) Many assume fecal matter already infected

Animal Fecal Wastes (1)

   All of the diseases associated with human fecal wastes

   (1) Animals serve as hosts, in the host/parasite relationship

Rodent-Borne Zoonoses (diseases of animals transmitted to man)--
   Echinostomiasis, hemorrhagic septicemica, histoplasmasis,
   lymphocytic choriomeningitis, plague, rat-bite fever, rat-
   mite dermatitis, rat tapeworm, Rocky Mountain spotted fever,
   salivary gland virus infections, salmonellosis, schistoso-
   miasis, belhargiasis, sporotrichosis, swine erysipelas,
   trichinosis, leptospirosis, leishmaniasis, relapsing fever,
   tularemia, rickettsial pox, marine typhus.

Mosquito-Borne Disease--dengue, encephalitis, filariasis, malaria,
   yellow fever.

Miscellaneous--soil fungus (associated with infected buried solid
   wastes).

   *Table compiled from Thrift G. Hanks, Solid Waste/Disease
Relationship.

Thus, the number of disease/solid waste relationships is
varied and complex. Each solid waste problem (i.e. generation,
collection, disposal) provides sufficient life support needs for
many diseases. When collection ceases and solid wastes accumu-
late, the chances of fly and rodent borne diseases rise rapidly.
This is especially true in large metropolitan centers, which
often have long public employee strikes. Similarly, improper disposal of disposable diapers is a disease danger, as is the large
number of feedlots, feral dogs, and domestic animals in both
rural and urban settings.

Obviously, the best way to avoid all of the aforementioned
diseases is proper disposal. Some wastes may contaminate soil
and ground water supplies. The effects of carcinogens and pesticides (as residues) and their relationship to man is still not
fully understood. Even the treated solid wastes (i.e. sewage
sludge) often contain harmful organisms.

If used in agriculture, viable organisms may be carried to
water supplies, while the pathogens also involve occupational
exposure to agricultural and sanitation workers. More research
is needed in this area. Fly control has been recognized as a
major problem relating to wastes and public health. For better
control of flies, research is needed in the following areas:
1. Better containers for garbage.
2. Improved methods of treatment of specialized wastes
    (e.g., manures, food processing wastes)
3. Better education and understanding
4. Pesticide applications (to home compactors, for example)
5. Development of new techniques for collection and dis-
    posal and/or treatment

Hanks states that the use of garbage grinders to eliminate garbage storage and collection, appears to be the best present
solution to the problem of flies in residential areas (Hanks, p.
159).

c. EFFECTS ON MARINE LIFE

While much literature is devoted to solid waste disposal
on land it should also be remembered that ocean disposal of solid
waste takes place. Smith and Brown (1971) reviewed the effects of
the disposal of certain industrial wastes upon marine surrounding
life in the immediate area of ocean disposal. Their results are
summarized in Table 4.12.

TABLE 4.12

SUMMARY OF ENVIRONMENTAL STUDIES ON INDUSTRIAL WASTES DISCHARGED AT SEA

Waste Type Industrial	Description of Disposal Area				Barging Characteristics		
	Distance from shore (miles)	Water depth (feet)	Lati- tude	Longi- tude	Amount of waste/ trip	Depth of dis- charge	Rates of discharge tons/min.
Spent sul- phuric acid	15 from New Jersey coast	80	40°20'N	73°40'W	3200 tons 5000 tons	15 feet	18 70
Chlorinated hydo- carbons	125 SE of Galveston, Texas	2400	27°36'N	94°36'W	1200 tons	12 feet	5
Paper mill wastes (black liquor)	125 SE of Galveston, Texas	2400	27°36'N	94°36'W	1300 tons	10 feet	5
Ammoniasulphate (mother liquor)	100 S of Freeport, Texas	2760	27°35'N	95°20'W	1700 tons		7
Waste liquor	70 S of Freeport, Texas	960	27°48'N	94°54'W	2400 tons		5-24
Chlorinated waste liquor	125 SE of Galveston, Texas	2400	27°36'N	94°36'W	1400 tons (proposed)		13-25 (recom- mended)
Sodium sludge (con- tainerized)	110 S of Galveston, Texas	2400	27°36'N	94°36'W	15 55-gal. drums (500- 570 pounds per drum)	Surface	Variable
Pesticides	95 SSE of Galveston, Texas	720	27°49'N	94°30'W	50 55-gal. drums per trip	1200 ft	1 barrel/2 mins. (600' intervals on bottom
Caprolactam wastes	35 S of Sabine Bank Light	60	29°10'N	93°40'W			

Source: Smith and Brown (1971).

Towing speed (knots)	Waste Characteristics		Laboratory Toxicity Studies		
	Given description	Type of test organisms	TLM (range)	Remarks	
6 7	Fe_2SO_4 (10%) H_2SO_4 (8.5%)	Marine phyto-plankton	2.7-35.5 mg/l 6-16 day test duration	Investigated effects of various concentrations of iron on growth of algae	
6	Beta-chloropropylene (22%) trichloropropane (5%), iso-propylchloride (38%), allyl-chloride (11%), misc. chlor-ides (33%), heavy ends (3%), pH--9.8, specific gravity--0.9-1.34	Marine phyto-, and zoo-plank-ton, anemones, brine shrimp, bacteria, fish	0.02-2.5% saturated 0.0005-1 g/l, 2-24 hr test duration	Investigated acute toxicity and in-hibition to photo-synthesis	
6	Paper mill wastes, 47% solids, BOD_5--100,000 ppm Na_2CO_3, Na_2SO_4, NaOH, etc. pH--13, specific gravity 1.27 at 60°C	Marine phyto-plankton zoo-plankton	0.001-1.0 g/l, 22 hr test duration	Investigated acute toxicity and inhibition to pho-tosynthesis	
4	Ammonium sulfate (23%), nitrogen (8%), carbon (12%), organics (29%) (alcohols, esters, amides), IOD--90 mg/l, BOD_5--57,000 ppm, pH--4.3, S.G.--1.23	Brineshrimp, top-water min-nows	1.25% by vol-ume 200 ppm, 24 hr test duration	Acute toxicity	
6	NA_2S (Na_2S_2) (6%) (Na_2S_3) NaHS (1%) S (total) (6%), NaCl (21%), organic (2%), solids (dissolved and sus-pended), specific gravity --1.24 at 60°C	Marine phyto-plankton, top-water min-nows, brine shrimp	0.0005-0.18% by volume, 24 hr test duration	Acute toxicity	
5 (recom-mended)	(Organic waste) chlorinated organics (10-15%), inorganic salts (Na_2SO_4) (5-6%); (acid) chlorinated organics (1%), sulfuric acid (10-15%), nitric acid (0.1%)	Marine phyto-plankton, top-water min-nows, brine shrimp	0.02-0.64% by volume, 24 hr test duration	Acute toxicity, waste acid more toxic to fish than brine shrimp	
10	Metallic sodium (75%), cal-cium (24%), barium, magnes-ium, potassium (1%)				
3	Anilines (chlordaniline, mo-nichlorobenzene), liquid or-ganics (methanol, p-xylene, chlorobenzene), dry chemi-cals--insoluble (thiram, thi-ram-E, thionex, zineb, fer-bam, monuron, carbon disul-fate)	Minnows, largemouth bass, salmon, bluegills, mos-quito fish, channel cat-fish, bluegill sunfish	1-135 mg/l, 48-96 hr test duration	Toxicity values obtained from literature	

TABLE 4.12 (Cont'd)

Waste Type		Reported Field Observations	
Industrial	Physical-Chemical	Biological	Observed effects
Spend sulfuric acid	pH, iron concentration (0-60'), wind, weather, sea state	Plankton (0-60'), benthic organisms, pelagic fish (30')	Water discoloration, plankton temporarily immobile, iron settled rapidly from surface layer, no appreciable accumulation of iron found in bottom sediments.
Chlorinated hydrocarbons	Temp. (0-900'), salinity oxygen, waste concentration (0-500'), surface currents, wind, weather, sea state, bottom mud	Plankton, O_2 evolution, C_{14} uptake, chlorophyll-A, visual inspection of sargassum weed	Water discoloration: fish plankton killed on direct contact of waste, no harmful effects seen after 2-4 hrs. Bulk of waste sank. Low diffusion of waste at depth.
Paper mill wastes (black liquor)	Temp. (0-900'), salinity (0-600'), waste concentration surface samples, pH, oxygen (0-600'), wind, weather, sea state	Plankton (0-100'), O_2 evolution, C_{14} uptake, chlorophyll-A	Slight water discoloration. No mortality to marine life. Bulk of waste sank.
Ammoniasulphate (mother liquor)	Waste concentration (0-150')		No fish mortality. No floating oil. Bulk of waste sank. Maximum waste concentration at depth.
Waste liquor	Waste concentration (0-150'), temp., salinity pH, oxygen, (0-600')	Plankton, pelagic fish, sargassum weed communities	No evidence of subsurface maximum waste concentration.
Chlorinated waste liquor			
Sodium sludge (containerized)	pH	Plankton, fish, sargassum weed	No mortality to fish. Flying debris hazardous to disposal personnel. 30% mortality to plankton due to collection methods.
Pesticides			
Caprolactam wastes	Temp. (0-60'), salinity (surface), wind, weather, sea state	Plankton, bottom samples, C_{14}, chlorophyll-A, -B, -C	

Source: Smith and Brown (1971).

Mixing Characteristics		General study conclusions
Initial dilution	Diffusion coefficient $cm^2/sec.$	
1:5,000	2.9×10^3	Mixing and diffusion of wastes occurs rapidly in the wake of the barge. No evidence to indicate adverse effects. Each new proposed waste disposal operation needs careful study prior to allowing ocean disposal.
	2.5×10^3 (average)	Disposal of toxic wastes at sea can be accomplished with only a slight effect on organisms in the biomass within a limited oceanic area. Each new waste disposal operation needs careful study prior to sanctioning it.
1:300,000	2.5×10^3 (average)	Disposal of "black liquor wastes" in the deep sea can be accomplished without determinable effects on marine biota. Ultimate disposal is expected to be accomplished by bacteria. Advisable to monitor each separate load of waste to determine toxicity in laboratory.
	9×10^2	No undesirable effects were observed. Diffusion great enough to ensure good dispersion to minimize harmful effects to biota.
1.10,000 1:100,000 in 2 hrs		Disposal should produce no significant mortality in the biota, nor any prolonged effects.
		No significant mortality would be expected from disposal of this waste in the open ocean. It is suggested that a full-scale disposal operation be properly monitored and continued to verify preliminary study results.
		Explosions caused by reaction of sodium with seawater had no significant effects on sargassum and zooplankton populations. Absence of fish-kiln was probably due to barrenness of disposal area.
100:1	0.002×10^3	Consideration of available toxicity and diffusion data from literature sources indicate that the zone of water containing toxic concentrations of waste surrounding each disposal drum will be limited in extent and duration and will not endanger motile aquatic life in the disposal area to a significant degree.
		Limited scale (one day) of survey precluded any significant results. Recommend future surveys be conducted on 3-day basis for better results.

There are many methods used by nature to change, filter or recycle so-called "pollutants" within nature's ecosystems. These methods, how they relate to natural systems, and how man uses similar methods for his own pollution control, are summarized in Table 4.13. Those methods which are directly related to solid waste materials are indicated.

TABLE 4.13

PHENOMENA AND PROCESSES UTILIZED BY NATURE
OR EXPLOITED BY ENGINEERED SYSTEMS FOR POLLUTION CONTROL

Phenomenon or Process	Function in Natural Systems	Exploitation by Engineered Systems
Sedimentation	1. Suspended organic and inorganic particles removed from flowing or ponded water	1. Commonly used in clarification of water for municipal and industrial supply
	2. Particles removed from percolating water	2. Used to reduce abrasiveness of water to be pumped
	3. Particles and droplets removed from the atmosphere	3. Commonly used to separate solid and liquid fractions of domestic sewage for treatment
	4. Gases or liquids having different temperature, salinity, or sediment load separated gravimetrically	4. Commonly used in industrial waste treatment
		5. Used to remove fly ash, etc., from industrial gases
	5. Stored or ponded water stratified	6. Limited use to clarify water for groundwater recharge
Filtration	1. Infiltering and percolating waters clarified in coils and aquifers	1. Widely used standard method of treating domestic and industrial water supplies (sand filter)
	2. Particulate matter in atmosphere reduced by trees and other vegetation	2. Widely used method of treating organic fraction of domestic and industrial wastes (biological filter)
	3. Suspended solids in surface runoff reduced by vegetation and debris	3. Limited use in spray disposal of organic wastes

TABLE 4.13 (Cont'd)

Phenomenon or Process	Function in Natural Systems	Exploitation by Engineered Systems
Filtration (Continued)	4. Surface strata of soil acts as biofilter to remove dissolved and suspended organic solids	4. Limited use in induced groundwater recharge from surface waters
Coagulation and Chemical Precipitation	1. Incompatible chemicals in water or in air removed	1. Widely used standard method of clarifying domestic and industrial water supplies 2. Common method of treating industrial waste waters 3. Common method of softening domestic and industrial water supplies
Flocculation and Coalescence	1. Particles in flowing and stored water, and in air, agglomerated, often leading to precipitation 2. Colloids in soils agglomerated	1. Commonly involved in treatment of domestic and industrial water supplies 2. Common phenomenon in waste-water treatment processes
Deflocculation	1. Occurs in soils receiving high-sodium waters 2. Probably occurs in many situations in subtle ways	1. No waste-oriented engineered systems
Mixing, Diffusion, and Dilution	1. Occurs in normal cycle of stratification and overturn of ponded water 2. Common phenomena in gas (oxygen) interchange between air and water 3. Gas from sanitary landfills diffuses into soil and groundwater 4. Aerosols and gases mixed in atmosphere 5. Liquids of different characteristics (e.g., salinity) mixed	1. Mixing commonly utilized in coagulating and flocculating water for domestic and industrial use 2. Diffusion structures widely used in dispersing waste waters in surface water mass to achieve dilution 3. Diffusion widely used to supply oxygen to microorganisms in waste-water treatment 4. Dilution by mixing waste streams commonly used in industrial waste disposal

TABLE 4.13 (Cont'd)

Phenomenon or Process	Function in Natural Systems	Exploitation by Engineered Systems
Flotation	1. Floatable solids separated from flowing and ponded water	1. Commonly used in separating solids from liquids in treatment of domestic and industrial waste waters
Ion-Exchange	1. Ions interchanged between percolating water and soil or groundwater	1. Widely used in softening and deionizing water for domestic and industrial supplies
		2. Removal of minerals added by use; in experimental stage
Oxidation	1. Stabilization of organic matter	1. Widely used in stabilization of domestic and industrial organic wastes
	2. Precipitation of inorganic salts	2. Widely used in domestic and industrial refuse incineration
	3. Oxidation of gases and particulates in the atmosphere	3. Limited use in afterburners in energy-production systems
	4. Burning of vegetation (forest fires)	
Biodegradation	1. Normal process of reduction of unstable organic matter in soil, water, and air to inorganic salts, gases, and water	1. Widely used in treatment of organic solids in domestic and industrial wastes
		2. Limited use in treatment of special industrial wastes
		3. Commonly used in composting organic wastes
Nutrient Removal a) Denitrification b) Phosphorous Removal	1. Anaerobic bacteria reduce nitrates to free nitrogen	1. Experimental and pilot studies on sewage effluent denitrification in progress
		2. Experimental and pilot plant studies on sewage plant effluents in progress
Molecular Entrapment	1. Large molecules in percolating water removed at intersection of particles	1. No engineered systems for waste management

TABLE 4.13 (Cont'd)

Phenomenon or Process	Function in Natural Systems	Exploitation by Engineered Systems

Adsorption	1. Adsorption on particulates
	  a) In the atmosphere
	  b) In the water
	  c) In soils and vegetation
		1. Widespread use in water treatment for domestic and industrial use
		
		2. Commonly used to remove volatile and nonreactive radionuclides
		
		3. Experimental and pilot studies in progress
		
		4. Widespread use in removal of exotic organics from polluted waters
		
		5. Widespread use in removal of odors from air
		
		6. Widespread use in control of humidity

Desorption	1. Desorption from particulate in water, air, soils, and vegetation	1. Essential part of ion-exchange systems
Change of State	1. Change of vapor to liquid state, i.e., rainfall 2. Silt load increased by weathering 3. Condensation removes small particulates <1 micron	1. Experimental use in desalination 2. Limited use to dewater radioactive wastes 3. Experimental and pilot studies in progress
Electrostatic Precipitation	1. Removes charged ions and particulates from atmosphere	1. Commonly used to collect fly ash, pollen, radioisotopes, etc.
Osmosis	1. Nutrient transfer in living cells 2. Osmotic-pressure effects in soil moisture	1. Experimental removal of salts from water 2. Experimental osmotic transfers in water treatment 3. Experimental and pilot studies in progress

TABLE 4.13 (Cont'd)

Phenomenon or Process	Function in Natural Systems	Exploitation by Engineered Systems
Reverse Osmosis		1. Experimental systems of desalination
Ionizing Radiation	1. Creation of radio-isotopes under cosmic-ray bombardment	1. Universal storage of wastes until stabilization or reduction occurs by decay
Evaporation and Prevention of Evaporation	1. Salts concentrated in soil or water 2. Air temperature reduced	1. Limited use in reducing volume of liquid wastes 2. Reduction in evaporation from stored water in experimental stage
Sterilization and Disinfection	1. Antibiotics produced in decaying organic matter 2. Low temperature delays biodegradation 3. Ultraviolet radiation reduces microorganisms 4. Ozone reduces microorganisms	1. Widely used in treating domestic and industrial water supplies 2. Widely used in treating waste waters containing organic matter 3. Limited use in groundwater recharge systems
Transpiration	1. Concentrates salts in soil 2. Phreatophytes concentrate salts in soil and water	1. No engineered systems
Microstraining	1. Bivalves remove bacteria and other food water 2. Plant roots reject salts in water	1. Commonly used in separating fine solids from liquid wastes
Synergism	1. Combined effect of two biospecies exceeds total of two separately 2. Catalyst effect in chemical reaction	1. No waste-oriented engineered systems

TABLE 4.13 (Cont'd)

Phenomenon or Process	Function in Natural Systems	Exploitation by Engineered Systems
Biological Antagonisms	1. One organism reduces rate of activity of another	1. No waste-oriented engineered systems
Clogging in Depth·	1. Agglomeration of soil particles increases rate of infiltration by vertical dispersion of clogging materials	1. Experimental studies of soil systems and sand filters
Magnetic Processes	1. Not important	1. Separation of ferritic materials from solid wastes
Dissolution	1. Leaching and transport of mineral salts and organics 2. Nutrient transfer in living cells	1. Leaching of solid-waste accumulations 2. Drainage systems to reduce salinity 3. Commonly used in treating industrial wastes
Capillary	1. Soil-moisture and plant-liquid transfer	1. Limited use for storing liquid wastes in unsaturated soils
Electrodialysis	1. Role in nature unclear	1. Commonly used for desalination of water 2. Experimental and pilot studies in progress
FeS Precipitation	1. Anaerobic organisms precipitate sulfur as ferous sulfide in degrading organic matter	1. No engineered system in use
Sonics	1. Role in nature unclear	1. Experimental use in treating polluted air and water

TABLE 4.13 (Cont'd)

Phenomenon or Process	Function in Natural Systems	Exploitation by Engineered Systems
Storage	1. All natural systems provide various volumes and durations of storage	1. "Permanent" storage to sequester wastes 2. "Temporary" storage to increase the reaction time of many of the processes listed above

Source: _____, Waste Management and Control, National Academy of Sciences, National Research Council, 1966, pp. 105-109.

2. WELFARE EFFECTS

What are the more general effects of solid wastes on the public welfare? Evidence is limited, but certain conclusions can be drawn together:

a. ECONOMIC CONSIDERATIONS

The 1968 National Survey of Community Solid Waste Practices indicated that the collection and disposal of solid wastes costs the taxpayer massive sums each year, contributing to the tendency to concentrate on the costs of solid wastes, rather than the benefits derived from proper disposal and/or re-use. Table 4.14 indicates the amount of monies expended per person per year by communities covered in the survey. Budgeted community funds indicate an 80-20 percent split between collection and disposal.

TABLE 4.14

BUDGETED COMMUNITY EXPENDITURES
(Dollars per Person per Year)

	Excluding Capital	Capital Only	Total
Disposal			
Average for all communities	1.17	0.25	1.42
Communities operating disposal systems	1.46	0.71	2.17
Collection			
Average for all communities	4.86	0.53	5.39
Communities operating 1/wk systems	4.85	0.75	5.60
Communities operating 2/wk systems	5.67	1.15	6.82

Source: Muhick, 14.

The scale of community involvement is indicated by the fact that one solid waste collector or driver is employed in the public or private sector for every 590 persons, for a total of 337,000 persons involved in the collection and transportation of solid waste.

5   NOISE POLLUTION

I. MEASUREMENT SYSTEMS

Noise has been defined as unwanted sound. Scientifically-based standards for acceptable community noise levels have yet to be determined, and thus standards set in municipal ordinances vary greatly across the country. Most current research focusses upon source delieation and source emission measurement, yet because no agreement has been reached upon measurement for systems community noise levels, different types of noise emissions are measured by different agencies on different measurement scales. There is a total absence of detailed surveillance systems or workable data in the majority of cases.

1. THE POLLUTANT

A simple direct measure of noise levels over the entire audible spectrum has been shown to be an inadequate measure of noise pollution. Scales of measurement have been developed, however, which do relate community responsiveness to physical measurements of noise. The aspects of noise considered in these scales are:

   (i) the magnitude of the noise,

  (ii) the frequency distribution of the noise, and

 (iii) the temporal distribution (time variation and duration) of the noise events.

Using these three aspects, five measurement scales have been developed:

   1) A Weighted Decibel Scale (dβA):

      This scale measures sound level in a way that emphasizes frequencies in a manner similar to human auditory systems. It was developed largely for use in measurement of motor vehicle noise.

   2) Perceived Noise Level (PNL) (L_{PN})

      This scale involves a complex combination of frequency components of the greatest importance to the most prominent frequency band. PNL is largely associated with the development of scales for the measurement of aircraft noise and is best suited for measurement of noises of a continuous nature.

3) Traffic Noise Index (TNI):

This scale includes both A-weighted sound levels and temporal statistics over a 24-hour period. TNI was developed to more realistically assess effects of highways on the noise environment.

$$TNI = 4 \ (L_{10} - L_{90}) + L_{90} - 3$$

where L_{10} and L_{90} are the A-weighted sound levels exceeded 10 and 90 percent of the time respectively.

4) Noise Pollution Level (NPL) (L_{NP}):

This measure consists of an A-weighted sound level or a perceived noise level and temporal statistics of noise over a specified period, usually day or night.

$$NPL = L_e + 2.56 \ S$$

where L_e = energy mean noise level in dβA

S = standard deviation, in dβA, of the time distribution of noise levels making up the composite noise environment.

The Noise Pollution Level is used to assess community noise levels with mixed noise sources.

5) Composite Noise Rating (CNR):

This measure is the sum of a time equivalent steady level, plus a correction for background noises, and other corrections, including one for time of day. The CNR is in effects a measure of the amount by which the offending noise level exceeds the prevalent ambient noise level.

2. SURVEILLANCE NETWORKS

Surveillance networks for community noise measurements do not exist on the national level. Noise measurement on the local level varies from area to area. Noise surveillance systems in some urban places involve stationary noise reporting equipment at various collection points while in others noise levels are established with periodic field checks throughout the urban area with mobile sensing units. How, when and where noise data are collected is left to the discretion of local authorities accounting for variation among local surveillance systems.

II. GENERATION OF NOISE

1. EMISSION SOURCES AND AMOUNTS

The major noise emission sources of noise pollution in urban places can be classified into two groups: (1) stationary sources, and (2) corridor sources. Stationary sources include

industrial noise, construction and demolition noise, and domestic
noise (air conditioners, lawnmowers, appliances, etc.) Corridor
sources involve urban transportation networks and aircraft flight
patterns.

The most frequently cited source of noise intrusions is
automobile noise, as shown in Figure 5.1. Different types of
motor vehicles produce different amounts of noise (Table 5.1).

TABLE 5.1

MOTOR VEHICLE NOISE GENERATION

Vehicle Type	Mean Sound Level (dβA)	Range for 80% of Vehicles
Cars	70 - 72	67 - 77
Heavy Commercial	81	76 - 86
Buses (London Transport)	83	80 - 85
Motorcycles	77	72 - 83

NOTES: (1) Straight level road; open site away from
junctions, etc.
(2) Readings from 25 feet from center of roadway;
(3) Minimum flow 120 vehicles/hour;
(4) Background noise below 55 dβA.

Source: Journal of Sound and Vibration (1971) 15 (1), p. 32.

Likewise, as Bolt Beranek and Newman show in their studies of
the urban noise environment, different traffic volumes produce
different noise levels (Figure 5.2). A comparison of the amount
of noise generated by various sources found in urban places is
shown in Figure 5.3.

The growth in noise sources over the past two decades is
summarized in Table 5.2.

2. THE INCIDENCE OF POLLUTION

Noise levels vary substantially by location and time of
day. This is shown in various ways in Figures 5.4 to 5.8: in
a range of environments across the nation (Figure 5.4); within
the urban environment (Figure 5.5); in relation to urban densities (Figure 5.6); in relation to freeways (Figure 5.7); and
also with respect to time of day (Figure 5.8).

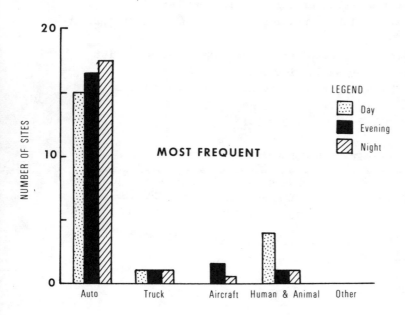

MOST FREQUENT

Source of figures: Bolt, Beranek and Newman (1970).

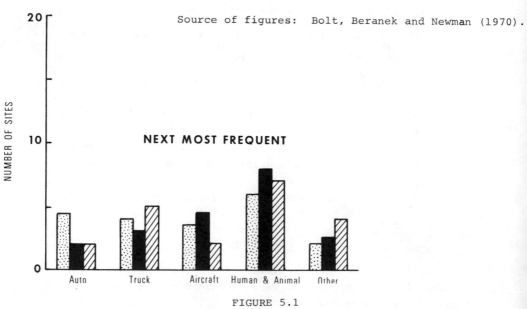

NEXT MOST FREQUENT

FIGURE 5.1

SOURCES OF NOISE INTRUSIONS

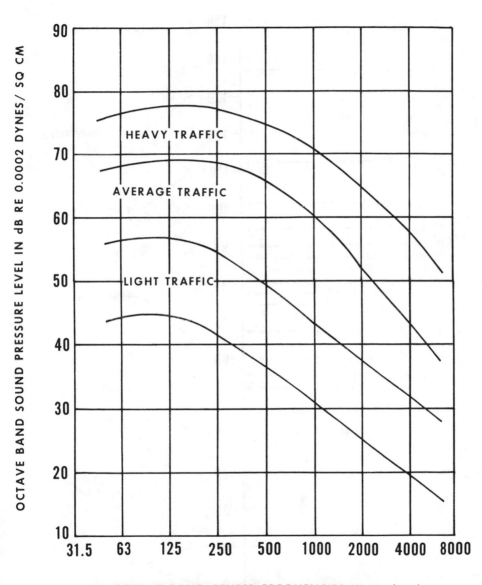

OCTAVE BAND CENTER FREQUENCIES IN Hz (cps)

FIGURE 5.2

NOISE OF CHICAGO STREET TRAFFIC, HEAVY, AVERAGE AND LIGHT, 1947

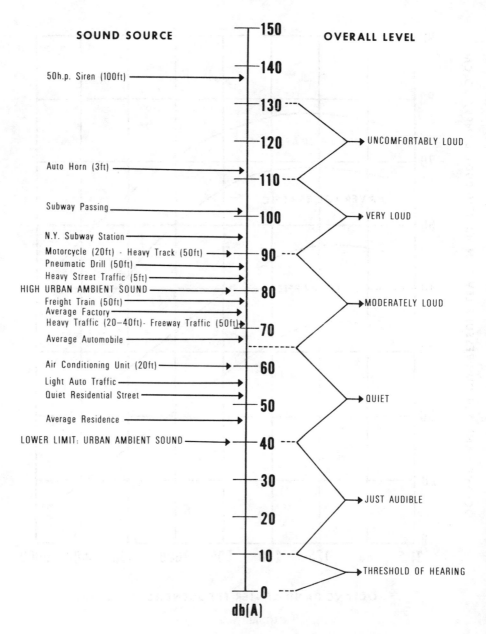

FIGURE 5.3

COMPARISON OF SOUND SOURCES AND OVERALL NOISE LEVELS

TABLE 5.2

GROWTH IN NOISE SOURCES*

(M = Million, TH = Thousand)

Year:	1950	1960	1970
Population (M) :	151	181	204
Transportation Vehicles			
Cars, Buses, Trucks (M)	49.2	73.9	106.3
Motorcycles (M)	0.45	0.51	3.0
Powered Boats (M)	2.6	4.7	5.8
Snowmobiles (TH)	0	2	1600
Commercial Aircraft (Turbofan)	0	202	1989
Private Aircraft (TH)	45	76.2	136
Outdoor Appliances (Approximate)			
Lawn Mowers (M)		10	17
Chain Saws (M)		.5	1.2
Home Appliances	**1953**	**1960**	**1970**
Dishwashers (M)	1.3	3.2	14.9
Clothes Washers (M)	32.2	42.0	57.6
Clothes Dryers (M)	1.5	9.0	25.3
Air Conditioners (M)	0.6	6.5	23.0
Food Mixers (M)	12.6	27.0	51.2
Food Waste Disposers (M)	1.4	4.8	14.4

*Based on EPA Reports

Source: Bolt, Beranek and Newman (1970).

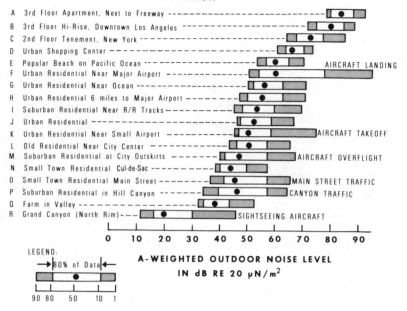

FIGURE 5.4

THE RANGE OF DAYTIME OUTDOOR NOISE READINGS FOR 18 LOCALES

DESCRIPTION	TYPICAL RANGE dB(A)	AVERAGE dB(A)
Quiet suburban residential	36 to 40 inclusive	38
Normal suburban residential	41 to 45 inclusive	43
Urban residential	46 to 50 inclusive	48
Noisy urban residential	51 to 55 inclusive	53
Very noisy urban residential	56 to 60 inclusive	58

FIGURE 5.5

QUALITATIVE DESCRIPTORS OF URBAN AND SUBURBAN DETACHED HOUSING RESIDENTIAL AREAS AND APPROXIMATE DAYTIME RESIDUAL NOISE LEVEL(L90)

Source: EPA, Community Noise, 1971.

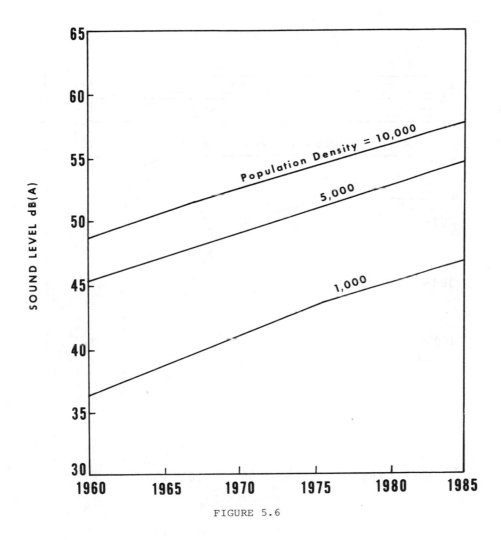

FIGURE 5.6

AMBIENT NOISE LEVEL FOR THREE DIFFERENT POPULATION DENSITIES
(after Dickerson, 1970)

218

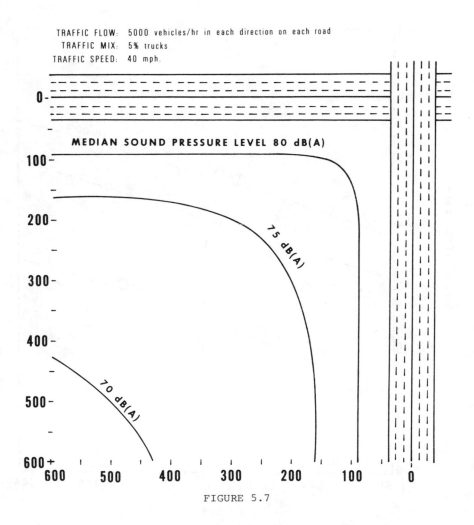

FIGURE 5.7

MEDIAN SOUND PRESSURE LEVEL CONTOURS
AT THE INTERSECTION OF TWO HIGHWAYS

(after Dickerson, 1970)

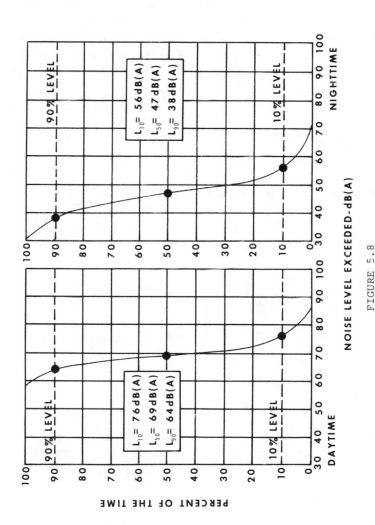

FIGURE 5.8

STATISTICAL DISTRIBUTION OF NOISE LEVELS AT URBAN SITE, SHOWING DIFFERENCE
BETWEEN DAYTIME (0700-2200) AND NIGHTTIME (2200-0700) NOISE EXPOSURE

(after Dickerson, 1970)

3. GENERATION FACTORS

Two sets of factors are involved in the generation of these different noise levels. These are (1) factors which affect initial emission of noise from the source, and (2) factors which affect the propagation of noise once it is emitted from the source. Factors affecting initial source emission of noise into the urban environment involve the physical engineering of the noise sources. Motor vehicle noise, for example, can be attributed to the factors outlined in Table 5.3.

TABLE 5.3

SOURCES OF AUTOMOBILE NOISE

Origin of Noise	Noise Inside the Vehicle	Noise Outside the Vehicle
Engine Vibration	Major Source of Low Frequency Noise	Not important
Engine Airborne Noise (and its transmission)	Major Source of High Frequency Noise	Major Source of High Frequency Noise
Engine Exhaust	Not important	Major Source of Low Frequency Noise
Engine Inlet	Not important	Major Source of Low Frequency Noise following Exhaust
Fan Noise	May be noticeable	Can be significant in low and middle frequency ranges
Road-Excited Vibration	Major Source of Low Frequency Noise	Not significant
Road-Excited Tire Noise	Not significant	Significant

Source: Journal of Sound and Vibration (1971) 15 (1), p. 64.

The second set of pollution generation factors involve the
properties of sound and its transmission into the surrounding
physical world. Once noise is produced, a number of variables
will affect the distance, the direction and the strength of noise
propagation. Most practical situations involve several of the
following effects:

Geometric spreading: The spreading of sound energy
through space causes an attenuation in sound levels by a
certain amount generally as distance travelled is doubled.

Refraction: Refraction is the bending of sound rays
caused by changes in the speed of sound. It is often the
effect of changes in humidity or wind conditions.

Air Absorption: Absorption of sound in air can be expressed as a change in sound level at a certain distance.
This form of sound attenuation is frequency dependent and
occurs at a fixed distance, commonly several decibels per
1000 feet. It is most significant for noise problems in
which propagation distance is rather long, such as aircraft
takeoffs and landings.

Surface Absorption: There are two ways sound can be
affected by surface absorption. When both the source and
the receiver are close to the ground sound waves reflected
from the ground may interfere with direct sound rays. More
improtant in terms of the urban noise environment, however,
is the loss of sound level that accompanies this reflection
process.

Scattering: Scattering occurs when sound rays encounter
a region of inhomogeneity in medium. When this occurs the
sound energy is redirected in many directions, unlike refraction or reflection when the major portion of sound
energy is redirected in cone principle direction. Scattering occurs in the physical environment when sound rays
encounter turbulent media, and rough or irregular surfaces
or obstacles (such as vegetation). This phenomena is important in terms of the changes in sound level it can cause.
For instance, if a region would normally be shielded from
noise by a barrier of some type, turbulence may cause a
scattering of sound rays and limit the effectiveness of the
barrier as a noise absorber.

Reflection: Reflection is the redirection of an entire
sound wave resulting in increased sound levels for receivers
in the path of the rebounding wave and decreased sound levels
for others. This is particularly important for sound propagation in urban places where experiments have shown that
significant amounts of sound pressure are present even after
a sound ray has been reflected off of four or five buildings.

Diffraction: Diffraction occurs when a sound ray is
reflected in such a manner that the sound effects are concentrated in a confined area with limited effects on the
overall sound level.

Wall Transmission: Consideration of the transmission
of sound through the exterior walls, doors, and windows of
buildings is of prime importance in establishing the noise
levels to which people are exposed in the urban environment.

III. QUALITY ASSESSMENT SYSTEMS

1. STANDARDS

There presently exist no noise emission standards on a national level either for community noise levels or for source emission levels. However, the Environmental Protection Agency plans to establish nationwide noise emission regulations for both motor carriers and rail carriers by November 1973 and to publish final emission regualtions for all major noise sources by May 1974.

Noise standards do exist on the state and local government levels. These standards are for the most part directed towards regulation of noise from specific types of emitters. The most prevalent of these are regulations for motor vehicle noise. Motor vehicle noise regulations fall into two categories: (1) qualitative noise regulations, and (2) quantitative noise regulations.

Quantitative standards for motor vehicle noise emission levels generally specify the type of vehicle, in some cases the travel speed, and the maximum noise limits permissible from the vehicle. The maximum noise level permitted by any State or City is 90 dβA of sound at 50 feet from the vehicle in use.

Quantitative noise ordinances for motor vehicles currently exist in the following U.S. cities: Anchorage; Cincinnati; Cleveland; Columbus; Los Angeles; Milwaukee; Peoria, Ill.; Seattle. There are also ordinances in the following states: California, New York.

Qualitative noise regulations for motor vehicles are more common than quantitative ordinances. These generally require an operating exhaust muffler system; they often specify restrictions on the use of horns and other signalling devices by motor vehicle operators; and in some areas the regulations put qualitative limits on loading and unloading noise.

Qualitative noise ordinances for motor vehicles presently exist in the following cities: Albuquerque; Akron, Ohio; Anchorage; Boston; Beverly Hills; Cincinnati; Atlanta; Birmingham; Buffalo; Dayton; Denver; Detroit; Fairlawn, N.J.; Hartford; Houston; Indianapolis; Kansas City, Mo.; Little Rock, Ak.; Las Vegas; Memphis; Miami, Fla.; Milwaukee; Minneapolis; Newark, N.J.; New Orleans; New York City; Norfolk; Peoria; Philadelphia; Pittsburgh; Portland, Ore.; Raleigh, N.C.; Rochester, N.Y.; Sac-

ramento; St. Louis, Mo.; Salt Lake City; San Antonio; San Diego;
San Francisco; Seattle; Tuscon, Az.; Washington, D.C. There
are also motor vehicle noise ordinances in the following states:
Alabama, Arizona, Arkansas, California, Colorado, Connecticut,
Delaware, Florida, Georgia, Hawaii, Idaho, Illinois, Indiana,
Iowa, Kentucky, Louisiana, Maine, Massachusetts, Michigan, Min-
nesota, Mississippi, Missouri, Montana, Nebraska, Nevada, New
Hampshire, New Mexico, New York, North Carolina, North Dakota,
Ohio, Oklahoma, Oregon, Pennsylvania, Rhode Isalnd, South Caro-
lina, South Dakota, Tennessee, Texas, Utah, Vermont, Virginia,
Washington, West Virginia, Wisconsin, Wyoming.

A number of U.S. cities have municipal ordinances which
quantitatively regulate noise from sources other than motor
vehicles: Anaheim; Beverly Hills; Buffalo; Chicago; Columbus;
Coral Gables; Dallas; Dayton; Fairlawn, N.J.; Indianapolis;
Inglewood; Los Angeles; Miami, Fla.; Minneapolis; New York City;
Orlando; Peoria, Ill.; Raleigh, N.C.; Salt Lake City; San Diego;
Tuscon, Az.; Warwick, R.I.; Washington, D.C. Most of these ordinances set permissible noise emission levels for specific
sources such as construction projects, loudspeakers or broad-
casting vehicles, air conditioning units or industrial sites.
These regulations all put restrictions on intrusive noise, with
one exception. Chicago is the one city which has legislated an
allowable ambient noise level.

A comparison of maximum noise levels for nonmotor vehicle
noise in a number of American cities shows the variation in standards throughout the nation (Figure 5.9).

2. ACHIEVEMENT OF STANDARDS

State and local standards on source emission levels are difficult to enforce. State motor vehicle regualtions are regulated
in most cases through state inspection systems but because of
ambiguity in the regualtions themselves most violation of ordinances is investigated and prosecuted on a case by case basis,
making an overall assessment of standard achievement difficult.
Chicago's ambient noise limitations were found to be exceeded at
certain points in the urban area twenty-four hours a day.

Bolt Baronek & Newman have attempted to set up, not standards,
but limitations on levels of acceptability of various noise levels
for various types of human activity as expressed in land use
form. Their proposals are shown in Figure 5.10 and Table 5.4.

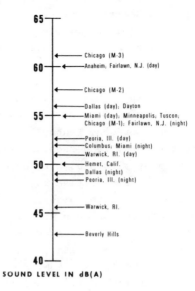

FIGURE 5.9

MUNICIPAL NOISE ORDINANCES
FOR NON-MOTOR VEHICLE
SOURCES: MAXIMUM NOISE
LIMITS AT RESIDENTIAL
BOUNDARY

SOUND LEVEL IN dB(A)

TABLE 5.4

NOISE COMPATIBILITY INTERPRETATIONS

Compatibility Code	Land Use Descriptors
A.	Satisfactory, with no special noise insulation requirements for new construction.
B.	New construction or development should generally be avoided except as possible infill of already developed areas. In such cases, a detailed analysis of noise reduction requirements should be made, and needed noise insulation features should be included in the building design.
C.	New construction or development should not be undertaken.
D.	New construction or development should not be undertaken unless a detailed analysis of noise reduction requirements is made and needed noise insulation features included in the design.
E.	New construction or development should not be undertaken unless directly related to airport-related activities or services. Conventional construction will generally be inadequate and special noise insulation features must be included. A detailed analysis of noise reduction requirements should be made and needed noise insulation features included in the construction or development.
F.	A detailed analysis of the noise environment, considering noise from all urban and transportation sources should be made and needed noise insulation features and/or special requirements for the sound reinforcement systems should be included in the basic design.
G.	New development should generally be avoided except as possible expansion of already developed areas.

225

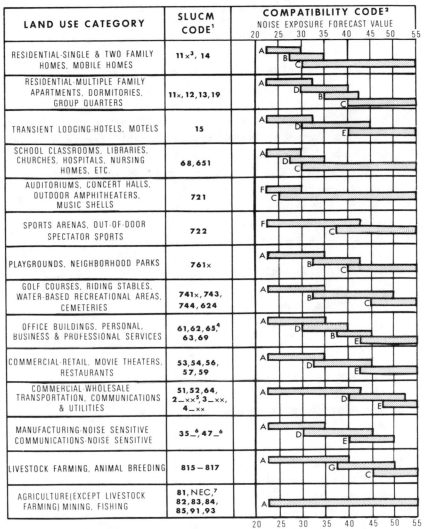

1. STANDARD LAND USE CODING MANUAL
2. CORRESPONDING LAND USE DESCRIPTORS ARE LISTED IN TABLE FOUR
3. X = A SLUCM CATEGORY BROADER OR NARROWER THAN, BUT GENERALLY INCLUSIVE OF THE CATEGORY DESCRIBED
4. EXCLUDING HOSPITALS
5. XX = SOME EXCEPTIONS MAY OCCUR FOR PARTICULAR OR SPECIALIZED NOISE SENSITIVE ACTIVITIES
6. DEPENDENT UPON SPECIFIC TASK REQUIREMENTS
7. NOT ELSEWHERE CLASSIFIED

FIGURE 5.10

LAND USE COMPATIBILITY CHART FOR AIRPORT NOISE

Source of figures: Bolt, Beranek and Newman (1970).

The Department of Housing and Urban Development has set up similar guidelines to be used in assessing the acceptability of the noise environment for location of projects under H.U.D. sponsorship. H.U.D. guidelines include noise from ground transportation, aircraft noise and overall site noise levels.

Noise control policy has two basic alternative directions which could be followed to achieve acceptable levels of noise in selected types of human environments. The location of land use forms can be regulated to insure that acceptable levels of noise will not be exceeded; this is analogous to the approach being used by H.U.D. with its noise assessment guidelines. Alternatively, source generation can be modified through engineering changes or muffling systems to obtain noise levels compatible with existing land use forms; this is the approach being taken in development of the 1973 Federal noise standards.

IV. EFFECTS OF NOISE POLLUTION

1. HEALTH EFFECTS

Whether a given noise should be considered "dangerous" and the amount of damage a given sound will impose on the listener depends on:

1) the level of the noise,
2) how long it lasts,
3) how many times it occurs daily,
4) over how many years daily exposure is repeated,
5) the effect on hearing considered to constitute damage,
6) individual susceptibility to this type of injury.

Table 5.5 provides guidelines for the relations between hearing threshold levels and the degree of hearing handicap. In a similar manner, general damage with criteria have been established for prolonged exposure to noise of different levels (Table 5.6).

It is difficult to specify allowable exposures for brief and intensive transportation noise exposures. A maximum tolerable limit can be set at 120-130 dB(A). Some investigators feel that a ten second exposure is the maximum tolerable level. One set of combinations of sound level, duration, and repetition considered acceptable for personnel exposures is described in Table 5.7. This table does not apply to: 1) noises of impacts, 2) brief noises lasting less than one second, 3) noises too variable to be measured with a standard sound meter.

TABLE 5.5

HEARING HANDICAPS RELATED TO THRESHOLD HEARING LEVELS

Class	Degree of Handicap	Average Hearing Threshold Level for 500, 1000, and 2000 Hz in the Better Ear		Ability to Understand Speech
		More Than	Not More Than	
A	Not significant		25dB	No significant difficulty with faint speech
B	Slight Handicap	25dB	40dB	Difficulty only with faint speech
C	Mild Handicap	40dB	55dB	Frequent difficulty with normal speech
D	Marked Handicap	55dB	70dB	Frequent difficulty with loud speech
E	Severe Handicap	70dB	90dB	Can understand only shouted or amplified speech
F	Extreme Handicap	90dB		Usually cannot understand even amplified speech

Source: U.S. Environmental Protection Agency, Effect of Noise on People, 1971, p.36.

TABLE 5.6

CRITICAL SOUND EXPOSURE LEVELS

Sound Level	Effect*
70-80 dB(A)	safe
85 dB(A)	hearing losses begin
90 dB(A)	serious losses begin
95 dB(A)	50% probability of a hearing impairment
105 dB(A)	losses in all exposed individuals

*Damage risk for prolonged exposures to noise over a period of several years.

Source: Dickerson (1970), p. 22.

TABLE 5.7

ACCEPTABLE EXPOSURES TO DANGEROUS NOISE

To use the table, select the column headed by the
number of times the dangerous noise occurs per
day, read down to the average sound level of the
noise and locate directly to the left in the first
column the total duration of dangerous noise allowed for any 24 hour period. It is permissible
to interpolate if necessary.

Total Noise Duration Per Day (24 hours)	Number of Times Noise Occurs Per Day						
	1	3	7	15	35	75	160 up
8 hrs.	89	89	89	89	89	89	89
6	90	92	95	97	96	94	93
4	91	94	98	101	103	101	99
2	93	98	102	105	108	113	117
1	96	102	106	109	114	125	125 (1 1/2 h)
30 min.	100	105	109	114	125		
15	104	109	115	124			
8	108	114	125				
4	113	125			A-Weighted		
2	123				Sound Levels		

Source: Chalupnik, 1970, p.107.

After hearing loss, the most easily detectable effect of
noise on the physiological state is the peripheral vegative functions. Certain noise levels have been shown to cause a vasocon-
strictive effect in the circulatory system. In test subjects
these effects were (i) noticeable at 52 dB(A), (ii) pronounced
at 72 dB(A) and (iii) considered dangerous at 85 dB(A).

Temporary Threshold Shift (T.T.S.) in acuity of hearing
varies with the individual and with the length and intensity
of exposure to noise. Noise exposure necessary for T.T.S. to
occur need not be severe, for some individuals a 12 hour automobile ride will produce a detectable loss in acuity. It is
unlikely that even high urban ambient noise levels could produce
T.T.S, however little is known about possible minor effects of
long term exposure to high levels of ambient noise.

Another possibly important but as yet unproven effect of
community noise, specifically traffic noise, is the hastening
of age induced hearing loss (presbycusis). Because age-deafening
progresses slowly and is expected as part of the life-cycle, an
individual adjusts to changes in hearing capacity and the effect
of the noise environment on the progression is generally unnoticed.

Other specific effects of noise on the human physical system include: muscular tension, sweating, metabolic changes,
reduced gastro-intestinal activity, nausea, headaches, tinnitus,
drowsiness and respiratory irregularities. The appearance and
intensity of these effects again depends on the intensity and
duration of the noise involved and to a great extent subjective
variables; no clear criteria for "dangerous" noise levels are
available for these physical effects.

2. WELFARE EFFECTS

   a. INTERFERENCE WITH SPECIFIC ACTIVITIES

      i. SLEEP DISTURBANCE

One of the chief complaints of transportation noise is interference with sleep or rest. The major "offender" is aircraft
noise.

Aggravated sleep loss can have a substantial effect on physical health and can become a significant variable in psychological well-being. The psychological consequences of repeated
sleep distrubance include paranoid delusions, hallucinations,
suicide and homicidal impulses.

While it is obvious that a sleeper who is awakened during
the night or kept from getting to sleep will have a less beneficial night's rest, it is not clear whether noise can reduce
the effectiveness of sleep without awakening the sleeper. Noise
which interrupts the deep sleep stage of the sleep cycle will
result in a less beneficial night's sleep.

While there are wide individual variations in the noises
which will awaken a sleeper, there are certain common parameters
for discussion of noise interference with sleep (Dickerson, 1970
1970;22):

1) the louder the noise, the greater the disturbance;

2) the more meaningful the sound, the greater the probability
of disturbance;

3) the more unexpected the sound, the greater the probability
of being awakened;

4) the greater the presence of personality variables
(neuroticism), the greater the sensitivity to noise;

5) the younger the child, the greater the susceptibility
to interference from noise; and

6) the greater the age or the poorer the health, the lower
the resistence to noise disturbance.

These and other variables combine to produce individual
levels of sensitivity to noise interference, making it difficult
to set criteria for acceptability. Estimates for threshold
noise levels for sleep disturbance range from 40-70 dB(A).

(ii)   AUDITORY COMMUNICATION

Communication difficulties will occur when background noise
exceeds certain levels. Again the frequency and time distribution of intruding noise play a role in auditory communication
interference; however the overall background level of noise is
the basis for evaluation of communication interference. General
interference with speech communication has been shown to be a
function of background noise levels, distance from speaker, voice
level and type of communication (Table 5.8).

Figure 5.11 shows the background noise levels, type of communication, voice level and the facility of speech communication.

(iii)   EFFECTS ON LEARNING & TASK PERFORMANCE

Numerous studies have been conducted which examine the effect of noise on learning and task performance. Most of this
research involves noise levels out of the range of present community noise; thus it is difficult to assess effects of the outdoor noise environment on the basis of this research.

The available literature indicates in some cases that
(i) noise has a decremental effect on task performance; in other
cases it indicates (ii) noise has no effect; and, still in
others, (iii) noise has been shown to have an incremental effect.
These conflicting conclusions may arise from the fact that high
noise levels can cause an actuation of psychic function which

TABLE 5.8

SPEECH INTERFERENCE LEVELS*

Voice Level Distance (ft)	Normal	Raised	Very Loud	Shouting
0.5	71	77	83	89
1	65	71	77	83
2	59	65	71	77
3	55	61	67	73
4	53	59	65	71
5	51	57	63	69
6	49	55	61	67
12	43	49	55	61

*(in dB re 0.0002 dyne/cm^2) which barely permit reliable conversation at the distances and voice levels indicated.

Source: Shih (1971), p. 61.

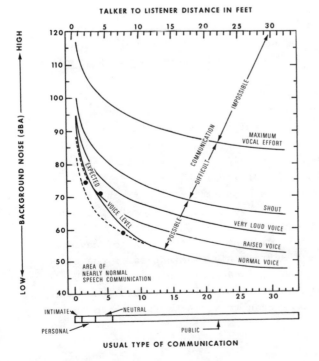

FIGURE 5.11

QUALITY OF SPEECH COMMUNICATION AS DEPENDENT ON THE A-WEIGHTED SOUND LEVEL (dBA) OF BACKGROUND NOISE AND DISTANCE BETWEEN TALKER AND LISTENER

After EPA, Effects of Noise on People (1971), p. 49

may lead to a decrease in performance. Test subjects may show increased task performance due to overcompensation.

Two factors have been shown to affect performance: loudness and distraction. However, the importance of these two factors has not been precisely determined. To the extent that certain urban noise intrusions (traffic noise for instance) are distracting, it may be expected that performance of mental tasks would be effected more than performance of physical tasks.

In recent experiments Singer & Glass (1972) found that random noises caused marked irritation and frustration as well as substantial declines in work performance, even after the noise had stopped. Glass suggests that an important negative factor in the effect of noise on performance may be the listener's perception of his powerlessness to change the situation. Given the nature of random intruding noises in the urban noise environment these findings may contribute significantly to further consideration of the effects of noise in urban areas.

b. ECONOMIC EFFECTS

Several studies have been conducted which examine the effect of noise on property values and apartment rents, as one approach to assessing the economic impact of noise pollution.

Colony, in research on the relationship between property values and expressway noise (1967) concludes that a residential property contiguous to a highway might be expected to decrease in value 20 to 30%, as compared with otherwise identical property not so located.

The percentage tends to decrease from the higher to the lower end of the range as the price of the property increases from $10,000 to $30,000. If a distance decay gradient of price decrease exists it is a steep one; no detrimental influence of the expressway can be detected outside of a narrow band about fifty feet wide along the right of way line.

From this research, it thus appears that traffic noise has a noticeable effect on the market value of a residential property immediately adjacent to the right of way--but that such influence decreases rapidly for parcels distant from the right of way.

According to McClure (1969) in his examination of the effect of jet noise on property values, a case can be made on the basis of insulation and easement costs that property exposed to jet noise is worth 10 to 20% less than it would be if it were not exposed to jet noise.

In a study of the effect of traffic noise and apartment
rents Towne (1966) generally concluded that freeway traffic noise
has a very small effect on the rent of units included in the
study.

His further conclusions include:

1) Freeway noise has some significant effect on rent differences when combined with other significant determinants.

2) Freeway noise had greater significance for explaining
   rent difference for units located in stories four and
   above than for those below.

3) The amount of effect of freeway noise is relatively small.
   The largest amount of variance in rent caused by freeway
   noise (though not the most significant) was about two
   cents per square foot per month, per decibel of noise,
   as measured at night.

4) The amount of effect of freeway noise on rent variations
   is both negative and positive. The latter may be considered illogical because of the assumption that noise
   is a disutility. In addition, intercorrelation between
   noise factors are high and this affects the sign of the
   noise coefficients.

Towne's final conclusion is deductive and appears plausible;
however, the data do not necessarily support the conclusion.
Freeway traffic noise may be a disutility and a nuisance to most
occupants of apartments. However, the analysis of the study
strongly suggests that the occupants' annoyance is not reflected
in rents. Two possible explanations are posited. The disutility
of noise is offset by the utility of other determinants; and
consumer preference may differ   among low and high rent apartment occupants, which was not controlled in the study.

c. OTHER EFFECTS: ANNOYANCE

Other effects of noise pollution have been considered under
the topic of annoyance. Variations of two general techniques
have been used to describe levels of annoyance within the community setting: (i) survey methods and (ii) examination of rates
and types of complaints.

Several surveys have shown that there is a relationship
between the sound level and level of expected annoyance. Figures
5.12 and 5.13 show this relationship for jet noise and traffic
noise respectively.

There are certain psychological-attitudinal factors which
correlate with the level of scaled annoyance:

1) general attitudes toward noise including personal differences in sound sensitivity;

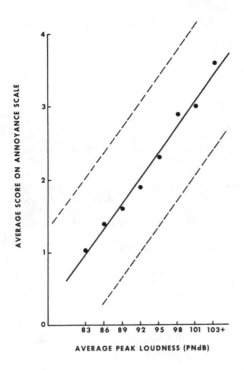

FIGURE 5.12

AVERAGE SCORES ON AN
ANNOYANCE SCALE FOR
PERSONS EXPOSED TO
VARIOUS LEVELS OF AIRCRAFT
NOISE

Source of figures: EPA,
Effects of Noise on People.

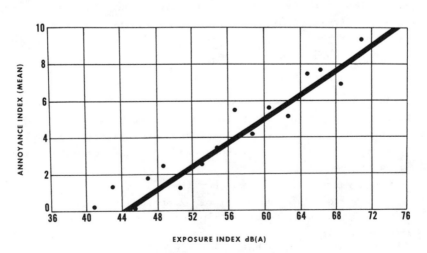

FIGURE 5.13

AVERAGE ANNOYANCE SCORES FOR PERSONS EXPOSED TO
VARIOUS LEVELS OF TRAFFIC NOISE

2) attitudes of the listener toward the noise generating source;

3) whether the listener believes the source operators are concerned about the effect of the emitted noise; and

4) factors specific to particular noise sources (i.e. fear of aircraft crashes).

Examination of the number and type of complaints as an indicator of community annoyance caused by noise has shown that reactions to annoyance vary with noise level and length of exposure (Figures 5.14 and 5.15).

The number of complaints may present only a small portion of the population actually "annoyed" by the noise. It has been determined (Tracor Strff, 1971) that in an area with a relatively high noise level, the number of highly annoyed households (h) can be predicted from the number of complaints per thousand (c) in the area by the formula:

$$h = 196 + 2c$$

Whether anti-noise complaint action is taken and when it does occur, the type of action which is taken is strongly affected by social, political and other factors which make up the whole of community dynamics. Community dynamics, which are poorly understood, substantially affect anti-noise actions.

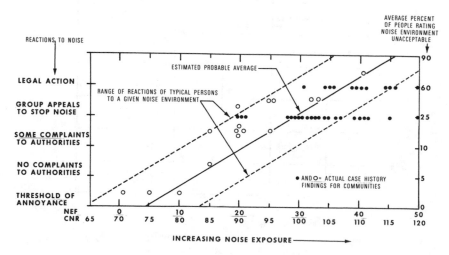

FIGURE 5.14

RELATIONS BETWEEN COMMUNITY NOISE LEVELS, JUDGMENTS OF UNACCEPTABILITY, AND COMMUNITY RESPONSES

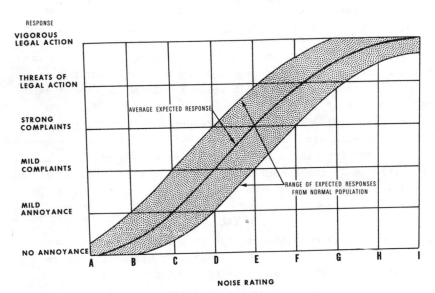

RESPONSE

VIGOROUS
LEGAL ACTION

THREATS OF
LEGAL ACTION

STRONG
COMPLAINTS

MILD
COMPLAINTS

MILD
ANNOYANCE

NO ANNOYANCE

AVERAGE EXPECTED RESPONSE

RANGE OF EXPECTED RESPONSES
FROM NORMAL POPULATION

A   B   C   D   E   F   G   H   I

NOISE RATING

CLASS	DEGREE OF HANDICAP	AVERAGE HEARING THRESHOLD LEVEL FOR 500, 1000 AND 2000 Hz IN THE BETTER EAR		ABILITY TO UNDERSTAND SPEECH
		MORE THAN	NOT MORE THAN	
A	NOT SIGNIFICANT		25dB	NO SIGNIFICANT DIFFICULTY WITH FAINT SPEECH
B	SLIGHT HANDICAP	25dB	40dB	DIFFICULTY ONLY WITH FAINT SPEECH
C	MILD HANDICAP	40dB	55dB	FREQUENT DIFFICULTY WITH NORMAL SPEECH
D	MARKED HANDICAP	55dB	70dB	FREQUENT DIFFICULTY WITH LOUD SPEECH
E	SEVERE HANDICAP	70dB	90dB	CAN UNDERSTAND ONLY SHOUTED OR AMPLIFIED SPEECH
F	EXTREME HANDICAP	90dB		USUALLY CANNOT UNDERSTAND EVEN AMPLIFIED SPEECH

FIGURE 5.15

RELATIONSHIP BETWEEN COMMUNITY RESPONSE,
NOISE EXPOSURE, AVERAGE HEARING
THRESHOLD LEVELS AND DEGREE OF HEARING HANDICAP

Source: EPA, Effects of Noise on People.

6   PESTICIDES

I.   MEASUREMENT SYSTEM FOR PESTICIDE RESIDUALS

    1. TYPES OF POLLUTANTS

/Pesticides include all insecticides, fungicides, rodent-icides, herbicides, and fumigants, or more generally, those bio-logically active chemicals used in pest control./ The minimum analytical schedule for pesticides contained in water (Feltz et. al., 1971) includes:

INSECTICIDES

Aldrin	Heptachlor
Chlordane	Lindane
DDD	Malathion
DDE	Methoxychlor
DDT	Methyl parathion
Dieldrin	Parathion
Endrin	Toxaphene

HERBICIDES

2,4-D
2,4,5-T
Silvex

    From an initial list of some 215 pesticides, the EPA has concluded that the following eight residuals are the most im-portant for present analysis of pesticide pollution (EPA, Strategic Environmental Assessment System, 1973).

Organochlorines
        1. DDT
        2. Dieldrin
        3. Heptachlor
        4. Heptachlor Epoxide
        5. Toxaphene
Organo Phosphorus
        6. Parathion/Paroxon

Herbicides

       7. Dioxin

       8. Picloram

2. SURVEILLANCE NETWORKS

The U.S. Geological Survey maintains a network of regularly sampled water quality stations where monthly samples are collected to determine the concentration and distribution of pesticides. (See Chapter 3.) The selected streams are ones whose waters are used for irrigation or are streams in areas where potential contamination could result from the application of the commonly used insecticides and herbicides.

Programs to monitor pesticides contained in food include (1) the Market Basket Study, which determines pesticide residues in what is considered to be the basic diet of a sixteen to nineteen year old male (statistically the nation's largest food consumer) to include 117 separate food items sampled in five geographical regions; (2) nationwide surveillance of unprocessed food and feed at seventeen field offices of the Food and Drug Administration; and (3) the surveillance program of the Consumer Protection Program, Consumer and Marketing Service, U.S. Department of Agriculture, for the analysis of meat and poultry samples taken at approximately 1,200 slaughtering plants.

II. GENERATION OF PESTICIDE POLLUTION

Total production of pesticides in the United States during 1970 amounted to approximately 1,203.9 million pounds (Haus, 1973). Three significant users, and thus generators feeding into the environment, of this pesticide production can be identified: farm, home and garden, and industry. Farm users include application to crops, livestock, poultry, seedbeds and transplants, and vector control. These various agricultural uses constitute over half of the pesticide usage in the United States. Several major concentrations of usage include: 41% of herbicides applied to corn, 68% of insecticides applied to cotton and corn, and most of the various fungicides applied to fruits and vegetables. According to a 1966 survey of 891 million acres of agricultural land use, only 5% was treated with insecticides, 12% with herbicides, and 0.5% with fungicides (Council on Environmental Quality, 1972).

Home and garden, or household usage, includes application for control both indoors and outdoors of insects, weed control of lawns

and gardens, rodent control, moth-proofing, insect control on pets,
etc. The four most important household pests controlled by pesticides in 1965 were roaches, mice, rats, and termites. The industrial use of pesticides includes all of the above, with the addition of use for preservation of wood and wood products, and the use
of some pesticides as raw materials for certain industrial processes.

Important in considering the generation of pesticides in addition to identification of users, is the cycling system which carries
the various pesticides to other locations within the environment
where their significance as an environmental pollutant may be multiplied many times. Three primary transport routes make up this
cycling system: the water route, the air route, and the food chain.
Surface run-off is generally considered to be the major route of
pesticide movement (Haus, 1973). Factors influencing the level of
pesticide transported from its site of origin by surface run-off
include: nature of the pesticide, extent of use, edaphic considerations, climatic factors, topography, and land use management practices. Atmospheric transportation occurs when pesticides are applied
aerially (some estimates place losses at 50%), through volatization
(vaporization) or by wind erosion of pesticides which have formed a
bond to the soil.

The food chain is potentially the most dangerous transport
route of pesticides. When animals eat plants or other organisms,
pesticides present in those organisims are ingested. The animal
then either biologically accumulates the pesticide in its body or
excretes it at a new location. With the repitition of this process
at every stage of the food chain, enormous magnifications of pesticide residues can occur which far exceed original environmental
concentrations. The increased level of these concentrations act
individually as new dangerous generators of pesticide hazards.

III. QUALITY ASSESSMENT SYSTEMS

The structure for assessing the level of pesticide pollution
was covered in an earlier section (Chapter 3, Section III on Water
Quality) where we found that a considerable degree of freedom
exists for the states to set their own levels of pollution control.

Listed below are the standards for the State of Illinois
which apply to waters designated for either public consumption
or food processing (see the above section on Water Quality for
a more complete statement of the standards).

(a) Water shall be of such quality that with treatment consisting of coagulation, sedimentation,
filtration, storage and chlorination, or other
equivalent treatment processes, the treated
water shall meet in all respects both the mandatory and the recommended requirements of the
Public Health Service Drinking Water Standards--
1962.

(b) The following levels of chemical constituents
shall not be exceeded:

CONSTITUENT	STORET NUMBER	CONCENTRATION (mg/l)
Arsenic (total)	01000	0.01
Barium (total)	01005	1.0
Cadmium (total)	01025	0.01
Chlorides	00940	250.
Carbon Chloroform Extract (CCE)	32005	0.2
Cyanide	00720	0.01
Iron (total)	01046	0.3
Lead (total)	01049	0.05
Methylene Blue Active Substance (MBAS)	38260	0.5
Nitrates plus Nitrites as N	00630	10.0
Oil (Hexane-solubles or equivalent)	00550	0.1
Phenols	32730	0.001
Selenium (total)	01145	0.01
Sulfates	00945	250.
Total Dissolved Solids	00515	500.

(c) Other contaminants that will not be adequately
reduced by the treatment processes noted in paragraph (a) of this Rule shall not be present in
concentrations hazardous to human health.

The level of pesticide pollution in each of the three food
sampling networks is assessed with different standards and procedures initially established by the Food and Drug Administration
and published in their Pesticide Analytical Manual. The Market
Basket Survey examines each commodity group for chlorinated organic pesticides, organic phosphate pesticides, herbicides, carbamates, arsenic, cadmium, mercury, polychlorinated biphenyl
residues, organochlorine, and organophosphorous residues. As
part of the nationwide surveillance unprocessed food and feed
are examined for chlorinated organic pesticides and organic
phosphate pesticides, with selected random sampling for chloro-
phenoxy compounds, carbaryl, and carbamates. Samples taken at
the some 1,200 slaughter houses are tested for chlorinated organic pesticide residues.

IV.   EFFECTS OF PESTICIDE POLLUTION

Two distinct levels of analysis are required in the investigation of the effects of pesticides--(1) the immediate effects
on humans and (2) the long range environmental effects, which
can only be analysed by use of complex ecological materials
balance types of approach. Man has been poisoned by at least
fifty different types of pesticides, from accidents or careless-
ness during manufacture or application, from accidents in the
home, from eating foods that contain pesticide residues,   from
environmental exposure. In 1963 it was estimated that 150 fatal-
ities per year occurred in the United States (Ingraham, 1963).
Health effects of pesticides to human beings are generally rather
well known, with statistical data available for some seven or
eight years to form a solid base line index for evaluating current content levels.

Chronic poisoning, or the long range effects, are more
elusive and much more difficult to analyse. It requires understanding of such phenomena as persistence--which causes the accumulation of pesticide residuals in the environment; and biological magnification--which creates high toxic concentration in
an organism even though the content of the pesticide in the
general environment is low.

7   RADIATION

I. MEASUREMENT SYSTEMS

1. TYPES OF POLLUTANTS

Radioactivity is found in the atmosphere of virtually all urban locations in the United States. In the form of beta radioactivity, it enters the urban environment as surface air particulates and as deposition from precipitation; in the form of radioactive tritium, it is found in both the atmosphere and the waterways.

The half dozen most important radionuclide residuals selected from an initial list of 78 sources are cobalt 60, Krypton 85, Strontium 90, Iodine 129, Iodine 131, and Cesium 137 (EPA, Strategic Environmental Assessment System, 1973).

2. SURVEILLANCE NETWORKS

Atmospheric beta radioactivity is sampled with the Radiation Alert Network which consists of a network of seventy stations located throughout the United States. Two sampling procedures are maintained--(1) gross beta radioactivity extracted from surface air particulates and, (2) measurement of the deposition of particulates to the earth as the result of precipitation.

Tritium is sampled and measured with the Tritium Surveillance System administered by the Office of Radiation Programs of EPA. Quarterly drinking water samples are obtained at the seventy Radiation Alert Network Stations, daily precipitation samples at eight of these stations, and quarterly samples at thirty-eight surface water stations.

II. GENERATION OF THE EFFLUENTS

Generation of radiation residuals will be reviewed by looking at six types of sources: natural, nuclear fuel cycle, medical, nuclear devices, electromagnetic devices, and other (Bisselle, 1973). Natural radiation, found at the general environmental level, is derived primarily from two sources: cosmic and terrestrial radiation. Cosmic radiation varies with altitude and geomagnetic latitude and terrestrial radiation results from the naturally radio-

isotopes which are released are: mining (radon gas - Rn-222, and
dust-absorbed daughter products - Po-218, Pb-214, Bi-214 and Po-214),
milling-refining (the same plus radium - Ra-226), conversion, enrichment, and fabrication (relatively little due to the extremely careful inventories maintained on this by non economically and strate-
gically valuable material); power plant (relatively few fusion or
activation products dangerous to man, gross alpha, beta and gamma
levels are monitored), fuel reprocessing (includes the possibility
of all previously mentioned radionuclides), disposal, and transportation (no releases of radionuclides in these final two phases of
the fuel cycle except accidentally).

Medical sources of radiation residues, X-ray machine, gamma
and neutron sources, and a wide range of pharmaceutical isotopes

TABLE 7.1

SUMMARY OF ESTIMATES OF ANNUAL WHOLE-BODY DOSE RATES
IN THE UNITED STATES (1970)

Source	Average Dose Rate* (mrem/yr)	Annual Person-Rems (in millions)
Environmental		
Natural	102	20.91
Global Fallout	4	0.82
Nuclear Power	0.003	0.0007
Subtotal	106	21.73
Medical		
Diagnostic	72**	14.8
Radiopharmaceuticals	1	0.2
Subtotal	73	15.0
Occupational	0.8	0.16
Miscellaneous	2	0.5
TOTAL	182	37.4

* Note: The numbers shown are average values only. For
given segments of the population, dose rates considerably
greater than these may be experienced.

** Based on the abdominal dose.

Source: National Academy of Sciences, 1972, p. 19.

which are used for diagnostic and therapeutic purposes, are by far
the largest contributor to the annual per capita radiation due
(Bisselle, 1973). Nuclear devices, as generators of radioactive
fallout, have decreased drastically since the 1963 atmospheric
test ban treaty. Underground testing, while contributing to the
general population dose, has not yet been found to be significant.
Electromagnetic devices, which include lasers, microwave, radio,
and television transmitters, emit non-ionizing radiation, however
levels of emission and significance of emission level to an exposed population have not been reliably estimated. Included in the
category other, are such items as television sets (X-rays), lumi-
nous watch dials, construction materials containing naturally
radioactive substances, etc. The per capita dose of exposure to
these items is relatively small.

III. QUALITY ASSESSMENT SYSTEM

The National Council on Radiation Protection and Measurements has recommended, and in 1960 the Federal Radiation Council
accepted, the figure of 170 mrem per year per individual person
as a standard radiation exposure. This population average was
calculated using a "medical balance" approach and is the same
total dosage estimate as used by the United Nations Scientific
Committee on the Effect of Atomic Radiation.

IV. EFFECTS OF RADIATION POLLUTION

In reviewing and updating the 1956 Biological Effects of
Atomic Radiation Report of the National Academy of Science, the
Advisory Committee on the Biological Effects of Ionizing Radiations in 1972 recommended four bases for assessment of genetic
risks of radiation pollution:

> (1) The risk relative to the natural background radia-
> tion. If the genetically significant exposure is kept well
> below this amount, we are assured that the additional con-
> sequences will be less in quantity and no different in kind
> from what we have experienced throughout human history.
> This base, although not quantitative, has the great merit
> that it is not necessary to make any quantitative assump-
> tions about human radiation genetics.

TABLE 7.2

ESTIMATED EFFECTS OF RADIATION
FOR SPECIFIC GENETIC DAMAGE*

	Current incidence per million live births	Number that are new mutants	Effect of 5 rem per generation	
			First generation	Equilibrium
Autosomal dominant traits	10,000	2,000	50-500	250-2,500
X-chromosome-linked traits	400	65	0-15	10-100
Recessive traits	1,500	?	very few	very slow increase

Estimates of cytogenetic effects from 5 rem per generation. Values are based
on a population of one million live births. Unbalanced rearrangements are
based on male radiation only.

	Current incidence	Effect of 5 rem per generation	
		First generation	Equilibrium
Congenital anomalies			
Unbalanced rearrangements	1,000	60	75
Aneuploidy	4,000	5	5
Recognized abortions			
Aneuploidy and polyploidy	35,000	55	55
XO	9,000	15	15
Unbalanced rearrangements	11,000	360	450

Source: National Academy of Sciences, (1972) pp. 54, 55.

*The range of estimates is based on doubling doses of 20 and 200 rem. The values given
are the expected numbers per million live births.

TABLE 7.3

ESTIMATED EFFECTS OF 5 REM PER GENERATION
ON A POPULATION OF ONE MILLION*

Disease classification	Current incidence	Effect of 5 rem per generation	
		First generation	Equilibrium
Dominant diseases	10,000	50-500	250-2500
Chromosomal and recessive diseases	10,000	Relatively slight	Very slow increase
Congenital anomalies	15,000		
Anomalies expressed later	10,000	5-500	50-5000
Constitutional and degenerative diseases	15,000		
Total	60,000	60-1000	300-7500

Source: National Academy of Sciences (1972), p. 57.

*This includes conditions for which there is some evidence of a genetic component.

(2) The risk of specific genetic conditions. Using the relative risk (or doubling dose) given above, an estimate of the increase in diseases caused by dominant and X-chromosome-linked recessive mutations can be made for the generation following radiation and for the equilibrium increase under continuous radiation. Estimates of cytogenetic effects can be made directly from mouse data. Numerical values are given in Tables 7.2 and 7.3.

(3) The risk relative to the current incidence of serious disabilities. Diseases caused by dominant and by X-chromsome-linked recessive mutations will eventually increase in proportion to the mutation rate increase. For congenital anomalies and constitutional diseases, we suggest that the mutational component (or the fraction of the incidence that is proportional to the mutation rate) is between five and fifty percent. Numerical values based on these assumptions are given in Table 7.4.

(4) The risk in terms of overall ill health. The contribution of the mutational component to ill health is arbitrarily taken as twenty percent. With this and a doubling dose between 20 and 200 rem a dose of 5 rem per generation would eventually lead to an increase of between 0.5 and 5.0 percent in all illness.

Certain effects of low-level irradiation must be considered as possible human health effects, however "no radiation injuries have been documented in man or other mammals under exposure conditions compatible with existing radiation guides" (Advisory Committee on the Biological Effects of Ionizing Radiations, 1972). Possible effects, however, include neoplasms, opacities of the lenses of the eye, impairment of fertility, defective development of the fetus, and of course, cancer.

The Special Studies Group of the EPA ("The Effects on Populations of Exposure," 1972, p.15) projects "that nuclear capacity in the United States will increase from 6,000 megawatts in 1970 to 800,000 megawatts in 2000. Associated with this increase, there is a postulated twentyfive-fold increase in uranium mining and milling, a fifteen-fold increase in fuel fabrication facilities, and establishment of about fifteen fuel reprocessing plants compared to one now in existence. For purposes of dose projections, the Special Studies Group has also assumed that a limit of five mrem per year per reactor at the site boundary will be met."

Evaluation of this projected growth and the possible environmental pollution of nuclear power is made difficult by the many undetermined values involved--the demand for electricity, potential shortage of certain types of fossil fuels, effects of present generating facilities on health and the environment and if new facilities are constructed, whether or not new technologies will offset the effects of increased nuclear consumption.

C   NATIONWIDE RELATIONSHIPS OF POLLUTION TO CITY CHARACTERISTICS

In Part B, it was shown that current surveillance of pollutants has many limitations and inadequacies: coverage is quite
variable from one type of pollutant to another and among different
regions of the country. Where national data systems have been
established, they work poorly at present. Rather than being the
sensitive information systems they ultimately must become, they
are today simply computerized storage devices into which every-
thing that might be of potential value is stored without checking
and quality control and with obstacles to both recovery and use
without substantial modifications and corrections. A similar situation exists with respect to environmental quality assessment.
The issue of standards remains unresolved in many cases, and even
where national standards are available there remains considerable
disagreement about the indices to be used to assess departures
of pollution levels from these standards, and indeed, about the
validity of the standards.

Despite these many difficulties presented by the current state
of environmental data systems, in this section we make an attempt
to develop the basic elements from which a sorting table relating
urban forms and land use to the native and intensity of environmental pollution might be fashioned, focusing on environmental
indexes for the period immediately following the 1970 census of
population. The focus is upon city-to-city variations, reserving
for Part D consideration of variations within urban regions. In
Chapter 8 we discuss the assembly of a nationwide data set. In
Chapter 8 we discuss the assembly of a nationwide data set. In
Chapter 9 a pollution-sensitive typology of urban regions is
derived and the format of a sorting table is suggested. Then,
in Chapter 10, relationships between selected city characteristics, measures of urban form, the nature of urban land use,
and environmental pollution are discussed, showing key relationships that can be discussed in the sorting table. Finally,
in Chapter 11, we address certain issues in the measurement
of agglomeration economies and environmental diseconomies.

The underlying concept in Chapter 10 and 11 is that the
size, density and economic base of the city, when filtered through

different urban forms, produce distinctive land use mixes and
patterns that, in turn, yield both the benefits and the diseconomies of urban life. Chapter 10 explores the individual conceptual links in this scheme, while in Chapter 11 the aggregate
interacting effects of the benefits and diseconomies of urban
life are considered, using total land and property values within
metropolitan regions as a key indicator.

8 A NATIONWIDE DATA SET

The first step was to assemble the best-possible nationwide
data set into a "sorting table" with urban regions in the rows
and with environmental indexes and other city characteristics in
the columns as a way of clarifying the availability and quality
of environmental data on a nationwide basis, and to enable the
relationships between environmental pollution and city characteristics to be studied. After much exploration, it was determined
that, because of constraints imposed by the availability of sufficient air quality data to compute the MAQI and EVI indexes,
the maximum feasible metropolitan data set would still have to
be restricted to observations made of the following seventy-six
urban areas: Even then, only 44 of the 76 had adequate water
quality data available, far less had data on pesticides and
solid wastes, and none on noise.

Akron	Memphis
Albuquerque	Miami
Allentown-Bethlehem-Easton	Milwaukee
Atlanta	Minneapolis-St. Paul
Baltimore	Nashville-Davidson
Birmingham	New Haven
Boston	New Orleans
Bridgeport	New York
Buffalo	Newark
Canton	Norfolk-Portsmouth
Charleston, W.Va.	Oklahoma City
Chattanooga	Omaha
Chicago	Paterson-Clifton-Passaic
Cincinnati	Philadelphia
Cleveland	Phoenix
Columbus, Ohio	Pittsburgh
Dallas	Portland, O.
Dayton	Providence-Pawtucket-Warwick
Denver	Reading
Des Moines	Richmond
Detroit	Rochester, N.Y.
El Paso	St. Louis
Flint	Salt Lake City
Fort Worth	San Antonio
Gary-Hammond-East Chicago	San Bernadino-Riverside-
Grand Rapids	Ontario
Hartford	San Diego
Honolulu	San Francisco-Oakland
Houston	San Jose
Indianapolis	Seattle-Everett
Jacksonville	Syracuse
Jersey City	Tampa-St. Petersburg
Johnstown	Toledo
Kansas City	Tulsa
Los Angeles-Long Beach	Utica-Rome
Louisville	Washington, D.C.

Wichita   York
Wilmington   Youngstown-Warren
Worcester

In every case, the Standard Metropolitan Statistical Area (SMSA),
as defined by the Office of Management and Budget in 1970, was
used as the operational unit.

　　Figure 8.1 maps the locations of these places. The set includes the fifty largest metropolitan areas in the nation. In
Table 8.1 is listed the total set of variables that was assembled
for as many of these metropolitan areas as possible. The nature
and sources of each subset is discussed below. As will become
painfully evident, the quality of national reporting is such that
the maximally-feasible data set of seventy-six urban regions was
quickly reduced to forty-four partially-reported areas in the
case of water quality data, and to only five in the case of pesticides. For solid wastes, synthetic data had to be generated,
and for noise surrogate variables had to be used to provide some
semblance of national coverage.

I. THE URBAN VARIABLES

　　1. CITY CHARACTERISTICS

　　The city characteristics selected for inclusion in the data
set were those reported by previous studies to have been most
consistently related to variations in environmental pollution
(size, density, manufacturing concentrations), as well as variables demonstrated in the City Classification Handbook to be
effective measures of other major dimensions along which urban
areas vary in the United States (Berry, 1972). Thus, median
family income indexes variations in the socio-economic status of
a city's population, and the median age of the city's population
reveals important life-cycle differences in the demographic composition of the city. The density and recent population change
variables together reveal the period of major growth of the urban
area, and the modal composition of its transportation infrastruc-
ture, etc. Also included in the data set was the total value of
real property in each SMSA, about which more will be said in
Chapter 11.

　　2. URBAN FORM INDICATORS

　　Three summary measures of urban form were created for use
in the city-to-city comparisons: the number of degrees of arc

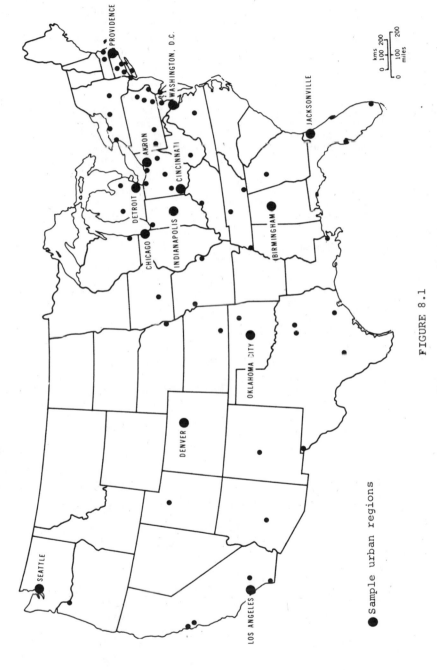

● Sample urban regions

FIGURE 8.1

MASTER SET OF METROPOLITAN AREAS

TABLE 8.1

LIST OF VARIABLES IN THE SORTING TABLE,
WITH UNITS OF MEASUREMENT

Variable		Unit of Measurement

1. CITY CHARACTERISTICS

1970	City Population	1000's
	SMSA Population	1000's
	City Density	Pop./sq. mile
	SMSA Density	Pop./sq. mile
	Density Ratio	(SMSA density/city density) x 100
1960-70	Population Change, CITY	percent
	Population Change, SMSA	percent
1970	Median Age of Population, CITY	years of age
	Median Age of Population, SMSA	years of age
	Median Family Income	$
	Percent of Labor Force Employed in Manufacturing	percent
	Land Area, CITY	sq. miles
	Land Area, SMSA	sq. miles
1967	Total Value of Real Estate, SMSA	$1,000,000's

2. URBAN FORM INDICATORS

Degrees of Arc of SMSA around CBD	0° to 360°
Transportation Radials,	number
Transportation Circumferentials, SMSA	number

3. AIR POLLUTANTS

Sulfur Dioxide	(a) Annual Mean ($\mu g/m^3$)
	(b) Annual Maximum ($\mu g/m^3$)
Total Suspended Particulates	(a) Annual Mean ($\mu g/m^3$)
	(b) Annual Maximum ($\mu g/m^3$)

4. AIR QUALITY INDEXES

MAQI (a) SO_2	index numbers
(b) TSP	index numbers
(c) NO_2	index numbers
(d) All pollutants	index numbers

TABLE 8.1 (cont'd)

Variable	Unit of Measurement

4. AIR QUALITY INDEXES (cont'd)

EVI	(a)	SO_2	index numbers
	(b)	TSP	index numbers
	(c)	All pollutants	index numbers

5. WATER CHARACTERISTICS

Temperature	°F
Color (Platinum-Cobalt Units)	P-C units
Turbidity	JTU's
pH	pH values
Fecal Coliform Bacteria	MPN/100 ml.
Total Dissolved Solid	ppm (residue at 180°C.)
Suspended Solids	ppm
Total Nitrogen	ppm
Alkalinity (as $CaCO_3$)	ppm
Hardness (Ca, Mg)	ppm
Chlorides	ppm
Total Iron and Manganese	ppm
Sulfate	ppm
Dissolved Oxygen	ppm

6. WATER QUALITY INDEXES

Water Quality Index, Drinking Use (PI_1)	index numbers
Water Quality Index, Recreation Use (PI_2)	index numbers
Water Quality Index, Industrial Use (PI_3)	index numbers
Mean Water Quality Index (of above 3)	index numbers

7. SOLID WASTE ESTIMATES

Single-Family Source Units, SMSA	1000's
Multi-Family Source Units, SMSA	1000's
Manufacturing Employees, SMSA	1000's
Total Solid Waste in Tons per Year:	
Single-Family (S.F.S.U. x 2858 lbs/year)	1000's tons/year
Multi-Family (M.F.S.U. x 1315 lbs/year)	1000's tons/year
Commercial (SMSA Pop x 3.5 lbs/cap/day)	1000's tons/year
Manufacturing (MFG emp x 7.6 tons/year)	1000's tons/year

TABLE 8.1 (cont'd)

Variable	Unit of Measurement

7. SOLID WASTE ESTIMATES (cont'd)

Simple	Demolition and Construction (500 lbs/cap/year)	1000's tons/year
	Sewage (SMSA Pop x 87.1 lbs/cap/year)	1000's tons/year
	Solid Waste Generation Figure	lbs/cap/day
	Total calculated from simple solid waste generation figure	1000's tons/year
	Total calculated from summation of generation figures for specific uses	1000's tons/year
	Same as above, but omitting manufacturing	1000's tons/year

8. SURROGATES FOR NOISE

Automobile Traffic Volume	No. of workers using private automobiles in commutation to work, SMSA
Air Traffic Volume	No. of scheduled aircraft arrivals and departures, SMSA

9. PESTICIDES

DDT	ppm
DDE	ppm
TDE	ppm
DIELDRIN	ppm
HEPTACHLOR EPOXIDE	ppm
BHC	ppm
Total Bromides	ppm
Lindane	ppm
Kelthane	ppm

10. RADIATION

Gross Beta Radioactivity, Max.	pci/m^2
Gross Beta Radioactivity, Ave.	pci/m^2
Rainfall	mm
Beta Radioactivity Deposition	mci/m^2

11. LAND USE

Residential	Percentage of total area
Commercial	Percentage of total area
Industrial	Percentage of total area
Extractive	Percentage of total area
Public and Semipublic	Percentage of total area
Transportation, Communications, Utilities (TCU)	Percentage of total area
Open Space	Percentage of total area

covered by the SMSA around its CBD, rounded off to the nearest
60°--compare Chicago's 180° half-circle west of Lake Michigan
with the full 360° of Dallas; the number of expressways and primary Federal aid highways radiating outwards from the city center;
and the number of circumferential highways providing beltway
access around the urban region. Various combinations of these
measures yield urban areas of differing structure ranging all the
way from the complete tessellation of a spider's web with many
radials and circumferentials covering a full 360° around the
center, permitting dispersed urban development to take place,
to more core-oriented radially-structured finger-like forms.
As will be seen in Chapter 10, the most important consequences
of these different forms appear to be for land use, the dispersed
forms producing more dispersed urban sprawl and the more focussed
core-oriented forms produced greater intensities of land use in
the accessible areas, yet retaining greater amounts of open space
at the same time.

Table 8.2 records the complete set of urban variables.

II. THE POLLUTION MEASURES

Much has already been said in Part B about specific pollution variables and environmental quality indicators. Therefore,
the description of the pollution measures incorporated into the
data set will be restricted to sources and to computational procedures where measures were developed by the project team. The
discussion follows the same sequence as in Chapters 2-7.

1. AIR QUALITY

All data are for 1970, and the bulk are derived from C.A.
Bisselle, S.H. Lubore and R.P. Pikul, National Environmental
Indices: Air Quality and Outdoor Recreation, The Mitre Corporation, Washington, D.C., 1972. This data base, developed by The
Mitre Corporation under contract to EPA is the only one which at
this time provides a standard system of reporting air emissions
on a national network of urban sampling sites and a computed set
of MAQI and EVI indexes. An attempt was made to fill gaps in
The Mitre Corporation's data set using recent Air Pollution Technical Documents as well as information requested directly from
EPA and discussed in more detail in Chapters 12 and 13. Table
8.3 records the air quality data set.

	City	Pop CITY	Pop SMSA	Den-sity CITY	Den-sity SMSA	Den. Ratio (S/C) x100	Pop Change CITY	Pop Change SMSA	Median Age CITY
1	Akron	275	679	5074	750	15	-5.1	28.2	29.0
2	Albuquerque	244	316	2968	270	9	21.2	18.1	25.2
3	AlBethEaston	182	544	10225	501	5	-1.5	19.8	33.5
4	Atlanta	497	1390	3779	805	21	2.0	68.6	27.5
5	Baltimore	906	2071	11571	917	8	-3.5	34.7	29.1
6	Birmingham	301	739	3786	272	7	-11.7	15.3	30.2
7	Boston	641	2754	13935	2790	20	-8.1	11.3	28.7
8	Bridgeport	157	330	5752	2021	21	-0.1	26.9	30.6
9	Buffalo	463	1349	11211	848	8	-13.1	14.5	31.4
10	Canton	110	372	5789	646	11	-3.1	15.6	30.5
11	Charleston	72	320	2647	254	10	-16.7	-5.5	34.6
12	Chattanooga	120	306	2286	308	13	-8.4	21.3	31.5
13	Chicago	3363	6974	15108	1875	12	-5.2	35.3	30.1
14	Cincinnati	452	1385	5787	644	11	-10.0	21.7	29.4
15	Cleveland	751	2064	9895	1359	14	-14.3	27.1	29.0
16	Columbus	539	916	4004	613	15	14.5	32.8	25.5
17	Dallas	844	1556	3178	341	11	24.2	61.8	27.5
18	Dayton	243	850	6345	498	8	-7.1	30.5	28.9
19	Denver	515	1228	5410	336	6	4.2	63.7	29.2
20	Des Moines	201	286	3180	481	15	-4.0	49.2	29.1
21	Detroit	1511	4200	10949	2152	20	-9.5	28.5	30.0
22	El Paso	322	359	2722	339	12	16.5	-0.7	23.2
23	Flint	193	457	5884	362	6	-1.8	38.3	25.2
24	Fort Worth	394	762	1922	474	25	10.4	69.9	28.1
25	GaryHammonDec	330	633	4209	676	16	-5.0	34.2	26.5
26	Grand Rapids	197	539	4388	380	9	11.5	20.0	27.4
27	Hartford	158	664	9080	988	11	-2.6	30.7	28.2
28	Honolulu	325	629	3974	1055	27	10.4	47.6	28.1
29	Houston	1232	1985	2839	316	11	31.4	56.7	26.1
30	Indianapolis	745	1110	1964	360	18	13.6	28.6	27.3
31	Jacksonville	529	529	691	691	100	-5.6	-5.6	26.0
32	Jersey City	261	609	17285	12957	75	-5.6	4.2	31.2
33	Johnstown	42	263	7368	148	2	-21.3	-2.8	36.3
34	Kansas City	675	1254	1809	453	25	6.6	21.0	30.0
35	LosAngLongBea	3175	7036	6196	1729	28	12.5	20.0	30.8
36	Louisville	361	827	6017	911	15	-7.5	39.0	30.7
37	Memphis	624	770	2870	565	20	25.3	-17.2	26.2
38	Miami	335	1268	5767	621	6	14.8	45.0	37.3
39	Milwaukee	717	1404	7547	964	13	-3.3	27.7	28.7
40	MinneapolisSP	744	1814	6940	861	12	-6.1	55.9	29.5
41	NashvilleDavi	448	541	882	332	38	12.1	45.7	28.1
42	New Haven	136	356	7500	1453	19	-9.4	29.1	28.4
43	New Orleans	593	1045	3009	530	18	-5.4	61.8	28.2
44	New York	7895	11572	26343	5418	21	1.1	25.7	32.7
45	Newark	382	1857	16255	2649	16	-5.6	14.8	26.0
46	NorfolkPortsm	419	681	5135	1004	20	-0.4	65.8	24.2
47	Oklahoma City	367	647	577	299	52	13.0	46.3	29.1
48	Omaha	348	540	4543	351	8	15.2	23.4	26.8
49	PatersonClipa	282	1359	12051	3183	26	1.0	18.7	32.0
50	Philadelphia	1949	4818	15167	1356	9	-2.7	22.6	31.4
51	Phoenix	581	968	2344	105	4	32.4	72.0	27.7
52	Pittsburgh	520	2401	9420	787	8	-13.9	4.4	31.7
53	Portland	382	1009	4287	276	6	2.7	39.5	33.0
54	ProvidencPaw	340	913	5502	1345	24	-4.8	23.0	32.4
55	Reading	88	256	8889	343	4	-10.7	17.8	36.8
56	Richmond	250	518	4146	433	10	13.5	24.3	30.1
57	Rochester	296	883	8063	381	5	-7.0	41.7	29.4
58	St. Louis	622	2363	10163	574	6	-17.0	28.5	31.8
59	Salt Lake City	176	558	2963	526	18	-7.2	47.8	28.4
60	San Antonio	654	364	3554	441	12	11.3	63.4	24.8
61	San Bernadino	308	1140	2227	42	2	38.4	42.2	26.9
62	San Diego	696	1357	2196	318	14	21.6	43.8	25.8
63	San Francisco	1077	3110	10901	1255	12	-2.8	31.9	33.7
64	San Jose	477	1065	3282	819	25	118.3	41.3	26.8

8.2

VARIABLES

Median Age SMSA	Median Family Income	Percent Employed in Mfg	Land Area CITY	Land Area SMSA	Property Values SMSA	Degrees of Arc	Radials CITY	Radials SMSA	Circumferentials SMSA
25.6	11047	39.3	54.2	905	5407	360	3	5	2
22.2	9031	8.6	82.2	1169	2122	360	3	3	0
31.6	10168	48.3	17.8	1086	3599	180	0	5	3
25.9	10695	19.8	131.5	1727	11249	240	9	10	4
27.6	10577	24.2	78.3	2259	9774	240	10	11	3
28.4	8295	28.0	79.5	2721	5122	360	6	6	0
29.9	11449	21.5	46.0	987	21022	240	11	12	4
30.4	11775	45.9	16.1	1193	13066	180	2	4	1
28.5	10430	34.0	41.3	1591	3842	180	4	5	2
28.3	10249	44.5	19.0	576	2735	360	3	4	3
29.0	8669	20.0	27.2	907	1818	360	2	4	0
28.3	8513	41.1	52.5	995	1213	240	1	4	2
27.4	11931	31.4	222.6	3720	50249	180	10	12	2
26.8	10257	33.3	78.1	2150	11240	180	7	8	0
29.6	11407	34.5	75.1	1519	19598	180	5	8	2
26.3	10460	23.8	134.6	1494	6846	360	7	10	3
25.4	10405	23.8	265.6	4564	11309	360	8	8	3
27.4	11234	38.2	38.3	1708	6737	360	4	7	1
24.9	10777	17.8	95.2	3660	7979	180	7	9	2
26.0	10682	19.3	63.2	594	2024	360	3	5	3
26.1	12117	37.6	138.0	1952	27861	180	12	13	3
20.5	7792	22.2	118.3	1058	1500	180	2	2	0
24.1	11172	46.8	32.8	1300	4138	360	1	4	2
25.8	10101	32.9	205.0	1607	724	360	7	9	2
24.9	11015	48.5	78.4	937	7483	120	6	10	1
24.6	10630	38.4	44.9	1420	2883	360	4	5	2
29.7	12282	29.0	17.4	672	6906	180	6	8	1
21.9	12035	7.4	83.9	596	4737	180	4	6	2
25.5	10191	19.2	433.9	6286	16271	360	7	7	1
26.6	10754	30.6	379.4	3080	6712	360	10	11	5
26.0	0671	13.0	766.0	766	2642	180	3	6	1
34.4	9698	41.7	15.1	47	2681	60	5	6	1
31.0	8310	32.2	5.7	1780	753	360	1	3	1
27.3	10568	24.8	373.1	2767	17735	360	9	11	0
28.5	10972	28.2	512.4	4069	81163	180	10	10	1
25.8	9614	34.8	60.0	908	4815	360	8	9	0
22.8	8542	21.9	217.4	1363	3534		4	5	2
33.0	9245	15.3	34.3	2042	8814	120	6	7	1
27.5	11338	35.8	95.0	1456	9274	180	7	7	1
23.9	11682	26.4	107.2	2107	13142	360	12	14	6
28.6	9187	27.7	507.8	1629	2882	360	8	8	0
30.9	11113	25.8	18.4	245	7161	240	3	6	1
24.7	8670	14.4	197.1	1975	6734	60	4	5	1
29.5	10870	20.9	299.7	2136	94578	60	12	15	2
32.5	11847	31.3	23.5	701	10250	180	12	14	3
23.7	8705	10.1	81.6	678	2907	120	2	3	0
25.0	9345	14.8	635.7	2143	4640	240	7	7	0
24.3	10204	19.0	76.6	1537	3588	360	4	5	2
32.5	12635	37.1	23.4	427	12252	360	10	12	1
28.4	10783	30.5	128.5	3553	15843	360	13	18	4
26.4	9856	21.6	247.9	9238	5791	360	2	2	0
31.7	9737	31.8	55.2	3049	10108	240	6	11	2
27.8	10463	22.5	89.1	3650	7539	360	4	5	1
29.1	9929	37.8	61.8	679	4622	300	4	5	0
32.4	10038	46.1	9.9	862	1169	360	2	2	1
27.6	10034	21.7	60.3	1196	2511	360	6	8	2
27.3	11969	41.6	36.7	2316	4398	360	4	6	2
27.5	10504	30.5	61.2	4118	14551	360	8	9	3
21.5	9952	14.9	59.3	1061	5177	360	3	5	1
22.9	7981	13.3	184.0	1960	2991	360	5	5	3
28.2	9272	17.9	158.3	27295	12582	360	7	8	2
25.5	10133	17.4	316.9	4262	10126	180	6	6	1
28.3	11802	16.1	98.8	2478	64027	180	9	10	0
26.8	12456	32.9	136.2	1300	10014	360	6	6	2

TABLE 8.2

City	Pop CITY	Pop SMSA	Den-sity CITY	Den-sity SMSA	Den. Ratio (S/C) x100	Pop Change CITY	Pop Change SMSA	Median Age CITY
65 SeattleEveret	585	1422	5182	336	6	-4.4	64.3	32.3
66 Syracuse	157	637	7636	263	3	-8.7	26.2	28.7
67 TampaStPeters	494	1013	3531	777	22	8.3	64.0	37.8
68 Toledo	384	693	4729	456	10	20.7	-1.2	29.2
69 Tulsa	332	477	1931	126	7	26.7	-7.6	29.1
70 UticaRome	142	341	1603	128	8	-6.8	11.2	30.7
71 Washington, D.C.	756	2861	12313	1216	10	-1.0	61.9	29.0
72 Wichita	277	389	3202	159	5	8.6	-11.1	27.3
73 Wilmington	80	499	6202	428	7	-16.1	31.5	32.3
74 Worchester	177	345	4723	728	15	-5.4	17.9	33.0
75 York	50	330	9434	280	2	-7.6	18.4	31.8
76 YoungstownWar	203	536	4452	520	12	-10.2	17.7	30.7

TABLE 8.3

THE AIR QUALITY

City	Total MAQI	Total EVI	SO$_2$ Mean	SO$_2$ Max Value	SO$_2$ MAQI
1 Akron	1.70	6.41	51.00	125.00	0.84
2 Albuquerque	2.42	1.60	5.00	21.00	0.09
3 AlBethEaston	2.98	5.22	37.00	235.00	0.94
4 Atlanta	2.60	3.44	20.00	104.00	0.32
5 Baltimore	4.17	15.15	54.00	162.00	0 89
6 Birmingham	5.05	16.13	8.00	23.00	0.14
7 Boston	2.12	1.09	47.00	150.00	0.76
8 Bridgeport	2.03	1.07	40.00	213.00	0.66
9 Buffalo	2.75	7.15	15.00	82.00	0.25
10 Canton	2.62	4.38	30.00	125.00	0.49
11 Charleston	4.20	19.28	27.00	104.00	0.45
12 Chattanooga	3.36	9.23	18.00	74.00	0.30
13 Chicago			73.00	296.00	
14 Cincinnati	2.86	4.35	10.00	23.00	0.17
15 Cleveland	3.82	10.09	64.00	250.00	1.07
16 Columbus	2.36	3.44	21.00	71.00	0.36
17 Dallas	2.18	2.07	7.00	20.00	0.11
18 Dayton	2.44	6.76	24.00	87.00	0.41
19 Denver			17.00	39.00	
20 Des Moines	2.19	4.62	11.00	59.00	0.18
21 Detroit	3.39	9.17	38.00	172.00	0.62
22 El Paso			23.00	116.00	
23 Flint			16.00	58.00	
24 Fort Worth	1.41		7.00	27.00	0.12
25 GaryHammonDec	4.22	25.63	57.00	197.00	0.95
26 Grand Rapids	2.00		13.00	48.00	0.21
27 Hartford	1.99		57.00	225.00	0.95
28 Honolulu					
29 Houston	2.59	1.19	10.00	42.00	0.16
30 Indianapolis	2.74	6.74	33.00	137.00	0.54
31 Jacksonville			14.00	33.00	
32 Jersey City	3.45	3.35	75.00	260.00	1.24
33 Johnstown	3.67	8.39	55.00	404.00	1.80
34 Kansas City	2.48	5.01	12.00	102.00	0.20
35 LosAngLongBea					
36 Louisville	2.48	2.41	23.00	99.00	0.38
37 Memphis	2.34	2.31	16.00	208.00	0.27
38 Miami	1.76		6.00	20.00	0.09
39 Milwaukee	2.69	6.41	15.00	39.00	0.26
40 MinneapolisSP	2.70	3.12	38.00	223.00	0.64

(Continued)

Median Age SMSA	Median Family Income	Percent Employed in Mfg	Land Area CITY	Land Area SMSA	Property Values SMSA	Degrees of Arc	Radials CITY	Radials SMSA	Circumferentials SMSA
25.5	11676	24.9	112.9	4229	12810	60	3	4	2
25.8	10450	27.9	25.8	2419	3172	360	3	5	1
37.1	7883	17.6	139.9	1303	5236	120	5	5	0
24.9	10932	33.3	81.2	1520	5476	180	3	6	2
29.0	9286	23.6	171.9	3781	3341	180	4	5	0
29.0	9726	35.2	88.6	2658	1119	360	3	5	0
25.9	12930	3.8	61.4	2352	24368	360	15	16	4
25.6	9413	28.4	86.5	2449	2753	360	4	5	3
26.3	10686	85.9	12.9	1165	3425	180	5	7	3
29.1	10713	34.8	37.4	474	2903	360	3	6	1
29.4	9828	45.8	5.3	1435	766	360	1	3	2
28.6	10390	43.7	46.5	1030	3743	360	4	7	3

(Continued)

DATA SET

SO$_2$ EVI	NO$_2$ MAQI	Total Suspended Particulate			
		Annual Mean	Max Value	MAQI	EVI
	0.94	94.00	169.00	1.93	6.41
	1.01	90.00	240.00	2.20	1.60
	1.42	114.00	228.00	2.44	5.22
	1.65	90.00	196.00	1.98	3.44
	1.80	114.00	468.00	3.65	15.15
	1.10	155.00	629.00	4.93	16.13
	0.96	80.00	163.00	1.72	1.09
	1.59	64.00	148.00	1.07	
	0.73	99.00	309.00	2.64	7.15
	1.52	101.00	182.00	2.08	4.38
	1.42	156.00	441.00	3.93	19.78
	1.16	113.00	377.00	3.14	9.23
		147.00	346.00		
	1.48	101.00	265.00	2.44	4.35
	1.83	116.00	251.00	2.56	10.09
	1.31	90.00	184.00	1.93	3.44
	0.84	102.00	160.00	2.01	2.07
	1.25	92.00	203.00	2.05	6.76
	0.79	94.00	193.00	2.03	4.62
	1.69	113.00	324.00	2.87	9.17
		69.00	106.00		
	0.56	78.00	133.00	1.29	
	1.21	177.00	390.00	3.93	25.63
	1.55	75.00	145.00	1.25	
	1.41	62.00	103.00	1.03	
		44.00	93.00		
	1.79	97.00	179.00	1.87	1.19
	1.19	106.00	246.00	2.41	6.74
		88.00	259.00		
	2.50	94.00	192.00	2.03	3.35
1.55	1.64	127.00	261.00	2.74	8.25
	0.73	103.00	245.00	2.36	5.01
		141.00	275.00		
	1.76	102.00	181.00	1.70	2.41
	1.41	78.00	196.00	1.85	2.31
	1.32	70.00	117.00	1.16	
	1.21	93.00	272.00	2.39	6.41
	1.42	74.00	275.00	2.21	3.11

TABLE 8.3

City	Total MAQI	Total EVI	SO2 Mean	SO2 Max Value	SO2 MAQI
41 NashvilleDavi	2.71	5.15	15.00	55.00	0.25
42 New Haven	2.62	4.46	39.00	215.00	0.65
43 New Orleans	1.73		6.00	20.00	0.11
44 New York	3.48	7.38	73.00	395.00	1.95
45 Newark	2.49	2.19	37.00	251.00	0.61
46 NorfolkPortsm	2.38	1.23	26.00	99.00	0.43
47 Oklahoma City	1.88	1.02	6.00	19.00	0.10
48 Omaha	2.89	12.80	14.00	108.00	0.24
49 PatersonClipa	3.08	4.35	28.00	131.00	0.46
50 Philadelphia	3.99	13.38	84.00	218.00	1.41
51 Phoenix	2.82	8.37	10.00	54.00	0.16
52 Pittsburgh	3.64	9.81	57.00	148.00	0.85
53 Portland	2.91	4.81	18.00	134.00	0.30
54 ProvidencPaw	2.97	2.98	67.00	291.00	1.58
55 Reading	2.88	8.65	29.00	131.00	0.49
56 Richmond	2.25	2.11	24.00	70.00	0.40
57 Rochester	2.84	5.16	32.00	227.00	0.53
58 St. Louis	4.41	13.15	58.00	278.00	1.44
59 Salt Lake City	2.17	1.06	8.00	34.00	0.14
60 San Antonio	1.61		6.00	17.00	0.10
61 San Bernadino	3.79	12.20	6.00	15.00	0.10
62 San Diego	2.67	4.65	10.00	32.00	0.16
63 San Francisco	1.78		8.00	28.00	0.13
64 San Jose			9.00	19.00	
65 SeattleEveret	2.36	1.38	21.00	77.00	0.36
66 Syracuse	2.48	2.73	12.00	46.00	0.21
67 TampaStPeters	2.27	1.11	17.00	92.00	0.27
68 Toledo	2.25	1.05	13.00	51.00	0.21
69 Tulsa	1.23		5.00	12.00	0.09
70 UticaRome	2.58	3.09	8.00	48.00	0.13
71 Washington, D.C.					
72 Wichita	2.26	2.55	6.00	17.00	0.09
73 Wilmington	2.51	2.27	17.00	78.00	0.29
74 Worchester	2.60	7.52	30.00	112.00	0.50
75 York	2.45	4.41	30.00	94.00	0.51
76 YoungstownWar	3.65	9.33	30.00	88.00	0.50

Source: EPA and Council on Environmental Quality

2.   WATER QUALITY

Since no national source of water quality data other than the
STORET system is available, the basic methodology followed in de-
veloping a national data set relevant for city-to-city comparisons
was taken from Benefits of Water Quality Enhancement, Department
of Civil Engineering, Syracuse University, 1970, pp. 13-33, sup-
plemented by Quality of Surface Waters of the United States, 1968,
Geological Survey Water Supply Paper 2099, Part ll, pp. 7-19.

Construction of the "Syracuse Index" was discussed in some
detail in Chapter 3. The number of pollutants which may be used
in the calculation of the index is limited only by the availability
of data concerning the particular pollutant's concentration, and
the permissible standards. Our choice of the fourteen variables
noted in Table 8.1 followed the Syracuse methodology, essentially
recognizing the limited availability of water quality data, and
development of standards for permissible pollutant levels.

(Continued)

| SO2 EVI | NO2 MAQI | Total Suspended Particulate | | | |
		Annual Mean	Max Value	MAQI	EVI
	1.64	89.00	231.00	2.14	5.19
	1.58	93.00	186.00	1.99	4.46
	1.20	74.00	128.00	1.24	
1.52	1.49	123.00	208.00	2.47	7.22
	1.64	81.00	171.00	1.77	2.19
	1.50	79.00	185.00	1.80	1.23
	1.05	70.00	153.00	1.56	1.02
	1.32	121.00	238.00	2.56	12.80
	1.99	86.00	273.00	2.31	4.35
	2.28	135.00	287.00	2.95	13.38
	1.26	121.00	225.00	2.52	8.37
	2.13	127.00	276.00	2.80	9.81
	0.89	87.00	351.00	2.75	4.81
2.15	1.77	88.00	151.00	1.78	1.01
	1.48	111.00	240.00	2.45	8.65
	1.34	83.00	165.00	1.76	2.11
	1.53	111.00	213.00	2.33	5.16
1.07	1.79	154.00	413.00	3.76	13.11
	1.31	82.00	159.00	1.73	1.06
	1.33	54.00	109.00	0.90	
	2.34	120.00	330.00	2.98	12.20
	1.72	97.00	214.00	2.03	4.65
	1.53	54.00	130.00	0.91	
		108.00	242.00		
	1.58	62.00	207.00	1.72	1.38
	1.19	95.00	220.00	2.16	2.73
	1.32	87.00	167.00	1.83	1.11
	1.51	77.00	157.00	1.65	1.05
	0.83	55.00	145.00	0.91	
	0.68	85.00	307.00	2.49	3.09
	1.04	83.00	220.00	2.26	2.55
	1.21	110.00	176.00	2.13	2.27
	1.14	110.00	204.00	2.23	7.52
	1.28	98.00	180.00	2.02	4.41
	1.45	117.00	401.00	3.31	9.83

It should be noted that the Syracuse method is heavily
weighted with respect to three parameters. Tolerance levels for
turbidity, suspended solids and fecal coliform bacteria are extremely low for aesthetic and industrial reasons. Color is related to turbidity and suspended solids. The latter two are a
function of flow.

Fecal coliform bacteria has long been monitored as an indicator of organic pollution, although its actual health effects
have not been sufficiently determined. Several water quality
investigations have deemphasized its importance and thus,
the Enviro-Control Corporation, in its report discussed in Chapter 3, eliminated fecal coliform from its analysis along with
pH, temperature, hardness, color and total coliform. Fecal
coliform bacteria, according to Enviro-Control, has only local
value because the effect of the parameter diminishes markedly
downstream. However, for purposes of this study, fecal coliform

readings were retained because they do indicate that organic
pollution is being added to the water body by the major urbanized area or areas within the SMSA.

Turbidity data proved difficult to employ because of the
lack of standardization of measurement. Many states still report turbidity in terms of ppm silica, which is not readily con-
vertible to Jackson Turbidity Units. No conversion tables have
ever been published. Data for this parameter are recorded in
terms corresponding to the standard method in use at the time.
The data are inconsistent and readings are subjective and often
inaccurate under 25 JTUs.

Suspended solids are normally an excellent indicator of pollutants in the water. However, the sensitivity of the parameter
decreases when receptor stations are located at or near dams.
Dams and reservoirs change flow and suspension characteristics
and readings taken can unduly influence the PI indexes.

Dissolved oxygen is a commonly measured indicator of pollution, although Enviro-Control assessment showed no strong trend
in organic pollution and little relation of DO with BOD and COD.
There are two explanations:

1) Stationary water quality stations do not monitor DO at
   its moving sag point.
2) DO readings are usually taken during the day at times
   when algae are contributing oxygen (photosynthesis).

Our own research confirmed the anomalous relationship between dissolved oxygen levels and pollution levels. In some
cases, cities with known pollution did not have low DO levels,
although other variables monitored indicated high pollutant
levels. In general it can be said that DO levels are higher upstream and lower downstream from cities.

Recognizing that many such questions remain open, forty-four
SMSA's out of the total set of seventy-six were evaluated using
one water-quality monitoring station for each SMSA. Station
locations were determined by the following criteria:

1) Location on the main stream a short distance downstream
   from the urbanized area was sought in order to register
   the maximum number of urban pollutant sources.
2) Where alternatives were available, refinement of the
   first criterion by basing final receptor selection on
   whichever station provided the maximum number of parameters needed for the Syracuse Index. In some instances,
   the number of parameters available for the data bank
   outweighed the distance factor in final determination
   of stations.

3) Further refinement was accomplished based on the frequency of readings and their distribution throughout the year. Stations proximal to and downstream from major urban centers were often discarded for ones with less favorable locations but with better seasonal distribution of a higher number of recorded parameters.

4) Monitoring stations on lakes, reservoirs, estuaries, bays or canals were chosen only in cases where receptors on flowing streams were lacking.

The source of most of the raw data was U.S. Geological Survey publications for individual states. Supplemental information was obtained from published texts of the numerous water pollution conferences. The USGS data are now included in STORET, and had the STORET System functioned better it would have been used. However, research time was limited, and it proved quicker to obtain needed data from USGS's publications than from STORET.

The mean was obtained for each parameter used. This necessitated calculation from raw data where means were not provided. The processed data were not corrected for flow unless source materials provided time-weighted averages. Some station data which were averaged out included some unusually high readings, possibly from storms, treatment plant failure, instrument failure, etc. If pollution concentrations were not already corrected for flow by the reporting agency, no further modification was made. If published, a weighted average was used. In uncorrected data, notation was made of any major deviations from average readings.

The results of application of the Syracuse Index to data for the selected forty-four cities are shown in Table 8.4. Total PI values for all but nine of the cities were above 1.000, thus classifying them as polluted. However, the results must be qualified before attempting interpretation, as many anomalies appear on the list.

The incongruities of PI values are explained in terms of the receptor stations' failure to meet one or more of the selection criteria:

1) Location on a main stream near the city was often unavailable. Distance-decay and dilution factors markedly decrease the sensitivity of certain variables, expecially fecal coliform and dissolved oxygen, to increasing downstream distance.

2) A lack of parameters for use in index calculation was by far the most common problem. Overall lack of data for fecal coliform bacteria, turbidity and suspended solids kept median index values relatively low. These variables weigh heavily in the Syracuse calculations. In certain cases, removal of one of the three parameters would radically alter the PI Indes. Sometimes not all data recorded at a monitor is published because of cost and page space limitations.

TABLE 8.4

WATER POLLUTION INDEX VALUES FOR SELECTED SMSA's

	SMSA	PI_1^a	PI_2^b	PI_3^c	PI^d	Comments
1	Akron	2.994	1.070	1.275	1.780	no readings late Jan. to mid-June
2	Albuquerque	0.614	0.535	0.849	0.666	conveyance channel; no flow Oct. 24-28, July 23-31, Sept. 21-30
3	Allentown - Bethlehem - Easton	2.119	0.519	0.476	1.038	water quality equipment being installed
4	Atlanta	13.940	9.320	0.905	8.055	excellent location; all 14 parameters available
9	Buffalo	11.800	7.800	0.900	6.800	
10	Canton	3.690	3.540	4.186	3.805	
11	Charleston	2.180	0.443	0.487	1.037	location on dam
13	Chicago	3.530	0.532	0.816	1.626	
14	Cincinnati	3.964	5.010	1.210	3.395	1000 ft. upstream from dam; high coliform level, but no fecal coliform given
16	Columbus	2.880	1.276	1.358	1.838	DO taken daily with large gaps in summer
17	Dallas	1.017	0.602	0.730	0.783	
18	Dayton	2.520	0.751	1.785	1.685	
19	Denver	3.300	0.222	1.219	1.580	June 11 - high readings (TDS, discharge, turbidity); turbidity in mg/l therefore not used
20	Des Moines	2.120	1.120	1.410	1.550	few readings; location 40-45 miles downstream
22	El Paso	4.120	4.689	5.228	4.679	location on rectified channel, 81.1 river miles downstream
24	Fort Worth	4.245	1.394	1.347	2.329	excellent location
27	Hartford	5.212	0.676	0.461	2.116	
30	Indianapolis	3.306	4.712	1.885	3.301	location 30 miles downstream from Union Stockyards and City Disposal Plant; coliform level extremely high, but no fecal coliform available for calculation
32	Jersey City	6.681	6.506	7.903	7.030	few readings, all in summer; location on Hackensack River (little discharge); TDS very high
33	Johnstown	3.097	6.324	2.466	3.962	location 40-50 miles downstream; pH average less than 3.5, may be due to mine wastes or steel plants
34	Kansas City	8.990	5.087	1.632	6.236	readings are 5-day composites taken in fall and winter; represent both wet (high runoff) and dry periods
39	Milwaukee	0.678	0.903	0.373	0.651	Milwaukee Harbor location--possible dilution effect
40	Minneapolis - St. Paul	3.345	3.069	0.953	2.456	location on downstream side of dam
43	New Orleans	1.058	0.715	0.664	0.812	
47	Oklahoma City	1.503	1.255	1.312	1.357	location on tributary parallel to main stream
48	Omaha	0.733	0.696	1.220	0.883	station located 50 miles downstream
50	Philadelphia	2.140	1.101	0.911	1.384	
51	Phoenix	5.501	4.638	4.931	5.023	location 35 miles downstream (above diversions and near dam); "Samples...believed to be representative of total flow..."
52	Pittsburgh	1.473	1.899	0.588	1.320	
53	Portland	0.533	0.390	0.453	0.459	station somewhat affected by tidal action
55	Reading	2.192	0.327	0.610	1.043	location about 60 miles downstream on fringe of Philadelphia; suburban pollution added
57	Rochester	8.100	3.500	0.600	4.100	
58	St. Louis	0.531	0.445	0.445	0.474	poor location 80 miles downstream

TABLE 8.4 (Continued)

	SMSA	PI_1^a	PI_2^b	PI_3^c	PI^d	Comments
59	Salt Lake City	0.611	0.586	1.669	0.995	near reservoir; only station in area; location vague
60	San Antonio	2.577	0.707	1.121	1.468	good location
61	San Bernadino - Riverside - Ontario	3.569	1.286	1.835	2.230	receptor station below dam
67	Tampa - St. Petersburg	7.426	7.119	8.023	7.523	only one reading; TDS and chloride levels high; approaching natural sea water levels; strongly affects index
68	Toledo	3.999	1.531	1.033	2.188	
69	Tulsa	0.835	0.944	0.830	0.870	station ninety miles downstream from Tulsa and below confluence of Arkansas and Canadian Rivers; includes pollution from Oklahoma City
70	Utica-Rome	1.800	0.800	0.700	1.100	
72	Wichita	1.412	1.404	1.412	1.409	location fifty miles downstream
73	Wilmington	3.559	3.508	4.119	3.729	center of navigation channel at entrance to Delaware Bay
75	York	2.272	0.445	0.498	1.072	few readings; exact location undetermined
76	Youngstown - Warren	8.883	4.245	1.138	4.755	

[a]Drinking Use

[b]Recreation Use

[c]Industrial Use

[d]Average Index

Source: water quality indexes computed by project staff using USGS data.

3) The lack of frequent and well distributed sampling data was the most prominent hindrance to reliable detection of trends in water quality. Single readings for Jersey City and Tampa-St. Petersburg precluded seasonal comparison of water quality and made the readings unusable, even though they seemed to indicate high pollution.

4) In several instances stations on or near reservoirs, estuaries and conveyance channels were used for lack of an alternative. Such locations certainly were not representative of normal flow characteristics. The effects of dilution and concentration must be acknowledged.

Although index values for the most of tested SMSA monitors therefore must be deemed unreliable, the PI values for those stations which best comply with selection criteria do provide insights into regional pollution problems. For example, Atlanta, with an average PI index of 8.055, illustrates the potential merits of the Syracuse Index. The receptor station is about ten miles downstream and regularly records the maximum number of Syracuse parameters. In all other respects, observations at this station are within normal range. However, fecal coliform bacteria levels are so much greater than permissible levels that even the averaging in of the other variables still produces the

highest of all of the index values, a consequence of untreated
sewage from Atlanta. It should be noted that the PI_3 Index for
Atlanta, which excludes fecal coliform, results in water unpolluted for industrial use.

3. SOLID WASTES

Solid waste generation was estimated using the linear expression

$$W = \sum_i a_i X_i$$

where W = the total waste generated
    W_i = the waste generated by source i
    a_i = a waste multiplier for source i
    X_i = the number of source units for source i

The sources, waste multipliers and units of measurement used are
the following:

Single Family Residence	2858.0 lb/unit/yr
Multiple Family Residence	1315.0 lb/unit/yr
Commercial	3.5 lb/cap/yr
Manufacturers	7.6 tons/emp/yr
Demolition and Construction	500.0 lb/cap/yr
Sewage	87.1 lb/cap/yr

The specific waste generation factors were derived from the California solid wastes investigations discussed in Chapter 4. By
obtaining population, single family and multiple family housing
statistics from the 1970 U.S. Census of Population and Housing
and the number of manufacturing employees from the 1967 U.S.
Census of Manufacturing, and from the population data calculating
amounts of sewage, demolition and construction, and commercial
solid wastes, it was possible to make estimates of total solid
wastes generated by each of the seventy-six urban regions. Table
8.5 shows the results of applying this process.

While the expression $W = \sum_i a_i X_i$ provides one method of estimating solid wastes, another less accurate method is often employed in solid waste planning. This involves the use of a single
generation figure per person. This figure is derived by taking
the total volume of solid waste generated by a city for one entire year, as indicated by quantities arriving at city dumps,
and then dividing this by the total population of the city. The
derived figure is expressed in pounds per person per day (i.e.
3.73). Unfortunately the amounts of waste which arrive at municipal dumps often are much less than the total amount produced

TABLE 8.5

SOLID WASTE COMPONENTS

ID	City	Single-Family Source	Multi-Family Units	Total Solid Waste in 1000s Tons/Year						
				MFG Employees	Single Family	Multi Family	Com-mercial	MFG	Dem+ Const	Sewage
1	Akron	166.0	47.0	101.1	970.3	446.4	433.7	768.4	169.8	29.6
2	Albuquerque	80.0	18.0	7.8	451.6	207.8	201.8	59.3	79.0	13.8
3	AlBethEaston*	137.0	44.0	102.6	777.4	357.7	347.5	779.8	136.0	23.7
4	Atlanta	296.0	154.0	117.2	1986.3	913.9	887.9	890.7	347.5	60.5
5	Baltimore	463.0	189.0	209.7	2959.5	1361.7	1322.9	1593.7	517.8	90.2
6	Birmingham	201.0	43.0	68.0	1056.0	485.9	472.0	516.8	184.8	32.2
7	Boston	391.0	500.0	316.2	3935.5	1810.8	1759.1	2403.1	688.5	119.9
8	Bridgeport	71.0	53.0	79.5	557.3	256.4	249.1	604.2	97.5	17.0
9	Buffalo	241.0	192.0	176.2	1927.7	887.0	861.7	1339.1	337.3	58.7
10	Canton	94.0	24.0	62.5	531.6	244.6	237.6	473.0	93.0	16.2
11	Charleston	65.0	13.0	20.9	328.7	151.2	146.9	158.8	57.5	10.0
12	Chattanooga 2	67.0	20.0	51.6	437.3	201.2	195.5	392.2	76.5	13.3
13	Chicago	1081.0	1208.0	983.1	9965.8	4585.4	4454.6	7471.6	1743.5	303.7
14	Cincinnati 3	212.0	146.0	166.8	1979.2	910.6	884.7	1267.7	346.3	60.3
15	Cleveland	403.0	273.0	306.8	2949.5	1357.1	1318.4	2331.7	516.0	89.9
16	Columbus	202.0	94.0	83.0	1309.0	602.3	585.1	630.8	229.0	39.9
17	Dallas	380.0	148.0	148.9	2223.5	1023.1	993.9	1131.6	389.0	67.8
18	Dayton	208.0	63.0	126.2	1214.6	558.9	542.9	959.1	212.5	37.0
19	Denver	287.0	121.0	74.1	1754.8	807.4	784.4	563.3	307.0	53.5
20	Des Moines	74.0	24.0	25.4	408.7	188.0	182.7	193.0	71.5	12.5
21	Detroit	943.0	374.0	584.5	6001.8	2761.5	2682.7	4442.2	1050.0	182.9
22	El Paso	74.0	27.0	18.9	513.0	236.0	229.3	143.6	89.8	15.6
23	Flint	126.0	23.0	*****	710.2	326.8	317.5	*****	124.3	21.6
24	Fort Worth	206.0	51.0	78.4	1088.9	501.0	486.7	595.8	190.5	33.2
25	Gary Hammond E.C.**	138.0	54.0	105.0	904.6	416.2	404.3	798.0	158.3	27.6
26	Grand Rapids	134.0	34.0	75.7	770.2	354.4	344.3	575.3	134.8	23.5
27	Hartford	120.0	92.0	110.6	948.9	436.6	424.1	840.6	166.0	28.9
28	Honolulu	102.0	71.0	19.5	898.8	413.6	401.8	148.2	157.3	27.4
29	Houston	505.0	161.0	138.1	2836.6	1305.1	1267.9	1049.6	496.3	86.4
30	Indianapolis	273.0	95.0	134.7	1586.2	729.8	709.0	1023.7	277.5	48.3
31	Jacksonville	138.0	36.0	23.1	755.9	347.8	337.9	175.6	132.3	23.0
32	Jersey City	30.0	185.0	107.2	870.3	400.4	389.0	814.7	152.3	26.5
33	Johnstown	64.0	20.0	25.1	375.8	172.9	168.0	190.8	65.8	11.5
34	Kansas City 2	318.0	67.0	129.4	1792.0	824.5	801.0	983.4	313.5	54.6
35	Los Angeles - Long Beach	1580.0	957.0	855.4	10054.4	4626.2	4494.2	6501.0	1759.0	306.4
36	Louisville 2	164.0	61.0	110.0	1181.8	543.8	528.2	836.0	206.8	36.0
37	Memphis 2	158.0	63.0	57.4	1100.3	506.3	491.8	436.2	192.5	33.5
38	Miami	263.0	186.0	58.3	1812.0	833.7	809.9	443.1	317.0	55.2
39	Milwaukee	247.0	199.0	216.5	2006.3	923.1	896.8	1643.4	351.0	61.1
40	Minneapolis - St. Paul	371.0	204.0	203.7	2592.2	1192.7	1158.7	1548.1	453.5	79.0
41	Nashville - Davidson	130.0	48.0	54.1	773.1	355.7	345.6	411.2	135.3	23.6
42	New Haven	61.0	56.0	46.1	508.7	234.1	227.4	350.4	89.0	15.5
43	New Orleans	205.0	140.0	55.5	1494.7	687.7	668.1	421.8	261.5	45.6
44	New York	1131.0	2835.0	1147.4	16536.4	7608.6	7391.6	8720.2	2893.0	504.0
45	Newark	285.0	313.0	263.0	2653.7	1221.0	1186.2	1998.8	464.3	80.9
46	Norfolk - Portsmouth	138.0	62.0	19.0	973.1	447.8	435.0	144.4	170.3	29.7
47	Oklahoma City	184.0	42.0	29.3	916.0	421.5	409.4	222.7	160.3	27.9
48	Omaha 2	24.0	4.0	36.6	771.7	355.0	344.9	278.2	135.0	23.5
49	Paterson - Clifton - Passaic	240.0	194.0	190.0	1942.0	893.5	868.1	1444.0	339.8	59.2
50	Philadelphia	1122.0	411.0	573.0	6884.9	3167.8	3077.5	4354.8	1204.5	209.8
51	Phoenix	253.0	84.0	59.3	1383.3	636.5	618.3	450.7	242.0	42.2
52	Pittsburgh	567.0	220.0	299.6	3431.0	1578.7	1533.6	2277.0	600.3	104.6
53	Portland 2	239.0	75.0	79.8	1441.9	663.4	644.5	605.5	252.3	43.9
54	Providence - Pawtucket	24.0	10.0	138.0	1304.7	600.3	583.2	1048.8	228.3	39.8
55	Reading	79.0	22.0	56.4	423.0	194.6	189.1	428.6	74.0	12.9
56	Richmond	127.0	45.0	51.4	740.2	340.6	330.9	390.6	129.5	22.6
57	Rochester	187.0	92.0	145.7	1261.8	580.6	564.0	1107.3	220.8	38.5
58	St. Louis 2	532.0	250.0	295.5	3376.7	1553.7	1509.4	2245.8	590.8	102.9
59	Salt Lake City	121.0	42.0	27.5	797.4	366.9	356.4	209.0	139.5	24.3
60	San Antonio	208.0	52.0	27.4	1234.7	568.1	551.9	208.2	216.0	37.6

*Allentown - Bethlehem - Easton   **E.C. = East Chicago

Source: compiled by project staff from U. S. census data

TABLE 8.5 (Continued)

ID	City	Single-Family Source Units	Multi-Family Units	Total Solid Waste in 1000s Tons/Year						
				MFG Employees	Single Family	Multi Family	Com-mercial	MFG	Dem+ Const	Sewage
61	San Bernardino	355.0	62.0	46.4	1629.1	749.5	728.2	352.6	285.0	49.6
62	San Diego	326.0	124.0	63.5	1939.2	892.2	866.8	482.6	339.3	59.1
63	San Francisco	670.0	459.0	197.8	4444.2	2044.8	1986.5	1503.3	777.5	135.4
64	San Jose	242.0	94.0	120.3	1521.9	700.2	680.3	914.3	266.3	46.4
65	Seattle - Everett	372.0	139.0	162.2	2032.0	935.0	908.3	1232.7	355.5	61.9
66	Syracuse	130.0	71.0	68.2	910.3	418.8	406.9	518.3	159.3	27.7
67	Tampa - St. Petersburg	317.0	77.0	46.7	1447.6	666.0	647.1	354.9	253.3	44.1
68	Toledo	140.0	46.0	77.7	990.3	455.6	442.7	590.5	173.3	30.2
69	Tulsa	141.0	30.0	41.9	681.6	313.6	304.7	318.4	119.3	20.8
70	Utica - Rome	67.0	42.0	42.9	487.3	224.2	217.8	326.0	85.3	14.9
71	Washington, D.C.	511.0	425.0	55.5	4088.4	1881.1	1827.5	421.8	715.3	124.6
72	Wichita	108.0	25.0	57.7	555.9	255.8	248.5	438.5	97.3	16.9
73	Wilmington 3	120.0	34.0	68.0	713.1	328.1	318.7	516.8	124.8	21.7
74	Worchester	57.0	51.0	50.9	493.0	226.8	220.4	386.8	86.3	15.0
75	York	88.0	20.0	57.0	471.6	217.0	210.8	433.2	82.5	14.4
76	Youngstown - Warren	139.0	28.0	82.9	765.9	352.4	342.4	630.0	134.0	23.3

Some generation figures have been developed by this method, however. But these represent only a portion of the total tonnages, as is shown in Table 8.6, which reveals the substantial differences between the method just described and the compositional estimates derived earlier.

4. NOISE

In the absence of national noise inventories, two surrogates for traffic noise were included in the data set: air traffic and commuter automobile traffic volumes. The air traffic data, with the exception of Honolulu, are for the year 1969 and were obtained from Tables 4.8, 4.9, and 4.10 (Aircraft Departures Scheduled, Aircraft Departures Performed, and Revenue Traffic at Large, -at Medium, -at Small, Air Traffic Hubs in the Contiguous 48 States; Domestic Operations at Large, -at Medium, -at Small, Hubs, 12 Months Ended December 31, 1969) in Transportation Planning Data for Ubanized Areas, U.S. Department of Transportation, 1970. The datum for Honolulu is The Reports, The State of Hawaii Department of Transportation, Honolulu, 1967.

Auto traffic data are all from Table 82 ("Mobility, Commuting, and Veteran Status, for Areas and Places: 1970" in The 1970 Census of Population: General Social and Economic Characteristics.

The two most general sources of noise emissions in the urban environment are highway and air flight traffic. The measures chosen were selected as those best reflecting noise emission potentials of a comparative nature across the national network of urban places. The data are listed in Table 8.7.

TABLE 8.6

SOLID WASTES DATA SET

		From Overall Multiplier		From Individual Multipliers	
ID	City	Total Lbs/Cap/Day	Total Tons/Year -1000s-	Total Tons/Year -1000s-	Total Tons/Year-1000s- Omitting MFG
1	Akron	3.73	462.	1670.	901.
2	Albuquerque	5.72	330.	480.	421.
3	Allentown - Bethlehem - Easton	3.73	370.	1512.	732.
4	Atlanta	3.43	870.	2711.	1820.
5	Baltimore	4.27	1614.	4310.	2717.
6	Birmingham	3.48	469.	1521.	1004.
7	Boston	4.60	2312.	5858.	3455.
8	Bridgeport	4.60	327.	1104.	500.
9	Buffalo	5.72	1408.	3067.	1728.
10	Canton	3.73	253.	972.	497.
11	Charleston	5.72	240.	475.	316.
12	Chattanooga 2	5.72	319.	786.	394.
13	Chicago	5.72	7280.	16312.	8841.
14	Cincinnati 3	3.74	945.	2958.	1690.
15	Cleveland	2.07	780.	5011.	2680.
16	Columbus	3.73	624.	1835.	1204.
17	Dallas	4.80	1363.	3223.	2091.
18	Dayton	3.73	579.	2090.	1131.
19	Denver	5.72	1282.	2198.	1635.
20	Des Moines	5.72	299.	581.	388.
21	Detroit	3.73	2859.	9951.	5509.
22	El Paso	3.20	210.	602.	458.
23	Flint	3.73	338.	*****	659.
24	Fort Worth	2.60	362.	1634.	1038.
25	Gary - Hammond - East Chicago	3.73	431.	1621.	823.
26	Grand Rapids	3.73	367.	1292.	716.
27	Hartford	4.60	557.	1692.	851.
28	Honolulu	5.72	657.	927.	779.
29	Houston	3.20	1159.	3728.	2678.
30	Indianapolis	3.73	756.	2511.	1487.
31	Jacksonville	3.48	336.	890.	714.
32	Jersey City	5.72	636.	1547.	732.
33	Johnstown	5.72	275.	541.	350.
34	Kansas City 2	5.72	1309.	2651.	1668.
35	Los Angeles - Long Beach	6.95	8924.	15948.	9447.
36	Louisville 2	5.72	863.	1881.	1045.
37	Memphis 2	5.72	804.	1421.	985.
38	Miami	3.75	868.	2123.	1680.
39	Milwaukee	3.73	956.	3438.	1793.
40	Minneapolis - St. Paul	3.73	1235.	3904.	2355.
41	Nashville - Davidson	5.72	565.	1133.	722.
42	New Haven	4.60	299.	806.	456.
43	New Orleans	3.48	664.	1782.	1360.
44	New York	4.10	8659.	22989.	14269.
45	Newark	2.30	779.	4343.	2344.
46	Norfolk - Portsmouth	5.41	672.	1017.	873.

TABLE 8.6 (Continued)

ID	City	From Overall Multiplier		From Individual Multipliers	
		Total Lbs/Cap/Day	Total Tons/Year -1000s-	Total Tons/Year -1000s-	Total Tons/Year-1000s- Omitting MFG
47	Oklahoma City	5.72	669.	1111.	888.
48	Omaha 2	3.75	370.	819.	540.
49	Paterson - Clifton - Passaic	5.72	1419.	3182.	1738.
50	Philadelphia	3.10	2726.	10720.	6365.
51	Phoenix	5.72	1010.	1757.	1306.
52	Pittsburgh	5.72	2506.	5470.	3193.
53	Portland 2	5.72	1053.	1938.	1332.
54	Providence - Pawtucket 2	5.72	953.	1941.	892.
55	Reading	5.72	309.	832.	403.
56	Richmond	5.72	541.	1085.	694.
57	Rochester	5.72	922.	2258.	1151.
58	St. Louis 2	3.73	1609.	5373.	3128.
59	Salt Lake City	5.72	582.	930.	721.
60	San Antonio	6.70	1056.	1345.	1137.
61	San Bernadino	9.28	1931.	1964.	1611.
62	San Diego	9.28	2298.	2295.	1813.
63	San Francisco	9.28	5267.	5662.	4159.
64	San Jose	5.72	1112.	2315.	1401.
65	Seattle - Everett	4.10	1064.	3181.	1949.
66	Syracuse	5.72	665.	1345.	826.
67	Tampa - St. Petersburg	3.48	643.	1803.	1448.
68	Toledo	3.73	472.	1467.	876.
69	Tulsa	5.72	498.	984.	666.
70	Utica - Rome	5.72	356.	767.	441.
71	Washington DC 3	4.79	2501.	4099.	3677.
72	Wichita	5.72	406.	972.	533.
73	Wilmington 3	5.72	521.	1176.	659.
74	Worchester	5.72	360.	823.	437.
75	York	5.72	344.	880.	447.
76	Youngstown - Warren	3.73	365.	1347.	717.

Source: compiled by project staff drawing on sources listed in
American Association of Public Wastes, Municipal Refuse Disposal
(1970), and from local publications.

TABLE 8.7

NOISE DATA SET

City	Auto Traffic Volume	Air Traffic Volume	City	Auto Traffic Volume	Air Traffic Volume
Akron	190657	9001	Milwaukee	368198	70776
Albuquerque	89183	39808	MinneapolisSP	500264	127278
AlBethEaston	153882	8816	NashvilleDavi	153506	57074
Atlanta	420807	324430	New Haven	99336	
Baltimore	502397	99854	New Orleans	211949	109488
Birmingham	194380	43548	New York	1552313	464152
Boston	630065	188152	Newark	455672	168654
Bridgeport	116194		NorfolkPortsm	177352	38860
Buffalo	331873	78268	Oklahoma City	205590	48578
Canton	105073	9001	Omaha	145959	42492
Charleston	54490	24794	PatersonClipa	37557	
Chattanooga	87667	21526	Philadelphia	1068741	16732
Chicago	1563220	797060	Phoenix	287568	79698
Cincinnati	356901	88296	Pittsburgh	531187	175458
Cleveland	546882	137984	Portland	287478	88926
Columbus	251177	61898	ProvidencePaw	256572	32234
Dallas	485108	116723	Reading	82765	
Dayton	243909	56726	Richmond	139130	27798
Denver	369130	161652	Rochester	231757	57016
Des Moines	87192	27552	St. Louis	614826	174826
Detroit	1132233	194394	Salt Lake City	156239	59066
El Paso	82243	36542	San Antonio	216178	53392
Flint	133444	12542	San Bernadion	309588	27750
Fort Worth	240382	116723	San Diego	365288	42560
GaryHammonDec	158655		San Francisco	814992	227593
Grand Rapids	150915	25906	San Jose	326631	13262
Hartford	191754	56682	SeattleEveret	397538	96842
Honolulu	176478	128182	Syracuse	159993	32520
Houston	585207	129276	TampaStPeters	266484	84504
Indianapolis	308660	70884	Toledo	194395	19772
Jacksonville	146912	43190	Tulsa	142971	40960
Jersey City	96883		UticaRome	83618	13482
Johnstown	52910		Washington, D.C.	748801	271354
Kansas City	375501	117032	Wichita	117217	27912
LosAngLongBea	2122131	328450	Wilmington	132699	
Louisville	225865	68532	Worcester	90526	
Memphis	189577	98976	York	98057	
Miami	351176	202126	Youngstown	150693	13352

Sources: U. S. Department of Transportation (1970), State of Hawaii (1967), and U. S. Bureau of the Census (1972).

5. PESTICIDES

The problems of obtaining an adequate data set on pesticides were reported in Chapter 6. In brief, the only data available for 1970 are those for five cities in the National Food Monitoring Program Reports published in The Pesticides Monitoring Journal (Table 8.8). The nine pesticide residues selected from this source for the present analysis were chosen for their extensive inclusion in each of the twelve classes of foodstuffs of the Market Basket Survey.

TABLE 8.8

PESTICIDES DATA SET

City	DDT	DDE	TDE	Di-eldrin	Hepta-chlor Epoxide	BHC	Total Bro-mides	Lin-dane	Kel-thane
5 Baltimore	0.031	0.018	0.017	0.018	0.010		12.200	0.003	0.200
7 Boston	0.067	0.063	0.066	0.027	0.041	0.032	8.700	0.007	0.121
34 Kansas City	0.048	0.023	0.027	0.044	0.015	0.025	6.300	0.055	0.067
39 LosAngLongBea	0.050	0.067	0.022	0.011	0.022	0.013	5.100	0.012	0.046
40 Minneapolis SP	0.047	0.020	0.017	0.023	0.012	0.019	4.900	0.009	0.068

Source: The Pesticides Monitoring Journal (1971).

6. RADIATION

All radiation data are for 1971 and derived from Radiation
Alert Networks (RAN) figures as reported in Radiological Health
Data and Reports and Radiation Data and Reports. This data set
gives the best national coverage of radiation levels and includes
the two significant factors of ambient atmospheric levels of
beta radioactivity and the beta radioactivity deposited with precipitation. See Table 8.9.

III. LAND USE DATA

Land use has been left for separate discussion because of
the special difficulties of deriving land use information for
metropolitan areas, and even for the few areas for which such
data are forthcoming, at a comparable point in time and for consistent categories.

These difficulties were such that it was decided that data
acquisition should be restricted to a sample of thirteen of the
seventy-six SMSA's (Table 8.10). The rationale for selection
of this sample is outlined in the next chapter. Even then, problems remained. The areas to be studied were SMSA's. Most land
use investigations are restricted to the areas within the boundaries of some municipality. The SMSA differs greatly from these

TABLE 8.9

RADIATION DATA SET

City	Gross Beta Radioactivity Maximum	Radioactivity Average	Rainfall	Beta Radioactivity Deposition
2 Albuquerque	5	1	65	
4 Atlanta	2	1	254	13
5 Baltimore	2		548	4
6 Birmingham	3	1	906	353
7 Boston	1		1041	
9 Buffalo	2	1		
11 Charleston	3	1	1031	148
15 Cleveland	2	1	911	256
16 Columbus	1	1		
19 Denver	8	2	195	
21 Detroit	1	1	505	62
22 El Paso	5	1		
23 Flint	1	1	505	62
27 Hartford	1		971	1
28 Honolulu	2		448	
30 Indianapolis	2	1		
31 Jacksonville	1		917	192
34 Kansas City	5	2	568	133
35 LosAngLongBea	3	1		
38 Miami			853	
39 Milwaukee	2	1	644	72
40 MinneapolisSP	2	1	691	128
41 NashvilleDavi	3	1	983	168
43 New Orleans			1517	
47 Oklahoma City	5	1	126	79
50 Philadelphia	2		1368	51
51 Phoenix	9	4		
53 Portland	1		1179	178
54 ProvidencePaw	2		142	
56 Richmond	1		522	141
58 St. Louis	4	1	564	11
59 Salt Lake City	4	1	268	92
60 San Antonio	8	2	316	
61 San Bernadino	3	1		
63 San Francisco	1		242	1
64 San Jose	1		242	1
65 SeattleEveret			648	
70 UticaRome	1			
71 Washington, D.C.	1			
74 Worchester	2	1	1199	
75 York	2		121	28

Source: Radiological Health Data and Reports and Radiation Data and Reports (1971-1972).

TABLE 8.10

LIST OF CITIES SURVEYED, YEAR OF SURVEY
AND AREA COVERED

	City	Year	Area
1	Akron	1970	SMSA
6	Birmingham	1965	Urbanized area
13	Chicago	1970	SMSA
14	Cincinnati	1965	SMSA + 1 county
19	Denver	1970	All of 2 SMSA counties, parts of 3 counties
21	Detroit	1965	SMSA
30	Indianapolis	1964	SMSA
31	Jacksonville	1968	SMSA
35	Los Angeles	1971	SMSA
47	Oklahoma City	1965	Urbanized area
54	Providence	1960	State of Rhode Island
65	Seattle	1971	SMSA
71	Washington, D.C.	1968	SMSA

legally-bounded areas, the responsibility of local planning agencies, because it approximates more closely the functional or "true" urban region. However, a complete set of data was gathered for a majority of the sample SMSA's, with the result that this study is perhaps the first to compare land use statistics for various SMSA's across the United States. It must be emphasized that the land use data remain far from perfect, though: not all data sets refer to the entire SMSA.

Incompatabilities also arose through inconsistencies in types and descriptions of land use. The types, through their titles, tend to be descriptive, for example "Residential" and "Commercial." Title alone, however, is not an adequate description of the detailed contents of each category. Differences in category contents cause great difficulty in comparing, combining, or dividing local data sets.

Related to the sphere of types and correlated descriptions is the problem of loss of data. Often original figures, detailing a number of minor uses, are destroyed after tabulation. Obviously, these figures then are no longer available for further research. The problem is compounded when dealing with a series of land units (traffic sectors, counties, etc.) that have been combined, and the separate data groups destroyed by the local

agency--an all too common experience. The opposite problem en-
tails the collection of detailed data that is not tabulated, and
not easily available for tabulation.

Land use figures are dated as to year of collection. Because
local and regional planning agencies collect such data as the
need arises, dates are irregular. 1970 was selected as the base
year for this study, although many agencies were unable to provide data for that year in particular (Table 8.10).

The land use statistics were made as conformable as possible
through a series of aggregations and divisions, using The Standard Land Use Coding Manual as guide (Table 8.11). The process
is illustrated by Table 8.12, showing Denver, Birmingham, and
Akron's land use information and how the figures were made compatible.

TABLE 8.11

A STANDARD SYSTEM FOR IDENTIFYING AND CODING LAND USE
ACTIVITIES--ONE- AND TWO-DIGIT LEVELS

Code	Category	Code	Category
1	Residential.	11	Household units.
		12	Group quarters.
		13	Residential hotels.
		14	Mobile home parks or courts.
		15	Transient lodgings.
		19	Other residential, NEC[1]
2	Manufacturing.	21	Food and kindred products-- manufacturing.
		22	Textile mill products-- manufacturing.
		23	Apparel and other finished products made from fabrics, leather, and similar materials-- manufacturing.
		24	Lumber and wood products (except furniture)-- manufacturing.
		25	Furniture and fixtures-- manufacturing.
		26	Paper and allied products-- manufacturing.
		27	Printing, publishing, and allied industries.
		28	Chemicals and allied products--manufacturing.
		29	Petroleum refining and related industries.

TABLE 8.11 (cont'd)

Code	Category	Code	Category
3	Manufacturing (cont'd).	31	Rubber and miscellaneous plastic products--manufacturing.
		32	Stone, clay, and glass products--manufacturing.
		33	Primary metal industries.
		34	Fabricated metal products--manufacturing.
		35	Professional, scientific, and controlling instruments; photographic and optical goods; watches and clocks--manufacturing.
		39	Miscellaneous manufacturing, NEC
4	Transportation, communication, and utilities.	41	Railroad, rapid rail transit, and street railway transportation.
		42	Motor vehicle transportation.
		43	Aircraft transportation.
		44	Marine craft transportation.
		45	Highway and street right-of-way.
		46	Automobile parking.
		47	Communication.
		48	Utilities.
		49	Other transportation, communication, and utilities, NEC.
5	Trade.	51	Wholesale trade.
		52	Retail trade--building materials, hardware, and farm equipment.
		53	Retail trade--general merchandise.
		54	Retail trade--food.
		55	Retail trade--automotive, marine craft, aircraft, and accessories.
		56	Retail trade--apparel and accessories.
		57	Retail trade--furniture, home furnishings, and equipment.
		58	Retail trade--eating and drinking.
		59	Other retail trade, NEC.

TABLE 8.11 (cont'd)

Code	Category	Code	Category
6	Services.	61	Finance, insurance, and real estate services.
		62	Personal services.
		63	Business services.
		64	Repair services.
		65	Professional services.
		66	Contract construction services.
		67	Governmental services.
		68	Educational services.
		69	Miscellaneous services.
7	Cultural, entertainment, and recreational	71	Cultural activities and nature exhibitions.
		72	Public assembly.
		73	Amusements.
		74	Recreational activities.
		75	Resorts and group camps.
		76	Parks.
		79	Other cultural, entertainment, and recreational, NEC.
8	Resource production and extraction.	81	Agriculture.
		82	Agricultural related activities.
		83	Forestry activities and related services.
		84	Fishing activities and related services.
		85	Mining activities and related services.
		89	Other resource production and extraction, NEC.
9	Undeveloped land and water areas.	91	Undeveloped and unused land area (excluding noncommercial forest development).
		92	Noncommercial forest development.
		93	Water areas.
		94	Vacant floor area.
		95	Under construction.
		99	Other undeveloped land and water areas, NEC.

---

[1] NEC--Not elsewhere coded.

Source: Urban Renewal Administration and U.S. Bureau of Public Roads, Standard Land Use Coding Manual, 1965.

TABLE 8.12

COMBINATION OF THREE SETS OF LAND USE
DATA ACCORDING TO SURVEY CODE

Project Code	Code No.	Akron	Code No.	Birmingham	Code No.	Denver
1. Residential	1.	Residential	1.	Residential	1.	Single-family residential
2. Commercial	1.	Single-family	2.	Retail		
3. Industrial	1.	Two-family	2.	Wholesale	1.	Multi-family residential
4. Extractive	1.	Multi-family	3.	Manufacturing	2.	Commercial
5. Public	1.	Mobile homes			2.	Services
6. T.C.U.	1.	Others	4.	Resources	3.	Industrial
7. Open space	2.	Retail goods	5.	Public	4.	Extractive
	2.	Retail services	6.	Transportation--communications, utilities	5.	Public & semi-public
	2.	Wholesale	7.	Recreation	6.	Transportation--communication*
	3.	Industrial	7.	Vacant		
	4.	Extractive industries	7.	Water	7.	Parks & recreation
	5.	Public--quasi-public (churches, schools,etc.)			7.	Agriculture
					7.	Vacant
	6.	Transportation--terminals & utilities				
	6.	Transportation--faculties (roads, airports, etc.)			*originally "Industry-transportation-communication." Agency calculated Industrial & extractive.		
	7.	Public--quasi-public open space				
	7.	Vacant				
	7.	Water				

All missing data were requested from and calculated by the agency involved, or the project. Percentages were calculated by dividing a cell figure by the true column totals. This was done (instead of using the given total) because of discrepancies in original agency tabulations.

The final set of land uses assembled, with their descriptions, is as follows. Table 8.13 provides the data.

1) RESIDENTIAL

Structures and associated land intended for use as a residence. Includes single family, multiple family, mobile and transient facilities, as well as garages and yards.

2) COMMERCIAL

Structures and associated land intended for consumer goods and services, office-type and wholesale facilities. Includes parking and other directly related land.

3) INDUSTRIAL

Structures and associated land intended for light or heavy manufacturing, industrially-oriented non-manufacturing. Warehousing and open yards included.

4) EXTRACTIVE

Land and associated structure intended for resource extraction. Includes mining, stone, gravel, clay and oil activity and production.

5) PUBLIC, QUASI-PUBLIC

Structures and associated land intended for educational, medical, religious, governmental, correctional, and other institutional purposes. Includes military installations, public, social, and cultural centers.

6) TRANSPORTATION-COMMUNICATION-UTILITIES

Structures and associated land intended for transportation terminals or facilities; streets, roads, alleys, expressways, and highways for the conveyance of passengers and freight. Includes all utilities, rights-of-way for railroads and highways, and automobile parking not directly associated with other uses.

7) AGRICULTURAL-RECREATIONAL-WATER-VACANT

All land and associated structures intended for agricultural (crop production or grazing) purposes. All recreational land, all permanent bodies of water, and all vacant or undeveloped land. Cemeteries are also included in this category.

TABLE 8.13

LAND USE AS PERCENTAGE OF TOTAL SMSA OR MEASURED AREA*

	Residential	Commercial	Industrial	Extractive	Public	T.C.U.	Open Space
Akron	11.19	1.77	.70	.77	.91	6.01	78.65
Birmingham[1]	15.58	1.23	2.27	2.44	1.77	9.68	67.03
Chicago	13.10	1.36	1.33	.99	3.25	9.19	70.78[2]
Cincinnati	9.13	.56	.53	.26[3]	1.23[4]	4.20	84.10
Denver	6.01	.65	2.15[5]	.24[5]	3.35[6]	3.74	83.86
Detroit	15.10	1.62	2.43	.82	4.19[6]	6.66[4]	69.17
Indianapolis	16.81	1.38	.80	.45	1.84	11.01	67.71
Jacksonville	6.95	.93	.55	.01	.69[6]	8.71[7]	82.16
Los Angeles	15.99	1.63	2.29	.75	5.13	1.34	72.87
Oklahoma City	4.88	.52	.67	.15	2.52	6.65	84.62
Providence	8.38	.90	.63	.18	2.61	5.63	81.68
Seattle	11.49	1.60	.91	.24	1.16	8.13	76.48
Washington, D.C.	11.14	1.21	1.00	.20	5.63	5.67	75.14

*Note that figures may not add to 100.00%
due to rounding.
1. All figures net data (excludes streets).
2. Excludes all water data.
3. Excludes Ohio County (Indiana) data.
4. Estimated by project.
5. Estimated by planning agency.
6. Includes cemetaries.
7. Includes protective services.

9   A POLLUTION-SENSITIVE TYPOLOGY OF THE URBAN REGIONS

Recalling what was said in Chapter 1, the purpose of the study was to isolate key relationships between urban form and land use on the one hand, and environmental pollution on the other, so that insights might be provided into the consequences of alternative land use policies. To accomplish this, a two-stage research process was initiated:

(a) A "sorting table" with urban regions in the rows and environmental variables in the columns was to be developed to assess the availibility and quality of pollutant survaillance systems on a nationwide basis, to evaluate the status of environmental quality indexes, and to study the relationships between urban characteristics and environmental pollution across the set of urban regions.
(b) For a sample of the urban regions representative of the universe in the sorting table, equivalent intra-urban data systems were to be developed as a basis for studying detailed local relationships between environmental pollution and land use.

The link between the two stages involved the development of a pollution-sensitive typology of the urban regions to be used as a sampling frame. It is this typology that is discussed in the present chapter. Chapters 10 and 11 then focus on the relationships of environmental pollution to the characteristics of the larger set of seventy-six urban regions. In Part D, the intra-urban relationships are discussed.

I. METHOD OF ANALYSIS

The method of analysis chosen to develop the typology was Q-mode factor analysis, with both orthogonal and oblique reference-axis rotation. In this method, one begins with a data matrix X of order n x m, where there are n observations (urban regions) and m variables (pollutant measures). Each of the m variables is transformed as needed to ensure linearity, creating a matrix X*, and then converted, for i regions and j variables, to standardized variates $Z_{ij} = \dfrac{x^*_{ij} - \bar{x}^*_{j}}{S_{x^*_j}}$, to correct for the fact that factors extracted from sample covariance matrices are not invariant under a change of measurement scales used. The matrix Z is then post-multiplied by its transpose to yield a sample covariance matrix Q in the following manner: $Q = \frac{1}{m} Z \cdot Z^T$ (1)

(n x n)$\phantom{ = \frac{1}{m} }$(n x m) (m x n)

Q is , of course, the sample correlation matrix of the urban regions, and is of order n x n. It is this matrix which is factored for its characteristic roots and vectors.

The underlying concept in such factoring is that Q is composed of two parts, a part derived from the expression of an underlying typological structure in the similarities of the urban regions with respect to their pollution characteristics, Q*, and a set of uniqueness and error terms U^2

$$Q = Q* + U^2 \tag{2}$$

with $\qquad Q* = \frac{1}{m} Z* Z*^T$ (3)

and $\qquad Z*^T = A \cdot C$ (4)

(m x n) (m x r) (r x n)

where the C are coefficients (factor loadings) assigning the cities to r classes, and the coefficients A are classification scores linking the actual pollution measures to the city types.

$$U^2 = \frac{1}{m} E^T \cdot E \tag{5}$$

(n x n)$\phantom{ = \frac{1}{m} }$(n x m) (m x n)

where the E are uniqueness and error terms left unaccounted for by the classification. The linear form of equation (4) assumes that the classes are orthogonal, while the errors are assumed to be independent of each other and of the r orthogonal factors.

From the above:

$$Q = \frac{1}{m} C^T \cdot A^T \cdot A \cdot C + U^2 \tag{6}$$

(n x n)$\phantom{ = \frac{1}{m} }$(n x r) (r x m) (m x r) (r x n) (n x n)

But if the classification scores have been standardized, and since the classes are orthogonal $A^T A = mI$, one derives:

$$Q* = Q - U^2 = C^T \cdot C \tag{7}$$

To obtain the C's, Q* may be solved for its characteristic roots and vectors by solving the characteristic equation

$$| Q* - \lambda I | = 0 \tag{8}$$

the roots of which yield the vectors F and eigenvalues λ viz:

$$Q* = F^T \Lambda F \tag{9}$$

and $\qquad C = \Lambda^{\frac{1}{2}} F$ (10)

so that $\qquad Q* = C^T \cdot C$ (11)

This method obtains r factors or groups of urban regions with common profiles across the initial m pollution variables. Viewed geometrically, the A are orthogonal reference axes on which the original n-variates (urban regions) in m-space (pollution characteristics) given by Z^T are projected using the coefficients C.

Once having obtained a solution using the principal axis method, it is useful both to check for the validity of the orthogonality assumption, and to rotate the reference axes to the position of "simple structure" in which the original vectors (urban regions) fall as closely as possible to only one reference axis, having the effect of allocating the urban regions as nearly as possible to disjoint subsets, a desirable typological goal. This was done using the OBLIMIN criterion to check orthogonality and the VARIMAX model to rotate to simple structure. Both of these criteria are discussed in detail in standard texts on factor analysis, and to conserve space will not be elaborated here. The information they provide determines whether or not one can work with a mutually exclusive classification of urban regions to types, and whether or not these types should be treated as co-equal, or as subsets of some higher order classification (Rummel, 1971).

II. DATA AND RESULTS

The methods described in the foregoing were applied to a data matrix which included the information on types of air, water, and land pollution, including solid wastes, pesticides, radiation and noise, recorded in the overall sorting table. Seventy-six urban regions were included in the investigation. Where problems of missing data existed, correlations were computed only across the available data set, however.

A six-factor solution was able to reproduce a very high proportion of the variance, as indicated by the vector of eigenvalues presented in Table 9.2 and the communalities of each of the seventy-six urban regions listed in Table 9.1. Moreover, the optimum oblique rotation of the factors showed the factor solution to be naturally near-orthogonal (Table 9.3).

The taxonomy was then derived using the 76 x 6 matrices of factor loadings for the principal axis, varimax rotated and oblimin rotated solutions in the following manner:

1. The group (factor) on which each urban region loaded most highly was identified in the varimax and oblimin solutions, as were all other larger loadings lying beyond the range -0.50 to +0.50.

TABLE 9.1

URBAN REGIONS INCLUDED IN THE ANALYSIS,
WITH PROPORTIONS OF VARIANCE ACCOUNTED FOR BY A
SIX-FACTOR MODEL

1	Akron	0.95909
2	Albuquerque	0.81815
3	Allentown-Bethlehem	0.93993
4	Atlanta	0.76499
5	Baltimore	0.96484
6	Birmingham	0.86774
7	Boston	0.98037
8	Bridgeport	0.89217
9	Buffalo	0.98062
10	Canton	0.95253
11	Charleston	0.97332
12	Chattanooga	0.97332
13	Chicago	0.97160
14	Cincinnati	0.70762
15	Cleveland	0.72660
16	Columbus	0.95821
17	Dallas	0.76780
18	Dayton	0.50343
19	Denver	0.89343
20	Des Moines	0.96685
21	Detroit	0.94162
22	El Paso	0.94084
23	Flint	0.94585
24	Fort Worth	0.96728
25	Gary-Hammond	0.93011
26	Grand Rapids	0.84280
27	Hartford	0.94653
28	Honolulu	0.96685
29	Houston	0.87825
30	Indianapolis	0.85657
31	Jacksonville	0.99271
32	Jersey City	0.86763
33	Johnstown	0.89400
34	Kansas City	0.73713
35	Los Angeles	0.98062
36	Louisville	0.84280
37	Memphis	0.95988
38	Miami	0.94084
39	Milwaukee	0.91401
40	Minneapolis	0.92985
41	Nashville	0.90461
42	New Haven	0.95253
43	New Orleans	0.96087
44	New York	0.89816
45	Newark	0.84179
46	Norfolk	0.84829
47	Oklahoma City	0.91310
48	Omaha	0.99271
49	Patterson	0.84542
50	Philadelphia	0.92983
51	Phoenix	0.73365
52	Pittsburgh	0.92983
53	Portland	0.98725

TABLE 9.1 (Cont'd)

54	Providence	0.88076
55	Reading	0.93785
56	Richmond	0.91761
57	Rochester	0.74876
58	St. Louis	0.91297
59	Salt Lake City	0.83433
60	San Antonio	0.87332
61	San Bernadino	0.70782
62	San Diego	0.92773
63	San Francisco	0.94891
64	San Jose	0.95909
65	Seattle	0.05793
66	Syracuse	0.84113
67	Tampa-St. Petersburg	0.98544
68	Toledo	0.94585
69	Tulsa	0.91310
70	Utica-Rome	0.83283
71	Washington, D.C.	0.98725
72	Wichita	0.86774
73	Wilmington	0.89230
74	Worcester	0.97160
75	York	0.91572
76	Youngstown	0.94207

TABLE 9.2

VARIANCE EXTRACTED BY THE SIX-FACTOR SOLUTION

Factor	Eigenvalue	Percentage of Variance	Cumulative Percentage
1	21.81287	28.7	28.7
2	14.91827	19.6	48.3
3	13.12157	17.3	65.6
4	9.77722	12.9	78.5
5	9.05012	11.9	90.4
6	7.20181	9.5	99.8

TABLE 9.3

CORRELATIONS AMONG FACTORS IN OPTIMUM OBLIMIN SOLUTION

	FACTOR 1	FACTOR 2	FACTOR 3	FACTOR 4	FACTOR 5	FACTOR 6
FACTOR 1	1.00000	0.05051	-0.00492	-0.14781	-0.01018	0.09101
FACTOR 2	0.05051	1.00000	0.08361	0.04017	-0.05146	-0.04503
FACTOR 3	-0.00492	0.08361	1.00000	0.02517	-0.06304	0.09662
FACTOR 4	-0.14781	0.04017	0.02517	1.00000	-0.08579	-0.02097
FACTOR 5	-0.01018	-0.05146	-0.06304	-0.08579	1.00000	0.02331
FACTOR 6	0.09101	-0.04503	0.09662	-0.02097	0.02331	1.00000

2. "Core" groupings were developed by identifying those urban regions with their highest loadings on the same factor in both the varimax and oblimin solutions.

3. The mirror-image couplets comprising centers with high
positive loadings at one extreme and high negative loadings at the other extreme were separated on the first
five factors (factor six had only strong positive loadings.)

4. Residual cases were allocated to the core groups on the
basis of the overall pattern of correlations with the
set of core-group members.

Table 9.4 shows the resulting eleven groups into which the urban
regions naturally cluster with respect to similarities in environmental pollution. The cases selected for detailed study in Part

TABLE 9.4

CORE GROUPS COMMON TO THE ORTHOGONAL AND
OBLIQUE Q-MODE FACTOR STRUCTURES

FACTOR	GROUP OF METROPOLITAN AREAS	
1+	Atlanta Boston Columbus Dallas Detroit Fort Worth Houston Miami	New Orleans New York San Antonio San Diego San Francisco San Jose Seattle Tampa-St. Petersburg
1-	Birmingham Charleston Chattanooga Dayton Des Moines Gary-Hammond	Johnstown Nashville Omaha Reading Utica-Rome Worcester
2+	Chicago Milwaukee Minneapolis Philadelphia	Pittsburgh Portland St. Louis
2-	Albuquerque El Paso Oklahoma City	Phoenix Tulsa Wichita
3+	Bridgeport Cleveland Hartford	New Haven Newark Providence
3-	Cincinnati Jersey City Kansas City	San Bernadino Syracuse Wilmington
4+	Baltimore Buffalo Indianapolis	Los Angeles Washington, D.C.

TABLE 9.4 (Cont'd)

4-	Denver	Salt Lake City
5+	Akron Allentown-Bethlehem Canton	Rochester Youngstown York
5-	Honolulu	Memphis
6+	Flint Grand Rapids Jacksonville Louisville	Norfolk Patterson Richmond Toledo

NOTES: Factors 1-6 near-orthogonal.
Bipolar + and - categories on a given factor have reverse-image pollution characteristics.
Cities underlined are cases for which more detailed intraurban investigations will be undertaken.

D are underlined. Rather than choosing sample cases on a randomized basis, the selection was made on the basis of adequacy of basic information on internal variations in environmental quality; hence, because base data were unavailable, no "5-" city was included in the studies in Part D.

III. DISCUSSION

On inspection, many of the groups appear, intuitively, to make good common sense--for example Group 2+ containing such industrial cities as Chicago, Milwaukee, Minneapolis, Philadelphia, Pittsburgh, Portland, and St. Louis certainly contrasts with the much cleaner set comprising Group 2--members Alburquerque, El Paso, Oklahoma City, Phoenix, Tulsa, and Wichita. But intuition is not enough. The questions that arise in terms of the initial "sorting table" approach to the research effort described earlier are these:

(a) How are the groups differentiated in terms of the pollution characteristics of their members?

(b) What characteristics of urban form and function discriminate among the groups?

(c) How do the pollution differences and urban variables covary, and what do the covariances imply?

Tables 9.5 and 9.6 provide an initial insight into these questions. The groups are arranged in mirror-image sequence in

TABLE 9.5

POLLUTION--VARIATIONS ACROSS THE GROUPS

	GRAND MEAN	S.D.	4+	2+	5+	1-	3+	6+	3-	1+	5-	2-	4-
WQI 1 (drinking)	3.3	2.7	7.6	1.7	4.7	2.1	5.2	4.0	5.4	4.7	n.a.	2.3	2.0
WQI 2 (recreation)	2.2	2.3	6.3	1.2	2.2	1.5	0.7	1.5	4.3	3.0	"	2.2	0.4
WQI 3 (industry)	1.8	1.8	1.4	0.6	1.4	1.2	0.5	1.0	3.3	2.0	"	2.4	1.4
WQI4 (average)	2.5	2.0	5.1	1.2	2.8	1.6	2.1	2.2	4.5	3.3	"	2.3	1.3
Temperature	61	9	58	59	63	58	57	58	61	69	"	62	51
Color	15	13	10	14	10	6	n.a.	20	24	20	"	12	n.a.
PH	7.3	0.9	7.4	7.4	6.8	6.9	6.7	7.7	7.1	7.3	"	8.0	7.7
TOT. Dissolved Solids	1945	5467	865	211	820	353	95	407	4765	4448	"	1894	445
TOT Nitrates	11	13	3	5	16	7	4	3	8	19	"	16	11
Hardness	483	947	335	148	333	226	42	234	874	886	"	561	264
Color	1146	3619	39	33	323	30	16	30	4885	2337	"	666	264
TOT Iron and Manganese	1.0	2.5	n.a.	0.5	0.9	2.1	0.2	n.a.	0.6	0.3	"	0.2	n.a.
Sulfate	235	435	n.a.	54	96	160	15	76	474	369	"	424	113
Dissolved Oxygen	6.9	2.1	7.2	8.0	5.3	7.8	7.1	7.9	7.0	6.9	"	4.9	n.a.
TOT MAQI	2.7	0.8	3.2	3.4	2.7	3.2	2.7	2.1	2.9	2.3	2.3	2.1	2.2
TOT EVI	6.0	5.0	9.7	8.4	5.9	10.2	4.2	2.2	5.0	3.5	2.3	3.4	1.1
SO2 AVE	27	21	34	49	38	25	51	20	22	19	16	9	13
SO2 MAX	117	93	127	191	149	117	241	74	87	80	208	40	37
SO2 MAQI	0.5	0.1	0.6	0.8	0.6	0.5	0.9	.3	0.4	0.4	0.3	0.1	0.1
NO2 MAQI	1.4	0.4	1.2	1.6	1.4	1.2	1.6	1.6	1.6	1.4	1.4	1.0	1.3
TSP AVE	97	25	115	117	106	119	84	82	104	85	61	84	82
TSP MAX	231	95	325	317	229	310	168	184	238	179	145	197	159
TSP MAQI	2.2	0.8	2.9	2.8	2.4	2.9	1.7	1.7	2.4	1.7	1.9	1.9	1.7
TSP EVI	6.1	5.0	9.7	8.4	5.9	10.6	4.4	2.2	5.0	3.5	2.3	3.4	1.1
AUTO. TRV.	342	362	803	705	155	120	278	193	239	515	183	154	263
AIR. TRV.	104	123	170	228	194	36	99	34	66	152	114	46	110
G.B.R. MAX	2.7	2.1	2.0	2.2	2.0	2.4	1.7	1.0	3.0	2.1	2.0	6.0	1.5
G.B.R. AVE	1.3	0.7	1.0	1.0	n.a.	1.0	1.0	1.0	1.5	1.3	n.a.	1.8	.231

TABLE 9.5 (Cont'd)

	GRAND MEAN	S.D.	4+	2+	5+	1-	3+	6+	3-	1+	5-	2-	4-
Rainfall	.641	.395	.548	.893	.121	1.030	.675	.648	.568	.624	.448	.095	.231
B.R.DEP	99	92	4	88	28	223	129	132	133	19	n.a.	79	92
S.W.G.F.1	4.89	1.43	5.09	4.49	4.39	5.04	3.98	4.66	5.98	4.75	5.72	5.30	5.72
S.W.G.F.4	n.a.	n.a.	5987	6737	1440	999	2482	1434	1940	4527	1174	984	1564
S.W.G.F.5	n.a.	n.a.	3811	3858	741	579	1287	914	1193	2938	882	712	1178
No. Cases	76		5	7	6	12	6	8	6	16	2	6	2

TABLE 9.6

SOME CHARACTERISTICS OF CITIES IN THE ELEVEN GROUPS

(GROUP AVERAGES)

	4+	2+	5+	1-	3+	6+	3-	1+	5-	2-	4-
Population of Central City	1209	1185	186	209	321	327	329	1152	475	354	346
Population of SMSA	2285	2969	557	448	1040	705	921	2267	700	525	893
Density of Central City	10669	10111	6966	4711	9630	8774	7553	7569	4285	3958	5380
Density of SMSA	6396	5911	3413	2048				6302	3586	637	2891
Growth Rate, Central City	1.7	-6.5	-5.8	-5.8	-6.1	3.9	0.8	14.2	17.9	19.7	-1.5
Growth Rate, SMSA	31.9	30.1	23.6	21.5	25.3	24.9	24.5	48.2	15.2	19.5	55.8
Md. Age of Central City Residents	29.5	31.3	30.8	31.0	29.1	28.1	29.8	29.4	27.2	26.9	28.8
Md. Age of SMSA Residents	27.4	27.7	28.5	28.0	30.4	26.2	28.1	27.4	22.4	24.8	23.2
Md. Family Income	11.1	10.9	10.6	9.7	11.4	10.3	10.2	10.4	10.3	9.1	10.4
Percent Employed in Manufacturing	24.2	29.8	43.9	32.5	34.0	29.4	30.3	22.0	14.7	19.9	16.4
Area of Central City	215	108	30	89	36	144	107	180	151	224	77
Area of SMSA	2670	3093	1225	1400	668	1027	5973	2519	980	3306	2361
Degrees of Arc: SMSA	264	291	330	330	210	285	250	225	240	280	270
Radial Highways: Central City	9.8	8.6	3.0	3.6	5.3	4.6	6.0	7.3	4.0	3.7	5.0
Radial Highways: SMSA	10.6	10.9	5.0	5.4	7.5	6.6	7.5	8.3	5.5	4.0	7.0
Circumferential Highways	3.0	2.7	2.5	1.5	1.6	1.7	1.8	2.4	2.0	3.0	1.5
Total Land + Property Values in SMSA	25.2	18.5	3.4	3.1	10.3	4.7	8.5	18.8	4.1	3.4	6.6

Both tables from the cities in groups 4+, 2+, 5+, and 1-, most heavily afflicted by air pollution, through groups 3- and 1+, with the greatest water pollution, to the least-polluted cities in groups 5-, 2-, and 4-. Where the pollution level exceeds the national average, the number in the table is underlined. Table 9.6 records related city characteristics in the same progression from group 4+ to group 4-.

What is indicated is the following: The largest metropolitan areas with the greatest population densities and average-to-high levels of manufacturing employment are afflicted by the highest levels of air pollution, the greatest auto and air travel volumes (and therefore presumably the greatest noise pollution), generate the greatest volumes of solid wastes, and are likely to be afflicted with water pollution problems, too. At the other extreme, small, low-density metropolitan areas with low levels of manufacturing employment have the lowest levels of environmental pollution, standing at with respect only to those things that may be regionally-determined, such as water hardness. Between these extremes are the large regional capitals of the West and South, plus New York, Boston and Detroit, seen as suffering in particular from severe problems of water pollution. The question that we now want to address is whether, holding these major effects of size, density manufacturing etc. constant, differences in urban form and land use have an incremental effect, either increasing or decreasing environmental pollution. This is the subject of the next chapter.

10   RELATIONSHIPS OF ENVIRONMENTAL POLLUTION, CITY CHARACTERISTICS, AND URBAN LAND USE

Urban life produces both "goods" and "bads." Chapter 11 will focus on the goods, examining the ways in which the aggregate net benefits of urban activity are capitalized as land values, and asking whether disbenefits are apparent in particular types of cities. In this chapter we focus on the bads--on the relationships of environmental pollution to city characteristics, taking into account the intervening role of urban form and land use.

The conceptual model we have in mind is diagrammed in Figure 10.1. An urban area is seen as deriving its basic properties (growth rate, size, incomes and demographic structure) from its economic base, the nature of which is determined exogenously by the position of the urban area in the national economy. From these basic properties are derived demands for land use, but these demands only result in a particular land use mix after translation through urban form, which is historically determined, and which controls the supply, location, and accessibility of land and urban densities, and hence the intensity of land use. In turn, the mix and pattern of land use is argued to control the nature, intensity and pattern of environmental pollution. The aggregate net benefits of urban life are capitalized as land values, and both land values and environmental pollution feed back to affect the relative role of the urban region in the national economy.

We begin by looking at the relationships between environmental pollution, city characteristics and urban form. Because land use plays an important intervening role, and this link is omitted in the initial equations, the direct relationships are identifiable, but relatively weak. Likewise, it is found that the direct relationship of land use to city characteristics is weak when the translating effects of urban form are omitted. But when land use is related to both city characteristics and urban form, the relationships are very strong, except for those types of land use (industry, transportation) reflecting activities whose location is determined exogenously to the urban region. Further, the relationships of environmental pollution to land use are direct and strong. These findings confirm the significance of urban form and land use in determining the nature and intensity of environ-

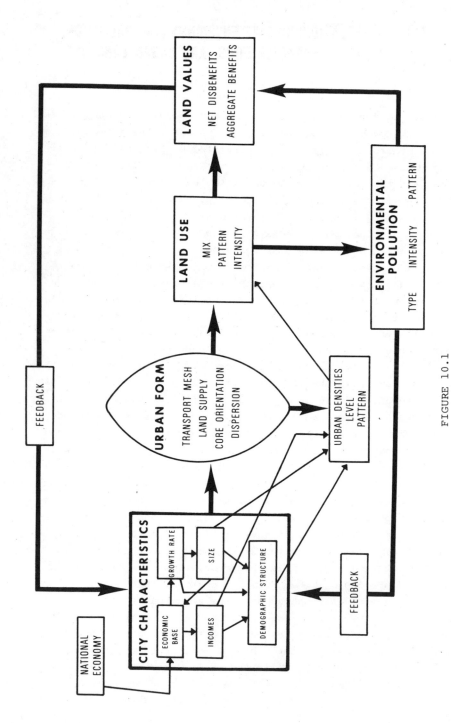

FIGURE 10.1

THE LINKS BETWEEN THE URBAN ECONOMY, LAND USE AND ENVIRONMENTAL POLLUTION

mental pollution.

I. ENVIRONMENTAL POLLUTION, CITY CHARACTERISTICS AND URBAN FORM

Table 10·1 shows clearly enough that environmental pollution does covary with city characteristics and urban form, but weakly when the relationships are estimated over the full set of 76 cities and land use is omitted. In this table, fourteen environmental quality indicators are regressed, first on city size, the ratio of SMSA to central city population density, median family income and percentage of the labor force engaged in manufacturing, and secondly on these four variables plus three additional variables describing the spatial form of the urban area--number of degrees of arc occupied by the city around its center and the number of radial and circumferential highways. In contrast to previous studies that have used much smaller data sets, the regression equations in all cases yield modest results. The R^2's vary from only 0.133 to 0.429. In general, raw environmental variables are more significant than the quality indexes.

Despite the low coefficients of determination a certain consistency in the results does emerge, however. Pollution levels increase with city size for air quality measures, with manufacturing concentrations for both air and water quality, and they are lower in higher income communities (which is more likely a consequence rather than a cause). Water pollution problems are greater in more dispersed lower-density urban regions where SMSA and central city densities are most similar. On the other hand, suspended particulate concentrations are worst in the highly centralized cities where central city densities are much greater than SMSA densities and the urban density gradients are relatively steep. On the other hand, SO_2 and NO_2 are, holding the effects of city size etc. constant in the model, greater problems in the more disposed city, which is consistent with greater use of the automobile. These results confirm what previous researchers have found about factors correlated with pollution, and they begin to show that there may be variations associated with different urban forms. Of the spatial form variables, only the number of radial highways is consistently significant in these crude models, however, and then only with respect

TABLE 10.1

REGRESSION RELATIONSHIPS BETWEEN CITY CHARACTERISTICS AND POLLUTION VARIABLES

Dependent Variable	Coefficients and t statistics for independent variables						t statistics and R^2 for model including spatial variables			
	SMSA Population	Density Ratio	Median Family Income	Manufacturing Percentage	Intercept	R^2	Degrees of Arc	Radials	Circumferentials	R^2
MAQI	0.135[1] (3.56)[2]	-0.063 (-.171)	-0.98 (-3.10)	0.252 (3.26)	8.47 (3.14)	0.303	(-0.92)	(2.57)	(-1.46)	0.387
EVI	0.218 (1.51)	-0.277 (-1.99)	-1.459 (-1.22)	0.987 (3.37)	10.88 (1.06)	0.257	(0.61)	(1.78)	(-1.11)	0.324
SO_2 AVE	0.300 (2.47)	0.153 (1.31)	-0.077 (-0.077)	1.076 (4.37)	-2.16 (-0.25)	0.371	(-1.50)	(0.81)	(1.33)	0.429
SO_2 MAX	0.245 (1.67)	0.169 (1.19)	0.205 (0.169)	0.957 (3.22)	-2.62 (-0.25)	0.253	(-0.89)	(0.24)	(1.27)	0.292
SO_2 MAQI	0.343 (2.57)	0.120 (0.93)	-0.434 (-0.39)	1.113 (4.10)	-3.27 (-0.34)	0.332	(-1.35)	(0.77)	(1.05)	0.378
NO_2 MAQI	0.146 (2.68)	0.003 (0.075)	-0.568 (-1.25)	0.161 (1.46)	4.01 (1.04)	0.133	(-1.14)	(1.16)	(-0.42)	0.166
TSP AVE	0.075 (2.08)	-0.078 (-2.26)	-0.764 (-2.56)	0.231 (3.17)	10.57 (4.26)	0.274	(0.10)	(2.40)	(-1.43)	0.362
TSP MAX	0.108 (1.84)	-0.118 (-2.09)	-0.966 (-1.98)	0.222 (1.86)	13.19 (3.17)	0.178	(0.04)	(1.97)	(-1.08)	0.247
TSP MAQI	0.090 (2.10)	-0.106 (-2.56)	-0.853 (-2.39)	0.223 (2.57)	7.61 (2.51)	0.255	(0.03)	(2.14)	(-0.98)	0.326
TSP EVI	0.206 (1.37)	-0.311 (-2.15)	-1.24 (-1.00)	0.912 (3.00)	9.32 (0.88)	0.237	(0.32)	(2.02)	(-0.97)	0.310
WPI 1	0.087 (0.46)	0.272 (1.55)	-0.746 (-0.50)	0.866 (2.31)	3.76 (0.30)	0.157	(-0.83)	(0.37)	(0.40)	0.177
WPI 2	0.185 (0.83)	0.461 (2.25)	-3.299 (-1.92)	1.055 (1.72)	25.0 (1.72)	0.203	(-0.38)	(0.02)	(0.81)	0.221
WPI 3	-0.050 (-0.31)	0.348 (2.30)	-3.077 (-2.43)	0.372 (1.15)	26.8 (2.51)	0.240	(-0.10)	(-0.39)	(0.56)	0.247
WPI 4	0.066 (0.383)	0.336 (2.10)	-1.68 (-1.26)	0.158 (2.22)	12.4 (1.10)	0.166	(-0.75)	(0.16)	(0.52)	0.184

[1]regression coefficient
[2]t-statistic
Note: t values of 2.0 or above significant at the .05 level, and 3.0 or above at the .01 level.

to air quality, indicating that the more radially-structured
urban region has greater inadequacies of air quality overall,
and suspended particulates in particular. The reversal of
signs on the measure of number of circumferentials is, again,
consistent with the patterns of automobile usage: The greater
the number of circumferential highways, the greater the dispersion of the urban region, the lower the TSP concentrations,
but also, the greater the water pollution.

II. LAND USE, CITY CHARACTERISTICS AND URBAN FORM

If environmental quality displays relatively weak direct
relationships to city characteristics and urban form, the opposite is true for urban land use. See Table 10.2. Actually,
however, this statement needs qualification. The power of
the regression models is not substantially greater than those
presented in Table 10.1 for models relating land use percentages
directly to the four key city characteristics (population, density ratio, median incomes, manufacturing proportion). However,
when the three urban form indicators are included, the coefficients of determination more than double for all land use types
except industrial and TCU (transportation, communications,
utilities) indicating that urban form plays a significant
intervening role in translating city characteristics into land
use. The two exceptions, industrial land use and TCU, are indeed
exceptions that prove the rule. In economic models, it is
commonly assumed that industrial location is determined exogenously by the role played by a city in the national economy, and that
TCU represents a key instrument variable that may be used to pattern land use i.e. that industry and transportation are determinants of urban structure rather than being determined by it.
The regression results confirm this common assumption.

As for the other land uses, the important intervening role
of urban form in determining the urban land use mix is clear.
For example, the percentage of land used for residential purposes varies directly with SMSA population, with a 1.0 percent
change in population producing an 0.6 percent change in the
residential percentage, inversely with the density ratio and income levels, and positively with manufacturing employment. The
less-than-proportionate rate of increase of residential land
use with city size is commensurate with the fact that city area
also increases at a slower rate than urban population, producing

TABLE 10.2

LAND USE AS A FUNCTION OF CITY CHARACTERISTICS

INDEPENDENT VARIABLES	Land Uses Used as Dependent Variables													
	LOG RESIDENTIAL		LOG COMMERCIAL		LOG INDUSTRIAL		LOG EXTRACTIVE		LOG PUBLIC USES		LOG T.C.U.		LOG OPEN SPACE	
LOG SMSA POPULATION	.232[1] (1.350)[2]	.608 (2.798)	.160 (.851)	.756 (3.431)	.576 (2.554)	.621 (1.304)	.688 (1.529)	.975 (1.489)	.592 (2.455)	.367 (.798)	-.349 (-1.245)	-.372 (-.672)	-.057 (-1.396)	-.124 (-2.674)
LOG DENSITY RATIO	-.105 (-.735)	-.092 (-.894)	-.002 (-.014)	-.312 (-1.673)	-.329 (-1.460)		-.899 (-2.415)	-.826 (-2.663)	-.007 (-.329)	-.056 (-.259)	-.005 (-.201)	-.085 (-.325)	.243 (.717)	.025 (1.142)
LOG MEDIAN FAMILY INCOME	-.218 (-.172)	-2.134 (-1.754)	.674 (.486)	-1.628 (-1.320)	-2.642 (-1.590)	-3.960 (-1.486)	-2.378 (-.717)	-2.039 (-.556)	-.626 (-.352)		.799 (.387)	-1.335 (-.431)	.180 (.596)	.710 (2.741)
LOG PERCENT MANUFACTURING	.179 (1.037)	.921 (.568)	.120 (.638)	-.135 (-.822)	-.042 (-.184)	-.001 (-.002)	.769 (1.760)	.860 (1.760)	-.132 (-.385)	-.319 (-1.317)	.028 (.100)	.152 (.369)	-.018 (-.428)	-.014 (-.413)
DEGREES OF ARC		.002 (1.828)		.002 (1.554)		-.000 (-.093)		.007 (2.253)		.002 (.695)		-.001 (-.295)		-.000 (-1.450)
RADIAL HIGHWAYS		-.081 (-1.470)		-.161 (-2.880)		.004 (.336)		-.018 (-.108)		.086 (.739)		.037 (.266)		.011 (.943)
CIRCUMFERENTIAL HIGHWAYS		.212 (2.431)		.287 (3.237)		.122 (.635)		-.040 (-.154)		-.149 (-.806)		.183 (.824)		-.054 (-2.895)
INTERCEPT	2.397 (.213)	17.524 (1.634)	-7.729 (-.629)	10.487 (.965)	21.328 (1.450)	32.942 (1.402)	15.970 (.544)	8.792 (.272)	3.419 (.217)	-6.756 (-.298)	-3.017 (-.165)	16.202 (.593)	3.070 (1.147)	-1.289 (-.565)
COEFFICIENT OF DETERMINATION	.420 (4.8)	.817 (7.5)	.318 (4.8)	.815 (7.5)	.540 (4.8)	.593 (7.5)	.647 (4.8)	.852 (7.5)	.597 (4.8)	.711 (7.5)	.202 (4.8)	.383 (7.5)	.300 (4.8)	.823 (7.5)
F-STATISTIC	1.449	3.187	.934	3.148	2.347	1.042	3.672	4.118	2.958	1.756	.506	.443	.855	3.328

NOTES:
1. Regression coefficient
2. t-statistic

increased residential densities, and is borne out by the inverse
relationship that exists between the residential percentage and
the density ratio: the percentage of residential land increases
as the density ratio falls. The density ratio falls when central
city densities are high relative to SMSA densities (i.e., a
situation in which the population density gradient is relatively
steep and the population of the urban area is core-oriented).
In other words, higher central city densities produce more
intensive land use.

The greatest elasticity of residential land use is with
respect to median incomes; a 1.0 percent increase in incomes
is associated with a 2.1 percentage point decrease in residential land use. Looking at the other equations, the compensating
factor is open space: the greater the median income of a community, the greater the open space, commensurate with national
attitudes regarding the quality of life.

The intervening role of the three urban form variables
reveals the specific mechanics of translation of city characteristics into land use. A positive relationship is seen
between the residential percentage and the degrees of arc of a
city. The higher the degrees of arc, the more area is available
for residential development, and the more extensive is land use.
On the other hand, residential land use varies indirectly with
the number of radials. Planners have advocated the use of a
radial urban design to cut down on urban sprawl. By concentrating
development along the radials, or "fingers," and restricting the
uses of the "wedges" between these fingers, according to the
argument, land development might be confined to the easily accessible areas along the fingers. The inverse relationship
shown here supports this argument, as does the positive relationship of the residential percentage to the number of circumferential highways. An increased number of circumferentials pro-
motes residential sprawl.

What are the mechanics of these urban from relationships?
What is indicated is that the demand for urban land is determined
exogenously by the role that the city plays in the national
economy. From such exogenous relationships arise the industry
mix, growth rate, size, and income levels of the urban region.
Urban form controls the supply of land of each access type
available for development. The greatest supply of land is
delivered by a circular urban region with many circumferential
highway rings; such supply conditions produce residential

sprawl. On the other hand a radially-structured urban region on a restricted site has higher residential densities, a steeper density gradient, a lower residential land use percentage (and more open space).

Similar relationships exist for the other land uses. The commercial, and extractive percentages increase with city size, are lower where the density gradient is steep, decrease with community income levels, and increase in manufacturing cities. They increase as the urban form approaches circularity, decrease in a radial structure and increase with the number of circumferentials.

Conversely, open space decreases with city size, manufacturing concentrations, and circumferential structure, increases with income levels, where the density gradient is steep, and with the number of radials, and--the only surprise--decreases as the degrees of arc increase. But a moment's reflection eliminates even that surprise. Departures from circularity are usually environmentally-determined by lakes and seashore, rivers and mountains, and where such environmental amenities exist, there has been effort to preserve them as open space.

III. ENVIRONMENTAL POLLUTION AND LAND USE

The final link in the chain therefore must be between land use and environmental pollution. Recall what was reported in Table 10.1: the direct associations of city characteristics and environmental pollution are relatively weak. But if, as in the case of land use, urban form plays an important role in translating city characteristics into land use, perhaps land use itself plays the important translational role between city characteristics and urban form on the one hand and pollution on the other.

Table 10.3 provides the evidence for four measures of air pollution that confirms this logic. Each pollutant is regressed twice on a series of land use percentage variables, the difference between the models in each pair being the elimination of the extractive land use percentage and the addition of open space in the second equation. That the power of the model does not differ in the two versions and the lack of significance of the open space variable is indicative of the fact that

TABLE 10.3

AIR POLLUTION AS A FUNCTION OF LAND USE MIX

	LOG SO2 AVE	LOG SO2 AVE	LOG SO2 MAX	LOG SO2 MAX	LOG TSP AVE	LOG TSP AVE	LOG TSP MAX	LOG TSP MAX
LOG RESIDENTIAL PERCENTAGE	-.251[1] (-.187)[2]	-.957 (-.187)	-.209 (-.177)	-.533 (-.118)	.781 (1.494)	.257 (.306)	1.079 (2.666)	.430 (.503)
LOG COMMERCIAL PERCENTAGE	2.727 (2.415)	2.880 (1.821)	3.181 (3.202)	3.253 (2.333)	-.587 (-1.360)	-.488 (-1.302)	-1.066 (-3.192)	-.786 (-2.065)
LOG INDUSTRIAL PERCENTAGE	-1.176 (-2.078)	-1.379 (-.921)	-1.510 (-3.032)	-1.602 (-1.215)	.294 (1.045)	.131 (.365)	.935 (4.301)	.935 (2.065)
LOG EXTRACTIVE PERCENTAGE	.020 (.073)		.006 (.023)		-.041 (-.393)		-.135 (-1.685)	
LOG PUBLIC USES PERCENTAGE	.940 (1.843)	.853 (1.074)	1.440 (3.208)	1.400 (2.000)	.017 (.083)	-.054 (-.250)	-.285 (-1.851)	-.369 (-1.665)
LOG T.C.U. PERCENTAGE	-1.364 (-1.580)	-1.973 (-.499)	-1.208 (-1.591)	-1.476 (-.423)	.007 (.041)	-.163 (-.484)	.207 (1.672)	.084 (.245)
LOG OPEN SPACE PERCENTAGE		-4.995 (-.155)		-2.211 (-.078)		-2.626 (-.529)		-1.424 (-.282)
INTERCEPT	5.730 (1.649)	30.232 (.189)	6.159 (2.014)	17.033 (.121)	2.744 (1.947)	15.751 (.660)	2.710 (2.485)	10.820 (.446)
COEFFICIENT OF DETERMINATION	.762	.763	.873	.873	.688	.697	.906	.842
F-STATISTIC	(6.4) 2.134	(6.4) 2.146	(6.4) 4.572	(6.4) 4.579	(6.4) 1.467	(6.4) 1.532	(6.4) 6.422	(6.4) 3.562

NOTES:
1. Regression coefficient
2. t-statistic

presence of open space per se does not reduce environmental pollution; it is the type of land use that determines pollution
levels. That the power of all of the models is substantial--
more than double that of Table 10.1--indicates that land use
does indeed play the important translational role.

In particular, where industrial land use is greatest,
suspended particulate problems are at their maximum, while inversely with this, devotion of a greater proportion of land to
commercial uses weighs most heavily on the sulfur oxides. The
amount of residential land use is not statistically significant,
but extensive public uses are also associated with greater
sulfur oxide concentrations.

IV. PRINCIPAL SORTING-TABLE CONCLUSIONS

Several important conclusions are forthcoming from the foregoing. Confirming previous research, the most important determinants of environmental pollution are city size, the scale of manufacturing concentrations, etc. However, given the levels of pollution determined by these variables, urban form and land use appear
to have important incremental effects, either elevating or reducing
the levels so determined, viz: The core-oriented city, with steep
density gradient and a radially-structured transportation system
has greater land use intensity, proportionately more open space,
and lower levels of air pollution than the dispersed city, with
broad circumferential transport arteries, uniform densities and
urban sprawl. Thus, the poorest air quality should be found in the
very large, dispersed urban region, with substantial manufacturing employment (examples: Indianapolis, Washington D. C.) whereas the best environmental quality on all counts should be in the
small, reasonably affluent, non-manufacturing, core-oriented urban
region (examples: Salt Lake City, Phoenix, and Tulsa). We will
return to these combinations in the final chapter, when issues of
contemporary urban dynamics are discussed, along with their likely
environmental consequences, and the resulting need for affirmative
guidance of the spatial form of environmental regions if environmental goals are to be met.

11 EFFECTS OF AGGLOMERATION ECONOMIES AND ENVIRONMENTAL DISECONOMIES ON URBAN PROPERTY VALUES

In Chapter 10 the focus was upon the urban variables related to environmental pollution. We now turn the discussion around and focus on the aggregate net benefits of urban life and the extent to which environmental diseconomies reduce them.

These benefits should, first of all, vary directly with the size of the metropolis. The larger the city, the greater the size of market that can be reached, the greater the access to information about new products and processes, the better the access to a wide range of specialized suppliers, and the easier it is to recruit and retain a specialized workforce.
In industries marked by uncertain and fluctuating demands, there are advantages in being located in a city where specialized inputs can be obtained quickly. For households, there are advantages of a larger range of potential employment opportunities, varied and specialized sources of consumer goods and services, and access to those cultural activities that are available only in the larger cities.

Such benefits should become manifest through improved productivity and a resulting stream of net benefits that therefore increases directly with city size (Edel, Harris and Rothenberg, 1972; Thompson, 1968). Given well-functioning markets, the price of any capital asset will equal the present value of the anticipated future stream of net benefits over the useful life of the asset. Thus, summing over the properties within any metropolitan area, aggregate property values should provide a first approximation to the measurement of the stream of net benefits expected to accrue to land users within that area, and a means of estimating the effects of economies of agglomeration on those benefits (Harris and Wheeler, 1971). In other words, the market for land and property within urban areas should capture and express the net benefits of urban growth.

If this is so, then one question that arises is whether, since urban form affects land use intensities and percentages, the stream of net benefits varies with differences in urban form. Urban planners frequently argue, for example, that disorderly

urban sprawl destroys property values. A second and more important question is whether these benefits are reduced by environmental pollution. Both economies and <u>diseconomies</u> of agglomeration will come into play with increasing metropolitan size.
New activities provide additional opportunities for specialization
or integration of activities or improved quality of information.
These can be either pecuniary or physical external economies in
production or consumption. If there are scale economies in provision of public services, additional population gives rise to
decreasing average costs of services, which will result in a
higher quality of services per tax dollar. At the same time,
diseconomies of agglomeration will result from congestion and
pollution, or from decreasing returns to scale in the public service sector.

I. A SET OF TESTABLE HYPOTHESES

A series of empirically-testable propositions arise from
the foregoing (Harris and Wheeler, 1971):

   (1) Aggregate property values and total population should
       move systematically together in the absence of net
       economies or diseconomies of agglomeration in a linear
       fashion.

   (2) If there are net economies of agglomeration over some
       range, property values will increase more than propor-
       tionally with population.

   (3) With net diseconomies, property values will increase
       less than proportionally with population, and if dis-
       economies become sufficiently severe, property values
       will actually decline as population increases.

   (4) Assuming that aggregate property values increase in an
       S-shaped logistic pattern with respect to population,
       it should then be possible to identify that point at
       which average land value per person is maximized, the
       population size which is optimal for all cities in the
       system in the long run, as well as that point (the
       lower inflection point) at which the marginal increment
       in land value from population is maximized. This latter
       point is that size at which the marginal contribution
       of population to land values is largest in the short
       run.

Similarly, from Chapter 10,

   (5) To the extent that manufacturing concentrations increase
       environmental pollution and environmental quality is
       better in higher-income communities, these variables
       should account for a significant portion of the variance
       from (1).

   (6) If the dispersed city, holding constant city character-
       istics, produces a land use mix delivering lower envi-
       ronmental quality, this should be reflected in appro-

priate statistically-significant partial relationships
of urban form and aggregate land values.

In testing the first four propositions in 1971, a measure
of aggregate property values was derived from assessment data in
the 1963 Census of Governments, adjusting them toward true market
value using the assessment ratios available in that publication
(Harris and Wheeler, 1971). Aggregate property values were then
regressed on a variety of SMSA characteristics to find the partial
relationship between SMSA size and property values. The analytic
results were consistent with the idea that there are increasing
and then decreasing economies of agglomeration over a range of
population up to about three million. For the total set of metropolitan areas, the maximum marginal increase of land value with
respect to population occurred around 500,000, maximum per capita
land value at about 750,000, and maximum total value at about
1,000,000. Beyond the million mark total land values actually
declined until a size of about three million has reached and
thereafter there seemed to be no limit to the concomitant rise of
population and land values roughly in proportion.

It also appeared that manufacturing cities experienced diminishing returns between 500,000 and 1,000,000. Beyond the million mark, total property values actually declined in cities without important regional headquarters functions. St. Louis and
Pittsburgh were the most notable examples of cities that seemed
to have grown larger than would be dictated by efficiency. In
those cities with a large number of corporate headquarters, however, there seemed to be no sign of diminishing returns to scale
until the population exceeded one million and then the net gains
diminished less rapidly than is the case with manufacturing-
based cities, although beyond a million and a half there seem to
be substantial diseconomies of growth. However, for the largest
cities, with populations in excess of three million, land values
and population rose proportionally and there was no evidence of
downturn in the net benefits as measured by land values.

The partial relationship between population and property
values was found by Harris and Wheeler to be significantly non-
linear, which was the basis for the observation of increasing
or decreasing returns to scale outlined above. It seemed reasonable to those authors to argue that the assembling of a large
labor pool coupled with scale economies in the provision of some
public services explained the zone of net agglomeration economies,
while diseconomies of scale in services and related congestion-

pollution phenomena explained the zone of diseconomies of scale.

II. REGRESSION RELATIONSHIPS

We repeat and extend the Harris and Wheeler analysis here.
The dependent variable, total property values, was derived in the
same manner as the Harris-Wheeler measure, but from the later
1967 Census of Governments. Figure 11.1 shows that the two
measures are consistent, with a constant rate of change apparent
over the whole set of cities. On the leading edge, with more
rapid growth of property values than the nation, are such metropolitan areas as San Francisco, Kansas City and Indianapolis.
On the other hand, in Philadelphia, Pittsburgh, Buffalo, Jersey
City and Utica, they actually declined.

The independent variables are those defined in Chapter 8
and already used in the analysis reported in Chapter 10. Figure
11.2 plots the observed property values against metropolitan
population. Our interest centers on the partial nature of this
relationship, holding constant a variety of factors, and on the
possible contributions of urban form and environmental pollution
to the variance.

Table 11.1 records the first series of regression relationships, and clearly bears out propositions (1) and (5): aggregate
property values and total population move systematically together,
with property values depressed by manufacturing concentrations
and assuming much higher levels in higher income communities.
Harris and Wheeler believed that to the extent that median incomes reflect real-wage differentials, they are the necessary
"bribes" that must be paid to attract and retain the urban labor
force in congested, polluted, inadequately serviced, dangerous,
and impersonal large cities. However, our earlier results belie
this supposition; environmental quality, at least, is much better
in higher- than in lower-income communities.

Inclusion of the urban form variables does not significantly
affect the power of the model, however, and thus proposition (6)
is called into question. Three of the signs are in the right
direction if property values are lower in the dispersed city
(degrees of arc -, radial highways +, and circumferential highways -) but the density ratio has the wrong sign (+), and none
of these variables is statistically significant.

Nor, for that matter, are the environmental variables. If,
for example, the environmental quality indicators are regressed

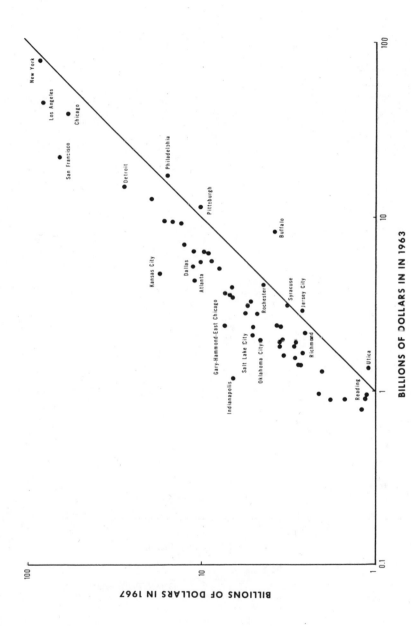

BILLIONS OF DOLLARS IN IN 1963

FIGURE 11.1

AGGREGATE PROPERTY VALUES OF SAMPLE SMSA'S IN 1963 AND 1967

Source of data: 1963 and 1967 Census of Governments

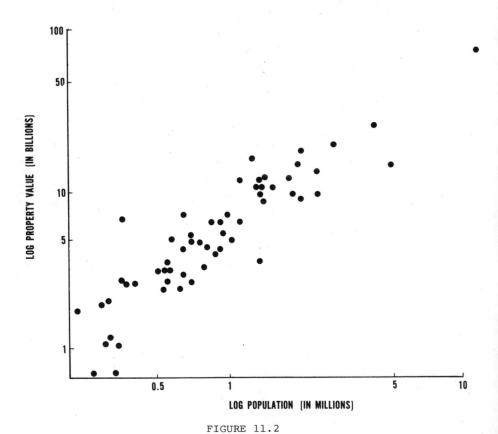

FIGURE 11.2

AGGREGATE PROPERTY VALUES RELATED TO SMSA POPULATION
Source of data: 1967 Census of Governments and 1970
Census of Population

TABLE 11.1

REGRESSION OF REAL PROPERTY VALUES ON SELECTED
CITY CHARACTERISTICS AND ON LAND USE MIX

Independent Variable*	Equations regressing property values on independent variables:			
	1	2	3	4
Population of SMSA	0.892 (13.59)		0.853 (8.18)	
Density Ratio--SMSA/C. City	0.109 (1.73)		0.070 (0.91)	
Median Family Income	2.143 (3.94)		2.335 (4.01)	
Percent Employment in Manufacturing	-0.375 (-2.82)		-0.381 (-2.75)	
Degrees of Arc of Urban Area			-0.000 (-0.15)	
Radial Highways in SMSA			0.018 (0.73)	
Circumferential Highways			-0.056 (-1.40)	
Residential Percentage		0.465 (0.301)		2.094 (0.835)
Commercial Percentage		0.831 (0.633)		0.664 (0.601)
Industrial Percentage		-0.222 (-0.343)		0.122 (0.229)
Extractive Percentage		0.063 (0.202)		
Public Uses Percentage		0.780 (1.654)		0.960 (1.808)
T.C.U. Percentage		-0.604 (-1.242)		0.066 (-.609)
Open Space Percentage				8.668 (0.629)
Intercept	-16.228 (-3.50)	8.728 (2.142)	-17.638 (-3.48)	-33.851 (-0.507)
Coefficient of Determination	0.875	0.708	0.879	0.724
F-Statistic	(4, 53) 92.531	(6, 6) 2.422	(7, 50) 52.165	(6, 6) 2.623

---

*All variables transformed to natural logarithms.
[1]Regression coefficient
[2]t-statistic
Note: t-statistics of 2.0 and above significant at .05 level, and at .01 level if over 2.5.

in turn on the property value residuals from the second equation
in Table 11.1, the results reported in Table 11.2 emerge. The
incremental effect of environmental pollution on aggregate property
values, holding constant the pollution effects arising directly
from size, manufacturing concentrations, and income, is statistically insignificant.

TABLE 11.2

R^2 OF POLLUTION VARIABLES REGRESSED ON
RESIDUALS FROM TABLE 11.1, EQUATION (2)

	Pollution Variable	Coefficient of Determination
1	MAQI	0.024
2	EVI	0.028
3	SO^2 AVE.	0.017
4	SO_2 MAX.	0.027
5	SO_2 MAQI	0.018
6	NO_2 MAQI	0.001
7	TSP AVE.	0.055
8	TSP MAX.	0.023
9	TSP MAQI	0.046
10	TSP EVI	0.030
11	WPI 1	0.000
12	WPI 2	0.011
13	WPI 3	0.020
14	WPI 4	0.004

Inclusion of the different subsets of environmental variables
into the basic equations, as in Table 11.3, provides no further
insights. The power of the model is scarcely affected by their
inclusion, and except in the case of the third model in the table,
the environmental variables are not statistically significant.
In the third model property values do appear to be marginally
lower where SO_2 concentrations are greater, but for TSP concentrations the sign of the coefficient is wrong, reaffirming the

311

TABLE 11.3

ENVIRONMENTAL VARIABLES INCLUDED IN BASIC REGRESSIONS

Independent Variables	Model 1 Regression Coefficients	Standard Errors	t Statistics	Model 2 Regression Coefficients	Standard Errors	t Statistics	Model 3 Regression Coefficients	Standard Errors	t Statistics
Population of SMSA	0.847*	0.194	8.10	0.860*	0.101	8.51	0.873*	0.097	8.93
Density Ratio - SMSA/City	0.115	0.083	1.38	0.155	0.082	1.88	0.170*	0.079	2.13
Median Family Income	2.617*	0.641	4.08	2.767*	0.603	4.58	2.821*	0.578	4.88
% Employment in Manufacturing	-0.478*	0.151	-3.15	-0.369*	0.153	-2.39	-0.376*	0.150	-2.49
Degrees of Arc	-0.000	0.000	-0.12	-0.000	0.000	-0.33	-0.000	0.000	-0.66
Radial Highways in SMSA	0.005	0.027	0.22	0.002	0.026	0.09	0.001	0.025	0.05
Circumferential Highways	-0.044	0.041	-1.08	-0.030	0.040	-0.76	-0.018	0.039	-0.46
MAQI	0.193	0.380	0.50						
EVI	0.058	0.099	0.58						
SO_2 MAQI				-0.130	0.073	-1.76			
NO_2 MAQI				0.199	0.178	1.11			
TSP MAQI				0.474*	0.217	2.18			
SO_2 AVE.							-0.163*	0.077	-2.12
TSP AVE.							0.732*	0.264	2.76
INTERCEPT	-20.210	5.727	-3.52	-22.399	5.328	-4.20	-25.24	5.553	-4.54
COEFFICIENT OF DETERMINATION	0.885			0.895			0.899		
F(9,68; 10,47; 9,48)	41.13			40.17			47.68		

*significant at .05 level

Yorkshireman's adage "Where there's muck there's money." Thus,
any effects on urban property values of environmental pollution
are contained <u>within</u> the <u>direct</u> relationships between the city
characteristics themselves and property values. No environmental
pollution variables appear to be of independent explanatory power
in accounting for any depressing effects on aggregate property
values. Rather, pollution effects are built into the parameters
relating size (etc.) to the stream of net urban benefits.

The questions posed in postulates (2)-(4) then arise. Table
11.4 and Figure 11.3 show that different city-size classes do
indeed appear to display different relationships between property
values and population size, with a zone of agglomeration economies
in the smaller size ranges, and net diseconomies setting in at
larger metropolitan sizes.

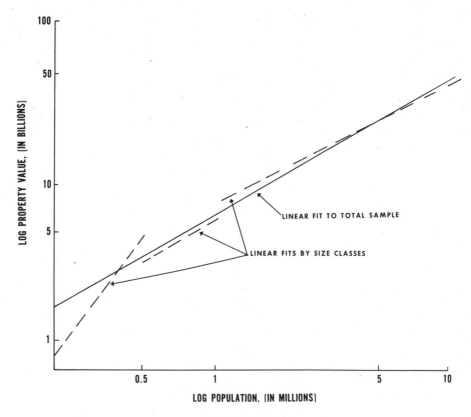

FIGURE 11.3

RELATIONSHIPS OF PROPERTY VALUES AND
POPULATION FOR THREE CITY SIZE CLASSES

TABLE 11.4

REAL PROPERTY VALUES REGRESSED ON CITY CHARACTERISTICS FOR THREE CITY SIZE CLASSES

Independent Variables*	SMSA Population 200,000 to 500,000			SMSA Population 200,000 to 500,000			SMSA Population 200,000 to 500,000		
	Regression Coefficient	Standard Errors	t Statistics	Regression Coefficient	Standard Errors	t Statistics	Regression Coefficient	Standard Errors	t Statistics
Log SMSA Population	2.063	0.839	2.46	0.890	0.249	3.57	0.786	0.183	4.30
Log Density - SMSA/City	0.440	0.188	2.34	0.158	0.082	1.94	0.128	0.117	1.10
Log Median Family Income	0.984	1.861	0.53	2.013	0.724	2.78	3.157	1.080	2.92
Log % Employed in Manu-facturing	-0.712	0.326	-2.19	0.002	0.190	0.01	-0.988	0.387	-2.56
Log SO_2 AVE.	0.338	0.266	1.27	-0.201	0.095	-2.11	-0.191	0.118	-1.61
Log TSP AVE.	0.122	1.047	0.17	0.561	0.277	2.39	0.739	0.476	1.55
INTERCEPT	-13.480	17.976	-0.75	-18.318	7.190	-2.62	-25.637	10.033	-2.56
Number of Observations	13			21			24		
Coefficient of Determination	0.833			0.665			0.8109		
Durbin-Watson Statistic	1.875			2.572			2.484		
F(6,6; 6,14; 6,17)	5.00			4.62			12.15		

* All variables transformed to natural logarithms

Even within size classes, city size remains an important determinant of property values, and manufacturing concentrations depress them. In the smallest cities, property values are greater, the greater the dispersion of the urban form (high SMSA/City density ratio), although this effect drops out in larger urban regions while income levels become progressively more significant in larger places. The two air quality variables included in Table 11.4 are statistically significant in the middle size-class, but again the signs of the coefficients raise more questions than they answer.

Table 11.5 and Figure 11.4 extend the argument a little further.

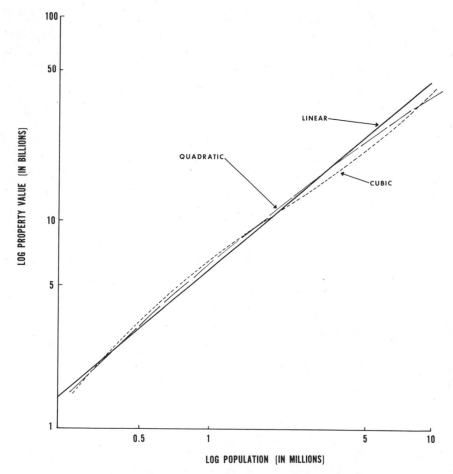

FIGURE 11.4: LINEAR, QUADRATIC AND CUBIC RELATIONSHIPS OF PROPERTY VALUES TO CITY SIZE

TABLE 11.5

PROPERTY VALUES REGRESSED ON CITY CHARACTERISTICS AND LINEAR, QUADRATIC AND CUBIC EXPRESSIONS OF POPULATION

Independent Variables*	Model 1			Model 2			Model 3		
	Regression Coefficient	Standard Errors	t Statistics	Regression Coefficient	Standard Errors	t Statistics	Regression Coefficient	Standard Errors	t Statistics
Log Density Ratio - SMSA/City	0.191	0.063	3.03	0.188	0.063	2.97	0.172	0.064	2.69
Log Median Family Income	2.683	0.533	5.03	2.662	0.533	5.00	2.723	0.533	5.11
Log % Employed in Manufacturing	-0.366	0.147	-2.49	-0.401	0.150	-2.67	-0.426	0.151	-2.82
Log SO_2 AVE.	-0.163	0.071	-2.29	-0.140	0.074	-1.90	-0.127	0.075	-1.71
Log TSP AVE.	0.722	0.240	3.00	0.784	0.246	3.18	0.811	0.246	3.29
Log SMSA Population	0.887	0.065	13.54	1.635	0.684	2.39	9.498	6.737	1.41
(Log SMSA Population)^2				-0.0536	0.0488	-1.10	-1.144	0.931	-1.23
(Log SMSA Population)^3							0.0496	0.0423	1.17
INTERCEPT	-24.216	4.996	-4.85	-26.828	5.524	-4.86	-46.067	17.297	-2.66
COEFFICIENT OF DETERMINATION	0.898			0.900			0.903		
DURBON-WATSON STATISTIC	1.931			2.918			2.005		
$F_{(6,51; 7;50; 8,45)}$	74.48			64.27			56.84		
Number of Cases = 58									

* All variables transformed to natural logarithms

Marginal improvements in fit emerge, moving from the linear
through the quadratic to the cubic formulations of the property
value-population relationship. In each case, there are significant partial effects of income and manufacturing employment.
The density ratio is significant throughout with a positive sign,
indicating that holding other variables constant, property values
are greater in the dispersed rather than the core-oriented city.
This would, of course, be the situation when the demand for land
of any given level of accessibility is relatively elastic, and
indicates that, the predilections of urban planners notwithstanding, urban sprawl produces the greatest stream of net benefits of urban growth, despite the greater pollution levels of
the dispersed city noted in Chapter 10 (which helps explain the
statistically-significant pollution variables with nonsensical
signs in Table 11.5).

Most of the results in Table 11.5 are consistent with those
of Harris and Wheeler (Table 11.6). However, in contrast to the
Harris-Wheeler results, we find no point at which there is an
absolute decrease of property values with increasing size.

In the quadratic model, property values are greater than in
the linear case in the range between 185,000 and 2,400,000 population. In the cubic formulation, the lower inflection point is
at 720,000 population (this is the point at which the marginal
increment in land value from population increase is maximized) and
the upper inflection point is at 6,600,000 population. Average
land value per person is maximized at 1,070,000 population, beneath which size there are increasing returns to urban scale, and
beyond which relative diseconomies of increasing size set in.
These diseconomies must, however, be those of congestion, crime,
etc., because the effects of environmental pollution are par-
tialed out by the independent variables included in the equation.

TABLE 11.6

PARTIAL EFFECT OF POPULATION SIZE ON
AGGREGATE LAND VALUE

Regression by Size Classes	Harris and Wheeler		Present Study		
	Sign	Statistic	Sign	Statistic	
50,000-250,000	+	7.7			
250,000-500,000	+	4.2	+	2.5	230,000-500,000
500,000-1,000,000	+	1.1	+	3.6	500,000-1,000,000
1,000,000-10,000,000	−	-1.4	+	4.3	1,000,000-11,600,000

Cubic Equation on Total Sample	Harris and Wheeler		Present Study		
	Sign	Statistic	Sign	Statistic	
Pop	+	1.1	+	1.4	Log Pop
$(Pop)^2$	−	-0.9	−	-1.2	$(Log\ Pop)^2$
$(Pop)^3$	+	3.9	+	1.2	$(Log\ Pop)^3$

D   LAND USE PATTERNS, URBAN FORM AND VARIATIONS IN ENVIRONMENTAL QUALITY WITHIN URBAN REGIONS

We now turn to the relationships between land use patterns within urban regions and the maps of pollution concentrations within these regions. Knowledge of the relationships should enable us to say which land use patterns are likely to produce the lowest levels of pollution. It is acknowledged, of course, that the nature of the pollution problem varies between urban regions because of external determinants of city size and the urban economic base. This is why, in the preceding pages, a pollution-sensitive typology of urban regions was developed. The strategy in this section is to study the internal land use-pollution relationships for each of the sample of thirteen urban regions selected on the basis of the typology to be representative of the range of environmental quality situations existing nationwide. Thus, any nationwide variations in the internal land use-pollution relationships themselves can be codified and generalized to the nation as a whole.

The materials are organized into several parts. In Chapter 12, we review what is known about the land uses producing air and water pollution, solid wastes and noise, using a simple, logical chain linking use of the land; pollution source; generation factor; emissions or discharges; diffusion, dispersion or transport; monitoring at receptors; and charting of the spatial distribution of pollution intensities from receptor data. This chain describes why the urban land use pattern and the pollution map should be related, although as will be evident in the review, there are many gaps in knowledge that need to be filled.

Chapter 13 follows with several analyses of urban form-environmental pollution relationships for the sample of thirteen urban regions in the attempt to fill some of the gaps. Many of the analyses are frankly experimental, because of the critical limitations imposed by data inadequacies and the unsatisfactory nature of monitoring networks within urban regions, together with the limited nature of what is known about land use-pollution relationships. Much of what is done in this section must, therefore, be viewed as <u>an attempt to open up lines of inquiry,</u> and much less as an effort producing irrefutible guidelines for public intervention.

12 THE LINKS BETWEEN LAND USE AND THE POLLUTION MAP

Suppose one has available a land use map of an urban region, and also a map showing concentrations of a particular environmental pollutant. The two maps will likely show some broad similarities. Why should this be so? A logical chain of relationships may be postulated, as in Figure 12.1.

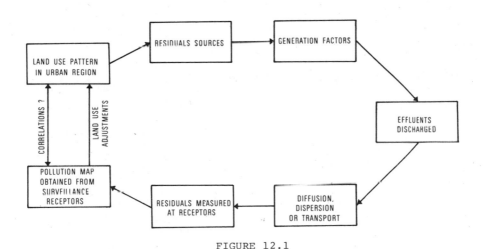

FIGURE 12.1

PATHS (→) LINKING LAND USE AND ENVIRONMENTAL POLLUTION, AND RESULTING CORRELATIONS OF THE TWO MAPS (↔)

In effect, the land use map can be interpreted as a spatial pattern of residuals sources. Different types and quantities of effluents are produced by these sources, both stationary and moving, whether of point-, line- or area-type, so the land use map can be converted into an effluent-production map. Because different dispersion, diffusion or transport mechanisms then come into play in transferring residuals from their sources to destinations where their direct consequences are experienced, the effluent map needs to be adjusted to reflect these mechanisms, if one is to produce a map of pollution as experienced by the urban resident. Residuals intensities at destinations are sensed by receptor monitoring devices at selected sampling points, and it is from this surveillance network data that the pollution map usually is drawn. Pollution concentrations may produce a chain of direct, indirect and market adjustments, including land use adjustments, and these are a second source of the high correlations that are observable between the maps of pollution and land use.

The paths linking land use and environmental pollution thus seem clear and straightforward. Can they be demonstrated in practice? This is the question addressed in the pages that follow. Looking at air, water, solid wastes and noise in turn, we examine the spatial patterns of emission sources; generation factors; diffusion, dispersion or transport mechanisms; receptor monitoring on a surveillance network; and the map-to-map relationships that can, as a result, be expected.

I. AIR POLLUTION AND THE LAND USE MAP

1. PATTERNS OF EMISSION SOURCES

There are several immediate considerations in understanding how land uses produce air pollution: (a) source mobility; (b) temporal variations; and (c) the spatial nature of emission sources.

a. MOBILITY

Emission sources are of two types, mobile and stationary. Stationary sources are classified as either "point" or "areal" sources and include industrial processes, solid waste disposal sites, and fuel combustion from space heating and at power generation sites. Mobile sources include all types of transportation -- automobiles, trucks, railroads and airplanes.

b. TIME

Time, at several scales, is significant for an understanding of the patterns of emission from these sources. The arcadian cycle of the flow of commuters from residence to place of employment and return influences the level of pollution each day. The evening commuter flow peak is especially high and temporal spreading of journeys can noticeably affect the volume of pollution (Figure 12.2).

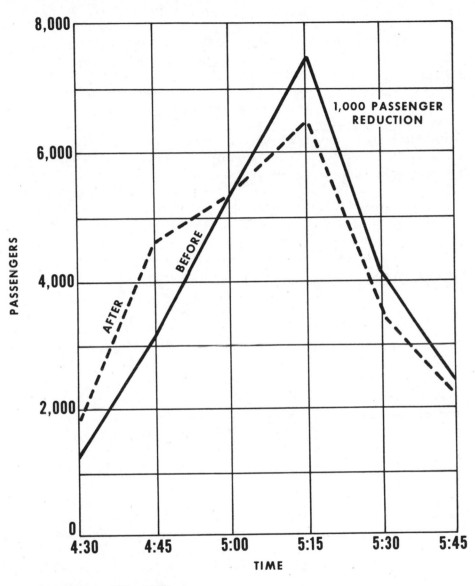

FIGURE 12.2

EFFECTS OF STAGGERED WORK HOURS UPON HUDSON TERMINAL
P.M. PASSENGER VOLUMES

c. SPATIAL UNITS

Emission sources assume three different spatial forms:
point, line, and area. By far the two most important point emission sources in the urban environment are power generation facilities and municipal incineration sites. Also to be included as
a point source is the isolated industrial emitter. The prime
example of line emission sources is of course the urban transportation system. The transportation system is of special note
as it is the source of the overwhelming proportion of the urban
environment's carbon monoxide and also the largest producer of
hydrocarbons. Significant types of land use which serve as area
emission sources include residential and industrial zones. Industrial processing and the space heating of residences are the
largest producers of atmospheric particulates in the urban environment. In New York City, space heating alone accounts for
over thirty-two percent of all particulate emissions (Eisenbud,
1970).

2. GENERATION OF EMISSIONS

Not only do air emission levels vary with city size (as
noted in earlier chapters), but also with very specific activities located within urban regions. Power generation plants
(stationary-point sources) and space heating (stationary-area
sources) generate the majority of sulfur oxide emissions. Industrial processes (stationary-area sources) produce the majority
of particulates, and the transportation system (consisting of
mobile point sources) accounts for the major proportion of carbon monoxide and hydrocarbon production.

In recent studies of Chicago, emissions were aggregated on
a square mile grid and land use was divided into three classes--
(1) Heavy Industrial (including all point sources except power
plants), (2) Light Industrial, and (3) Large Residential and
Commercial (office buildings, high-rise areas, heavy residential
coal use areas, outlying commercial centers, etc.) The resulting
emission densities are shown in Table 12.1. These figures demonstrate the significant differences in level of emissions when
the urban region is divided into a simple trichotomy of land
uses.

TABLE 12.1

CHICAGO REGION EMISSION DENSITIES[a] BY SQUARE MILE
(Largest 300 Miles -- 1968 Emission Inventory)

		Max.	Mean[b]	Min.
Total	SO_2	555.43	16.1	2.74
	Particulates	509.03	9.7	1.27
Heavy	SO_2	772.2	9.9	0
Industrial	Particulates	507.3	5.4	0
Light	SO_2	40.6	5.2	1.1
Industrial	Particulates	21.9	2.7	0.56
Large	SO_2	28.4	1.25	0
Residential	Particulates		0.55	0
Commercial				

[a]$Tons/day/mi^2$.

[b]Computed as $\frac{1}{300} \sum\limits_{i=1}^{300} \left(\frac{E_i^m}{z_i^m} \right)$ where E_i^m - emissions in class m,

z_i^m - zoning in class m.

Source: Hagevik, 212.

3. DIFFUSION MECHANISMS

Given differences in emission densities, diffusion of air
pollutants is affected by two overriding factors--(1) the urban
area's regional climatology and (2) specific elements of the
man-made urban environment. Factors important to the regional
climatology include topography, as when the Los Angeles basin
produces atmospheric inversions, and the probability that the
urban area will receive necessary and adequate fluxing movement
of air. Factors affecting the diffusion of air emissions specifically related to the urban environment include roughness of
the surface (including both the natural physiography and the
built-up environment), the nature of the urban heat island and

its relationship to the land use mix.

A number of efforts have been made to accurately describe and spatially plot the diffusion process of various air emissions (Air Pollution Control Office, 1970). For example, researchers at the Center for Environmental Studies of the Argonne National Laboratories have developed a computerized, multiple source, atmospheric diffusion model which has undergone preliminary validation and testing for inventorying sulfur dioxide air quality levels in the City of Chicago.

Argonne's "integrated puff" model consists of a series of algorithms assembled around a kernel that represents the transporting and diffusion of pollutant types from both point and area sources, according to a three-dimensional Gaussian distribution. The kernel, representing a three-dimensional puff of smoke, is integrated according to a series of piecewise constant wind vectors, and piecewise constant atmospheric stability parameters to simulate the transient behavior of a continuous smoke plume.

A statistical sample of 2300 data points of SO_2 measurements from five Chicago air quality monitoring stations has thus far been used to validate the diffusion model. The ratio of standard deviations to mean values for all hourly SO_2 predicted values is 0.93, for six hour predicted values--0.64, and for twenty-four hour predicted values--0.43. Over 66% of the twenty-four hour average SO_2 predictions were within ± 0.05 parts per million (ppm) of observed values and approximately 90% were within ± 0.1 ppm of actual amounts.

4. THE AIR QUALITY SURVEILLANCE NETWORK

Receptors that monitor diffused emissions yield actual air quality readings of the atmosphere surrounding the immediate environment of the station. The stations, while providing actual pollution levels for the various points in the urban system do not necessarily bring us very close to a full understanding of the actual source areas of pollution as generators, because of the intervening effect of diffusion. Unless the monitoring network consists of a dense array of stations within the urban region, it is dangerous to interpolate air quality levels at receptors across the urban region. Likewise, in the absence of well-developed diffusion models, it is very difficult to trace emissions observed at monitoring stations back to their sources.

Hence the current problem that exists in specifying exactly what
the links are between air quality and the spatial distribution
of land uses within urban regions.

5. THE EMISSIONS AND THE LAND USE MAPS RELATED

For the above reasons, few studies have so far actually
related the land use map to the spatial pattern of emissions, and
even less have clarified which zones of the city serve as emitters
(industry, transportation corridors, residences, etc.) and which
serve to ameliorate the levels of pollution (most significantly,
green areas). The relationship of emission level to land use
has been demonstrated in the city of Cincinnati, both cross-
sectionally and diurnally, however (Figures 12.3 and 12.4).

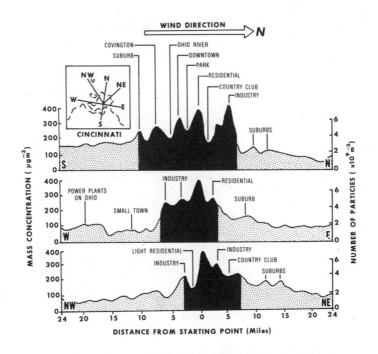

(The Heavily Shaded Mark the Extent of the Dust Dome on September 12, 1969, a Calm, Polluted Day)

FIGURE 12.3

THE URBAN DUST DOME AS A FUNCTION
OF LAND USE, CINCINNATI

(after Detwyler and Marcus, 1972, p. 87)

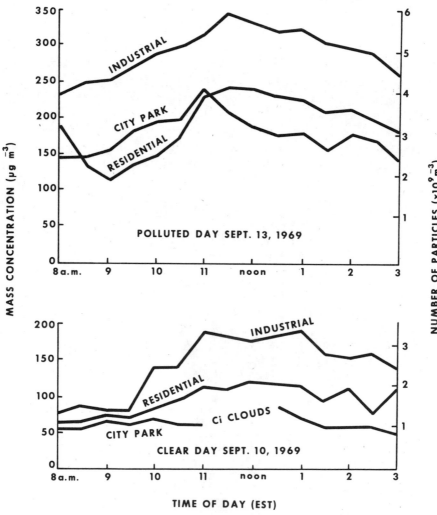

FIGURE 12.4

DIURNAL VARIATION OF PARTICULATE CONCENTRATION AS A
FUNCTION OF LAND USE, CINCINNATI

(after Detwyler and Marcus, 1972, p. 85)

II. WATER POLLUTION AND LAND USE

  1. PATTERNS OF EFFLUENT DISCHARGE SOURCES

The 1972 amendments to the Water Quality Act have the intent
of regulating the amount of pollutants being discharged from particular point sources. The Act defines point sources as any discernible, confined, and discrete conveyance from which pollutants
are or may be discharged. The perspective is a much different
one than that of regulating the amount of pollutants in a given
body of water by setting water quality standards. Under State
government administration and enforcement, no discharge is permitted except as authorized by a discharge permit.

When fully implemented the discharge permit program will
provide a reasonably complete picture as to patterns and sources
of effluent discharges. As of the summer of 1973, the various
Regional Offices of the Environmental Protection Agency only had
available partial data for major discharges. This information
may include the permit application number, the applicant name,
Basin number, SIC code, receiving water, and city/county code.
Once operational as a computer program, the permit application
data will supplement STORET and other data and allow for intensive urban analysis. This, however, is not yet possible, and
so the best we can do in Chapter 13 is to undertake an exploratory case study in the Seattle region.

Figure 12.5 summaraizes a generalized pattern of surface
effluent discharge sources, some of which will be required to
make permit applications. Figure 12.6 describes an idealized
sampling pattern available for recording the actual discharges.

  2. GENERATION OF EFFLUENTS

There are eight general categories of pollutants generated
by municipal and industrial discharges, the principal sources of
water pollution. These are: common sewage and other oxygen-
demanding wastes; disease-causing agents; plant nutrients; synthetic organic chemicals; inorganic chemicals and other mineral
substances; sediment; radioactive substances; and heat (Table
12.2). Most wastes are a mixture of these eight types, making
the problem of treatment and control that much more difficult.

Municipal wastes usually contain oxygen-consuming pollutants, synthetic organic chemicals such as detergents, sediments,
and other types of pollutants. The same is true of many indus-

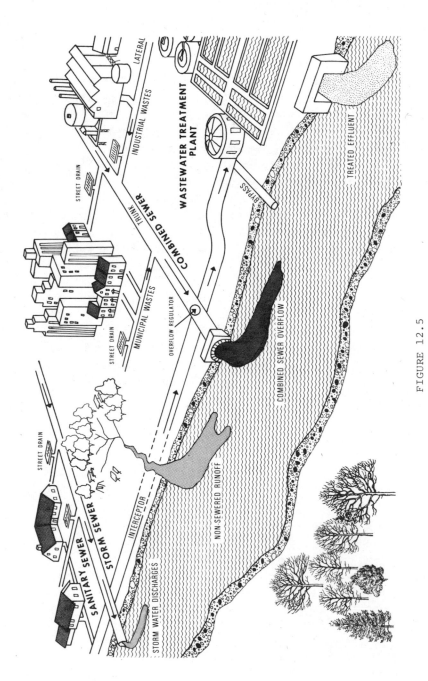

FIGURE 12.5

TYPES OF EFFLUENT DISCHARGES

331

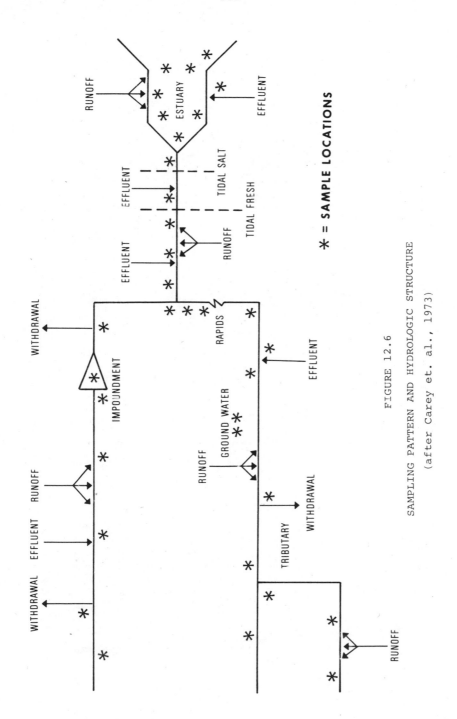

✳ = **SAMPLE LOCATIONS**

FIGURE 12.6

SAMPLING PATTERN AND HYDROLOGIC STRUCTURE

(after Carey et. al., 1973)

TABLE 12.2

POLLUTANTS GENERATED BY MUNICIPAL AND INDUSTRIAL SOURCES

Pollutant	Description
OXYGEN-DEMANDING WASTES	These are the traditional organic wastes and ammonia contributed by domestic sewage and industrial wastes of plant and animal origin. besides human sewage, such wastes result from food processing, paper mill production, tanning, and other manufacturing processes. These wastes are usually destroyed by bacteria if there is sufficient oxygen present in the water. Since fish and other aquatic life depend on oxygen for life, the oxygen-demanding wastes must be controlled, or the fish die.
DISEASE-CAUSING AGENTS	This category includes infectious organisms which are carried into surface and ground water by sewage from cities and institutions, and by certain kinds of industrial wastes, such as tanning and meat packing plants. Man or animals come in contact with these microbes either by drinking the water or through swimming, fishing, or other activities.
PLANT NUTRIENTS	These are the substances in the food chain of aquatic life, such as algae and water weeds, which support and stimulate their growth. Carbon, nitrogen and phosphorus are the three chief nutrients present in natural water. Large amounts of these nutrients are produced by sewage, certain industrial wastes, and drainage from fertilized lands. Biological waste treatment processes do not remove the phosphorus and nitrogen to any substantial extent--in fact, they convert the organic forms of these substances into mineral form, making them more usable by plant life. The problem starts when an excess of these nutrients over-stimulates the growth of water plants which cause unsightly conditions, interfere with treatment processes, and cause unpleasant and disagreeable tastes and odors in the water.
SYNTHETIC ORGANIC CHEMICALS	Included in this category are detergents and other household aids, all the new synthetic organic pesticides, synthetic industrial chemicals, and the wastes from their manufacture. Many of these substances are toxic to fish and aquatic life and possibly harmful to humans. They cause taste and odor problems, and resist conventional waste treatment. Some are known to be highly poisonous at very low concentrations. What the long-term effects of small doses of toxic substances may be is not yet known.
INORGANIC CHEMICALS AND MINERAL SUBSTANCES	A vast array of metal salts, acids, solid matter, and many other chemical compounds are included in this group. They reach our waters from mining and manufacturing processes, oil field operations, agricultural practices, and natural sources. Water used for irrigation picks up large amounts of minerals as it filters down through the soil on its way to the nearest stream. Acids of a wide variety are discharged as wastes by industry, but the largest single source of acid in our water comes from mining operations and mines that have been abandoned. Many of these types of chemicals are being created each year. They interfere with natural stream purification; destroy fish and other aquatic life; cause excessive hardness of water supplies; corrode expensive water treatment equipment; increase commercial and recreational boat maintenance costs; and boost the cost of waste treatment.
SEDIMENTS	These are the particles of soils, sands, and minerals washed from the land and paved areas of communities into the water. Construction projects are often large sediment producers. While not as insidious as some other types of pollution, sediments are a major problem because of the sheer magnitude of the amount reaching our waterways. Sediments fill stream channels and harbors, requring expensive dredgings, and they fill reservoirs, reducing their capacities and useful life. They erode power turbines and pumping equipment, and reduce fish and shellfish populations by blanketing fish nests and food supplies. More importantly, sediments reduce the amount of sunlight penetrating the water. The sunlight is required by green aquatic plants which produce the oxygen necessary to normal stream balance. Sediments greatly increase the treatment costs for municipal and industrial water supply and for sewage treatment where combined sewers are in use.
RADIOACTIVE SUBSTANCES	Radioactive pollution results from the mining and processing of radioactive ores; from the use of refined radioactive materials in power reactors and for industrial, medical, and research purposes; and from fallout following nuclear weapons testing. Increased use of these substances poses a potential public health problem. Since radiation accumulates in humans, control of this type of pollution must take into consideration total exposure in the human environment--water, air, food, occupation, and medical treatment.

TABLE 12.2 (Cont'd)

Pollutant	Description
HEAT	Heat reduces the capacity of water to absorb oxygen. Tremendous volumes of water are used by power plants and industry for cooling. Most of the water, with the added heat, is returned to streams, raising their temperatures. With less oxygen, the water is not as efficient in assimilating oxygen-consuming wastes and in supporting fish and aquatic life. Unchecked waste heat discharges can seriously alter the ecology of a lake, a stream, or even part of the sea.
	Water in lakes or stored in impoundments can be greatly affected by heat. Summer temperatures heat up the surfaces, causing the water to form into layers, with the cooler water forming the deeper layers. Decomposing vegetative matter from natural and man-made pollutants deplete the oxygen from these cooler lower layers with harmful effects on the aquatic life. When the oxygen-deficient water is discharged from the lower gates of a dam, it may have serious effects on downstream fish life and reduce the ability of the stream to assimilate downstream pollution.

Source: EPA, A Primer on Waste Water, 1973

trial wastes which may contain, in addition, substantial amounts of heat from cooling processes. Water that drains off the land usually contains great amounts of organic matter in addition to sediment, and may contain radioactive substances and pollutants washed from the sky, vegetation, buildings, and streets during rainfall.

3. TRANSPORT OF WATER POLLUTION

As pollutants enter water bodies, there are both time and distance effects, as diagrammed in Figure 12.7 in the case of an organic pollutant discharge. Within the water body, the dynamics of water residual diffusion can be understood from the following outline, which summarizes materials presented in Chapter 3 and, later, in Chapter 13.

Physical Models	Social, Economic and Behavioral Models	Scale of Reactions/Effects
- Runoff	- Health effects	- National
- Absorption	- Economic damages	- Regional
- Leaching	- Water demand/use	- River Basin
	- Population Exposure	- SMSA
	- Epidemiologic	- Local
	- Consumption Pattern	
	- Migration	
	- Abatement	

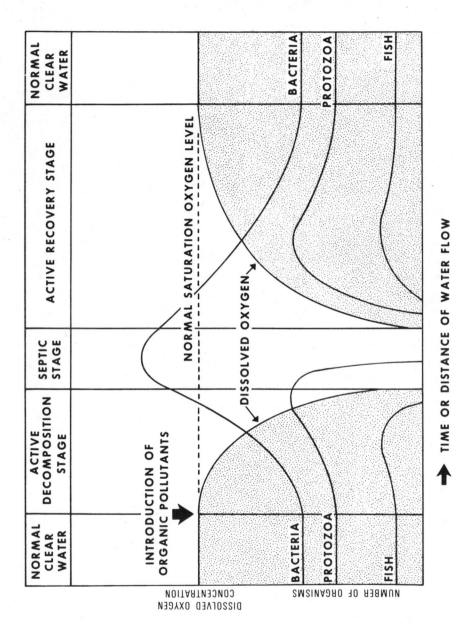

FIGURE 12.7: EFFECT OF ORGANIC POLLUTANTS ON WATER CONDITIONS
(after Grava, 1969)

4. MONITORING WATER-BORNE EFFLUENTS

Once effluents have entered a water body, physical and chemical alterations commence. Pollutants become less concentrated
through dispersion and react with natural elements in the stream
and the air and also with other parts of the effluent. At any
given point along the course of the stream, the quality of the
water will vary and can be measured.

Measurement of water quality is accomplished through collection of representative water samples at strategic locations
and subsequent analysis of those samples at the site or in a
laboratory. Sample site determination should be based on the
specific needs and design of the entire surveillance network.
Data obtained from each site should be taken at uniform times
along the length of the stream to give a representative picture
of the basin at a particular time. Figure 12.6 illustrates an
idealized surveillance network which analyzes water as it enters
or leaves the system as well as along the length of it.

Two types of monitoring stations are in use:

1) Automatic or robot monitors electronically measure a
   limited number of water quality parameters every few
   minutes. Specific conductivity, pH, dissolved oxygen
   and water temperature are the most commonly measured
   variables. These machines save lab work and facilitate
   data transfer by telemetering information to a data
   bank. However, they are extremely costly and perhaps
   unnecessary in some cases. They also require manual
   support and maintenance. In some water bodies readings
   need not be taken as frequently as in others. Moreover,
   coutinuous-recording monitors are not capable of recording several parameters which are extremely sensitive
   to pollution.

2) The most common method of sampling water quality is the
   manual method. Specimens are obtained at various time
   intervals using depth-integrating samplers or point
   samplers. Dissolved gas determinations, BOD and samples
   susceptible to aeration necessitate other specialized
   equipment. At each location several samples are usually
   taken at different parts of the stream and made into a
   more representative composite sample. Manual surveillance stations are often placed near a water gauging
   station so that flow conditions which might affect water
   composition can also be observed. Stations should not
   be placed near bridges or banks where turbulence is
   evident.

Sampling frequency at the receptor can vary from continuous
automatic testing every fifteen minutes to "grab" samples. "Grab"
samples refer to manual sampling performed only occasionally at
irregular locations, usually in response to a specific need or
crisis or unusual hydrologic event. The greater the number of

samples and sampling points, the greater the sampling accuracy
will be. The minimum interval between samplings should be such
that no major event altering water quality is absent from the
record. Samples taken as infrequently as once a month are occasionally acceptable, depending on the type of water body and
sampling technique and the accuracy required for each parameter
measured. However, it is more advantageous to have samples taken
at least once a week where feasible.

The final step in monitoring the effluent is to transfer
the data acquired to an official repository, preferably computerized, for long term storage and reuse in scientific studies
and planning. The STORET system of EPA and OWDC of USGS are
examples of such a data bank.

5. RELATIONSHIP BETWEEN WATER DISCHARGES AND LAND USE

Water is perhaps the most important physical factor influencing land use patterns. Developers and planners have recognized the recreational and aesthetic value water provides; this
in addition to the obvious economic and municipal uses. In the
past, urbanization has encroached upon both large and small
streams, lakes, and larger water bodies. This encroachment has
often been led by industries which utilize the resource, transport, and disposal opportunities water provides. How these land
uses have affected personal usage is therefore of great importance.

Some studies have begun to codify the nature of this usage.
A recent paper by The Regional Science Research Institute (1972),
for example, has examined the relationship of water quality and
distance of residence from a stream. Figures 12.8 and 12.9 illustrate both the base level use of a stream site by distance of
residence from the stream; and more importantly, the effect of
water pollution on use of stream sites.

III. SOLID WASTES AND LAND USE

There exists no map of solid waste generation related to
land uses. The closest approximation to such a map would be the
solid waste density map found in the New York Solid Waste Management Plan (Figure 12.10). Even this map indicates little
other than those areas where population and population densities
are greatest, however. The following discussion therefore is

337

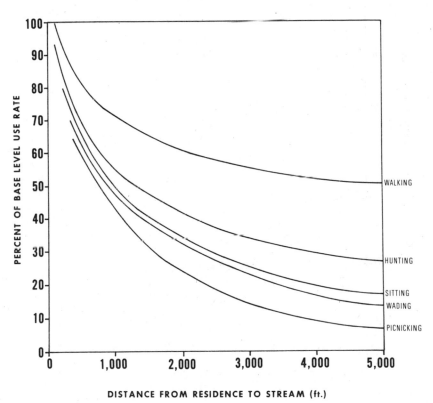

(Distance is Stright-Line Distance from Residence to Nearest Point on Stream).

FIGURE 12.8

PERCENT OF BASE LEVEL USE OF STREAM SITE BY DISTANCE
OF RESIDENCE FROM STREAM, FOR SELECTED ACTIVITIES

(after Coughlin et. al., 1972)

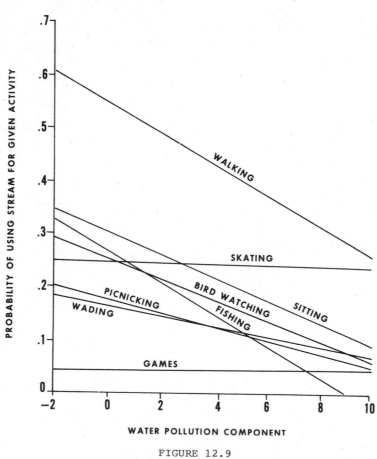

FIGURE 12.9

EFFECT OF WATER POLLUTION ON USE OF STREAM SITES

(after Coughlin et. al., 1972)

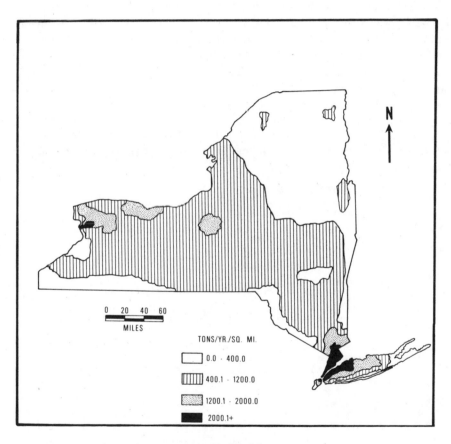

FIGURE 12.10

TOTAL WASTE DENSITY:
NEW YORK STATE, 1970

an attempt to show the links between land use, population, population density and the pollution map.

1. RESIDUAL SOURCES

    a. THE SOURCES SUMMARIZED

        (i) STATIONARY SOURCES

All types of land use, whether residential, recreational, industrial, commercial or institutional, generate their own type, amount and composition of solid waste. No matter what man's activities are, residual by-products of his affluent society will be found. The question is simply how much of what limits arises under what circumstances.

        (ii) MOBILE SOURCES

At the same time modern man is mobile. The routes traveled serve as receptacles for sources of solid wastes discarded during travel, or at destinations.

    b. SPATIAL PATTERNS

The stationary and mobile sources can be classified, as in the cases of air and water discharges, into point, line and area types.

        (i) POINT SOURCES

Point sources are of two kinds:

1) Those points (generation centers) where an unusually large or uniquely different solid waste type is gener ated.

2) All points which contribute to the total solid waste volume (i.e., houses, stores, offices, industry). Usually, how such points are aggregated to areas such as neighborhoods.

        (ii) LINE SOURCES

Each mode and artery of a transportation system is a _line_ source of solid wastes, including all residential streets, rail-lines, and expressways.

        (iii) AREA SOURCES

Area sources of solid wastes are those land use types which are of similar character throughout space and have similar generation characteristics. Examples would be single-family residential areas, multiple-family apartment areas, commercial areas, recreational areas.

c. TEMPORAL DIMENSIONS

Amounts of solid wastes generated vary according to amount
and type both seasonally, and regionally. This is true for all
of the spatial types (point, line, and area). For example,
Sheaffer et. al. (1960) concluded in Chicago:

1) Solid wastes accrue in a very clear seasonal pattern.
2) Not only the volume of solid wastes shifts seasonally,
    but also its determinants. (IV-83)

Seasons have their effects upon street cleaning and catch-basin
cleaning, lawn maintenance, the cleaning of garages or basements,
special services pick ups (i.e., Christmas trees, appliances,
ashes), and vacuum leaf collections, to name but a few examples.
Such seasonal variations can have dramatic effects upon the total
amount of solid wastes from any one source. They are, of course,
more noticeable in regions of the country which experience substantial seasonal changes.

2. GENERATION FACTORS

As noted in Chapter 4, the most common generation factor
used in solid waste studies is the total amount of solid wastes
collected in a city as weighted at dispersal sites, divided by
the total population, to produce an indication of how many pounds
per person per day is generated. Such a summary provides little
insight into land use differences in solid waste generation.

a. COMPOSITION OF SOLID WASTES

However, specific studies have produced information on the
composition of refuse for several locations and by household.

A survey conducted by the University of Louisville indicated that paper constituted the largest percent by weight of
most household waste generation. (See Table 12.3.) Similar
characteristics have been indicated in the twenty sample areas
of Table 12.5. Estimated annual average national refuse composition similarly indicates the same ranking (Tables 12.4 and
12.6).

b. HOUSEHOLD WASTES

Solid waste generation varies by population type and density
class of residential area (Tables 12.7 and 12.8, and Figure 12.11).
There is also some evidence that it varies by social class,
since the higher the income, the greater the amount of heavily-
packaged material that is purchased.

TABLE 12.3

COMPARISON OF WASTE GENERATION RATES
(lbs/household/wk)

Material	Measured by Univ. of Louisville Study		
	Low	Medium	High
Paper	24.9	29.7	37.8
Garbage	4.8	9.9	12.6
Glass	3.8	5.3	6.7
Metal	3.9	4.7	6.0
Minerals	0	0.7	3.1
TOTAL	37.40	50.30	66.20

Source: Boyd and Hawkins (1971).

TABLE 12.4

ESTIMATED ANNUAL AVERAGE NATIONAL REFUSE COMPOSITION*

Component	Mean Weight (%)
Glass	9.9
Metal	10.2
Paper	51.6
Plastics	1.4
Leather, rubber	1.9
Textiles	2.7
Wood	3.0
Food Wastes	19.3
TOTAL	100.0

*On a yard-waste-free and miscellaneous-free basis.

Source: Niessen and Chansky (1970).

TABLE 12.5

REFUSE - COMPOSITION DATA

Location	Notes	Food Wastes	Yard Wastes	Misc.	Glass, Ceramics	Metal	Paper Product	Plastics, Leather, Rubber	Textiles	Wood	Oil, Paint, Chemicals, etc.	Total
4-City, New Jersey Region	Average for Paterson, Clifton, Passaic, Wayne	8.3	13.3	8.96	6.44	9.44	43.87	2.66	4.52	2.96	---	100.49
Composite	As collected, includes 9.05% adjusted moisture	8.40	6.88	10.01	---	6.85	52.70	2.28	0.76	2.29	0.76	99.98
Hempstead, Long Island, N.Y.	Predominantly residential, as received	10.9	17.6	---	9.6	8.5	42.6	4.6	3.1	3.2	---	100.1
Hempstead, Long Island, N.Y.	Including residential and commercial excluding bulky and industrial	12.0	---	28.0	---	---	46.0	4.0	3.0	7.0	---	100.0
Johnson City, Tennessee	Residential, 10/67	26.1	1.6	1.0	11.0	10.9	45.0	2.7	1.4	0.4	---	100.01
Johnson City, Tennessee	Municipal, 7/68	34.6	2.3	0.2	9.0	10.4	34.9	5.8	2.0	0.8	---	100.0
Weber County, Utah	Residential and commercial, 4/68	8.5	4.2	5.9	4.6	3.4	61.8	2.5	2.0	2.2	---	100.1
Cincinnati, Ohio	Residential, 10/66	28.0	6.4	---	7.5	8.7	42.0	2.6	1.4	2.7	---	99.3
Memphis, Tennessee	Residential, 7/68	19.7	12.1	12.5	9.8	6.6	29.8	3.0	4.8	1.7	---	100.0
Alexandria, Virginia	Residential and commercial, 5/68	7.5	9.5	3.4	7.5	8.2	55.3	3.1	3.7	1.7	---	99.9
San Diego, California	Residential and commercial, 1967	0.8	21.1	---	8.3	7.7	46.1	5.0	3.5	7.5	---	100.0
Genesee County, New York	As collected, includes commercial, industrial, domestic, and demolition wastes	7.11	1.99	23.62	3.34	4.64	20.39	1.49	3.01	22.41	12.00	100.0

--- not reported or not specified.

Source: Niessen, W.R., and S.H. Chansky, "The Nature of Refuse," Proceedings of 1970 National Incinerator Conference, The American Society of Mechanical Engineers, New York, 1970, p.3.

TABLE 12.6

ESTIMATE OF NATIONAL ANNUAL AVERAGE COMPOSITION OF
MUNICIPAL REFUSE*

Component	Data[†] Samples Utilized	Mean Weight Percent	Mean (100% Total)	Standard Deviation S(X)	Confidence Limits (95%)
Glass	23	9.7	9.9	4.37	1.89
Metal	23	10.0	10.2	2.18	0.93
Paper	23	50.3	51.6	11.67	5.04
Plastics	9	1.4	1.4	.96	0.74
Leather, rubber	9	1.9	1.9	1.62	1.25
Textiles	17	2.6	2.7	1.80	0.93
Wood	22	2.9	3.0	2.39	1.06
Food wastes	23	18.8	19.3	10.95	4.73
		97.6			

*Excluding yard-waste and miscellaneous categories.
†Several data sets were not presented in a form suitable for extracting the weight fractions of all of the above refuse components.

Source: W.R. Niessen and S.H. Chansky (1970).

TABLE 12.7

MUNICIPAL SOLID WASTES COLLECTION RATES[1]

pounds/capita/day

Population	Waste Collection by Population Density Ranges		
r	0-3,999/sq.mi.	4,000-6,999/sq.mi.	7,000+/sq.mi.
0 - 4,999	3.3	–	–
5,000-19,999	3.6	5.0	4.6
20,000-99,999	4.1	4.1	4.6
100,000	4.6	5.1	5.6

[1]Consultant's Analysis

SOURCE: New York Solid Waste Management Plan, Status
Report 1970, U.S.E.P.A., 1971, Chapter 13,
p. 11.

TABLE 12.8

SOLID WASTE GENERATION BY DWELLING TYPE

	Single family	Multifamily	Apt. House
Pounds/capita/week	12.54	9.83	6.91
Gallons/capita/week	14.07	11.00	5.61
Pounds/cubic yard	179.97	180.50	248.87

SOURCE: Davidson, George R., <u>Residential Solid Waste Generated in Low Income Areas</u>, E.P.A., 1972, p. 2.

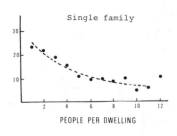

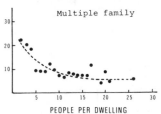

FIGURE 12.11

SOLID WASTE GENERATION RATES BY DWELLING TYPE

AVERAGE GENERATION RATE (lbs/capita/week)

c. INDUSTRIAL WASTES

Chapter 4 provided a great deal of information about solid
wastes generated by industrial sources. The greatest of these
industrial sources is food processing. Hudson indicates that
of the 33.5 million tons of raw materials used per year, the
food processing industry discharges 28% as a residual (Hudson,
1971). This amounts to about 9.3 million tons. Of this residual, approximately 79% (or 7.3 million tons) is reused as by-
products for animal feed and fertilizers. The remaining 21%,
about 2 million tons/year, is food waste. The following simplified flow diagram indicates the types of wastes and disposal
methods (Figure 12.12). Tables 12.9 and 12.10 and Figures 12.13-
12.15 indicate the tons of food residuals released in solid and
liquid form, revealing that the major pollution problem of the
food processing industries is the pollution of water bodies and
sewer systems with liquid wastes.

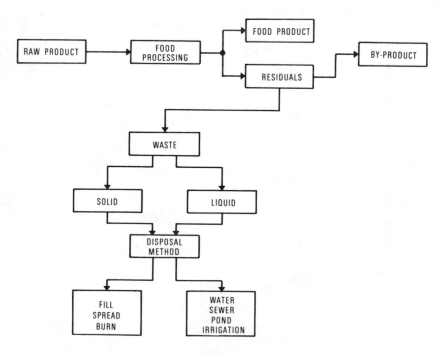

FIGURE 12.12
FLOW OF SOLID WASTE IN THE FOOD PROCESSING INDUSTRY
(adapted from Hudson, 1971)

TABLE 12.9

TONS OF FOOD RESIDUALS DISPOSED OF AS SOLID WASTES

TONS OF FOOD RESIDUALS DISPOSED OF AS SOLID WASTES BY FOOD PROCESSING
INDUSTRY PER 1,000 TONS OF RAW FOOD

| Product | Amount | Disposal Method | | |
		Filling	Spreading	Burning
Vegetable	1,037	467	566	4
Fruit	526	279	246	1
Speciality	93	77	8	8
Seafood	25	13	9	3
TOTAL	1,681	836	829	16

Source: Hudson (1971).

TABLE 12.10

TONS OF FOOD RESIDUALS DISCHARGED IN LIQUID FORM

TONS OF FOOD RESIDUALS DISCHARGED IN LIQUID FORM BY FOOD PROCESSING
INDUSTRY PER 1,000 TONS OF RAW FOOD

| Product | Amount | Disposal Method | | | |
		Water	Sewer	Pond	Irrigation
Vegetable	160	63	79	16	2
Seafood	94	82	12	0	0
Fruit	39	31	6	0	2
Specialty	26	0	19	7	0
TOTAL	319	176	116	23	4

Source: Hudson (1971).

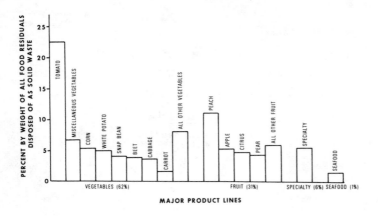

FIGURE 12.13

PRODUCT SOURCES OF FOOD RESIDUALS DISPOSED OF AS SOLID WASTE

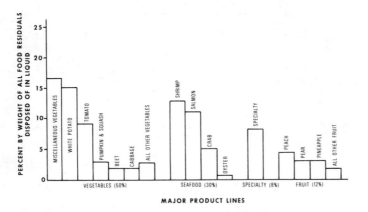

FIGURE 12.14

PRODUCT SOURCES OF FOOD RESIDUALS DISPOSED OF IN LIQUID

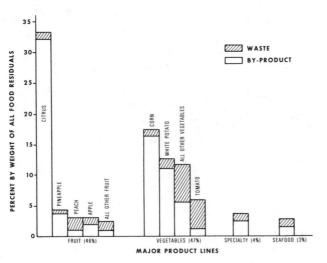

FIGURE 12.15

PRODUCT SOURCES OF FOOD RESIDUALS

d. RECREATIONAL WASTES

The waste generated by type of recreation area is indicated in Table 12.11.

TABLE 12.11

WASTE GENERATION RATES FOR RECREATION SITES

Recreation site	Average rate of waste generation 90 percent confidence interval
Campgrounds (lb/camper day)	1.26 ± 0.08
Campgrounds (lb/visitor day)	0.92 ± 0.06
Family picnic area (lb/picnicker)	0.93 ± 0.16
Group picnic area (lb/picnicker)	1.16 ± 0.26
Organization camps (lb/occupant day)	1.81 ± 0.39
Jobs Corps Civilian Conservation Corps Camps	
Kitchen waste (lb/corpsman day)	2.44 ± 0.63
Adminstrative and dormitory waste (lb/corpsman day)	0.70 ± 0.66
Resort areas	
Rented cabins (with kitchens) (lb/occupant day)	1.46 ± 0.31
Lodge rooms (without kitchens) (lb/occupant day)	0.59 ± 0.64
Restaurants (lb/meal served)	0.71 ± 0.40
Overnight lodges in winter sports areas (wastes from all facilities) (lb/visitor day)	1.87 ± 0.26
Day lodge in winter sports areas (lb/visitor day)	2.92 ± 0.61
Recreation residences (lb/occupant day)	2.13 ± 0.54
Observation sites (lb/incoming axle)	0.05 ± 0.03
Visitor centers (lb/visitor)	0.02 ± 0.008
Swimming beaches (lb/swimmer)	0.04 ± 0.01
Concession stands (lb/patron)	0.14 (1 site)
Administrative residences (lb/occupant day)	1.37 ± 0.35

e. ROADSIDE LITTER

In a study of twenty-nine states by the Research Triangle
Institute for Keep America Beautiful Inc. the following conclusions were drawn about roadside litter:

1) Approximately one cubic yard of litter was accumulated
    per month for each mile of interstate and primary high-
    ways.

2) The composition of these wastes was: 59% paper, 16%
    cans, 6% plastic, 13% miscellaneous, 6% glass bottle
    and jar.

Tables 12.13 and 12.14 give the number of litter items per
mile, a summary of percent of items by class and total litter
volumes for ten domains of average daily trafic and a list of
special items picked up.

3. COLLECTION, TRANSPORTATION AND MONITORING

The collection of solid wastes for any geographic area usually involves three separate systems--public, private and individual (Table 12.12)--working together to bring the wastes together at disposal sites--incinerators, sanitory landfills, or
open dumps. It is at these disposal sites that, as noted before,
most solid wastes are measured.

TABLE 12.12

COLLECTION OF SOLID WASTES

	Public	Private	Individual
Household Wastes	56%	32%	12%
Commercial Wastes	25%	63%	13%
Industrial	13%	57%	30%

Source: An Interim Report, p. 10.

As Table 12.14 indicates, various haulers haul different
types of wastes. Municipal refuse collection services provide
basically for residential wastes. Multi-family dwellings of substantial sizes are often omitted as well as downtown areas (e.g.,
Chicago). Larger apartment houses, commercial establishments,
and industrial plants use private or individual haulers which

TABLE 12.13

NUMBER OF LITTER ITEMS PER MILE

	FIRST PICKUP		SECOND PICKUP	
	Items Per Mile	% of Total	Items Per Mile	% of Total
Newspapers or magazines	58	1.77	25	1.89
Paper packages or containers	352	10.73	150	11.52
Other paper items	1195	36.44	601	46.08
Total number of paper items	1605	48.94	776	59.49
Beer cans	710	21.65	153	11.75
Soft drink cans	143	4.36	40	3.11
Food cans	33	1.00	8	0.64
Other cans	43	1.31	11	0.82
Total number of cans	929	28.32	213	16.31
Plastic packages or containers	63	1.92	34	2.57
Other plastic items	92	2.80	42	3.20
Total number of plastic items	155	4.71	75	5.78
Auto parts and accessories (not tires)	27	0.83	11	0.83
Tires (or tire pieces)	99	3.01	39	3.00
Lumber or construction items	87	2.66	52	3.97
Unclassified items	151	4.59	62	4.73
Total number of miscellaneous items	364	11.09	163	12.53
Number of special interest items	9	0.28	4	0.28
Returnable beer bottles	13	0.41	5	0.41
Nonreturnable beer bottles	90	2.74	30	2.31
Returnable soft drink bottles	53	1.62	21	1.62
Nonreturnable soft drink bottles	26	0.78	7	0.51
Wine or liquor bottles	25	0.77	8	0.64
Food bottles or jars	8	0.25	3	0.22
Other bottles or jars	12	0.36	2	0.17
Total number of bottles and jars	227	6.93	77	5.88
Total litter volume (cubic feet)	82		29	
Total of all items	3279		1304	

351   Source: Research Triangle Institute (1969).

TABLE 12.14

SUMMARY OF PERCENT OF ITEMS BY CLASS AND TOTAL LITTER VOLUME
FOR TEN DOMAINS OF AVERAGE DAILY TRAFFIC
(Second Pickup)

Average Daily Traffic	Sample* Size	Total Litter Volume	Percent of Total for each Domain				
			Paper	Cans	Plastics	Bottles	Miscel-laneous
Less than 400	19	9	49	21	7	9	14
400-999	43	17	53	25	6	8	8
1000-1999	57	20	55	16	9	7	13
2000-2999	45	23	56	18	10	8	7
3000-3999	19	31	59	18	4	7	12
4000-4999	18	56	48	24	7	9	12
5000-9999	26	56	66	18	3	3	10
10000-14999	17	43	68	7	8	4	13
15000-19999	6	71	78	5	7	2	7
20000 & over	9	120	55	11	2	6	25

* Number of segments, each two-tenths of a mile in length.
Source: Research Triangle Institute (1969).

must also use privately owned disposal facilities often considerable distances from the generation source.

4. LAND USE RELATIONSHIPS

The best summaries of solid waste relationships to land use
at source remain those of the California solid Wastes management
studies (Tables 12.15 and 12.16).

TABLE 12.15

ESTIMATES OF MUNICIPAL WASTES

Waste Source	Multipliers
Household Garbage and Rubbish	
Single Family Unit	1.42910 tons/unit/year
Multiple Family Unit	0.62755 tons/unit/year
City Streets: Leaves, Litter, Sweepings, and Tree Trimmings	42.9 lb/capita/year
Refuse Collected Along Highway Right-of-Way	
Freeway Refuse	8.0 tons/mile/year
County Roads Refuse	3.3 tons/mile/year
Sewage Treatment Residue	87.1 lb/capita/year
Local Parks and Playgrounds	5.4 lb/capita/year
Regional Parks	
TOTAL WASTE	

TABLE 12.16

ESTIMATES OF MANUFACTURING WASTES

Industry	Multipliers[b] tons/employee/year
Seasonal Foods	5.56570
Other Foods	4.81655
Total Food Products	
Paper, Printing, and Publishing	12.87060
Chemicals	8.21075
Textiles and Apparel	.52575
Rubber and Plastics	1.54810
Leather	2.49365
Total Other Nondurables	
Stone, Clay, Glass, and Concrete	18.11425
Primary and Fabricated Metals	6.7300
Electrical and Nonelectrical Machinery	3.58040
Lumber and Wood Products	21.68805
Furniture and Fixtures	20.15545
Transportation Equipment	3.39330
Instruments	2.51700
Total Other Durables	

[a] Multipliers for the manufacturing industries were developed and reported in Table VI, Comprehensive Studies of Solid Waste Management, Second Annual Report. The multiplier for the categroy Paper, Printing and Publishing (SIC 26 and 27) is a simple average of the separate multipliers for SIC 26 and 27. Also, the multiplier for the category Electrical and Nonelectrical Machinery (SIC 35 and 36) is a simple average of the separate multipliers for SIC 35 and 36.

At _disposal_ _point_, the issues are those of the siting of
what are generally perceived to be undesirable or noxious land
uses--incinerators, landfills, etc.--and the avoidance of them
by most other uses.

IV. NOISE

1. PATTERNS OF EMISSION SOURCES

As in the case of air pollution, it is useful to consider
noise emissions with respect to three dimensions: mobility, time,
and spatial scale.

a. MOBILITY DIMENSION

It is useful to distinguish mobile and stationary sources
of noise. Mobile sources include all forms of transportation:
automobiles, trucks, rail and aircraft. Stationary sources include industrial sites, noise from residential buildings (air
conditioners, for example), and construction and demolition
noise.

b. TIME DIMENSION

From these mobile and stationary sources, noise levels in
the urban environment vary markedly with time of day. Differences
between daytime and nighttime hours are most significant (Figure
12.16). In addition, peak hour travel times tend to have higher
noise levels than off peak hours.

c. SPATIAL SCALE DIMENSION

Noise emissions arise from three spatial types of sources:
point sources, line sources, and area sources.
Motor vehicles, although themselves mobile point sources,
produce in combination a line source of noise in the urban environment, the highway. Individual industries which act as noise
emitters fall into the category of point sources; however, when
a number of noise-producing industries are located in a given
area, an ambient industrial noise level for the area may be obtained, and treated as an area source. Residential areas, too,
are generally treated as area sources. The combination of residential traffic noise and outdoor domestic noise constitute the
major elements contributing to residential area noise levels.
Finally, aircraft overlight patterns tend to be treated as areas
of intruding noise.
In the sense of these spatial noise sources, the map of

a) VARIOUS MEASURES OF THE OUTDOOR NOISE LEVEL

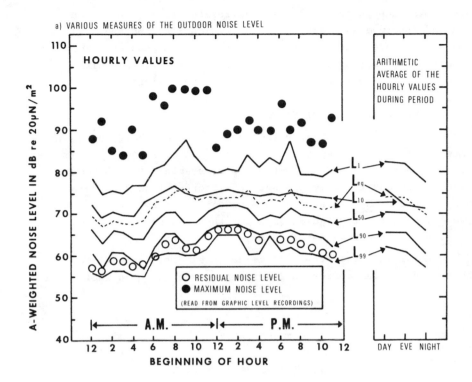

b) HISTOGRAMS OF THE PERCENTAGE OF TIME NOISE WAS IN EACH 5 dB INTERVAL FOR THREE TIME PERIODS

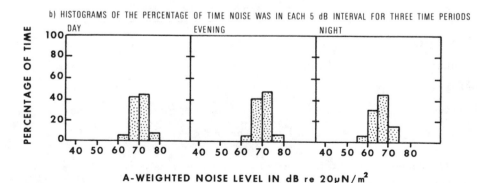

A-WEIGHTED NOISE LEVEL IN dB re 20μN/m²

FIGURE 12.16

SUMMARY OF THE 24-HOUR OUTDOOR NOISE LEVELS
AT LOCATION C-SECOND FLOOR TENEMENT

Source: EPA, Community Noise, 1971.

noise emissions in an urban area, as related to land use, can thus be conceived as a set of areas, residential and industrial, with given ambient noise levels, crossed by line sources along the arterial, expressway and public transport networks, with intrusive point sources and with aircraft overflight contours.

2. GENERATION OF EMISSIONS

How, then, can such an emissions map be related to a map of noise incidence at receptors? Determination of area source generation of noise is based on average noise readings for the combination of sources typically present in different land use areas. Noise levels within these land use categories vary with density; however, no definitive guidelines for the density-noise level relationship have been established.

General land use areas and noise levels associated with these land use categories in Inner London are shown in Table 12.17.

TABLE 12.17

LAND USE AND NOISE LEVELS IN INNER LONDON

Type of Area	dB(A) Day	Night
Residential	65	53
Industrial	66	54
Shopping	70	58
Offices	69	58
Railway	68	57

Levels based on Inner London: London Noise Study
Source: Greater London Council (1966).

Likewise, Table 12.18 shows levels of noise in five different types of residential areas in the U.S.

TABLE 12.18

QUALITATIVE DESCRIPTORS OF URBAN & SUBURBAN
DETACHED HOUSING (L_{90})

Description	Typical Range	Average dB(A)
Quiet Suburban Residential	36 to 40 inclusive	38
Normal Suburban Residential	41 to 45 inclusive	43
Urban Residential	46 to 50 inclusive	48
Noisy Urban Residential	51 to 55 inclusive	53
Very Noisy Urban Residential	56 to 60 inclusive	58

Source: U.S. Environmental Protection Agency, Report to the President and Congress on Noise, December 31, 1971, Table 2.2

As noted above, it is helpful to consider these ambient area noise levels as baseline levels for noise in sections of the urban area. The baseline levels can be overlaid by intruding noise sources (line sources and point sources) to bive an overall picture of the total urban noise environment.

Areas affected by intruding aircraft noise can be projected based on the concept of the noise exposure forecast (NEF). This involves a detailed correlation of (i) projected air traffic growth, (ii) types of aircraft involved (different jets produced different noise configurations) and (iii) pattern of operations throughout the twenty-four hour period each day. An example of NEF noise contours for the city of Chicago is shown in Figure 12.17.

The amount of noise generated by expressways, the principle line noise source in urban places, is a function of the number and speed of automobiles on the highway:

$$dB(A) = 37 + 10 \log_{10}m + 20 \log_{10}v$$

with

m = flow in automobiles/second
v = average speed in miles/hour.

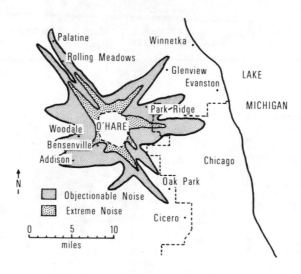

FIGURE 12.17

1970 NOISE EXPOSURE CONTOURS FOR AREAS SURROUNDING
CHICAGO'S O'HARE INTERNATIONAL AIRPORT

(after Mecklin, 1969).

Typical highway noise levels at fifty feet from the source are
as follows:

Heavy traffic	90 dB(A)
Average freeway traffic	72 dB(A)
Light auto traffic	56 dB(A)

Thus, the noise climate as a percentage of the time [dB(A)] is
as shown in Table 12.19.

TABLE 12.19

NOISE CLIMATE AS PERCENTAGE OF TIME

Location	Daytime	Nighttime	Level of Inter-mittent Peaks [dB(A)]	
Main Streets with heavy vehicles	68 - 80	50 - 70	85 - 92	at
Secondary Streets	60 - 70	44 - 55	up to 92	25
Residential Streets with local traffic only	51 - 60	43 - 49	occasionally up to 92	feet

Noise levels have been recorded for a few of the most typical industrial noise offenders; however, most industrial noise
generators tend to be industrial-facility specific. An average
factory emits approximately 70-75 dB(A) of noise. Construction
noise generally reaches intermittent peak levels of 110 dB(A)
(at ten feet). These point sources, although present in urban
places generally, play a minor role in the overall urban noise
environment relative to line and area sources.

3. NOISE DIFFUSION

Free flowing traffic noise is made up of two components with
different diffusion patterns. First, noise from quasi-steady-
state noise from the flow of automobiles distributed along a
line (highway) radiates with cylindrical symmetry to adjacent
areas. This radiation gives rise to a decrease in the sound pressure level of three decibels for each doubling of distance from
the line source (neglecting atmospheric attenuation). The second
component is associated with discrete moving sources. Because
of the localized nature of the source, noise from trucks radiates
with spherical symmetry, giving rise to a drop-off of six decibels
per doubling of distance from the source, the rate for point
sources. The passage of each truck gives rise to a peak in sound
pressure level, superimposed on the "background" of automobile
noise, which tends to remain fairly steady for constant flow and
average vehicle speed.

A case study of traffic noise generation and diffusion shows
the different levels of noise produced by different types and
volumes of traffic and the diffusion rates for these noise levels
(Figure 12.17). As the figure indicates, once the traffic volume
falls below a threshold level it is superseded by the surrouding
ambient noise levels and no longer acts as an intruding noise
source.

As is described in Chapter 2, diffusion of noise is affected
by a number of factors. Land form immediately adjacent to the
expressway plays a major role in the rate of diffusion of expressway noise levels is shown in Figure 12.19.

4. MONITORING NOISE LEVELS

Because of the lack of community noise standards in most
urban areas, one finds a corresponding lack of comprehensive

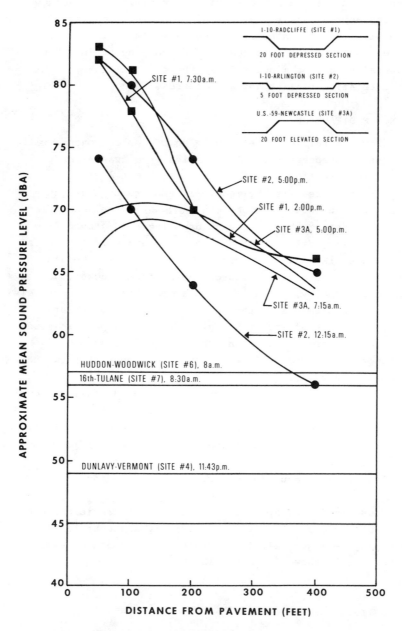

FIGURE 12.18

MEAN dBA VALUES AT HOUSTON SITES
(after Texas Transportation Institute, 1971)

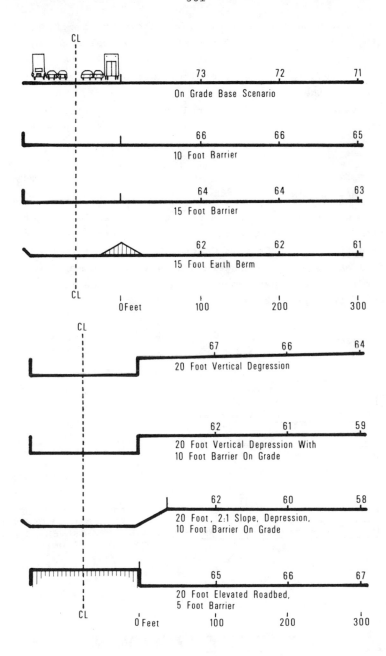

FIGURE 12.19

ESTIMATED MEDIAN A-WEIGHTED SOUND LEVELS--SIX LANE HIGHWAY,
1550 VEHICLES/HOUR/LAND, 10% TRUCKS,
AVERAGE SPEED 50-60 MPH
(after Paulin and Safeer, 1972)

noise receptor data. In some cities, notably Chicago (the only city with an ambient noise ordinance), data is collected by mobile sensing units. However, even in these areas data is too limited to give an adequate, useful picture of the overall noise environment of the urban area.

Some researchers have conducted noise <u>receptor</u> <u>studies</u> of their study areas. Jacoby (1972) has done this for the city of Detroit.

5. RELATIONSHIP BETWEEN THE MAP OF NOISE LEVELS AND THE MAP OF LAND USE

To show a direct comparison of average noise levels determined from receptor data and land use types three transverses were drawn through the Detroit Central City area (for which both noise data and land use data were available). A comparison of noise levels and land use types for this urban area is shown graphically in Figure 12.20.

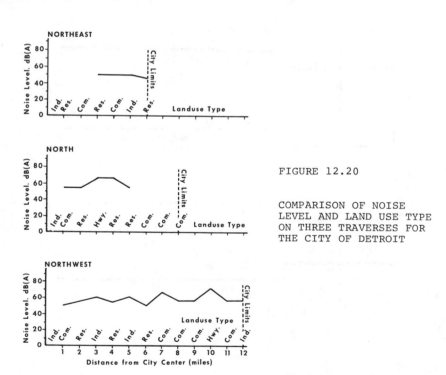

FIGURE 12.20

COMPARISON OF NOISE LEVEL AND LAND USE TYPE ON THREE TRAVERSES FOR THE CITY OF DETROIT

Note: derived from data presented in Jacoby (1970).

13   URBAN FORMS AND POLLUTION PATTERNS

We have already shown that variations in urban form, via
their effects on the mix of urban land uses, have significant
effects on levels of environmental pollution when city size, the
urban economic base, and income levels are held constant. But
the relationships developed in Part C were aggregative; each city
was treated as a single observation. The question that now must
be addressed is exactly how these relationships play themselves
out in the internal structure of the city when sample observations
of pollution concentrations are available for many locations
within each urban region.

In Chapter 12, the chain of causal connections was discussed.
To this will now be added comparative empirical evidence, assembled
either for each of the thirteen urban regions sampled to be representative of the range of environmental pollution found in urban
America, or for exemplary case studies where comparative evidence
for the thirteen is weak or absent. First, we review the ways
in which the form of each urban region was summarized to permit
comparative analysis to be undertaken. Second, sample analyses
of relationships between environmental pollution and urban structure are presented. Finally, certain comparative generalizations
are made, within--of course--the limits of the experiments undertaken.

I. ELEMENTS OF URBAN FORM

In Chapter 12, it was pointed out that for purposes of pollution analysis, land uses can be treated as either point, line
or area sources. Because urban land use has a spatial logic, the
area sources can, in turn, be arranged under the umbrella of an
urban density gradient, diminishing in intensity from core to
periphery. The line sources form the urban transport network.
Point sources are those which generate sufficiently large quantities of pollution that they stand out above the combined den-
sity- and transport-related pollution-source map in the cases of
air and noise pollution and solid wastes. In the case of water
pollution, the majority of sources have to be treated as within
a distinct spatial framework, however, as points on the hydrologic network, thus requiring a different scale and mode of

analysis.

1. THE URBAN DENSITY GRADIENT

The urban density gradient describes how the population
per square mile of an area drops off with distance from the center of the city. It has been shown in many studies that the rate
of decline is negative exponential, i.e.,

$$D_r = D_0 e^{-br}$$

where D_r is the population density at distance r from the city
center, D_0 is the imputed density at the city center, and b is
the density gradient.

For the thirteen sample urban regions, density gradients
were created using five sets of variables taken from the 1970
census of the population:

P_c Central City population

P_r Population of the "ring" area outside the central city
but within the SMSA

A_c Land area of the central city

A_r Area within the SMSA but outside the central city

S   The number of degrees of arc occupied by the urban
region, to take account of major topographic features,
such as the location of Chicago on Lake Michigan.

The population and area variables were combined to calculate the population density for the central city ($D_c = P_c/A_c$)
and for the ring or remainder of the SMSA, ($D_r = P_r/A_r$). These
derived densities define two ordinates which lie on the density
gradient when corresponding values of distance from the city
center are calculated for the abcissa.

In order to find this distance, the radius of a circle of
area A was calculated, where A is the area of the SMSA or central
city in question. However, since some cities cannot expand
radially in all directions a correction was made for the topographic constraints that tend to channel the direction of growth.
Hence the formula for the area sector S became

$$A = (\pi/360)Sr^2,$$

which was rewritten to solve for r by

$$r = \sqrt{A/(\pi S/360)}.$$

Note that when S = 360° the city can grow in all directions,
and the equation reduces to finding the radius of a simple circle.
Hence, using the previously defined variables the central city
radius (r_c) is given by,

$$r_c = \sqrt{A_c/(\pi S/360)},$$

while in the case of the SMSA the ring and central city areas
were combined to give a total SMSA radius which defines the regions
perimeter and is given by

$$r_r = \sqrt{(A_c + A_r)/(\pi S/360)}.$$

Thus, two points for each sample region were found, (r_c, D_c)
and (r_r, D_r). These lie on the density gradient, and if the negative exponential gradient is linearized by taking the natural
logs of the densities, these two points define a straight line
as described in Figure 13.1.

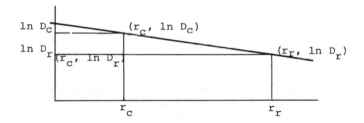

FIGURE 13.1

THE GRADIENT DEFINED BY $(r_c, \ln D_c)$ AND $(r_r, \ln D_r)$

The slope of this line is simply,

$$b = \frac{\ln D_c - \ln D_r}{r_c - r_r}$$

However, it appears that this line represents the upper
bound of an area through which the density gradient would pass.
The lower limit of this region may be defined as a line parallel
to the slope of the upper bound but passing through $(r_c, \ln D_r)$.
That is, in the case of the upper bound, the average densities
of the ring and central city were imputed to be at the perimeter

of each, while in the case of the lower bound the gradient is defined as passing through a point on the perimeter of the central city corresponding to the average density of the ring. See Figure 13.2.

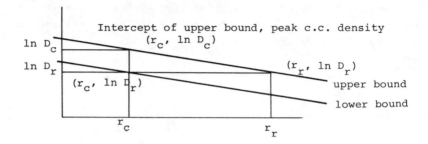

FIGURE 13.2

THE DENSITY GRADIENT: UPPER AND LOWER BOUNDS
AND PEAK DENSITY

The intercept of the upper bound is

$$\ln a = r_c - b \ln D_c,$$

and is given by $(0, \ln a)$ on the graph. Assume that this intercept gives the peak density. Then assume that density tapers off to the lower bound level at the extreme perimeter of the SMSA (r_r). This point is defined by $(r_r, 0)$, $(r_r, \ln D_r)$ or $x = r_r$. See Figure 13.3.

Since the y-axis and the line given by $(r_r, 0)$ and $(r_r, \ln D_r)$, i.e., $x = r_r$, are parallel and define a parallelogram in the area between them and the upper and lower boundary lines (shaded are in Figure 13.3), the distance from $(r_r, \ln D_r)$ to the perimeter density is equal to $\ln D_c - \ln D_r$, since those are the points of intersection of the line given by the points $(r_c, 0)$, $(r_c, \ln D_c)$, $x = r_c$, (parallel to the y-axis) and the upper and lower bounds. Thus, perimeter density is given by

$$\ln D_p = \ln D_r - (\ln D_c - \ln D_r).$$

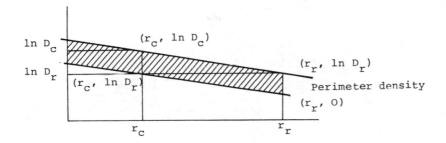

FIGURE 13.3

THE DENSITY GRADIENT: PERIMETER DENSITY

Since the density gradient passes through the peak density
(0,ln a) and perimeter density $(r_r, \ln D_p)$, we find the slope of
the density gradient as

$$B = \frac{\ln a - \ln D_p}{-r_r}$$

which intercepts the y-axis at ln a and defines the equation of
the density gradient as

$$Y = \ln a + BX.$$

Table 13.1 shows the data and results for 1970. A gradient was
not calculated for Jacksonville because the city and the SMSA
are the same political unit, as a result of city-county consoli-
dation.

For purposes of later analysis, the urban regions were ranked
in two ways, using the results shown in Table 13.1: (a) according
to their relative compactness (steepness of the density gradient);
and (b) according to their relative crowding (peak central city
densities). From the most compact to the most dispersed urban
form, within the constraints of S, the ranking is:

TABLE 13.1

DENSITY GRADIENT DATA, 1970

Region	S	P_c	A_c	D_c	r_c	a	P_r	A_r	D_r	r_r	D_p	B
Akron	360	275	54.2	5073.8	4.1536	10931.4	404	850.8	474.847	16.9726	44.4	-.3244
Birmingham	360	301	79.5	3786.16	5.03047	7216.1	438	2541.5	165.815	29.4299	7.3	-.2345
Chicago	180	3363	222.6	15107.8	11.9043	36022.5	3611	3497.4	1032.48	48.6644	70.6	-.1281
Cincinnati	180	452	78.1	5787.45	7.05123	10558.9	933	2071.9	450.311	36.9963	35.0	-.1543
Denver	180	515	95.2	5409.66	7.78499	10198.9	713	3564.8	200.011	48.2703	7.4	-.1498
Detroit	180	1511	138	10949.3	9.37301	22590.4	2689	1814	1482.36	35.2516	200.7	-.1340
Indianapolis	360	745	379.4	1963.63	10.9894	8347.4	365	2700.6	135.155	31.3112	9.3	-.2171
Jacksonville	180	518	344.3	1504.5	14.805		10	421.7	23.7135	22.0828		
Los Angeles	180	3175	512.4	6196.33	18.0611	16152.4	3861	3556.6	1085.59	50.896	190.2	-.0873
Oklahoma City	240	367	299.1	1227.01	11.9503	4322.0	274	1843.4	148.638	31.9838	18.0	-.1714
Providence	300	340	61.8	5501.62	4.85858	11867.1	573	617.2	928.386	16.1046	156.7	-.2687
Seattle	60	585	112.9	5181.58	14.6841	9752.1	837	4116.1	203.348	89.8709	8.0	-.0791
Washington	360	756	61.4	12312.7	4.42088	29302.3	2105	2290.6	918.973	27.3617	68.6	-.2080

TABLE 13.2

DENSITY GRADIENT DATA, 1960

Region	S	P_c	A_c	D_c	r_c	a	P_r	A_r	D_r	r_r	D_p	B
Akron	360	290	54.2	5350.55	4.1536	12712.5	315	850.8	370.24	16.9726	25.6	-.3657
Birmingham	360	341	79.5	4289.31	5.03047	8637.3	380	2641.5	143.858	29.4299	4.8	-.2545
Chicago	180	3550	222.6	15947.9	11.9043	42667.3	2671	3497.4	763.71	48.6644	36.6	-.1451
Cincinnati	180	503	78.1	6440.46	7.05123	12626.5	765	2071.9	369.226	36.9963	21.2	-.1727
Denver	180	494	95.2	5189.08	7.78499	10672.4	435	3564.8	122.026	48.2703	2.9	-.1703
Detroit	180	1670	138	12101.4	9.37301	28353.3	2092	1814	1153.25	35.2516	110.0	-.1575
Indianapolis	360	476	379.4	1254.61	10.9894	3659.5	468	2700.6	173.295	31.3112	24.0	-.1606
Jacksonville	180	201	344.3	583.79	14.805		254	421.7	602.324	22.0828		
Los Angeles	180	1504	512.4	2935.21	18.0611	4643.2	4535	3556.6	1275.09	50.896	553.9	-.0418
Oklahoma City	240	324	299.1	1083.25	11.9503	4434.7	148	1843.4	101.985	31.9838	9.6	-.1918
Providence	300	207	61.8	3349.51	4.85858	5659.3	614	617.2	994.815	16.1046	295.5	-.1833
Seattle	60	557	112.9	4933.57	14.6841	9982.9	550	4116.1	133.622	89.8709	3.6	-.0882
Washington	360	764	61.4	12443.	4.42088	22559.7	1300	2290.6	567.537	27.3617	25.9	-.2474

TABLE 13.3

DENSITY GRADIENT DATA, 1950

Region	S	P_c	A_c	D_c	r_c	a	P_r	A_r	D_r	r_r	D_p	B
Akron	360	275	54.2	5073.8	4.1536	13750.6	199	850.8	233.897	16.9726	10.8	-.4213
Birmingham	360	326	79.5	4100.63	5.03047	8438.4	327	2641.5	123.793	29.4299	3.7	-.2630
Chicago	180	3621	222.6	16266.8	11.9043	52165.4	1557	3497.4	445.188	48.6644	12.2	-.1718
Cincinnati	180	504	78.1	6453.26	7.05123	13830.9	525	2071.9	253.391	36.9963	10.0	-.1987
Denver	180	416	95.2	4369.75	7.78499	10135.7	196	3564.8	54.982	48.2703	1.0	-.1956
Detroit	180	1850	138	13405.8	9.37301	40281.6	1166	1814	642.778	35.2516	30.9	-.2036
Indianapolis	360	427	379.4	1125.46	10.9894	3895.1	306	2700.6	113.308	31.3112	11.4	-.1863
Jacksonville	180	205	344.3	595.411	14.805		99	421.7	234.764	22.0828		
Los Angeles	180	1970	512.4	3844.65	18.0611	10550.5	2182	3556.6	613.507	50.896	97.9	-.0919
Oklahoma City	240	244	299.1	815.781	11.9500	3253.5	148	1843.4	80.2864	31.9838	7.9	-.1882
Providence	300	249	61.8	4029.13	4.85858	7955.1	515	617.2	834.414	16.1046	172.8	-.2378
Seattle	60	468	112.9	4145.26	14.6841	8727.9	377	4116.1	91.5916	89.8709	2.1	-.0931
Washington	360	802	61.4	13061.9	4.42088	26888.8	706	2290.6	308.216	27.3617	7.3	-.3002

City	Slope	
Akron	-.3244	compact
Providence	-.2687	
Birmingham	-.2345	
Indianapolis	-.2171	
Washington	-.2080	
Oklahoma City	-.1714	
Cincinnati	-.1543	
Denver	-.1498	
Detroit	-.1340	
Chicago	-.1281	
Los Angeles	-.0873	
Seattle	-.0791	dispersed

In terms of imputed peak densities, the order is as follows (average population densities of the central city are added for comparison.):

City	Peak Density	Average Density of Central City
Chicago	36,022	15,107
Washington	29,302	12,312
Detroit	22,590	10,949
Los Angeles	16,152	6,196
Providence	11,867	5,501
Akron	10,931	5,073
Cincinnati	10,558	5,787
Denver	10,198	5,409
Seattle	9,752	5,181
Indianapolis	8,347	1,963
Birmingham	7,216	3,786
Oklahoma City	4,322	1,227

For later comparative use, the analysis was repeated using census data for 1960 and 1950 (Tables 13.2 and 13.3, respectively). Most of the density gradients are seen to have decreased in the past two decades, as decentralization of people and jobs has proceeded apace.

In all three years, the density gradient was related to population size, viz:

$$B_{1950} = -0.799 + 0.042 \ln P_s \qquad R = 0.41$$

$$B_{1960} = -0.923 + 0.052 \ln P_s \qquad R = 0.55$$

$$B_{1970} = -0.935 + 0.053 \ln P_s \qquad R = 0.63$$

This means that in any given year, the larger SMSA's are more dispersed than the smaller ones, and that all SMSA's have become more dispersed since 1950, holding size constant.

Similarly, for central densities:

$$D_{c,1950} = -172,000 + 13,553 \ln P_s \qquad R = 0.76$$

$$D_{c,1960} = -111,600 + 8,790 \ln P_s \qquad R = 0.62$$

$$D_{c,1970} = -105,600 + 8,348 \ln P_s \qquad R = 0.83$$

Central density increases with population size, but has done so
less rapidly in later years than in 1950. Not only are the urban
regions decentralizing; they are also showing significant decreases
in levels of crowding in the inner city. Progressively, all
SMSA's are converging on a similar pattern of population densities
uniformly dispersed throughout the urban region.

    2.   TRANSPORT NETWORK CONFIGURATIONS

    In their study concerning implications of highway planning
for air pollution control, Vorhees, et. al. (1971) used computer
simulation models of travel patterns for a hypothetical metropolitan area based on four ideal types of highway networks: a
basic arterial grid, freeways along major arterials, major radial
freeways with outer and inner beltways, and additional radials
freeways with a middle beltway added. A hierarchical classification of transportation networks has been developed for purposes of this study using these ideal types.

    Cities are ranked on the basis of the centrality of focus
of the transportation network. In this way cities with a very
heavy flow of traffic aimed towards the CBD can be distinguished
from those with a more diffuse set of travel path alternatives.
From the most dispersed to the most centralized, the transport
network configurations identified are these:

    I.   Multiple beltways without interior radials

        A.   Outer and mid beltways
        B.   Outer and inner beltways
        C.   Mid and inner beltways

   II.   Multiple beltways with interior radials

        A.   Outer and mid beltways
        B.   Outer and inner beltways
        C.   Mid and inner beltways

  III.   One beltway without interior radials

        A.   Outer beltway
        B.   Mid beltway
        C.   Inner beltway

   IV.   One beltway with interior radials

        A.   Outer beltway
        B.   Mid beltway
        C.   Inner beltway

    V.   Radial highways only

See Figure 13.4. Figures 13.5 to 13.17 show the highway networks of each urban region. The order is that of their population density gradients. Other details are included on the maps to
provide further background relating to each of the sample regions.

MULTIPLE BELTWAYS WITHOUT INTERIOR RADIALS

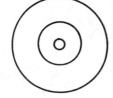

I.

MULTIPLE BELTWAYS WITH INTERIOR RADIALS

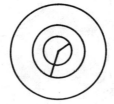

II.

ONE BELTWAY WITHOUT INTERIOR RADIALS

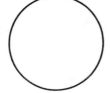

III.

ONE BELTWAY WITH INTERIOR RADIALS

IV.

RADIAL LIMITED ACCESS HIGHWAY ONLY

V.

FIGURE 13.4

NETWORKS RANKED IN ORDER OF
INCREASING CENTRALITY OF FOCUS

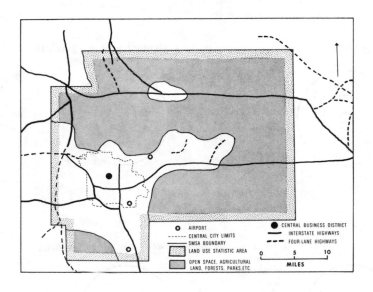

FIGURE 13.5

AKRON

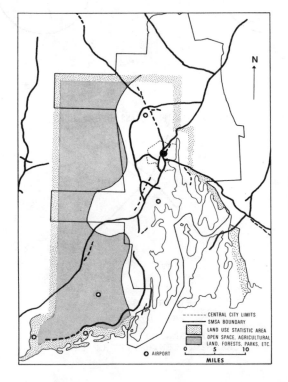

FIGURE 13.6

PROVIDENCE

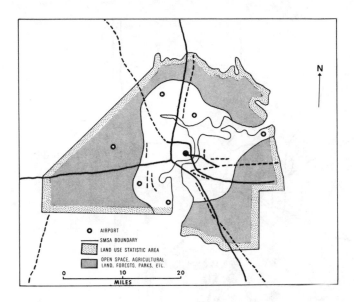

FIGURE 13.7

JACKSONVILLE

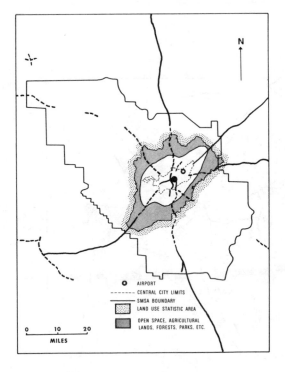

FIGURE 13.8

BIRMINGHAM

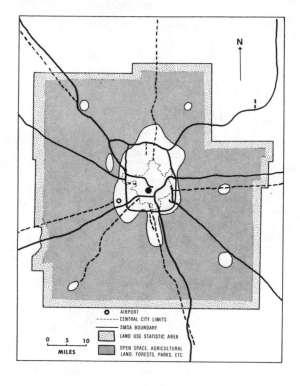

FIGURE 13.9

INDIANAPOLIS

AIRPORT
CENTRAL CITY LIMITS
SMSA BOUNDARY
LAND USE STATISTIC AREA
OPEN SPACE, AGRICULTURAL LAND, FORESTS, PARKS, ETC.

0   5   10
MILES

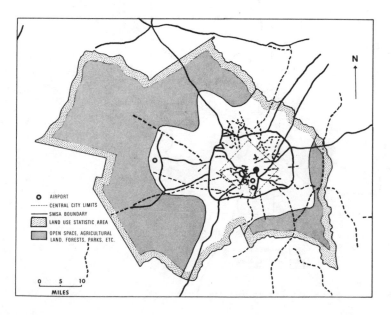

FIGURE 13.10

WASHINGTON, D.C.

AIRPORT
CENTRAL CITY LIMITS
SMSA BOUNDARY
LAND USE STATISTIC AREA
OPEN SPACE, AGRICULTURAL LAND, FORESTS, PARKS, ETC.

0   5   10
MILES

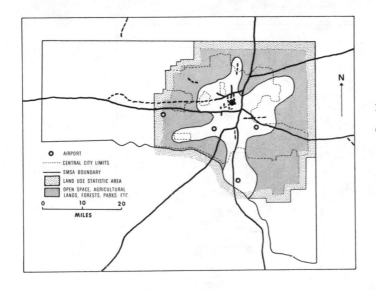

FIGURE 13.11

OKLAHOMA CITY

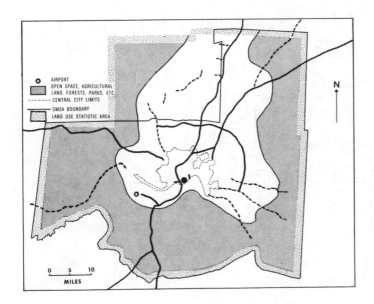

FIGURE 13.12

CINCINNATI

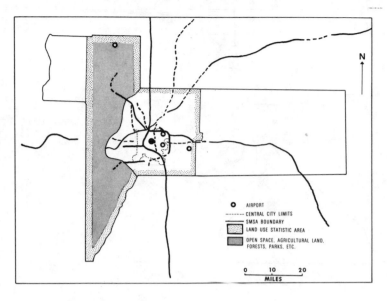

FIGURE 13.13

DENVER

AIRPORT
CENTRAL CITY LIMITS
SMSA BOUNDARY
LAND USE STATISTIC AREA
OPEN SPACE, AGRICULTURAL LAND, FORESTS, PARKS, ETC.

0   10   20
MILES

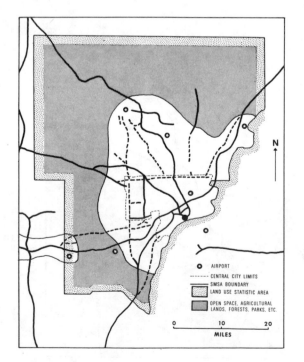

FIGURE 13.14

DETROIT

AIRPORT
CENTRAL CITY LIMITS
SMSA BOUNDARY
LAND USE STATISTIC AREA
OPEN SPACE, AGRICULTURAL LANDS, FORESTS, PARKS, ETC.

0   10   20
MILES

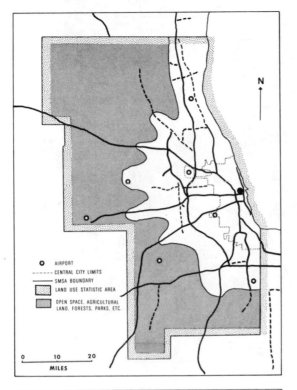

FIGURE 13.15

CHICAGO

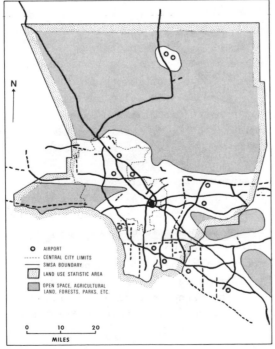

FIGURE 13.16

LOS ANGELES

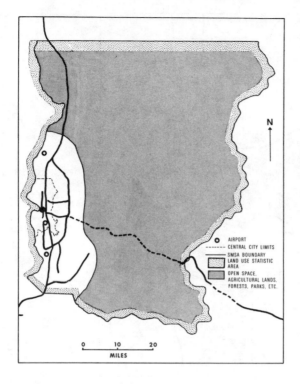

FIGURE 13.17

SEATTLE

AIRPORT
CENTRAL CITY LIMITS
SMSA BOUNDARY
LAND USE STATISTIC
AREA
OPEN SPACE,
AGRICULTURAL LANDS,
FORESTS, PARKS, ETC.

0   10   20
MILES

3.   INTRUSIVE POINT SOURCES

The definition of intrusive point sources may be illustrated
by using noise as an example. That the background noise levels
within an urban region are density-related has already been
demonstrated clearly enough in the earlier chapters, although
systematic studies of the metropolitan noise environment are
scarce. Thus, the urban density gradient can be converted into
an urban residential noise gradient by means of a simple noise-
density function. This would produce peak noise levels at the
city center and declining noise levels with increasing distance
from this point in the manner described in Section 2.

The effects of the transport network may be superimposed
on the noise-distance map. Traffic-related noise levels are
known, and they disperse in a known manner until they blend into
the background of density-related noise.

Intrusive point sources are those noise generators that
create higher noise levels than can be predicted by combining
area- and line-sources in the manner described above. Examples
include airports, with intrusive noise radiating from them along

aircraft flight paths, particularly noisy industrial plants or
railroad classification yards, etc. The type and location of
such intrusive point sources are unique to each case.

II. SAMPLE DENSITY RELATIONS

Theoretically, it is possible to calculate pollution intensity gradients in a manner analogous to the population density
gradient for almost any type of pollutant by plotting observed
pollution intensities at distances from the city center and
fitting a regression line to these observations. As has been
made clear in the preceding pages, there is a wide range of pollutants and pollutant types, however, and not all measurements of
the same effluent generate strictly comparable results. While
standardized effluent measurement systems such as the National
Air Surveillance Network, the Continuous Air Monitoring Project
and the use of Air Quality Control Regions has made progress
towards getting comparable information across regions in the
case of air quality, much material is lacking on many pollutants
within SMSA's at this time.

We will thus begin with a sample case involving one air
pollutant in one city at one point in time. The analysis may
be extended to other geographic areas and other pollutant types
as such data become available. Given the results thereby produced, orderings based on peak pollution intensity and pollution
intensity gradients can be compared with peak population density
gradients to examine how they covary. Further, as pollution
data are accumulated over time we may examine the pattern of
pollution changes and compare these with changing density data,
because if the preceding sections of the report are correct, con-
tradictory trends should be evident: as densities decline and
the urban system becomes more highly dispersed, problems of environmental pollution should increase, holding size and economy
constant.

The particular pollutant chosen for sample study was SO_3
and Detroit was taken as the sample city. While SO_3 is not as
commonly measured as SO_2, particulates, or CO it serves as a
useful example. Figure 13.18 maps the average annual SO_3 concentrations, as measured by the lead peroxide method. Such concentrations arise from both industrial by-products entering the
air, and from residential heating in densely populated areas.

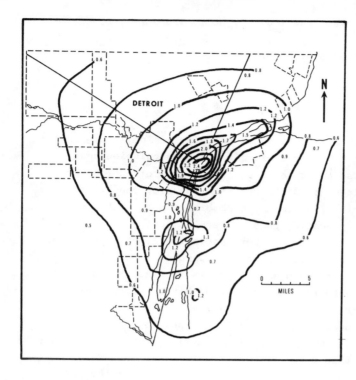

FIGURE 13.18

ANNUAL
AVERAGE SO₃
RATES IN THE
DETROIT-
WINDSOR AREA

The distance-density relationship to the city core is evident.

The figure shows the sample points on the air surveillance
network, and also three vectors used to obtain points to approximate the pollution intensity gradient. Where each of the contour
lines crosses a vector an observation was recorded, giving the
value of the contoured pollution intensity and the distance along
the vector from the city center to the intersection with the contour. In this particular case, 32 observations of intensity by
distance were taken. Of course, the actual SO_3 and distance
figures could also have been taken for the monitoring network
stations.

Transforming the distance variable to logarithmic form yields
the standardized distribution of the 32 observations shown in
Figure 13.19. The gradient is clearly   inverse,   with
the regression relationship

$$SO_{3,r} = 2.1569 - 0.5631 \ln r \qquad R = 0.96$$

This equation shows that the peak pollution intensity for the
Detroit area is 2.1569 mg $SO_3/100$ cm^2 - day with a standard
error of .044165 mg $SO_3/100$ cm^2 - day. The slope is -.5631 indicating a drop of .5631 mg $SO_3/100$ cm^2 - day per unit of log
distance with a standard error of .029417 mg $SO_2/100$ cm^2 - day.

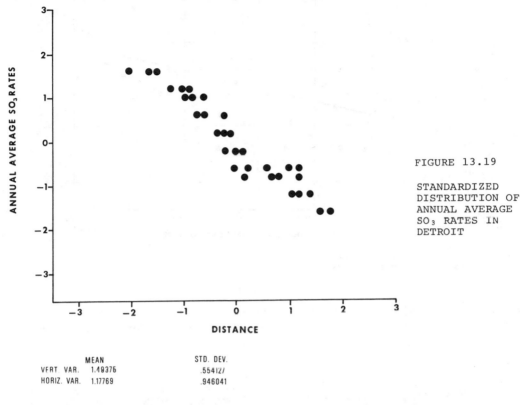

FIGURE 13.19

STANDARDIZED
DISTRIBUTION OF
ANNUAL AVERAGE
SO₃ RATES IN
DETROIT

	MEAN	STD. DEV.
VERT. VAR.	1.49376	.554127
HORIZ. VAR.	1.17769	.946041

Such relationships can also be computed for other pollutants. The case of noise has already been discussed. Similar
suggestive evidence is available for solid wastes. New York
State Solid Wastes Inventory data yield a relationship of per
capita waste collections to population density in that state
for the year 1967-1968, for example (Figure 13.20). The fitted
curve is of the form

$$W_D = k + c \ln D$$

where W_D is waste collected (lbs/cap/day) where population density is D, k is a constant and c is a coefficient of proportionality. Increments to density generate progressively less wastes,
the higher the density. The reason is to be found in land use:

> The general trend is for per capita collection to
> increase up to a certain density and then decrease.
> The apparent range for this transition is around
> 8,000 to 10,000 people per square mile, which is also
> the density range generally marking the transition
> from single-family dwelling communities to multi-
> family dwelling communities. The multi-family dwell-

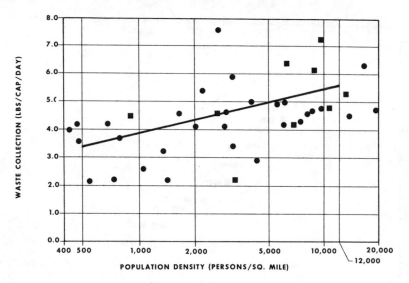

FIGURE 13.20

MUNICIPAL WASTE COLLECTION VS POPULATION DENSITY

Source: EPA, <u>New York Solid Waste Plan. States</u> Report, 1970 (1971),
Fig. B-1.

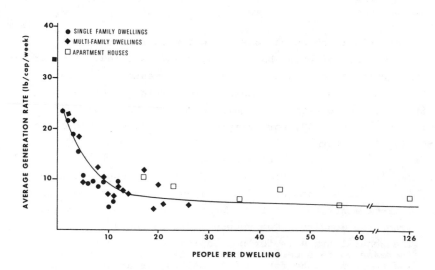

FIGURE 13.21

SOLID WASTE GENERATION FROM SINGLE-FAMILY,
MULTI-FAMILY AND APARTMENT HOUSES

Source: Davidson (1972), p. 12.

ing units have less lawn and garden cuttings, tend to
operate their own incinerators, and are generally occupied by families with lower income, a factor directly proportional to refuse production. Also, the
larger stores in the urban areas tend to practice
more salvage of paperboard and other similar wastes
than do the smaller stores associated with the less
densely populated areas.

New York Solid Waste Plan, 13-4

See Figure 13.21.

III. WATER QUALITY MEASURED AT POINTS ON A HYDROLOGIC NETWORK

So far in this chapter, pollutants have been discussed in
their raw form, not converted to quality indices. The problems
inherent in this further computational step, as well as the difficulties that beset comparative metropolitan analysis of water
quality because of the uniqueness of the hydrologic net and locations of discharges, may be illustrated in a case study of the
Seattle-Everett SMSA. The Syracuse Index, discussed earlier, is
adapted for the task.

Several factors make Seattle an ideal test case:

1) There are three major drainage basins which are located
entirely within the SMSA.

2) There is much physical diversity within the region,
ranging from mountainous headwaters to alluvial lowlands.

3) Location on Puget Sound provides an excellent opportunity
for applying a general water quality index to marine waters.
Heretofore, the Syracuse index was only applied to rivers or lakes.

4) The City of Seattle contains a heavily-industrialized
estuary, a CBD on a bay, the largest freshwater lake within a
metropolitan area and numerous rivers.

5) The area east of Lake Washington is expanding and is
expected to continue to do so, presenting a problem in water
resource planning.

6) Waters from the mountains reach the lowlands in unpolluted condition. There are no major SMSAs upstream from Seattle-
Everett.

7) There is adequate cooperation and transfer of data between all agencies which monitor water quality in the region
(i.e. Department of Ecology, EPA, METRO and U.S. Geological Survey).

8) The City of Seattle has experienced and reversed serious
degradation of its waters.

1. HYDROLOGIC SETTING

The major urbanized areas of western Washington are located
on Puget Sound and the rivers draining into it. The region was
heavily glaciated during the Pleistocene and present surface
features reflect their origin. The flat-lying till plains and
alluvial valleys bordering the Sound are known as the Puget
Sound Lowland. To the east are the rugged mountains of the Cas-
cade Range which provide Seattle, Tacoma, Everett and surrounding
communities with ample fresh water for drinking, agriculture and
industrial use.

Climate in the region ranges from a cool-summer mild-winter
marine type with an average of 30 inches pf precipitation near
the Sound to a more severe alpine climate with more than 150
inches of precipitation in the Cascades (Richardson et al,
1968 p. 8). Precipitation in the mountains is in the form of
snowfall. The snowpack serves as a moisture reservoir and its
thickness regulates stream discharge later in the year.

Three major drainage systems lie entirely within the
Seattle-Everett SMSA (King Co.-Snohomish Co.). It is to each of
these basins that the Syracuse method of water quality analysis
will be applied (see Figure 13.22).

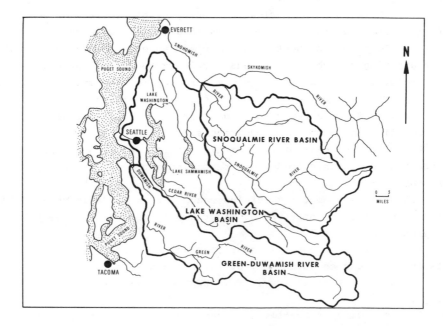

FIGURE 13.22: MAJOR DRAINAGE BASINS IN SEATTLE REGION

The Green-Duwamish River basin is the remnant of a much larger drainage system comprised of the Green, Black and White Rivers which once emptied into the Duwamish estuary. Diversion of the White River in 1906 and lowering of the level of Lake Washington in 1916 left the Green River as the main tributary of the Duwamish. The headwaters of this river serve as the municipal supply for Tacoma and are dammed to insure adequate flow and prevent flooding. From Auburn north to the mouth, the Green River flows in a broad valley in which the agricultural, industrial and population centers are located. Associated with the floodplain and the low summer discharge it receives are the major pollution problems of the basin.

The Lake Washington Basin consists of Lake Washington, 19.5 miles long and 200 feet deep, Sammamish Lake, 8 miles long and 100 feet deep and several small tributaries, the largest of which are the Cedar and Sammamish Rivers. The headwaters of the former serve as Seattle's water supply and the floodplain of the latter is a rapidly expanding suburban area. Lake Washington, which once flowed south into the Green-Duwamish Basin, now has its outlet to Puget Sound through Lake Union and the Washington Ship Canal. The urbanized character of the land surrounding the Lake has resulted in significant pollution problems in the past. The availability of fresh water during low summer flows will weigh heavily in maintenance of water quality in the Lake Washington Basin.

The largest basin in the SMSA is that of the Snohomish River and its tributaries, the Snoqualmie and Skykomish Rivers. The headwaters of this drainage network receive the heaviest precipitation in the region. Much of the West Fork of the Snoqualmie has been logged but the remainder of the basin is rugged and densely forested. The Snohomish River flows through a broad valley and empties into Puget Sound at Everett. The mouth of the Snohomish is heavily industrialized and polluted in the vicinity of the numerous sulfite mills.

2. HISTORY OF POLLUTION CONTROL

The seaport of Seattle was established in 1865 and grew rapidly. Its sewage was discharged into Puget Sound, but as the community grew, wastes also began to be discharged into Lake Washington. Rapid urbanization along the lake required diversion of all sewerage into Puget Sound in the 1930's.

Residential and commercial expansion on the eastern and northern shores of Lake Washington caused deterioration of the lake to recommence as both raw and treated sewage again flowed into it. In 1955, the appearance of Oscillatoria rubescens, an algal species indicative of impending eutrophication, marked the decline of the recreational value of the lake. Coincident with deterioration of water quality, Lake Washington experienced an increase in nutrient levels, a decline in fish populations and an overall decrease in dissolved oxygen concentrations (Edmondson in METRO, 1969, pp. 22-23).

Recent pollution in Seattle has not been limited to Lake Washington and its tributaries. Algal blooms in Green Lake within Seattle resembled those of Lake Washington. The Duwamish River estuary received untreated or partially treated industrial and domestic sewage, lowering dissolved oxygen levels and endangering the anadromous fish populations for which the river is famous. High bacterial levels in Elliot Bay and elsewhere along the Sound caused closing of coastal beaches as recently as the late 1960's. Before 1957, 70,000,000 gallons per day of raw sewage were discharged into Puget Sound. Pulp mills along the Sound, especially near Everett, had a very pronounced local pollution effect. To complicate the situation, there existed numerous new communities, each with an independent sewer district lacking the finances to release sewage anywhere but in the nearest water body. It was evident that the deterioration of the waters around Seattle would not cease unless radical and innovative changes were enacted. The answer to the problem was to be found on a regional scale in the Metro project.

In 1956, the Metropolitan Problems Advisory Committee was established by the mayor of Seattle and the Board of King County Commissioners. This committee formulated legislation proposing an organization with the powers to solve the pollution-generated problems plaguing the Seattle metropolitan area. The plan was ratified by the Washington State Legislature in 1957 and authorized, pending voter approval, creation of a metropolitan corporation empowered to handle six governmental functions: sewage disposal, transportation, comprehensive planning, park administration, water supply and garbage disposal. After one failure, a modified version of the proposal was ratified by the voters in 1958, establishing a Metropolitan Council empowered to regulate sewage disposal in King County.

Citizen participation in a larger-scale volunteer effort succeeded
in gaining majority approval. The officials of the Metro Council were the elected officials of all local municipal governments. The organization was officially entitled Municipality
of Metropolitan Seattle (METRO). This was the first time that
an independent municipal governmental unit was established with
the sole purpose of fighting urban water pollution. Beginning
in 1961, a ten-year construction program costing $125,000,000
established an overall sewage network (Figure 13.23) to eliminate the discharge of untreated wastes anywhere in the Metro
district. Two major treatment plants and three minor ones con-
solidated facilities and provided secondary treatment of all
influent. The West Point plant now services the west side of
Lake Washington, while the Renton treatment plant handles the
eastern side of the lake. Three minor treatment plants are
located on Puget Sound at Richmond Beach, Carkeek Park and Alki.
The construction was financed by a two dollar per month sewage
charge per unit. Construction was completed eighteen months
ahead of schedule and subsequent plans for expansion of service
were formulated. The massive network was expanded by annexa-
tion and contract affiliation during the initial ten year construction period. As urbanization progresses into the northern
and eastern suburbs, sewage trunk lines will also be extended.

Other characteristics of the Metro Comprehensive Sewage
Plan included

1) Disposal of all sludge in a treatment lagoon at the
West Point plant. Sludge had previously been dis-
posed of via a diffuser into Puget Sound off West
Point with no adverse effects noted since 1965.

2) The CATAD system (Computer Augmented Treatment and
Disposal) a series of computer-controlled regulator
and pumping stations which are designed to minimize
overflows of sewage and stormwaters.

3) A widespread comprehensive water quality monitoring
network which records all data in computerized form.

After 1961, discharge of effluent into Lake Washington was
gradually reduced until disposal in the lake was discontinued
by 1968. Lake Washington reacted to the diversion by reverting
back to its earlier unpolluted condition, slowly at first,
but with improving clarity as the algal blooms moderated.
Nutrient levels decreased and dissolved oxygen levels improved

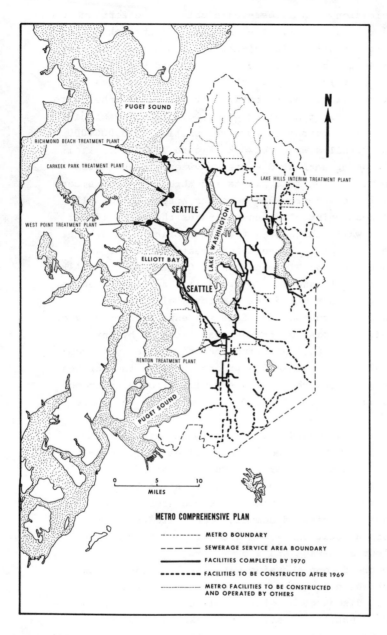

PUGET SOUND

RICHMOND BEACH TREATMENT PLANT

CARKEEK PARK TREATMENT PLANT

LAKE HILLS INTERIM TREATMENT PLANT

SEATTLE

WEST POINT TREATMENT PLANT

LAKE WASHINGTON

ELLIOTT BAY

SEATTLE

RENTON TREATMENT PLANT

PUGET SOUND

N

0   5   10
MILES

METRO COMPREHENSIVE PLAN

---------- METRO BOUNDARY

— — — SEWERAGE SERVICE AREA BOUNDARY

——— FACILITIES COMPLETED BY 1970

------- FACILITIES TO BE CONSTRUCTED AFTER 1969

.... METRO FACILITIES TO BE CONSTRUCTED
AND OPERATED BY OTHERS

Figure 13.23

SEWERAGE
NETWORK OF
THE SEATTLE
REGION

to the point that swimming and recreational activities were completely resumed.

The construction of the Metro sewer system reduced the number of sewage outfalls in the Seattle area from forty-six to zero within ten years. The overall water quality improved to where it is very much in evidence in the low overall PI values arrived at for stations in King County. (See Table 13.8 in Section d following.)

The Seattle CBD on Elliot Bay is expected to be revitalized as the quality of the waters improves. Many new parks and beaches are being constructed along the shores, especially around Fort Lawton at West Point. The recreational value of Green Lake has been reestablished as the algal blooms have been checked by an innovative experiment. The lake is flushed several times a year by pumping in water from the nutrient-poor municipal water supply.

3. DERIVATION OF WATER QUALITY INDEXES

a. WATER USE GROUPINGS

As in the original Syracuse Index, multiple-use groupings were established to derive water quality indexes for the region. In the case of Seattle, this necessitated a double set of groupings, one for freshwater streams and lakes and one for marine waters. Refinement of the multiple-use groupings was required to conform to the regional economy. Table 13.4 lists freshwater and marine water uses.

Three general use categories comparable to the original Syracuse categories were employed. The first category (j=1) included any water uses which involved immediate or eventual human consumption. This included waters used in food preparation which must meet rigid standards comparable to those for drinking water. Direct-contact recreational sports such as swimming and water skiing were considered human consumption water uses because of the potential ingestion of pollutants associated with them.

The second category (j=2) encompasses all agricultural uses and fish and wildlife habitats. The components of this group are products which may eventually be consumed by humans after being processed and cooked, that is, after subsequently being transferred to a first category water use group. The monitoring of toxic elements and pesticides is crucial for this group to prevent their absorption into animal tissue and vegetable fiber.

The final use grouping (j=3) contains all remote contact

TABLE 13.4

MULTIPLE USE GROUPINGS FOR FRESH AND MARINE WATERS

Use Grouping	Fresh Waters	Marine Waters
Human Consumption and Direct Contact Uses (j=1)	Drinking use Swimming and water skiing (direct recreational use) Beverage manufacturing } eventual Industrial food prepar- } human con- ation } sumption	Human water contact use--swimming and water skiing Food fish canning and preparation
Wildlife Habitat and Indirect Contact Uses (j=2)	Fish and shellfish reproduction, rearing and harvest Agricultural use (irrigation and stock watering) Wildlife habitat	Salmon rearing Other food fish Shellfish Wildlife habitat
Recreational and Industrial Remote Contact Uses (j=3)	Aesthetic and recreational (picnicking, hiking, fishing, boating and palin visitation) Commerce and navigation Power production Fish passage Industrial cooling water Industrial process use Log storage and rafting Liquid waste transport	Fish passage Aesthetics (environmental) Recreational (boating, picnicking, hiking and plain visitation) Commercial fishing and fish passage Industrial water use Navigation Log storage and rafting Liquid waste transport

uses which do not involve human contact or consumption. Recreational and industrial activities account for most uses of the water body. Fish passage and recreational and commercial fishing are also included with the assumption that the fish are spawned and reared elsewhere in waters meeting quality limits for the j=2 grouping and that they will be processed or cooked in waters meeting the criteria of the first use grouping. A great amount of diversity exists in tolerance levels for individual uses in the third category, especially for industrial requirements.

b. PERMISSIBLE QUALITY LEVELS FOR USE GROUPINGS

The criteria against which the water quality data were tested were derived from a combination of the water quality standards for the State of Washington and suggested criteria for specific water uses gleaned from a multiplicity of sources.

The water quality standards of Washington State are fairly high but are justifiable because of the overall good natural quality of water in the state. As is the case throughout the country, Washinton standards are nebulous. Only five of the many parameters monitored by the several state or local agencies have legislated minimum values. Minimum values for other parameters have not been established because of the need for additional research on their effects and their complex relationship to the water body. In other cases no toxic level is known or else toxicity levels may vary too greatly to permit a criterion to be extablished for a specific parameter. Legislated standards often specify a certain level above natural (and thus arbitrary) conditions.

The Washington State standards were established in 1967 and 1970 and approval of 1973 revised standards is pending. Only minor changes are expected and those deal with expanding watercourse classification. The waters of the state are divided into five watercourse classifications, with a specific set of standards allotted to each. The standards do not permit degradation of water quality in any of the five classifications and are oriented towards protecting local fisheries and recreational uses.

To permit full application of the Syracuse Index, additional criteria were developed for the parameters not covered by the state standards. Values were ascertained from a plethora of acknowledged works on water quality standards. For each multiple-use grouping, a median was chosen based on minimum accepted cri-

teria for each use within the grouping. The median was used instead of the average to minimize the tendency of the more liberal
water use tolerances to create an average criterion unacceptable
for many of the other uses. This alteration of the original
index construction was made feasible by the availability of more
data on suggested criteria for each use. The state standards
served as a guideline for establishing use groupings based on
watercourse classification. The A, B and C classifications contained criteria for the j=1, j=2, j=3 use groupings, respectively.
Table 13.5 shows the criteria used to evaluate the water quality
data.

For marine stations, only those five parameters with numerical criteria specified in the state standards were used. Few
variables other than those five are monitored by networks in
Puget Sound (Table 13.6).

The standards against which to measure recorded data tended
to be stringent because of the decision to use median values.
Selections were also influenced by a previous work proposing
water quality criteria for Washington. Sylvester and Rambow
(1968) advocated high water quality standards for long range
benefits and favored goal-oriented rather than standard-oriented
planning. Three basic principles were recognized by them:

1) Maintain original water quality;

2) Maintain the value of each parameter at that point dictated by the most critical use of the water in question;

3) Set requirements more restrictive than necessary to serve
   beneficial uses, to assume high water quality with expanded usage in the future.

The authors tended to favor the third principle as is indicated by their comment "In other words, high standards are proposed in an attempt to preserve the high quality of rivers at
least long enough for assimilative capacity and waste transport
capacity to be more effectively distributed among the maximum
number of users." (Sylvester and Rambow, p. 118)

c. DATA SOURCES AND CHARACTERISTICS

Data were obtained from the EPA STORET system through the
Region X office in Seattle. A PGM-INVENT request was made for
all stations within the general boundaries of the Seattle-Everett
SMSA for all data recorded between 1970-1972. Because of STORET
delays, data for the other twelve regions were unavailable, and when
Chicago materials were delivered, errors were found that caused
STORET to re-examine and then to modify its basic programs. Even
the Seattle data finally had to be hand pulled for the study to be
done on time.

TABLE 13.5

PERMISSIBLE QUALITY LEVELS FOR VARIOUS
FRESHWATER USES IN THE STATE OF WASHINGTON

Use	Parameter*													
	1	2	3	4	5	6	7	8	9	10	11	12	13	14
(A) j=1	18.5	5	5	6.5-8.5	240	500	5	10	150	100	250	.35	250	8.0
(B) j=2	21.0	10	10	6.5-8.5	1000	500	10	10	150	125	250	.35	250	6.5
(C) j=3	24.0	10	10	6.0-9.0	1000	500	10	45	75	100	250	.11	250	5.0

TABLE 13.6

PERMISSIBLE QUALITY LEVELS FOR VARIOUS
MARINE WATER USES IN THE STATE OF WASHINGTON

Use	Parameter*				
	1	3	4	5	14
(A) j=1	16.0	5	7.8-8.5	70	6.0
(B) j=2	19.0	10	7.8-8.5	1000	5.0
(C) j=3	24.0	10	6.0-9.0	1000	4.0

Source: Water Pollution Control Commission, State of Washington, "A Regulation Relating to Water Quality Standards for Interstate and Coastal Waters of the State of Washington and a Plan for Implementation and Enforcement of Such Standards, 1967.

*Parameters:

	Units	STORET Number
1 Temperature	° C	00010
2 Color	Platinum-Cobalt Units	00080
3 Turbidity	Jackson Turbidity Units	00070
4 pH	Standard Units	00400, 00403
5 Total Coliform Bacteria	/100 ml	31501, 31504
6 Total Dissolved Solids	mg/l	70300, 70301
7 Suspended Solids	mg/l	00530
8 Total Nitrogen	mg/l	00605, 00610, 00615, 00620, 71850
9 Total Alkalinity	mg/l	00410
10 Total Hardness	mg/l	00900
11 Chloride	mg/l	00940
12 Total Iron and Manganese	mg/l	01045, 01055
13 Sulfate	mg/l	00945
14 Dissolved Oxygen	mg/l	00300

Source for parameters 1, 3, 4, 5, 14: Water Pollution Control Commission, State of Washington, "A Regulation Relating to Water Quality Standards for Interstate and Coastal Waters of the State of Washington and a Plan for Implementation and Enforcement of Such Standards," 1967.

Remaining criteria derived from the following:
a) American Water Works Association, "Water Quality and Treatment," 1950.
b) Eugene Brown, M.W. Skougstad and M.J. Fishman, "Methods for Collection and Analysis of Water Samples for Dissolved Minerals and Gasses," U.S. Geological Survey Techniques of Water-Resources Investigation, 1970.
c) California State Water Pollution Control Board, 1952.
d) California State Water Quality Control Board, Water Quality Criteria, 1963.
e) John D. Hem, "Study and Interpretation of the Chemical Characteristics of Natural Water," 1970.
f) R.O. Sylvester and Carl A. Rambow, Methodology in Establishing Water-Quality Standards in Water Resources Management and Public Policy, 1968.
g) U.S. Federal Water Pollution Control Administration, Committee on Water Quality Criteria, 1968.
h) U.S. Public Health Service, "Drinking Water Standards," 1962.

The parameters selected for use in the index were the same as used in our earlier application, with these changes:

1) Total coliform bacteria replaced fecal coliform because of the greater availability of the former in the data record.

2) Total hardness was used instead of carbonate hardness because the latter was not monitored in most cases.

3) The metric system was used to conform to the terms in which the data were recorded. (Since 1967, the U.S. Geological Survey has used the metric system and it is expected that other monitoring agenices will also switch to the system.)

4) Water temperature was recorded in degrees Centigrade and used in that form.

In general, nine to twelve of the fourteen parameters were available for each station, a marked contrast from the paucity of data encountered in preliminary testing of the Syracuse Index and reported in Part B. Total Iron and Manganese and Suspended Solids were the least available parameters for our Seattle data set.

Mean annual water temperatures ranged from below freezing in the mountains to greater than 15°C near Puget Sound. Although temperature is usually indicative only of thermal pollution, it is a factor which regulates the levels of the other constituents of the water body and maintenance of the state's fisheries. The lack of frequent and well-distributed readings at some stations may have altered the effectiveness of the index slightly.

Color levels were relatively high when measured against the goals of 5 to 10 mg/l. The tolerable color values for nearly all states or agencies which suggest color standards specify 5 or 10 mg/l above natural levels. Since natural levels vary seasonally and areally, no number can be assigned to be a standard 5 or 10 mg/l above natural levels. However, since the water quality index measures suitability of water for multiple uses, the goal values were used to evaluate total color.

Color intensity is related to turbidity, suspended solids and the presence of iron and manganese. High natural amounts of those parameters in the streams near Seattle are attributable to the glacial outwash environment and the competence of those streams to transport large amounts of silt.

Total iron and manganese were included in the list of parameters investigated because of their reported abundance in groundwater in parts of King County, making them the sole restriction on an otherwise excellent water source. The two minerals are derived from the weathering of volcanic rock and enter the system as surface runoff or in springs or groundwater inflow. For purposes of this study, total iron and manganese proved to be a disappointment because most river stations do not monitor the parameter and only lake stations provided the data.

Total coliform bacteria per 100 ml was used in the water quality evaluation because of their availability in the records of most monitors. Several tests are used by collecting agencies but the results differ only slightly. Fecal coliform bacteria are monitored by the METRO network but those data were not yet available from the STORET system. Fecal coliform are still considered a better indicator of pollution than total coliform and should be used when available.

Total dissolved solids (residue at 180°C), when not given, were determined approximately by multiplying specific conductance by the conversion factor of .65. Although the conversion factor varies from stream to stream under different climatic conditions, it was deemed applicable to freshwater streams of Washington. Total dissolved solids were not determined for marine stations because of the nonlinearity of the regression line at higher conductivity values. Extreme dilution also affects the conductivity-TDS relationship, but in a converse manner and not as strongly as salinity. Its influence is not observable near the headwaters. (Hen, 1971, p.96-102)

In several instances, total dissolved solids (residue at 105°C) were determined by subtracting non-filtrable residue (STORET # 00530) from total solids (STORET # 00500). Residues at 105°C differ only slightly from those at 180°C in that not as many trace minerals precipitate out at the lower temperature.

Total nitrogen as used in the index is the sum of nitrogen in its several forms found in water. The major component of this parameter is nitrate. Ammonia nitrogen, nitrite and organic nitrogen are also present but the absence of one or more of them in the data record will not significantly alter the sensitivity of the parameter to industrial, organic and agricultural pollutants. Nitrogen, especially nitrate, is important for selecting drinking water sources since levels above 10 mg/l can cause cyanosis in infants.

Alkalinity of natural waters is usually the product of weathering of carbonates. High alkalinity values are associated with contamination by hydroxides of industrial and sewage origins. They may also indicate controlled water flow such as irrigation or modification by flood control ditches.

Hardness is an important variable in measuring industrial and drinking water quality. High values indicate pollution by an excess of magnesium from industrial sources.

The chloride and sulfate tolerance levels chosen were the generally accepted 250 mg/l although more conservative estimates have been proposed. Sylvester and Rambow suggested 20 mg/l for chloride and 30 mg/l for sulfate standards.

In the Seattle area many factors, both freshwater and marine, cause variations in dissolved oxygen concentrations. For this reason DO readings are taken frequently both manually or electro-chemically by automatic monitors. A saturation level of 10 mg/l was assumed for calculations. Saturation concentrations are usually slightly higher in cold freshwater streams and slightly lower in marine waters.

d.   RESULTS OF DATA ANALYSIS--PI INDEX VALUES

PI values were calculated for a total of 160 receptor stations. Of that amount ninety stations were located on rivers and lakes and seventy were located in marine waters (Figure 13.24). The unavailability of METRO data from STORET did not permit as thorough a coverage of the Duwamish estuary as was hoped but the abundance of water quality stations along Puget Sound and upstream from the estuary provided a sufficient overall view of Seattle's waters. Several lake stations were included within the river grouping.

Tabel 13.7 lists the refined data used in the index. All calculations were done by computer in two separate runs, one for freshwater stations and one for marine stations. The results are shown in Table 13.8. All overall PI values for freshwater stations were below one, thus classifying the waters around them as unpolluted. Only eight of the ninety freshwater stations had specific PI values above one and those were all in the human consumption use category, which used the highest water quality standards. Results for the marine stations were uniformly worse, however. The use of only five parameters and the high criteria for each are believed responsible for the results obtained.

By comparing the range of index values for each station with the water quality criteria used, one can detect the influence of each parameter on the index number for each of the three use groupings. The weight of one pollutant for which the criteria vary can easily be observed in some stations when that pollutant

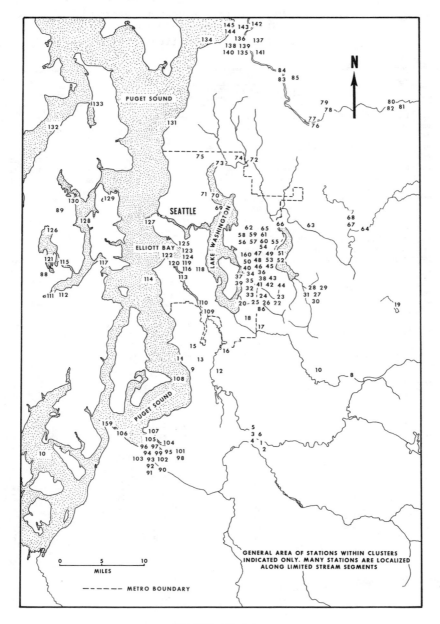

FIGURE 13.24

THE SAMPLING NETWORK OF 160 STATIONS

TABLE 13.7

WATER POLLUTION DATA FOR SEATTLE REGION
MONITORING NETWORK, 1970-1972

(a) Freshwater Stations

NAME	TEMP °C	COLOR	TURBIDITY JTU	pH	TOTAL COLIFORM/ 100 ml	TOTAL DISSOLVED SOLIDS mg/l	SUSPENDED SOLIDS mg/l	TOTAL NITROGEN mg/l	ALKALINITY	HARDNESS mg/l	CHLORIDES mg/l	TOTAL Fe+Mn mg/l	SULFATE mg/l	DO mg/l
01	11.1	14.4	4.2	7.3	279.5	30.0		.30	24.9	21.8	1.5		3.1	11.8
02	11.2	13.1	4.3	7.3	250.6	30.0		.28	25.2	21.8	1.5		3.1	11.8
03	10.3	5.0		7.3	670.6	52.6			29.2	27.2	1.7		4.4	10.7
04	10.1	47.5	5.4	7.4	1291.5	72.4	25.5	.73						10.9
05	10.5	26.3	3.1	7.3	801.1	72.2		.77	38.2	38.1	2.7		7.9	11.2
06	10.0	40.9	4.7	7.4	1048.8	67.6		1.68	37.6	37.4	2.9		8.2	11.4
07	11.1	16.6	4.7	7.2	582.8	44.3		.43	25.1	27.9	4.6			11.5
08	7.6	10.6	2.3	7.5	97.8	35.9		.20						11.9
09	9.9	59.0	7.9	7.5	4263.0	138.4		1.26						10.8
10	7.3	17.0	2.7	7.4	251.4	39.5		.29						11.8
11	11.4	23.2	5.6	7.1	947.1	54.1		.46	29.3	27.2	3.6		4.1	10.7
12	11.4	23.2	5.5	7.1	947.1	53.0		.50	30.2	27.9	3.8		4.1	10.7
13	10.3	69.1	21.5	7.3	5943.5	135.1		1.15						10.3
14	10.3	51.3	11.5	7.6	14718.2	146.6	37.7	1.36						10.8
15	10.2	53.6	10.5	7.4	23217.6	140.9	32.8	1.52						10.6
16	11.3	6.7		7.2	1404.4	69.9		1.57	34.6	32.8	6.1		5.2	10.4
17	10.1	11.5	3.0	7.2	397.6	49.6		.31	30.0	28.6	1.2		3.8	11.6
18	9.0	16.6	3.8	7.3	416.8	50.0		.40						11.8
19	10.3	3.3		6.9	983.3	20.3		.67	10.3	10.3	.7		1.8	11.5
20	10.7	64.8	6.5	7.5	2185.0			1.07						10.8
21	7.3		2.5	6.7	186.7	38.8		.44	20.7					12.1
22	12.8		14.7	7.4	59.0	135.8		.65	59.7	94.7				8.9
23	11.9		59.5	6.0		345.8		.17	197.2	260.7				2.4
24	12.2		6.0	7.8	2.8	654.4		.12	393.8	416.6				10.2
25	12.4		5.0	7.9	43.0	671.9		.14	381.4	412.8				10.1
26	13.3		7.4	7.6	45.3	340.7		.34	74.2	196.7				9.4
27	7.1		2.1	6.6	356.7	39.3		.36	20.7					10.6
28	10.0	30.1	4.9	7.2	1362.5	68.5		4.16						11.3
29	7.8		3.4	6.9	653.3	90.1		1.29	31.0					11.9
30	7.5		3.9	6.8	176.3	51.3		.54	28.7					12.0
31	10.2	24.3	4.9	7.2	1311.3	75.0		3.99	40.6	41.3	2.5		6.8	11.3
32	13.9		11.6	8.1	374.5	512.0		.24	281.7	293.2				9.6
33	14.0		8.0	7.5	224.5	513.0		.46	260.9	283.9				9.4
34	14.8		9.5	7.9	192.5	131.6		.78	75.8	74.4				9.4
35	15.1		8.9	7.9	447.5	470.0		.37	251.5	263.7				9.9
36	13.3		7.9	8.1	221.6	550.1		.21	302.3	315.8				10.0
37	13.1		5.1	8.2	76.8	567.7		.19	356.4	377.8				10.0
38	14.1		6.3	7.7	344.0	223.3		.48	64.0	140.5				9.5
39	15.4		8.1	7.6		444.0		.37	235.3	267.4				10.3
40	15.6		11.4	7.6	695.0	433.8		.31	244.0	257.7				9.9
41	14.5		6.4	7.5	286.7	116.9		.74	68.5	65.8				8.8
42	12.8		11.1	7.3	373.3	132.9		.64	83.0	76.7				6.9
43	12.7	103.5	6.1	7.3	1577.3	131.5	15.8	.52						7.5
44	19.6		10.0	7.5	283.3	141.7		.10	103.3	83.0				1.7
45	15.4		10.6	7.4	377.5	117.5		.34	72.4	67.6				8.6
46	15.0		13.1	7.3	501.3	115.5		1.58	79.3	66.3				8.0
47	12.2	101.6	5.3	7.7	2456.5	118.1	16.2	.75						10.4
48	15.7		12.8	7.4	434.2	99.1		.44	60.2	60.9				8.5

TABLE 13.7 (Cont'd)

NAME	TEMP °C	COLOR	TURBI-DITY JTU	pH	TOTAL COLI-FORM/ 100 ml	TOTAL DISSOLVED SOLIDS mg/l	SUS-PENDED SOLIDS mg/l	TOTAL NITRO-GEN mg/l	ALKA-LINITY	HARD-NESS mg/l	CHLO-RIDES mg/l	TOTAL Fe+Mn mg/l	SUL-FATE mg/l	DO mg/l
49	18.1		14.2	7.7	707.5	157.2		.35	73.6	69.4				8.4
50	18.2		29.1	7.4	586.6	102.4		.24	69.5	69.1				7.2
51	16.1		13.8			117.9		.79	88.0	74.4				4.6
52	15.1		14.1	7.3	732.8	121.9		.82	79.3	81.5				6.3
53	16.8		12.0	7.8	636.3	102.7		.32	60.4	73.4				8.6
54	15.8		12.3	7.5	1045.7	95.7		.70	58.8	60.9				7.7
55	17.2		13.8	7.5		90.4		.47	58.4	56.5				6.1
56	16.3		14.5	7.7	1003.3	89.0		.51	58.7	57.6				9.3
57	11.0	130.2	3.8	7.6	4506.8	98.0		.90						10.5
58	15.9		11.7	7.6	725.8	90.7		.56	58.5	57.7				8.8
59	15.9		34.4	7.6	1153.8	92.3		.51	59.2	59.7				8.1
60	15.6		9.1	7.7	1152.5	98.3		.43	57.2	55.8				8.4
61	10.8	107.5	14.4	7.3	11800.0	91.8		.89						9.8
62	11.9		2.7	7.5		105.3		.31	62.6	60.0				10.0
63	7.8		3.5	6.5	119.7	51.8	23.8	.57	27.0					11.9
64	11.4	3.3		7.1	144.0	32.0		.73	17.0	18.3	.7		3.7	11.5
65	13.2		7.3	7.6	1006.3	94.1		1.63	61.3	56.7				8.6
66	9.5		4.8	6.9	154.3	76.3	4.2	.38	29.3					11.4
67	8.3	24.2	5.5	7.0	1077.0	31.0		.27	15.4	13.8	1.1		2.6	11.7
68	8.8	22.7	4.6	7.0	1175.5	30.8		.27	15.4	13.8	1.1		2.6	11.6
69	10.8	45.0	6.7	7.7	10847.7	151.1	20.3	1.22						10.9
70	11.4	35.3	4.9	7.8	4488.6	170.6	13.2	1.34						10.6
71	10.7	41.7	4.6	7.8	7634.1	146.6	10.7	1.31						10.9
72	12.3	43.4	4.5	7.2	2457.2	86.4		.58	42.8	48.7	3.5		13.9	10.2
73	10.6	45.2	6.5	7.7	5631.8	132.5		1.37						10.8
74	11.7	55.3	4.5	7.1	2408.1	79.6		.61						10.3
75	12.9	51.5	4.9	7.6	917.3	110.8		.46						9.8
76	8.6	17.9	4.3	7.0	579.5	23.9		.22	11.9	14.7	3.0			12.0
77	9.7	6.2	6.2	6.9	544.3	26.9		.26	14.0	18.4	3.3			11.4
78	8.3	15.3	3.5	7.0	168.8	21.3		.15	11.7	12.9	2.4		2.4	12.2
79	10.3	45.8	4.8	7.0	5613.0	45.6		.94	24.1	24.6	3.2		3.8	11.2
80	8.6	13.9	3.3	7.0	187.0	21.4		.19	13.5	11.9	1.2		1.9	12.2
81	9.9	21.6	3.3	6.9	148.5	19.7		.17	11.1	10.7	.5		2.1	11.7
82	9.8	19.4	3.3	6.9	138.2	18.7		.37	12.5	12.3	1.0		2.3	11.7
83	9.5	18.4	5.2	6.9	951.6	27.4		.39	15.7	15.2	1.3		2.8	11.4
84	9.4	23.8	5.2	6.9	900.0	24.9		.31	15.1	14.2	1.3		2.9	11.6
85	11.8	40.9	9.3	7.0	1194.8	37.1		.51	20.7	20.8	2.2		4.2	11.1
86	9.5					59.0	21.0	.81	32.8	40.5	2.8		6.8	
87	7.8	11.1		6.9		17.2		.12	7.0		.9	.02	1.1	
88	16.4	16.7		7.6		62.0			34.3				2.9	
89	15.0	16.8		7.2		38.0		.14	12.7	13.0	3.0	.16	4.1	
160	18.5		26.4	8.7	873.3	110.4		.32	77.6	69.4				8.7

TABLE 13.7 (Cont'd)

(b) Marine Stations

NAME	TEMP °C	COLOR	TURBI-DITY JTU	pH	TOTAL COLI-FORM/ 100 ml	TOTAL DISSOLVED SOLIDS mg/l	SUS-PENDED SOLIDS mg/l	TOTAL NITRO-GEN mg/l	ALKA-LINITY	HARD-NESS mg/l	CHLO-RIDES mg/l	TOTAL Fe+Mn mg/l	SUL-FATE mg/l	DO mg/l
90	10.3		44.7	7.5	4889.4									
91	11.8		4.3	7.6	17568.7									12.3
92	10.7		53.8	7.6	5140.0									8.4
93	11.6		3.5	7.7	6620.0									11.8
94	11.7		9.2	7.7	912.2									8.5
95	11.8		5.6	7.8	474.7									7.9
96	11.2		3.1	7.8	2291.1									9.9
97	10.9		39.7	7.7	2273.3									8.8
98	12.5		6.4	7.8	990.1									7.7
99	11.1		11.0	7.7	1067.0									7.7
100	10.8		1.3	7.9	2.5									8.0
101	12.1		4.3	7.8	161.9									9.6
102	11.7		4.7	7.8	279.6									7.5
103	11.1		2.2	7.8	245.3									8.0
104	11.8		4.7	7.7	154.9									8.9
105	11.7		4.8	7.8	194.1									7.5
106	11.2		2.1	7.8	71.3									9.2
107	10.9		5.1	7.8	415.3									8.7
108	10.8		1.8	7.8	5.1									8.8
109	11.1		32.5	7.3	7100.0									9.0
110	11.8		13.8	7.5	10616.7									13.1
111	12.9		5.2	8.0	56.5									10.0
112	12.4		2.3	8.0	62.3									8.6
113	11.3		9.2	7.8	11300.0									10.9
114	11.1		2.8	7.9	107.7									9.9
115	12.6		1.3	8.1	65.3									9.7
116	11.6		3.5	7.9	66550.0									10.6
117	11.8		2.0	8.0	20.3									9.1
118	10.8		7.6	7.8	193000.0									10.7
119	11.2		6.4	7.8	6816.7									9.3
120	11.2		2.6	7.9	815.0									8.8
121	12.7		3.2	8.1	28.0									9.1
122	10.8		6.0	8.0	157.0									8.8
123	11.1		5.8	7.9	91700.0									9.5
124	11.9		3.8	8.0	41600.0									9.1
125	12.1		5.0	8.1	15600.0									9.6
126	12.8		2.5	8.1	50.5									9.2
127	11.3		4.5	8.0	62.3									10.8
128	12.3		2.5	8.1	4.0									9.9
129	11.7		4.3	8.0										11.1
130	13.0		7.0	8.0	277.3									10.6
131	11.7		3.0	8.1	96.5									9.9
132	11.4		2.3	8.1										9.5
133	11.0		1.7	8.0										8.1
134	11.0		1.8	7.8	310.4									9.0
135	9.0		9.8	7.0	787.5									8.6
136	11.5		5.7	7.2	3922.2									11.4
137	10.8		12.3	7.0	3284.4									7.0
138	11.4		3.8	7.5	4925.5									10.5
139	11.4		4.3	7.5	6020.0									6.3
140	11.4		4.9	7.4	6804.0									6.3
														5.8

TABLE 13.7 (Cont'd)

NAME	TEMP °C	COLOR	TURBI-DITY JTU	pH	TOTAL COLI-FORM/ 100 ml	TOTAL DISSOLVED SOLIDS mg/l	SUS-PENDED SOLIDS mg/l	TOTAL NITRO-GEN mg/l	ALKA-LINITY	HARD-NESS mg/l	CHLO-RIDES mg/l	TOTAL Fe+Mn mg/l	SUL-FATE mg/l	DO mg/l
141	10.2		12.7	7.1	1800.0									10.6
142	11.6		1.3	7.4	6348.8									5.6
143	11.5		8.4	7.5	1713.8									8.2
144	11.9		4.9	7.4	3856.7									4.7
145	11.4		9.3	7.4	2422.2									8.2
146	11.3		16.6	7.4	2674.4									8.6
147	11.3		2.3	7.8	328.4									8.4
148	11.1		13.1	7.2	1840.0									9.9
149	11.7		14.1	7.3	2411.1									9.4
150	10.3		1.7	7.9	3.3									7.3
151	11.1		2.8	7.8	11.0									8.8
152	10.2		2.7	7.7	827.1									8.2
153	10.1		2.6	8.0	12.7									7.7
154	11.5		2.9	8.0	12.3									8.4
155	10.0		4.7	7.9	23.7									7.7
156	9.8		3.4	8.0	16.7									7.4
157	9.3		1.9	7.9	4.3									7.1
158	10.4		23.7	7.7	235.8									8.6
159	10.2		1.8	7.7	7.9									7.6

is far in excess of desired levels. High color and total coliform levels for freshwater stations had the strongest influence
on the results. Coliform concentrations and a more limited pH
range in the marine station data produced slightly higher index
values for that category. However, despite the diversity of
values for each of the PI indexes, the overall index for the
stations selected indicate that Seattle area water quality is
basically good, although some parts of the water body are more
suited to specific uses than others.

    e. POLLUTANT SOURCES

Pollutants of water in the Seattle-Everett SMSA fall into
three source groupings--natural pollutants, agricultural pollutants and industrial and municipal wastes.

Natural pollutants can be either chemical or biological and
either point or area in origin. An example of a natural chemical
pollutant emanating from an area source is the abundance of iron
in groundwater and springs near Puget Sound. The sources may
be very localized or may cover an extensive area. The high hard-

TABLE 13.8

WATER QUALITY INDEXES FOR
SEATTLE MONITORING STATIONS

Obs. No.	PI_1	PI_2	PI_3	Overall PI	Obs. No.	PI_1	PI_2	PI_3	Overall PI
1	0.6165	0.5985	0.3463	0.5204	81	0.5069	0.6007	0.3065	0.4714
2	0.6293	0.5978	0.3488	0.5253	82	0.5059	0.6005	0.3042	0.4702
3	0.7285	0.6172	0.4937	0.6131	83	0.4778	0.7019	0.6916	0.6238
4	0.7199	0.6165	0.3910	0.5758	84	0.5080	0.6674	0.6550	0.6101
5	0.5517	0.6205	0.5896	0.5873	85	0.6788	0.6875	0.6747	0.6803
6	0.7065	0.6108	0.3781	0.5651	86	0.7337	0.7280	0.3202	0.5940
7	0.6943	0.6105	0.4366	0.5804	87	0.7185	0.7156	0.2885	0.5742
8	0.4450	0.5853	0.2279	0.4194	88	0.7219	0.7180	0.4887	0.6428
9	0.9077	0.6257	0.5670	0.7001	89	0.7280	0.7232	0.4479	0.6330
10	0.4487	0.5907	0.2227	0.4207	90	1.3241	0.6390	0.3047	0.7559
11	0.5066	0.7033	0.6936	0.6345	91	1.7162	0.8969	0.3526	0.9886
12	0.5068	0.7034	0.6937	0.6346	92	1.3398	0.6436	0.3170	0.7668
13	1.0174	0.6311	0.3095	0.6527	93	1.4147	0.6652	0.3465	0.8088
14	1.2974	0.8548	0.3099	0.8207	94	0.8041	0.6775	0.6641	0.7152
15	1.4354	0.9921	0.3078	0.9118	95	0.7288	0.7296	0.4070	0.6218
16	0.5689	0.6221	0.4936	0.5615	96	1.0975	0.7251	0.3350	0.7192
17	0.4709	0.6021	0.3230	0.4653	97	1.0888	0.6684	0.3234	0.6935
18	0.5578	0.5956	0.3063	0.4866	98	0.8376	0.7385	0.7117	0.7626
19	0.4964	0.7174	0.7079	0.6406	99	0.8523	0.6591	0.3293	0.6136
20	0.8067	0.6162	0.4652	0.6294	100	0.6362	0.6523	0.3215	0.5367
21	0.5901	0.5923	0.3875	0.5233	101	0.7339	0.7249	0.3634	0.6074
22	0.6985	0.6391	0.6881	0.6752	102	0.7379	0.7264	0.3535	0.6059
23	0.7880	0.7094	0.7239	0.7404	103	0.7297	0.7228	0.3327	0.5951
24	0.5097	0.6254	0.4343	0.5231	104	0.6822	0.6673	0.3542	0.5679
25	0.7419	0.6322	0.3772	0.5838	105	0.7357	0.7254	0.3526	0.6045
26	0.5403	0.6403	0.7228	0.6345	106	0.7234	0.7210	0.3340	0.5928
27	0.6519	0.6530	0.4357	0.5802	107	0.7271	0.7278	0.3707	0.6086
28	0.7300	0.6101	0.3570	0.5657	108	0.7231	0.7198	0.3214	0.5881
29	0.5082	0.6030	0.4792	0.5301	109	1.4385	0.6347	0.3293	0.8008
30	0.5803	0.5951	0.3449	0.5067	110	1.5588	0.7407	0.3489	0.8828
31	0.7404	0.6179	0.4114	0.5899	111	0.6501	0.6623	0.3881	0.5669
32	0.5584	0.6303	0.4232	0.5373	112	0.6525	0.6419	0.3706	0.5550
33	0.6830	0.6322	0.5771	0.6308	113	1.5820	0.7781	0.6564	1.0055
34	0.6128	0.7100	0.6954	0.6727	114	0.6404	0.6541	0.3326	0.5424
35	0.6956	0.7082	0.6954	0.6997	115	0.6767	0.6411	0.3762	0.5647
36	0.6835	0.6346	0.5757	0.6313	116	2.1275	1.3083	0.3497	1.2618
37	0.5304	0.6320	0.4023	0.5215	117	0.6268	0.6425	0.3523	0.5405
38	0.5599	0.6376	0.6288	0.6088	118	2.4527	1.6400	0.5459	1.5462
39	0.6506	0.6587	0.6468	0.6521	119	1.4259	0.7351	0.4591	0.8733
40	0.6457	0.6439	0.6344	0.6414	120	0.7790	0.6665	0.5846	0.6767
41	0.5764	0.6470	0.6711	0.6315	121	0.6472	0.6561	0.3806	0.5613
42	0.6098	0.6654	0.5587	0.6113	122	0.6357	0.6563	0.4325	0.5748
43	0.9605	0.7461	0.4427	0.7265	123	2.2215	1.4082	0.4193	1.3497
44	0.6984	0.7482	0.7321	0.7262	124	1.9817	1.1622	0.3590	1.1676
45	0.6166	0.6439	0.7047	0.6551	125	1.6804	0.8608	0.3655	0.9689
46	0.6097	0.6571	0.4895	0.5854	126	0.6293	0.6405	0.3830	0.5510
47	0.9549	0.7411	0.3858	0.6940	127	0.6647	0.6511	0.3405	0.5521
48	0.6274	0.6449	0.5907	0.6210	128	0.6186	0.6376	0.3679	0.5413
49	0.7266	0.6579	0.7255	0.7033	129	0.6297	0.6452	0.3514	0.5421
50	0.7307	0.6702	0.6825	0.6945	130	0.6364	0.6570	0.5051	0.5995
51	0.6706	0.6972	0.5391	0.6356	131	0.6364	0.6508	0.3517	0.5463
52	0.6323	0.6804	0.5995	0.6374	132	0.6474	0.6598	0.3412	0.5495
53	0.6753	0.6513	0.6015	0.6427	133	0.6399	0.6547	0.3283	0.5410
54	0.6358	0.6475	0.5731	0.6188	134	0.7300	0.7230	0.3301	0.5944
55	0.6794	0.6651	0.5664	0.6370	135	0.7615	0.7170	0.7059	0.7281
56	0.6564	0.6318	0.5739	0.6207	136	1.2517	0.6795	0.4097	0.7803
57	1.0337	0.8124	0.3313	0.7258	137	1.2000	0.6480	0.3222	0.7234
58	0.6367	0.6446	0.5793	0.6202	138	1.3260	0.6815	0.3396	0.7824
59	0.6485	0.6501	0.5776	0.6254	139	1.3884	0.6830	0.3401	0.8038
60	0.6284	0.6724	0.6708	0.6572	140	1.4275	0.6885	0.3518	0.8226
61	1.2252	0.7858	0.3219	0.7776	141	1.0154	0.6442	0.3038	0.6545
62	0.5191	0.6205	0.6047	0.5814	142	1.4004	0.6856	0.3441	0.8101
63	0.7389	0.7274	0.4850	0.6504	143	0.9979	0.6680	0.5990	0.7550
64	0.4965	0.6000	0.3487	0.4817	144	1.2542	0.6934	0.3561	0.7679
65	0.5659	0.6459	0.6036	0.6052	145	1.1047	0.6768	0.6633	0.8149
66	0.7171	0.6096	0.3637	0.5635	146	1.1371	0.6612	0.3347	0.7110
67	0.5120	0.6016	0.4032	0.5056	147	0.7318	0.7239	0.3396	0.5985
68	0.6844	0.6022	0.3409	0.5425	148	1.0225	0.6499	0.3298	0.6674
69	1.1996	0.7687	0.4848	0.8177	149	1.1054	0.6549	0.3470	0.7024
70	0.9426	0.6292	0.3631	0.6449	150	0.6590	0.6693	0.3071	0.5452
71	1.0999	0.6571	0.3406	0.6992	151	0.7265	0.7210	0.3311	0.5929
72	0.7679	0.6375	0.4338	0.6130	152	0.7760	0.6658	0.5917	0.6779
73	0.9928	0.6273	0.4699	0.6967	153	0.6555	0.6648	0.3028	0.5410
74	0.7782	0.6270	0.3559	0.5870	154	0.6503	0.6605	0.3442	0.5517
75	0.7491	0.6787	0.6620	0.6966	155	0.6881	0.6694	0.3385	0.5653
76	0.6358	0.6013	0.4276	0.5549	156	0.6604	0.6675	0.2949	0.5409
77	0.4678	0.6201	0.4684	0.5188	157	0.6608	0.6705	0.2779	0.5364
78	0.5315	0.5911	0.2638	0.4621	158	0.5490	0.6585	0.3100	0.5392
79	1.0086	0.6272	0.3618	0.6659	159	0.6513	0.6625	0.3032	0.5390
80	0.5821	0.5908	0.2697	0.4809	160	0.7440	0.6623	0.6543	0.6869

ness values in Coal Creek is another illustration of a chemical
pollutant.

Agricultural pollutants are composed chiefly of nitrates
from fertilizers, high alkalinity levels from irrigation ditches
and biological wastes in the form of runoff from pastures. These
contaminants would be most evident in the alluvial valley of the
Green River where the main agriculture is carried on.

The third category of pollutant sources is entirely man-
made and is the major source of pollution in the Seattle area.
Nearly all municipal sewage is discharged into the Metro sewer
system. A good deal of the industrial sewage in the district is
also discharged to the sewer system. However, much of the industrial wastes are discharged into the Duwamish and Cedar Rivers
and into Puget Sound. The heaviest concentration of these discharges is in the Duwamish waterway where the major industrial
sources are grouped. To evaluate the effect of industrial wastes
on water quality, a RAPP retrieval was requested from the EPA
STROET system for the year 1971. Detailed information was obtained for all industries which have filed an application for a
permit to discharge effluent into the waterways within the EPA
region. Only a portion of the total discharge is accounted for
by the retrieved information but it is sufficient to elucidate
the concentrations of industry. Figure 13.25 shows the locations
of pipes discharging effluent into the region's waterways. The
heaviest grouping of industrial discharges is at the mouth of
the Duwamish River. (RAPP is STORET's Retrieval and Report Procedure)

f. DIFFUSION OF EFFLUENTS

The high volumes of water in the region tends to diffuse
the effluent to tolerable levels within a short distance downstream from the discharge point. The circulation in the Sound
causes rapid dissipation of pollutants throughout the year except
in areas of highly concentrated discharge near pulp mills of
Tacoma and Everett. During low-summer flow the problem of pollution becomes more serious because of the lessened volume of
the transport medium.

g. MONITORING OF EFFLUENTS BY RECEPTOR NETWORK

Several governmental agencies maintain water-quality moni-
toring networks in the Seattle-Everett SMSA. They include the
Municipality of Metropolitan Seattle (METRO), the Washington
State Department of Ecology, the U.S. Geological Survey and the
Environmental Protection Agency. Figure 13.26 shows the locations

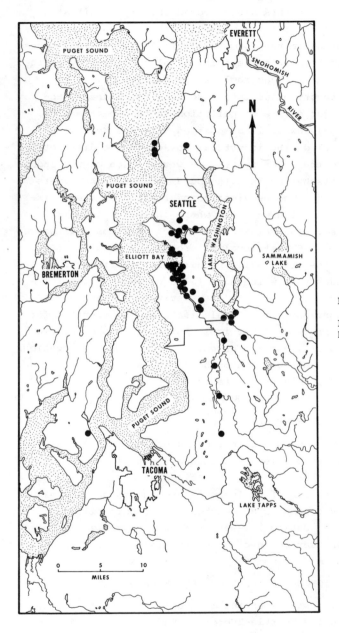

FIGURE 13.25

LOCATION OF
DISCHARGES

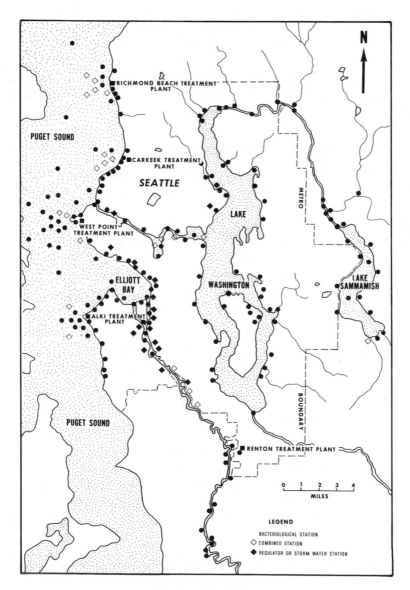

N

RICHMOND BEACH TREATMENT PLANT

PUGET SOUND

CARKEEK TREATMENT PLANT

SEATTLE

LAKE

METRO

WEST POINT TREATMENT PLANT

ELLIOTT BAY

WASHINGTON

LAKE SAMMAMISH

ALKI TREATMENT PLANT

PUGET SOUND

BOUNDARY

RENTON TREATMENT PLANT

```
0  1  2  3  4
    MILES
```

LEGEND

● BACTERIOLOGICAL STATION
◇ COMBINED STATION
◆ REGULATOR OR STORM WATER STATION

FIGURE 13.26

SEATTLE'S RECEPTOR NETWORK

of water quality monitoring stations within the METRO area.
These stations are operated on a cooperative basis between METRO
and the other agencies and include several automatic monitors
which measure temeprature, pH, DO and specific conductance. Many
other receptor stations are located within the SMSA and sample
daily, weekly or monthly. Supplemental data are generated by
cooperative research programs aimed at correlating changes in
land use and sewerage network planning with their effects on the
water body as detected at the monitors. The Fisheries Research
Institute and the University of Washington participate in these
programs.

     h.   DATA STORAGE AND RETRIEVAL

    Water quality data recorded by network monitors are collected
by participating agencies and transferred to the STORET system of
EPA. Information is freely exchanged and available for regional
planning uses.

    Variables recorded by automatic monitors are telemetered
hourly to receiving centers and converted electronically to tape-
punched or printed form for storage. All other data are eventually computerized including lists of major dischargers into
individual drainage basins as well as sewage data.

IV. AIR QUALITY AND URBAN FORM: SOME COMPARISONS

    Earlier, it was suggested that, holding city size and the
urban economic base constant, the more dispersed urban form
should have the more serious problems of environmental quality.
To examine this relationship in more detail, a request was made
to the Environmental Protection Agency that data be provided on
air pollution measures for all stations on the National Air
Sampling Network (NASN) recording information in the National
Aerometric Data Bank for the thirteen sample urban regions and
for the larger Air Quality Central Regions within which they are
located. The information returned was of quarterly frequency
distribution readings for two pollutants, particulates and sulfur dioxide, with stations classified according to location
(central city-suburbs) and also according to land use in the area
within which the monitoring station is located (commercial, industrial, residential). Numbers of stations of each type for
which data were provided for each city are indicated in Table
13.9. Table 13.10 shows the geometric means available for each

TABLE 13.9

DISTRIBUTION OF NASN STATIONS

| | Central City | | | Suburbs | | | |
	Commercial	Industrial	Residential	Commercial	Industrial	Residential	Totals
Chicago	3	4	16	0	0	1	24
Washington	4	1	2	0	0	1	8
Detroit	4	2	4	0	0	0	10
Los Angeles	0	1	0	0	0	0	1
Providence	1	3	0	0	0	0	4
Akron	0	0	0	0	0	0	0
Cincinnati	5	0	0	2	2	3	12
Denver	4	0	1	0	1	2	8
Seattle	3	0	0	1	0	0	4
Indianapolis[a]	1	0	0	0	0	0	1
Birmingham	2	2	0	0	0	2	6
Oklahoma City	3	1	0	3	0	5[b]	12
Jacksonville	0	0	0	0	0	0	0

[a]fifteen other stations provided without location or land use.

[b]includes "rural."

TABLE 13.10

AIR POLLUTION BY LAND USE AND LOCATION
Data are geometric means in parts per cubic meter.

| | | Central City | | | Suburbs | | |
		Commercial	Industrial	Residential	Commercial	Industrial	Residential
Chicago	Part.	66.6	26.4	32.3	-----	-----	23.2
	SO_2	17.5	0.2	0.2	-----	-----	0.1
Washington	Part.	84.5	66.6	85.5	-----	-----	51.5
	SO_2	14.9	-----	20.3	-----	-----	-----
Detroit	Part.	106.8	176.5	101.8	-----	-----	-----
	SO_2	9.5	-----	-----	-----	-----	-----
Los Angeles	Part.	-----	134.6	-----	-----	-----	-----
	SO_2	-----	17.9	-----	-----	-----	-----
Providence	Part.	110.4	86.6	-----	-----	-----	-----
	SO_2	18.3	52.6	-----	-----	-----	-----
Akron	Part.	-----	-----	-----	-----	-----	-----
	SO_2	-----	-----	-----	-----	-----	-----
Cincinnati	Part.	96.5	-----	-----	83.3	109.8	68.3
	SO_2	15.7	-----	-----	-----	-----	-----
Denver	Part.	134.2	123.2	69.7	-----	114.1	83.0
	SO_2	4.3	-----	-----	-----	-----	-----
Seattle	Part.	53.4	-----	-----	42.4	-----	-----
	SO_2	18.2	-----	-----	-----	-----	-----
Indiana-polis	Part.	86.4	-----	-----	-----	-----	-----
	SO_2	9.2	-----	-----	-----	-----	-----
Birmingham	Part.	131.1	189.7	-----	-----	-----	-----
	SO_2	6.0	-----	-----	-----	-----	-----
Oklahoma City	Part.	95.0	115.5	-----	54.1	-----	55.0
	SO_2	3.0	-----	-----	-----	-----	-----
Jackson-ville	Part.	-----	-----	-----	-----	-----	-----
	SO_2	-----	-----	-----	-----	-----	-----

land use type and location, revealing the enormous gaps in air
quality information that exist.

Enough information was available for particulates in seven
of the thirteen cases to compute pollution intensity gradients,
however, using the same methodology as was used to compute the
thirteen population density gradients earlier in the chapter
(Table 13.11). The results are shown in Table 13.12, using the
following notation:

X_c, X_r pollution concentrations in central city and suburban ring, respectively

A_c, A_r areas

r_c, r_r calculated radii of central city and ring

a_x peak central city intensity

X_p perimeter intensity

B_x pollution intensity gradient

TABLE 13.11

COMPARATIVE POPULATION DENSITY
AND POLLUTION INTENSITY DATA

| | Population Density | | | Pollution Level: Particulates | | |
	Central City	Suburban	Ratio	Central City	Suburban	Ratio
Birmingham	3,786.16	165.815	22.83	168.875	122.073	1.383
Chicago	15,107.80	1,032.48	14.63	32.858	23.289	1.411
Cincinnati	5,787.45	450.318	12.85	96.462	86.328	1.117
Denver	5,409.66	200.01	27.05	131.493	88.079	1.493
Oklahoma City	1,227.01	148.64	8.26	106.673	55.304	1.929
Seattle	5,181.58	203.35	25.48	53.757	42.357	1.269
Washington, D.C.	12,312.70	918.97	13.39	82.046	51.470	1.594

TABLE 13.12

POLLUTION INTENSITY GRADIENTS

Region	X_c	A_c	r_c	a_x	X_r	A_r	r_r	X_p	B_x
Birmingham	168.8	79.5	5.03047	178.428	122.1	2641.5	29.4299	75.4	-3.5008
Chicago	32.8	222.6	8.41758	35.9088	23.2	3497.4	34.4109	13.6	-0.648307
Cincinnati	96.4	78.1	4.98598	98.7783	86.3	2071.9	26.1604	76.2	-0.863071
Denver	131.5	95.2	5.50482	139.845	88.1	3564.8	34.1323	44.7	-2.78755
Oklahoma City	106.6	299.1	9.75737	137.201	55.3	1843.4	26.1147	4	-5.10062
Seattle	53.7	112.9	5.99476	55.9264	42.3	4116.1	36.6896	30.9	-0.682111
Washington	82	61.4	4.42088	87.8776	51.5	2290.6	27.3627	21	-2.4442

If the resulting coefficients are used to rank the seven
cases by order of their peak pollution intensities, the results
are as follows: a_x

Birmingham	178.428
Denver	139.845
Oklahoma City	137.201
Cincinnati	98.7783
Washington	87.8776
Seattle	55.9264
Chicago	35.9088

This ranking is <u>inversely</u> <u>related</u> to that of peak population
densities (a_p) viz:

$$a_x = 147.82 - 0.0028\ a_p \qquad R = 0.679$$

In other words, the urban regions with the lowest density central
cities apparently have the greatest central city particulate
concentrations.

On the other hand, the pollution intensity gradient and
the population density gradient are directly related. The ranking is: B_x

Oklahoma City	-5.10062
Birmingham	-3.5008
Denver	-2.78755
Washington	-2.4442
Cincinnati	-0.86307
Seattle	-0.682111
Chicago	-0.648307

and the regression equation is:

$$B_x = 0.94 + 20.1\ B_p \qquad R = 0.611$$

E   CONCLUSIONS

Once again imagine a "sorting table" as on the following page, with the rows representing the nation's urban regions, the columns reserved for various contaminants of the nation's air, water and land resources, and the cells containing whatever information is currently available on the level, intensity and spatial distribution of environmental pollution in each urban region. What relationships between city characteristics and environmental pollution can be discerned in such a matrix? What role do urban form and the pattern and mix of urban land uses play in producing or reducing pollutant concentrations, and in enhancing or reducing the quality of life in the nation's urban areas? These are the questions that have been addressed in this study, which has thus been directly responsive to Russell E. Train's statement in the October, 1972 editorial of <u>Science</u> that "we know that land use is a basic component of environmental quality, but at this point it is not clear what aspects of land use we should be measuring."

Some of our conclusions are consistent with the results of previous research that has shown environmental pollution to be the direct consequence of wastes being introduced into natural systems in greater quantities than can be absorbed and dispersed by natural processes, this in turn being a result of the growth of large, high-density, industrial cities and increasing reliance on the automobile. The most obvious sorting-table relationship thus is one with the large, high-density, industrial city at one extreme and the smaller, low-density, service-oriented city at the other. The former is afflicted by the worst air, water and noise pollution, and generates the most solid wastes.

What we have added to the previous literature is firm evidence that urban form plays a significant role in translating these basic city characteristics (size, density and the economic base) into land use, and that the land use pattern, as shaped by urban form, is directly related to the nature and intensity of environmental pollution. Most importantly, <u>holding the effects of city size and manufacturing concentration constant</u>, and controlling for an inverse relationship between income levels

SUMMARY SORTING TABLE

GROUP OF CITIES

	4+	2+	5+	1-	3+	6+	3-	1+	5-	2-	4-
	Baltimore	Chicago	Akron	Birmingham	Bridgeport	Flint	Cincinnati	Atlanta	Honolulu	Albuquerque	Denver
	Buffalo	Milwaukee	Allentown-Bethlehem	Charleston	Cleveland	Grand Rapids	Jersey City	Boston	Memphis	El Paso	Salt Lake City
	Indianapolis	Minneapolis	Canton	Chattanooga	Hartford	Jacksonville	Kansas City	Columbus		Oklahoma City	
	Los Angeles	Philadelphia	Rochester	Dayton	New Haven	Louisville	San Bernadino	Dallas		Phoenix	
	Washington D.C.	Pittsburgh	Youngstown	Des Moines	Newark	Norfolk	Syracuse	Detroit		Tulsa	
		Portland	York	Gary-Hammond	Providence	Patterson	Wilmington	Fort Worth		Wichita	
		St. Louis		Johnstown		Richmond		Houston			
				Nashville		Toledo		Miami			
				Omaha				New Orleans			
				Reading				New York			
				Utica-Rome				San Antonio			
				Worcester				San Diego			
								San Francisco			
								San Jose			
								Seattle			
								Tampa-St. Petersburg			
KEY URBAN INDICATORS:											
Population (in thousands)	2,285	2,969	557	448	1,040	705	921	2,267	700	525	893
Percent employed in manufacturing	24.2	29.8	43.9	32.5	34.0	29.4	3C.3	22.0	14.7	19.9	16.4
Median family income (in thousands)	11.1	10.9	10.6	9.7	11.4	10.3	10.2	10.4	10.3	9.1	10.4
Urban property values (billions)	25.2	18.5	3.4	3.1	10.3	4.7	8.5	18.8	4.1	3.4	6.6
URBAN FORM INDICATORS:											
Central density (sample city)	17,000	36,022	10,931	7,216	11,867	-	10,558	15,500	-	4,322	10,198
Density gradient (sample city)	-.168	-.1281	-.3244	-.2345	-.2687	-	-.1543	-.107	-	-.1714	-.1498
Radial highways	10.6	10.9	5.0	4.4	1.5	6.6	7.5	8.3	5.5	4.0	7.0
Circumferential highways	3.0	2.7	2.5	1.5	1.6	1.7	1.8	2.4	2.0	3.0	1.5
Open Space Percent	71.1	70.7	78.5	67.3	81.6	82.1	64.1	73.0	-	84.6	83.8
ENVIRONMENTAL QUALITY INDICATORS:											
1. Water											
Dissolved oxygen	7.2	8.0	5.3	7.8	7.1	7.9	7.0	6.9	-	4.9	-
Dissolved solids	865	211	820	353	95	407	4765	448	-	1,894	445
Nitrates	16	16	16	4	4	3	8	19	-	11	11
Average WQ Index	5.1	1.2	2.8	1.6	2.1	2.2	4.5	3.3	-	2.3	1.3
2. Air											
Average SO_2	34	49	38	25	51	20	22	19	16	9	13
Average TSP	115	117	106	119	84	82	104	85	61	84	82
Average AQ Index	3.2	3.4	2.7	3.2	2.7	2.1	2.9	2.3	2.3	2.1	2.2
Average EV Index	9.7	8.4	5.9	10.6	4.2	2.2	5.0	3.5	2.3	3.4	1.1
3. Solid Wastes Generated by individual multipliers	5,897	6,737	1,440	999	2,482	1,434	1,940	4,527	1,174	984	1,564
4. Noise Air travel index	170	228	194	36	99	34	66	152	114	46	110
5. Beta Radiation Deposition	4	88	28	223	129	132	133	19	-	79	92

and pollution (probably an effect of pollution rather than a
cause, via migration of people and activities to the least polluted amenity-rich environments in the past two decades), we
have found that:

1) The core-oriented urban region with a radial transportation network and a steep density gradient

   a) displays greater intensity of land use, a lower per-
      centage of land developed and used for residential
      and commercial purposes, and more open space, and

   b) as a consequence of this land use mix and pattern,
      has superior air and water quality to:

2) The dispersed urban region, which has a less focussed
   transport network and lower, more uniform population
   densities. This urban form

   a) displays urban sprawl, with a higher percentage of
      residential and commercial land use and less open
      space than in the core-oriented case, and

   b) as a consequence of this land use mix, has inferior
      air and water quality.

In what ways are these circumstances of environmental pollution reflected in levels of welfare within cities? It has
been shown that properly-structured economic models of property
values can be given a direct interpretation in terms of the individual's willingness to pay for environmental quality. Does
the same relationship hold between the aggregate property values
of an urban region and the levels of environmental pollution in
that region? If aggregate property values do express streams
of net benefits accruing to land uses within an urban area,
taking into account all benefits and costs, including agglomeration economies and negative externalities, then properly-structured economic models should be capable of interpretation in
terms of the aggregate willingness of urban residents to pay for
whatever advantages their urban region has to offer.

In fact, we have found that the aggregate property values
of urban regions vary directly with their population size (the
elasticity lying between 0.85 and 0.89) and median income levels
(elasticity between 2.14 and 2.33), and inversely with manufacturing concentrations (elasticity between -0.37 and -0.48). A
cubic relationship to city size reveals that net agglomeration
economies are present in urban regions up to a size of 2.5 millions, with maximum property values per capita in urban regions
of around 1 million people, that net diseconomies of greater size
take their toll between 2.5 and 6.0 millions, and that increas-

ing returns are found once again in the largest urban regions.
Most importantly, variables representing levels of environmental
pollution add no explanation to the model not already provided
by size, economic base and income levels. Any depressing effects
of pollution, congestion and crime on the quality of urban life
are expressed in the fact that the elasticity of property values
with respect to population size is less than one, that the coefficient attached to manufacturing concentrations is negative,
and that there is a self-selectivity reflected in the fact that
the relationship to income levels is positive and large.

To complicate matters, the levels of aggregate property
values associated with different urban forms are exactly <u>reverse</u>
of what might be predicted from levels of pollution. Controlling
for the basic city characteristics once again, aggregate property
values are <u>greater</u> in the lower-density dispersed urban region
than in the high-density, core-oriented urban center. This means
either that there are certain real advantages of dispersion that,
in balance, offset the greater pollution levels associated with
this urban form or that there are other negative externalities
present in the core-oriented cities of the U.S. that offset any
positive effects on property values imbued by their relatively
superior levels of environmental quality. Whichever of these
reasons is correct, the rapid continuing decentralization of
American urban regions is consistent with adjustments to urban
form in response to the net benefits of dispersion, while carrying with it the probability that environmental quality will, as
a result, worsen. It is to the issues for public policy raised
by these divergent findings that we turn in the final chapter.

14 THE ENVIRONMENTAL CONSEQUENCES OF ALTERNATIVE URBAN FUTURES

What do the conclusions of this study hold for the evaluation by the Environmental Protection Agency of alternative land use policies? The question resolves itself into two parts: (a) What is the present trend of urban development, and the consequences of the resulting land use patterns for environmental quality? (b) What would be the consequences of achieving some alternative urban form, and which alternative would be least subject to environmental pollution? As a corollary of the second question: Would achievement of the environmentally-superior alternative result in an <u>overall</u> increase or decrease of welfare when additional criteria deriving from a broader concept of the quality of life are considered? It is to these questions that we now turn, in response to EPA's charge to carry out a program that will result in the protection of the environment of the nation by abating or avoiding pollution, and in particular to the charge to EPA's Office of Research and Development to pursue six goals:

1) The development of appropriate science and technology for setting and enforcing pollution control standards.

2) The full understanding of the environmental impact of that which the Agency is mandated to control.

3) The knowledge of what it "costs" to meet environmental quality standards.

4) Knowledge of the "costs" of not meeting environmental standards (i.e., the benefits to be derived from meeting them).

5) Monitoring, to meet environmental goals.

6) Establishing the means to forecast the long-range effects of societal actions so as to avoid deleterious environmental impacts.

I. CONTEMPORARY URBAN DYNAMICS

To report that decentralization is proceeding apace in American urban regions is neither novel nor startling. Thus, to complement the ample information available elsewhere, we offer two further pieces of evidence about the nature and pace of decentralization particularly relevant to the discussion of urban form: the rapid decline of core-orientation in America's metropolitan regions as evidenced by the rapid decline of retailing in the nation's central business districts; and the changing transport mix in metropolitan regions, as indexed by the decay of public transportation.

1. THE DECLINE OF THE AMERICAN C.B.D.

Data can now be assembled for twenty-five years of change in the retail structure of American urban regions, and several conclusions stand out:

1) Throughout the period the central business district has remained relatively more important in smaller urban regions than in larger ones:

   a) CBD sales as a percentage of total SMSA retail sales continue to decline with population size.

   b) Major outlying retail centers have always accounted for a higher proportion of SMSA retail sales in larger urban regions.

2) But the strength of these relationships has changed dramatically in the period 1948-1967. The slope and intercept of the regression line relating the CBD sales percentage to SMSA population have both declined radically since the Second World War.

3) The declines in CBD shares in all urban regions have been greater than would have been expected on the basis of population growth alone.

4) The change in CBD convenience goods sales has been consistent across all sizes of urban regions. The CBD's of the largest SMSA's were most affected by the decline of shopping goods trade in the period 1958-1963, with losses in smaller urban regions accelerating 1963-1967 as new major outlying retail centers were opened in these regions, too.

Figures 14.1-14.8 provide the evidence. Figure 14.1 shows the declining regression relationship between the CBD sales percentage and the log of SMSA population. Figures 14.2-14.5 show the actual declines of the CBD sales percentage of individual SMSA's in relation to their population growth for each of several regions. Figure 14.6 plots the regressions of the CBD convenience goods sales percentage on polulation, and Figure 14.7 the shopping goods percentage on population. Finally, Figure 14.8 charts the rise of the major outlying regional center.

The evidence is that of the emergence of increasingly uniformly dispersed multi-nodal urban regions; traditional core-orientation is a thing of the past.

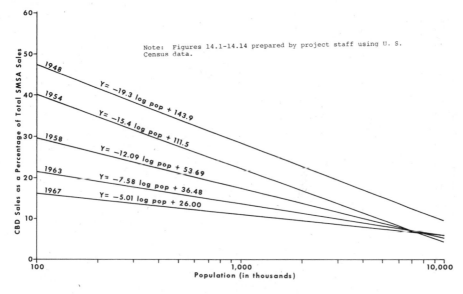

FIGURE 14.1

CBD SALES PERCENTAGE RELATED TO
SMSA POPULATION, 1948-1967

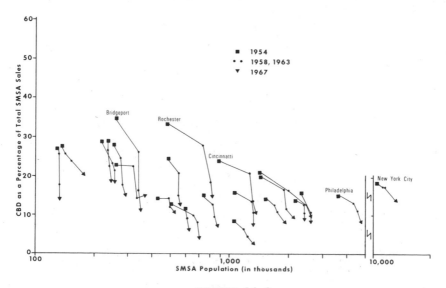

FIGURE 14.2

CHANGES IN THE CBD SALES PERCENTAGE:
CITIES IN THE NORTHEAST

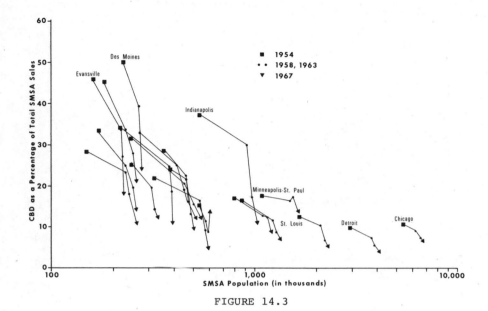

FIGURE 14.3

CHANGES IN THE CBD SALES PERCENTAGE:
MIDWESTERN CITIES

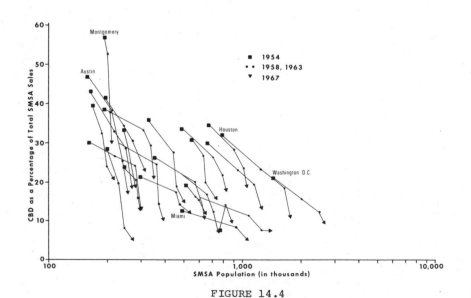

FIGURE 14.4

CHANGES IN THE CBD SALES PERCENTAGE:
SOUTHERN CITIES

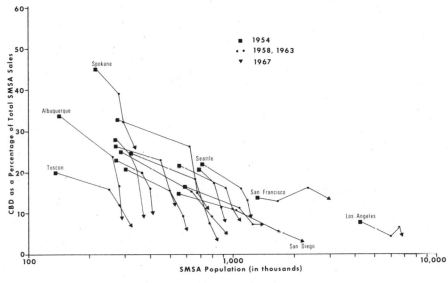

FIGURE 14.5

CHANGES IN CBD SALES PERCENTAGE:
WESTERN CITIES

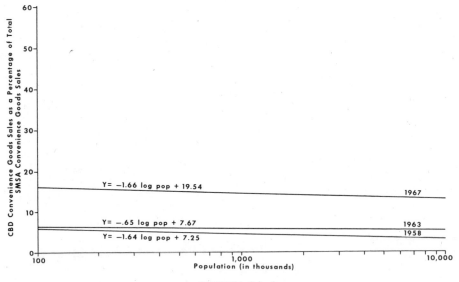

FIGURE 14.6

CHANGES IN CBD CONVENIENCE GOODS SALES, 1958-1967

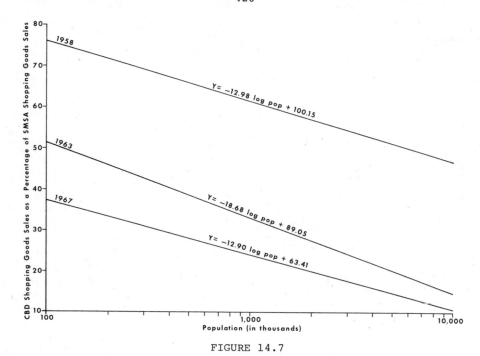

FIGURE 14.7

CHANGES IN CBD SHOPPING GOODS SALES. 1958-1967

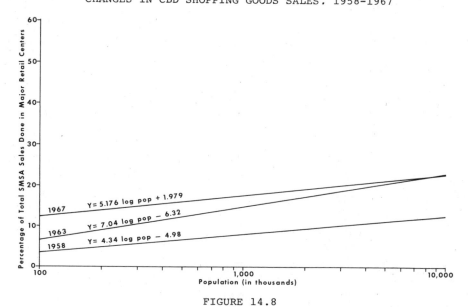

FIGURE 14.8

CHANGES IN THE RETAIL SHARES OF
MAJOR REGIONAL SHOPPING CENTERS, 1958-1967

2. THE DECLINE OF PUBLIC TRANSPORTATION

In the case of public transportation (bus, street car, subway, elevated train and railroad) the relationship of the proportion of the labor force using public transportation in the journey-to-work to city size is positive, although with important regional differences. In all regions, however, increasing automobile usage accompanying decentralization is evident.

Figure 14.9 shows the relationships of public transport use for commuting to SMSA size in 1970, by region. In all regions, it is evident that the greater concentration of population in the largest cities supports greater public transport shares of work trips. The successively lower regression lines as one progresses from the eastern seaboard to California and the southwest reflects differences in development history, for the "heartland" cities of the eastern seaboard and the manufacturing belt grew in the pre-automobile era at higher densities, mass-transportation oriented, while the "rimland" urban regions have grown up in the automobile era, lacking the denisties and concentration supportive of public transportation.

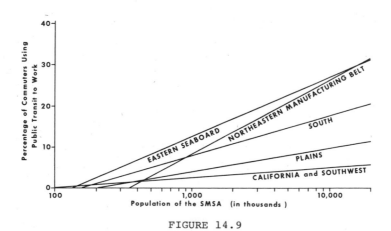

FIGURE 14.9

REGIONAL DIFFERENCES IN THE RELATIONSHIP OF PUBLIC
TRANSIT USE FOR COMMUTING TO SIZE OF SMSA

In all regions, public transportation usage is declining (Figures 14.10 to 14.14), with the rate of decline more rapid in larger than in smaller SMSA's. The uniform low densities of today's dispersed urban regions are supporting uniformly low levels of patronage of public transportation.

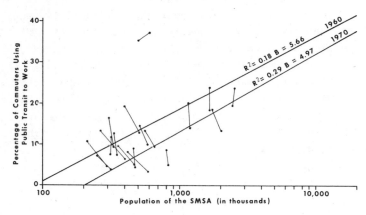

FIGURE 14.10

CHANGES IN PUBLIC TRANSIT USE:
EASTERN SEABOARD SMSA'S

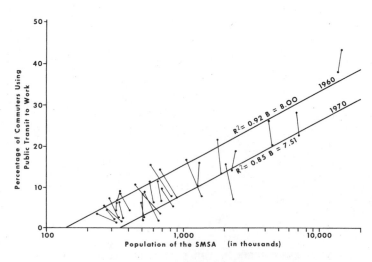

FIGURE 14.11

CHANGES IN PUBLIC TRANSIT USE:
MANUFACTURING BELT CENTERS

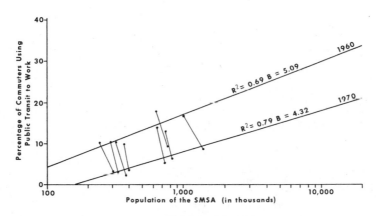

FIGURE 14.12

CHANGES IN PUBLIC TRANSIT USE:
MIDWESTERN AND SOUTHERN SMSA'S

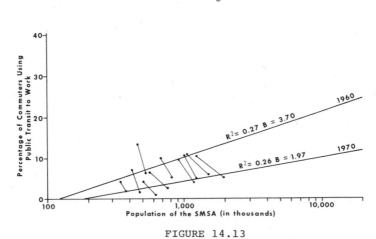

FIGURE 14.13

CHANGES IN PUBLIC TRANSIT USE:
PLAINS SMSA'S

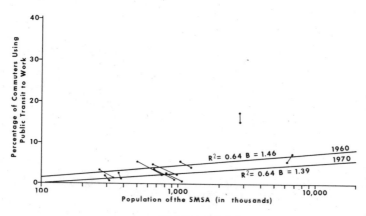

FIGURE 14.14

CHANGES IN PUBLIC TRANSIT USE:
CALIFORNIA AND THE SOUTHWEST

II. THE SPECTRUM OF POLICY ALTERNATIVES

All trends point in the same direction: increasing size,
increasing dispersion, and increasing automobile usage are producing the very urban forms and land use patterns that will increase rather than decrease environmental pollution.

Grava (1969) provides a picture of the policy alternatives
that arise (Figure 14.15). One can, he suggests, change pollution by:

1) Removing, changing and dispersing pollutants produced
   by existing activities.

2) Changing the nature of these activities.

3) Changing urban forms through relocation of people and
   activities.

Currently, EPA's regulatory approaches focus on the first of
these alternatives. Much of today's ecoactivism is directed to
the second. What is suggested by the results of this study, and
supported by the work of others, is that the third represents

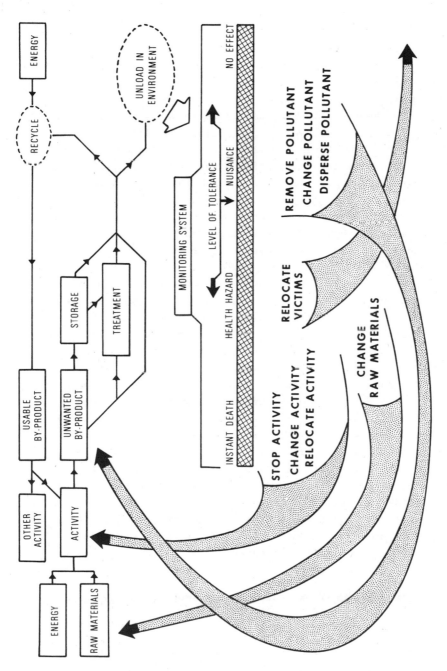

FIGURE 14.15: THE WASTE CYCLE
(after Grava, 1969)

an alternative worthy of consideration, too.

1.   URBAN FORM AS A BASIC VARIABLE

The urban form variable is, of course, quite complex. It can be specified microscopically in terms of the detailed locations of jobs, residences, commercial areas, recreation areas, and vacant, non-urban land, with particular attention to the location of heavy polluting facilities (power stations, for example). At a higher level of generalization, it can be specified in terms of its density (areal intensity of activities and elements), the mixture or separatedness of uses, type and structure of the transportation network, and the time dimension of the utilization of its space. Or, at the most generalized level, urban form may be approached in terms of plausible spatial configurations: compact versus dispersed, single nuclei versus multiple nuclei, those which adapt to growth as contrasted with those which have predetermined size.

Findings at all levels complement our own. For example, Greenberg et. al. (1973) show in a study of the New York region that the secondary treatment plants now in existence or currently being built to provide biological treatment with a maximum average of 25 ppm. BOD will be insufficient to allow more than half the Raritan stations to meet present water quality standards through 1985. Moreover, major regional sewage treatment plants would create as many problems as they solve; a wider spatial distribution of smaller effluent discharges would be preferred to make efficient use of the natural assimilative capacity of streams. Finally, if present water quality standards are to be used, portions of the Raritan Basin will have to be depopulated, zoning ordinances drastically revised and unrecorded discharges halted.

Similarly, in the case of air pollution, Voorhees (1971) reports on the environmental consequences of alternative regional forms in a variety of cases:

Hartford. Air quality would be improved by corridor development rather than sprawl.

Chicago. Significant air quality improvements would result from a radial finger plan.

Seattle. Emissions would be reduced by corridor development.

In all cases, Voorhees noted that improved regional development patterns should reduce auto emissions and the number of persons

exposed to pollutants from both vehicles and stationary sources.
He recommended strict land use controls on location of stationary sources in relation to local and regional dispersion characteristics, along with increased use of performance zoning and
the establishment, as in Britain, of "smokeless zones" via air
zoning. Further, control of land uses around sources was recommended, with special attention to buffers, and particularly, to
the design of transport networks to minimize pollution. Important considerations involved include multi-modal planning to reduce the proportional automobile usage.

Voorhees also experimented with eight different urban patterns (sprawl; moderate, heavy, rotated and extreme rotated corridors; satellite cities; and centralized employment with either
sprawling or radial population), four highway networks (a basic
arterial grid, freeways along major arterials, major radial freeways with an outer beltway and inner loop, additional radials
and an inner beltway), and three basic transit networks (bus,
rapid radial rail with bus, radial and outer loop rail) and concluded that greater clustering of employment and higher residential densities along radials would promote transity usage and
significantly improve air quality. Basic goals for transport
network design that were derived to promote improved air quality
included: reducing trip lengths and automobile travel, moving
traffic at faster and more consistent speeds, supporting expanded
transit usage, and preventing increased traffic flows into already
congested areas. Recommended techniques for improving traffic
flow, rated for probable effectiveness (1--least effective, to
5--most effective) were:

Technique	Probable Effectiveness
(a) Freeways	
1. Reverse-lane operations	3
2. Driver advisory displays	1
3. Ramp control	2
4. Interchange design	2
(b) Arterials	
1. Alignment	1
2. Widening intersections	3
3. Parking restrictions	2
4. Signal progression	2
5. Reversible lanes	3
6. Reversible one-way streets	3
7. Helicopter reports	2

Technique	Probable Effectiveness
(c) Downtown Distribution	
1. Traffic responsive control	5
2. One-way street operations	3
3. Loading regulations	3
4. Pedestrian control	1
5. Traffic operations program to increase capacity and safety	5

Similarly, to reduce pollution concentrations, recommended techniques were:

Technique	Probable Effectiveness
(a) Staggered Work Hours	3
(b) Roadway Concentrations	2
(c) Cross-sections	2
(d) Elevated, At-grade, Depressed Roadways	2

Finally, techniques recommended for reducing auto traffic included:

Technique	Probable Effectiveness
(a) Transit Operations	
1. Bus lanes on city streets	1
2. Bus lanes on freeways	1
3. One-way streets with two-way buses	1
4. Park-ride, kiss-ride	3
5. Service improvements and cost reductions	2
(b) Regulation	
1. Parking bans	4
2. Auto-free zones	4
3. Gasoline rationing	5
4. Idling restrictions	2
5. Four-day, forty-hour week	2
(c) Pricing Policy	
1. Parking policy	2
2. Road-user tax	5
3. Gasoline tax	5
4. Car pool incentives	2
(d) Planned Unit Development	2

2. THE POLICY PROBLEM

One cannot help feeling that Voorhees is grasping at straws in his suggestions, however, for what the evidence indicates is that _if environmental pollution is to be changed by changing_ _urban form, nothing less than reversal of present urban develop-_

ment directions must be achieved. But to state this is to highlight the nation's current urban policy problem, which is that
there is no national urban policy except to accept the consequences of current developments. The lack of national will in
this regard was highlighted no more clearly than in President
Nixon's Report on National Growth 1972 (pp. 30-1), in which it
was stated:

> Patterns of growth are influenced by countless deci-
> sions made by individuals, families and businesses.
> These decisions are aimed at achieving the personal
> goals of those who make them, and reflect healthy
> free choices in our society. Locational shifts by
> individuals reflect, in part, a search for better
> job opportunities or for a better climate, while
> businessmen relocate where they can operate most er-
> rectively and therefore make the most profit.
>   The factors that influence these decisions may
> be susceptible to changes that will alter the emerg-
> ing growth patterns, but, in a Nation   that values
> freedom in the private sector and democratic choice
> in the public, the decisions themselves cannot be
> dictated....It is not feasible for the highest
> level of government to design policies for develop-
> ment that can operate successfully in all parts of
> the Nation. (Emphasis added.)

What, then, are "the factors that...may be susceptible to
change"? In the words of the Nixon report, they include "local
tax levies; the location of public facilities and roads; the ex-
tension of sewer, water, electric, and gas services; specific
zoning and building regulations; and the approval of development
plans." Even to make changes with respect to these factors at
a local level will demand that the present limits of land use
planning be extended in at least three ways, however (Kaiser,
et. al., 1973):

1) By redefining comprehensive planning to reflect environmental objectives.

2) By including environmental system information, concern
   for physical processes operating in the biosphere, and
   related evaluation criteria, in the land use planning
   process.

3) Through development of an adequate land use guidance
   system, involving use of public facility decisions to
   control the spatial locations and timing of development.

But, to achieve these extensions so that new urban development
can be cast into more desirable urban forms will demand that
land use planning decisions be made and policing power be applied
effectively at their currently weakest level, that of the metropolis, so that reasonable closure be achieved with respect to
the land use system whose development path it is hoped to re-

direct. The fact that most land development decisions remain
private today, reflecting the prevailing attitude that land is
a private commodity rather than a public resource, combined with
a balkanization of available land guidance techniques among competing local governments, serve to produce our urban future by
incremental drift. Radical changes in attitudes are required,
involving nothing less than a new land ethic, if national environmental policy is to be promoted by changed directions of
urban development.

431

LITERATURE CITED

I. AIR POLLUTION

Anderson, R.J., and T.D. Crocker. "Air Pollution and Residential Property Values," Urban Studies. Vol. 8, No. 2 (October, 1971).

Babcock, Jr., L.R. "A Combined Pollution Index for Measurement of Total Air Pollution, " Journal of the Air Pollution Control Association. Vol. 20, No. 10 (October, 1970).

Council on Environmental Quality. National Environmental Indices: Air Quality and Outdoor Recreation. The MITRE Corporation MTR-6159. Washington, D.C., 1972.

Croke, E.J., and and J.J. Roberts. Chicago Air Pollution Systems Analysis Program Final Report. Argonne National Laboratory. Chicago, 1971.

Eisenbud, M. "Environmental Protection in the City of New York," Science. Vol. 170, November, 1970.

Freeman III, A.M. "Air Pollution and Property Values: A Methodological Comment," Review of Economics and Statistics. Vol. 53, No. 4, (November, 1971).

Hagevik G. (ed.). The Relationship of Land Use and Transportation Planning to Air Quality Management. Center for Urban Policy Research and Conferences. Rutgers University, 1972.

Hickey, R.J., D.E. Boyce, E.B. Harmer, and R.C. Clelland. Ecological Statistical Studies Concerning Environmental Pollution and Chronic Disease. Summary in Digest of Technical Papers, 2nd International Geoscience Electronics Symposium, IEEE, Washington, D.C., April, 1970.

Highway Research Record No. 465. "Air Pollution Controls for Urban Transportation", Washington: NAS, 1973.

Justus, CG. et. al. Economic Costs of Air Pollution Damage. Atlanta: Science, Technology and Research, Inc., 1973.

Lave, L., and E. Seskin. "Air Pollution and Human Health," Science. Vol. 169, No. 3947 (August, 1970).

Lave, L. "Air Pollution Damage: Some Difficulties in Estimating the Value of Abatement," in Allen V. Kneese and Blair T. Bower, Environmental Quality Analysis. Baltimore: Johns Hopkins Press, 1972.

McMullen, T.B. Comparison of Urban and Nonurban Air Quality. 9th Annual Indiana Air Pollution Control Conference, Purdue University, October, 1970.

Morris, D.E. The Cost of Controlling Air Pollution: A Study in Economies of City Size. Unpublished paper, 1972.

Ridker, R.B., and J.A. Henning. "The Determinants of Residential
Property Values with Special Reference to Air Pollution,"
Review of Economics and Statistics. Vol. 49, No. 2 (May,
1967).

Ridker, R.G. Economic Costs of Air Pollution, Studies in Measurement. New York: Frederick A. Praeger, 1967.

Stern, A.C. (ed.). Air Pollution. Vol. I (1968) Academic Press,
New York.

Strotz, R.H. "The Use of Land Rent Changes to Measure the Welfare Benefits of Land Improvement," (ditto), 1966.

U.S. Department of Housing and Urban Development. Urban Mass
Transit Planning Project. Abstract City Analysis. Alan M.
Voorhees & Associates. McLean, Virginia: September, 1968.

U.S. Environmental Protection Agency. "National Primary and
Secondary Ambient Air Quality Standards," Federal Register.

_____. Office of Air Programs. A Guide for Reducing Air Pol-
lution Through Urban Planning. Alan M. Voorhees & Associates, Inc. and Ryckman, Edgerley, Tomlinson & Associates.
Washington D.C., December, 1971.

_____. Guide for Air Pollution Episode Avoidance. Washington,
D.C.: U.S. Government Printing Office, 1971.

_____, Office of Air Programs. Federal Air Quality Control
Regions. Washington: G.P.O., 1972.

The National Air Monitoring Program: Air Quality and Emissions
Trends; Annual Report. Research Triangle Park North Carolina: Office of Air Quality Planning and Standards, 1973.

Voorhes, Alan M. and Associates, Inc., and Ryckman, Ederley. Tomlinson and Associates. A Guide for Reducing Air Pollution
through Urban Planning. A Report prepared for the Office
of Air Programs, E.P.A., 1971.

Walther, E.G. "A Rating of the Major Air Pollutants and Their
Sources by Effect," Journal of the Air Pollution Control
Association. Vol. 22, No. 5 (May, 1972).

II. WATER POLLUTION

American Public Health Association. Standard Methods for the
Examination of Water, Sewage and Industrial Waste. New
York: American Public Health Association, Inc., 1955.

Bartsch, A.F. "Induced Eutrophication--A Growing Water Resource
Problem," Algae and Metropolitan Wastes. USPHS, SEC TR
W61-63.

Carey, G.W., et. al. Urbanization, Water Pollution, and Public
    Policy. New Brunswick, New Jersey: Center for Urban Policy
    Research, Rutgers University, 1972.

Coughlin, R.E., T.R. Hammer, T.G. Dickert, S. Sheldon. "Percep-
    tion and Use of Streams in Suburban Areas: Effects of
    Water Quality and of Distance from Residence to Stream,"
    RSRI Discussion Paper Series: No. 53, March, 1972.

Council on Environmental Quality. National Assessment of Trends
    in Water Quality. Enviro Control, Inc. Washington, D.C.,
    June, 1972.

Davis, R.K. The Range of Choice in Water Management. Baltimore,
    Md.: The Johns Hopkins Press, 1968.

Edmondson, W.T. "Water-Quality Management and Lake Eutrophica-
    tion: The Lake Washington Case." Department of Zoology.
    Washington University, Seattle, 1969.

Edmondson, W. T. 1969. "The History of Lake Washington" in METRO -
    The First Ten Years. Seattle: Municipality of Metropolitan
    Seattle.

Grava, Sigurd. Urban Planning Aspects of Water Pollution Control.
    New York: Columbia University Press, 1969.

Greenberg, M.R., G.W. Corey, L. Zolder, and R.M. Hordon. "A
    Statistical Dissolved Oxygen Model for a Free-flowing River
    System," Journal of the American Statistical Association.
    Vol. 69, 1973.

Grima, Angelo. Residential Water Demand. Toronto: University
    of Toronto Press, 1972.

Hem, J. D. 1970. Study and Interpretation of the Chemical Charac-
    teristics of Natural Water. U. S. Geological Survey Water
    Supply Paper 1473. Washington, D. C.: Government Printing
    Office.

Hutchinson, G.E. "Eutrophication," American Scientist. Vol. 61
    (May-June, 1973).

Leopold, L.B. "Hydrology for Urban Land Planning--A Guidebook on
    the Hydrologic Effects of Urban Land Use," U.S. Geological
    Survey Circular. Vol. 554 (1968).

Municipality of Metropolitan Seattle 1969. METRO - The First Ten
    Years. Seattle: Municipality of Metropolitan Seattle.

Richardson, D., J. W. Bingham, and R. J. Madison. 1968. Water
    Resources of King County, Washington. U. S. Geological
    Survey Water-Supply Paper 1852. Washington, D. C.: Govern-
    ment Printing Office.

Santos, J. R., and J. D. Stoner. 1972. Physical, Chemical, and
    Biological Aspects of the Duwamish River Estuary, King County,
    Washington 1963-67. U. S. Geological Survey Water-Supply
    Paper 1873-C. Washington, D. C.: Government Printing Office.

Sylvester, R. O., and C. A. Rambow. 1968. "Methodology in Estab-
    lishing Water-Quality Standards," in Water Resource Management
    and Public Policy. Seattle: Washington University Press.

Sylvester, R.O., and C.A. Rambow, "Methodology in Establishing Water Quality Standards," in T.H. Campbell and R.O. Sylvester, Water Resource Management and Public Policy. Seattle: Washington University Press, 1968.

Sylvester, R.O. "Nutrient Content of Drainage Water from Forested, Urban and Agricultural Areas," Algae & Metropolitan Wastes. USPHS, SEC TR W61-63, 1970.

Todd, D. K. 1970. The Water Encyclopedia. Port Washington, New York: Water Information Center.

U.S. Department of Health, Education and Welfare. Public Health Service. Effects of Land Disposal of Solid Wastes on Water Quality. Rodney L. Cummins. (Washington, D.C., U.S. Government Printing Office, 1968).

_____. Drinking Water Standards. Publication No. 956. (Washington, D.C.: U.S. Government Printing Office, 1962).

U.S. Department of the Interior. Federal Water Pollution Control Administration. Interim Report of the National Technical Advisory Commission on Water Quality Criteria. (Washington, D.C.: U.S. Government Printing Office, 1967).

_____. The Cost of Clean Water. Vol. I and II. (Washington, D.C.: U.S. Government Printing Office, 1968).

_____. Industrial Waste Guide on Thermal Pollution. (Washington, D.C.: U.S. Government Printing Office, 1968).

_____. 1968 Inventory of Municipal Waste Facilities. Three Volumes. (Washington, D.C.: U.S. Government Printing Office, 1969).

_____. Water Pollution Aspects of Urban Runoff. The American Public Works Association, Report No. WP-20-15, (January, 1969).

_____. Storm Water Pollution from Urban Land Activity. Water Pollution Control Research Series. (Washington, D.C.: U.S. Government Printing Office, 1970).

_____. The Nations Water Resources. (Washington, D.C.: U.S. Government Printing Office, 1968).

U. S. Department of the Interior. Federal Water Pollution Control Administration. 1968. Committee on Water Quality Criteria. Washington, D. C.: Government Printing Office.

U.S. Environmental Protection Agency. Benefits of Water Quality Enhancement. Department of Civil Engineering, Syracuse University, 1970.

_____. Water Quality Criteria Data Book. Vol. I, II, III, IV. (Washington, D.C.: U.S. Government Printing Office, 1970).

_____. Study and Interpretation of the Chemical Characteristics of Natural Water. U.S. Geological Survey Water Supply Paper 1473. (Washington, D.C.: U.S. Government Printing Office, 1968).

_____. The Economics of Clean Water. Two Volumes. (Washington, D.C.: U.S. Government Printing Office, 1972).

U. S. EPA (1971). Water Quality Office. A Primer on Waste Water Treatment. (Washington: U. S. Government Printing Office, 1971)

U.S. Geological Survey. Methods for Collection and Analysis of Water Samples for Dissolved Minerals and Gases. (Washington, D.C.: U.S. Government Printing Office, 1970).

_____. Techniques of Natural Resources Investigations of the U.S. Geological Survey, Book 5, Laboratory Analysis. (Washington, D.C." U.S. Government Printing Office, 1970).

_____. Quality of Surface Waters of the United States, 1968. U.S. Geological Survey Water-Supply Paper 2099. (Washington, D.C.: U.S. Government Printing Office, 1972).

Water Pollution Control Commission, State of Washington. 1967. A Regulation Relating to Water Quality Standards for Interstate and Coastal Waters of the State of Washington and a Plan for Implementation and Enforcement of Such Standards.

Westman, W.E. "Some Basic Issues in Water Pollution Control Legislation." American Scientist. Vol. 60, 1972.

Willrich, T.L., and G.E. Smith (eds.) Agricultural Practices and Water Quality. Ames, Iowa: The Iowa State University Press, 1970.

Zwick, D. and M. Benstock. Water Wasteland. New York: Grossman Publishers, 1971.

III. SOLID WASTES

American Public Works Association. 1970. Municipal Refuse Disposal, Chicago: Institute for Solid Wastes.

Boyd, Gail B., Hawkins, Myron B., 1971. Methods of Predicting Solid Waste Characteristics. U. S. Environmental Protection Agency.

Davidson, George R., 1972. Residential Solid Waste Generated in Low Income Areas, U. S. Environmental Protection Agency, Solid Waste Management Office.

Hudson, Henry J., 1971. Solid Waste Management in the Food Processing Industry. U. S. Environmental Protection Agency, Solid Waste Management Office.

Muhich, Anton, 1970. "Sample Representativeness and Community Data", An Interim Report: 1968 National Solid Waste Survey, U. S. Dept. of Health, Education and Welfare.

National Academy of Sciences. National Research Council. Waste Management and Control. Washington, D.C., 1966.

Niessen W. R., Chansky, S. H., 1970. "The Nature of Refuse", Proceeding of 1970 National Incinerators Conference. The American Society of Mechanical Engineers.

Research Triangle Institute, 1969. A National Study of Roadside Litter. Keep America Beautiful Inc., New York.

Shaeffer, J. R. et. al., 1971. Decision Making and Solid Waste Disposal. Centers for Urban Studies, University of Chicago, Chicago.

Smith, David, Brown, Robert P., 1971. Ocean Disposal of Barge-Delivered Liquid and Solid Wastes From U. S. Coastal Cities. U. S. Environmental Protection Agency. Solid Waste Management Office (SW-19c).

State of California. Department of Public Health. Status of Solid Waste Management in California. 1968.

U.S. Department of Health, Education and Welfare. Solid Waste/Disease Relationships. T.G. Hanks. (Washington, D.C.: U.S. Government Printing Office, 1967).

U.S. Environmental Protection Agency. Bureau of Solid Waste Management. Systems Analysis for Solid Waste Disposal by Incineration. FMC Corp., Santa Clara Study, 1968.

U.S. Environmental Protection Agency. "National Solid Wastes Survey Report Summary and Interpretations," in An Interim Report. Richard D. Vaughan. (Washington, D.C.: U.S. Government Printing Office, 1970).

U.S. Environmental Protection Agency. Solid Waste Management Office. (SW-2tsg). California Solid Waste Management Study (1968) and Plan (1970). (Washington, D.C.: U.S. Government Printing Office, 1971).

U.S. Environmental Protection Agency. New York State Department of Health. New York Solid Waste Management Plan, Status Report 1970. Roy Weston, Environmental Scientists and Engineers. (Washington, D.C.: U.S. Government Printing Office, 1971).

Washington State University. Department of Ecology. Regulations Relating to Minimum Functional Standards for Solid Wastes Handling. 1972.

IV. NOISE

Bolt, Beranek and Newman, Inc. Chicago Urban Noise Study. Report No. 1411-1413. Downers Grove, Illinois, November, 1970.

_____. HUD Noise Assessment Guidelines. HUD TE/NA 171. Washington, D.C., August, 1971.

_____. Noise in Urban and Suburban Areas: Results of Field Studies. Washington, D.C.: U.S. Government Printing Office, January, 1967.

Burt, M.E. "Aspects of Highway Design and Traffic Management," Journal of Sound and Vibration. Vol. 15, No. 1. March, 1971.

Chalupnile, J.D. (ed.) Transportation Noises: A Symposium on Acceptibility Criteria. University of Washington Press: Seattle, 1970.

Colony, D.C. Expressway Traffic Noise and Residential Properties. Toledo, Ohio: Research Foundation, University of Toledo, July, 1967.

Dickerson, D.O., et. al. Transportation Noise Pollution: Control and Abatement. Springfield, Va.: National Technical Information Service, N71-15557, 1970.

Greater London Council. Traffic Noise. London: Greater London Council, February, 1966.

Glass, D.C. and J.E. Singer. "Behavioral Aftereffects of Unpredictable and Uncontrollable Aversive Events," American Scientist. Vol. 60, No. 4, 1972.

Jacoby, L.R. Perception of Air, Noise, and Water Pollution in Detroit. Ann Arbor: Michigan Geographical Publication No. 7, 1972.

Lyon, R.H. "Propagation of Environmental Noise," Science. Vol. 179, No. 4078, March, 1973.

McClure, P.T. Indicators of the Effect of Jet Noise on the Value of Real Estate. Santa Monica: The Rand Corporation, 1969.

Paullin, R.L. and H.B. Safeer. Motor Vehicle Noise Generation and Potential Abatement. New York: Society of Automotive Engineers, January, 1972.

Priede, T. "Origins of Automotive Vehicle Noise," Journal of Sound and Vibration. Vol. 15, No. 1. (March, 1971).

Shih, H.H. A Literature Survey of Noise Pollution. Washington, D.C.: Institute of Ocean Science and Engineering, Catholic University of America, March, 1971.

Texas Transportation Institute. Urban Traffic Noise Reduction: Final Report. Report No. TT1-2-8-71-16614F. College Station, Texas, August, 1971.

Towne, Robin and Associates, Inc. An Investigation of the Effect of Freeway Traffic Noise on Apartment Rents. Springfield, Va.: Clearinghouse for Federal Scientific and Technical Information, October, 1966.

U. S. Bureau of the Census. Census of Population: 1970; General Social and Economic Characteristics. Washington: U. S. Government Printing Office, 1972.

U. S. Department of Transportation. Transportation Planning Data for Urbanized Areas. Washington: U. S. Government Printing Office, 1970.

U.S. Environmental Protection Agency. Community Noise. Report No. NT1D300.3 (Washington, D.C.: U.S. Government Printing Office, December, 1971).

_____. The Economic Impact of Noise. Report No. NT1D300.14. (Washington, D.C.: U.S. Government Printing Office, December, 1971).

_____. Effects of Noise on People. Report No. NT1D300.7. (Washington, D.C.: U.S. Government Printing Office, December, 1971).

_____. Fundamentals of Noise: Measurement, Rating Schemes, and Standards. Report No. NT1D300.15. (Washington, D.C.: U.S. Government Printing Office, December, 1971).

_____. The Social Impact of Noise. Report No. NT1D300.11. (Washington, D.C.: U.S. Government Printing Office, December, 1971).

V. PESTICIDES

Federal Committee on Pest Control. Pesticides Monitoring Journal. Vol. 1, No. 1, June, 1967 through Vol. 5, No. 3, December, 1971.

Haus, S. A., Strategic Environmental Assessment System: Pesticide Residuals. Report for Office of Research and Development, Washington Environmental Research Center, Environmental Protection Agency, 1973.

State of New York. New York State Joint Legislative Committee on Natural Resources. The Use and Effect of Pesticides. Albany, N.Y., 1963.

U.S. Federal Committee on Pest Control. Catalog of Federal Pesticide Monitoring Activities in Effect July 1967. Washington, D.C., 1967.

VI. RADIATION

Bisselle, C. A. Strategic Environmental Assessment System: Radiation Residuals. Report for the Office of Research and Development, Washington Environmental Research Center, Environmental Protection Agency, 1973.

Howells, H., and H.J. Dunster. "Environmental Monitoring in Emergencies," Environmental Surveillance in the Vicinity of Nuclear Facilities. Springfield, Ill.: Charles C. Thomas, 1970.

National Academy of Sciences. Advisory Committee on the Biological Effect of Ionizing Radiations. The Effects on Populations of Exposure to Low Levels of Ionizing Radiation. Washington, D.C., 1972.

Sternglass, E.J. "Environmental Radiation and Human Health," Proceedings of the 6th Berkeley Symposium on Mathematical Statistics and Probability. Berkeley: The University of California Press, 1971.

VII. OTHER

Alonso, William, "A Theory of the Urban Land Market" Papers and Proceedings of the Regional Science Association. Vol. 6 (1960).

Benarde, M.A. Our Precarious Habitat. New York: W.W. Norton &
     Co., Inc., 1970.

Berry, B.J.L. (ed.) City Classification Handbook. New York:
     Wiley-Interscience, 1972.

Clawson, M. (ed.) Modernizing Urban Land Policy. Baltimore:
     The Johns Hopkins University Press, 1973.

Detwyler, T.R., and M.G. Marcus. Urbanization and Environment.
     Belmont, California: Duxburg Press, 1972.

Edel, M., J.R. Harris and J. Rothenberg. "Urban Concentration
     and Deconcentration." Paper prepared for the National
     Academy of Sciences--National Research Council Committee
     on the Concept of Community, 1972.

Forrester, J.W. Urban Dynamics. Cambridge: The M.I.T. Press,
     1969.

Friedman, J. and J. Miller (1965) "The Urban Field," Journal of
     the American Institute of Planners. 31, 312-319.

Harris, J.R. and D. Wheeler, "Agglomeration Economies: Theory
     and Measurement." Paper presented at the Urban Economics
     Conference, University of Keele, 1971.

Hoch, I.B. "Urban Scale and Environmental Quality," Population,
     Resources, and the Environment, Vol. III, 1972.

James, Preston E. and C. F. Jones. American Geography: Inventory
     and Prospect. Syracuse: Syracuse University Press, 1954.

Kahn, H. and Wiener, A. J., (1967) "The Next Thirty-three Years:
     A Framework for Speculation," Daedalus. 96, 705-32.

Kaiser, E.J., et. al. Promoting Environmental Quality Through
     Urban Planning and Controls. Center for Urban and Regional
     Studies, University of North Carolina. Six Volumes. Chapel
     Hill, N.C., 1973.

Lowenthal, David et. al. "Report of the AAG Task Force on Environ-
     mental Quality," The Professional Geographer. Vol. 25, No. 1,
     (February, 1973).

Niedercorn, John H. and Hearle, Edward, F. R., "Recent Land-Use Trends
     in Forty-Eight Large American Cities. Santa Monica: The Land
     Seperation, 1963.

Office of Research and Monitoring, Environmental Studies Division
     Environmental Protection Agency, The Quality of Life Concept.
     (1973).

State of Hawaii. Department of Transportation. The Reports.
     Honolulu, 1967.

State of New York. Department of Environmental Conservation.
     Environmental Plan for New York State. Albany, 1973.

Thomas, W.A. (ed.) Indicators of Environmental Quality. New
    York: Plenum Press, 1972.

Thompson, W.R. "Internal and External Factors in the Development
    of Urban Economies," in H. Perloff (ed.) Issues in Urban
    Economics. Baltimore: The Johns Hopkins Press, 1968.

U. S. Council on Environmental Quality. Environmental Quality.
    THIRD Annual Report of the Council on Environmental Quality:
    (Washington, D. C.: U. S. Government Printing Office, 1972).

U. S. Environmental Protection Agency, Environmental Studies Divi-
    sion. The Environment: 1972 EPA Summer Jellous Project,
    in summary draft form, 1972.

_____. Office of Research and Monitority. Strategic Environ-
    mental Assessment System: (SEAS) May, 1973.)

U.S. Council on Environmental Quality. Environmental Quality.
    Second Annual Report of the Council on Environmental Quality.
    (Washington, D.C.: U.S. Government Printing Office, August,
    1971).

U.S. Department of Transportation. Federal Highway Administration.
    Bureau of Public Roads. Standard Land Use Coding Manual.
    (Washington, D.C.: U.S. Government Printing Office, 1969).

U.S. Department of Transportation. Transportation Planning Data
    for Urbanized Areas. (Washington, D.C.: U.S. Government
    Printing Office, 1970).

THE UNIVERSITY OF CHICAGO
DEPARTMENT OF GEOGRAPHY
RESEARCH PAPERS (Lithographed, 6×9 Inches)

(Available from Department of Geography, The University of Chicago, 5828 S. University Ave., Chicago, Illinois 60637. Price: $5.00 each; by series subscription, $4.00 each.)

48. BOXER, BARUCH. *Israeli Shipping and Foreign Trade* 1957. 176 pp.

53. ACKERMAN, EDWARD A. *Geography as a Fundamental Research Discipline* 1958. 40 pp. $1.00

56. MURPHY, FRANCIS C. *Regulating Flood-Plain Development* 1958. 216 pp.

62. GINSBURG, NORTON, editor. *Essays on Geography and Economic Development* 1960. 196 pp.

71. GILBERT, E. W. *The University Town in England and West Germany*
1961. 79 pp. 4 plates. 30 maps and diagrams. (Free to new subscribers)

72. BOXER, BARUCH. *Ocean Shipping in the Evolution of Hong Kong* 1961. 108 pp.

74. TROTTER, JOHN E. *State Park System in Illinois* 1966. 152 pp.

84. KANSKY, K. J. *Structure of Transportation Networks: Relationships between Network Geometry and Regional Characteristics* 1963. 155 pp.

91. HILL, A. DAVID. *The Changing Landscape of a Mexican Municipio, Villa Las Rosas, Chiapas*
NAS-NRC Foreign Field Research Program Report No. 26. 1964. 121 pp.

94. MC MANIS, DOUGLAS R. *The Initial Evaluation and Utilization of the Illinois Prairies, 1815–1840*
1964. 109 pp.

97. BOWDEN, LEONARD W. *Diffusion of the Decision To Irrigate: Simulation of the Spread of a New Resource Management Practice in the Colorado Northern High Plains* 1965. 146 pp.

98. KATES, ROBERT W. *Industrial Flood Losses: Damage Estimation in the Lehigh Valley*
1965. 76 pp.

102. AHMAD, QAZI. *Indian Cities: Characteristics and Correlates* 1965. 184 pp.

103. BARNUM, H. GARDINER. *Market Centers and Hinterlands in Baden-Württemberg* 1966. 172 pp.

105. SEWELL, W. R. DERRICK, et al. *Human Dimensions of Weather Modification* 1966. 423 pp.

106. SAARINEN, THOMAS F. *Perception of the Drought Hazard on the Great Plains* 1966. 183 pp.

107. SOLZMAN, DAVID M. *Waterway Industrial Sites: A Chicago Case Study* 1967. 138 pp.

108. KASPERSON, ROGER E. *The Dodecanese: Diversity and Unity in Island Politics* 1967. 184 pp.

109. LOWENTHAL, DAVID, ET AL. *Environmental Perception and Behavior.* 1967. 88 pp.

110. REED, WALLACE E. *Areal Interaction in India: Commodity Flows of the Bengal-Bihar Industrial Area* 1967. 210 pp.

112. BOURNE, LARRY S. *Private Redevelopment of the Central City: Spatial Processes of Structural Change in the City of Toronto* 1967. 199 pp.

113. BRUSH, JOHN E., and GAUTHIER, HOWARD L., JR. *Service Centers and Consumer Trips: Studies on the Philadelphia Metropolitan Fringe* 1968. 182 pp.

114. CLARKSON, JAMES D. *The Cultural Ecology of a Chinese Village: Cameron Highlands, Malaysia*
1968. 174 pp.

115. BURTON, IAN, KATES, ROBERT W., and SNEAD, RODMAN E. *The Human Ecology of Coastal Flood Hazard in Megalopolis* 1968. 196 pp.

117. WONG, SHUE TUCK. *Perception of Choice and Factors Affecting Industrial Water Supply Decisions in Northeastern Illinois* 1968. 96 pp.

118. JOHNSON, DOUGLAS L. *The Nature of Nomadism* 1969. 200 pp.

119. DIENES, LESLIE. *Locational Factors and Locational Developments in the Soviet Chemical Industry*
1969. 285 pp.

120. MIHELIC, DUSAN. *The Political Element in the Port Geography of Trieste* 1969. 104 pp.

121. BAUMANN, DUANE. *The Recreational Use of Domestic Water Supply Reservoirs: Perception and Choice* 1969. 125 pp.

122. LIND, AULIS O. *Coastal Landforms of Cat Island, Bahamas: A Study of Holocene Accretionary Topography and Sea-Level Change* 1969. 156 pp.

123. WHITNEY, JOSEPH. *China: Area, Administration and Nation Building* 1970. 198 pp.

124. EARICKSON, ROBERT. *The Spatial Behavior of Hospital Patients: A Behavioral Approach to Spatial Interaction in Metropolitan Chicago* 1970. 198 pp.

125. DAY, JOHN C. *Managing the Lower Rio Grande: An Experience in International River Development* 1970. 277 pp.

126. MAC IVER, IAN. *Urban Water Supply Alternatives: Perception and Choice in the Grand Basin, Ontario* 1970. 178 pp.

127. GOHEEN, PÉTER G. *Victorian Toronto, 1850 to 1900: Pattern and Process of Growth* 1970. 278 pp.

128. GOOD, CHARLES M. *Rural Markets and Trade in East Africa* 1970. 252 pp.

129. MEYER, DAVID R. *Spatial Variation of Black Urban Households* 1970. 127 pp.

130. GLADFELTER, BRUCE. *Meseta and Campiña Landforms in Central Spain: A Geomorphology of the Alto Henares Basin* 1971. 204 pp.

131. NEILS, ELAINE M. *Reservation to City: Indian Urbanization and Federal Relocation* 1971. 200 pp.

132. MOLINE, NORMAN T. *Mobility and the Small Town, 1900–1930* 1971. 169 pp.

133. SCHWIND, PAUL J. *Migration and Regional Development in the United States, 1950–1960* 1971. 170 pp.

134. PYLE, GERALD F. *Heart Disease, Cancer and Stroke in Chicago: A Geographical Analysis with Facilities Plans for 1980* 1971. 292 pp.

135. JOHNSON, JAMES F. *Renovated Waste Water: An Alternative Source of Municipal Water Supply in the U.S.* 1971. 155 pp.

136. BUTZER, KARL W. *Recent History of an Ethiopian Delta: The Omo River and the Level of Lake Rudolf* 1971. 184 pp.

137. HARRIS, CHAUNCY D. *Annotated World List of Selected Current Geographical Serials in English, French, and German* 3rd edition 1971. 77 pp.

138. HARRIS, CHAUNCY D., and FELLMANN, JEROME D. *International List of Geographical Serials* 2nd edition 1971. 267 pp.

139. MC MANIS, DOUGLAS R. *European Impressions of the New England Coast, 1497–1620* 1972. 147 pp.

140. COHEN, YEHOSHUA S. *Diffusion of an Innovation in an Urban System: The Spread of Planned Regional Shopping Centers in the United States, 1949–1968* 1972. 136 pp.

141. MITCHELL, NORA. *The Indian Hill-Station: Kodaikanal* 1972. 199 pp.

142. PLATT, RUTHERFORD H. *The Open Space Decision Process: Spatial Allocation of Costs and Benefits* 1972. 189 pp.

143. GOLANT, STEPHEN M. *The Residential Location and Spatial Behavior of the Elderly: A Canadian Example* 1972. 226 pp.

144. PANNELL, CLIFTON W. *T'ai-chung, T'ai-wan: Structure and Function* 1973. 200 pp.

145. LANKFORD, PHILIP M. *Regional Incomes in the United States, 1929–1967: Level, Distribution, Stability, and Growth* 1972. 137 pp.

146. FREEMAN, DONALD B. *International Trade, Migration, and Capital Flows: A Quantitative Analysis of Spatial Economic Interaction* 1973. 202 pp.

147. MYERS, SARAH K. *Language Shift Among Migrants to Lima, Peru* 1973. 204 pp.

148. JOHNSON, DOUGLAS L. *Jabal al-Akhdar, Cyrenaica: An Historical Geography of Settlement and Livelihood* 1973. 240 pp.

149. YEUNG, YUE-MAN. *National Development Policy and Urban Transformation in Singapore: A Study of Public Housing and the Marketing System* 1973. 204 pp.

150. HALL, FRED L. *Location Criteria for High Schools: Student Transportation and Racial Integration* 1973. 156 pp.

151. ROSENBERG, TERRY J. *Residence, Employment, and Mobility of Puerto Ricans in New York City* 1974. 230 pp.

152. MIKESELL, MARVIN W., EDITOR. *Geographers Abroad: Essays on the Problems and Prospects of Research in Foreign Areas* 1973. 296 pp.

153. OSBORN, JAMES. *Area, Development Policy, and the Middle City in Malaysia* 1974. 273 pp.

154. WACHT, WALTER F. *The Domestic Air Transportation Network of the United States* 1974. 98 pp.

155. BERRY, BRIAN, J. L., et al. *Land Use, Urban Form and Environmental Quality* 1974. 464 pp.